# Inglorious Revolutions:
# State Cohesion in the Middle East
# after the Arab Spring

**The Moshe Dayan Center for Middle Eastern and African Studies** seeks to contribute by research, documentation, and publication to the study and understanding of the modern history and current affairs of the Middle East and Africa. The Center is part of the School of History and the Lester and Sally Entin Faculty of Humanities at Tel Aviv University.

# Inglorious Revolutions: State Cohesion in the Middle East after the Arab Spring

edited by
Brandon Friedman and Bruce Maddy-Weitzman

The Moshe Dayan Center
for Middle Eastern and African Sudies

Tel Aviv University

# Table of Contents

# Preface

In 2010 and 2011, Tunisia and Egypt, and then Libya, Yemen, Bahrain, and Syria erupted in a great convulsion of popular revolt. Like most mass uprisings, it took everyone by surprise and triggered a wave of instant interpretation and explanation. Historian David Bell tells us that up until the mid-eighteenth century, the word "revolution" meant little more than "political upheaval." According to Bell, revolutions of this sort were sudden, unpredictable, and uncontrollable. Most important, Bell points out that "Revolutions were things that happened to people, not things that people themselves were seen as capable of consciously directing."[1] Yet the French Revolution of 1789 generally changed that perception of revolution; rather than a quick explosion of political change, revolution came to be understood as a political process of cascading radicalism.[2] This type of revolution as conceived by revolutionaries such as Leon Trotsky and Mao Zedong, was an "ongoing, consciously directed process" with the ultimate goal of transforming society.[3] The essays in this volume primarily address the impact of the 2010–2011 "Arab Spring" uprisings in terms of the pre-French Revolution perception of revolution as "political upheaval." It is still too early to adequately assess whether there are broader revolutionary processes taking place. Nevertheless, it is not too early to begin grappling with how the 2010–2011 political upheaval affected the cohesion of the state throughout the Middle East.

Henry Kissinger once wrote that "when social cohesiveness is slight, the struggle for control of authority is correspondingly more bitter."[4] The essays in this volume make no over-arching assumptions about the social cohesiveness of the states of the Middle East on the eve of the Arab uprisings in 2010–2011, yet the popular movements against state authorities beg a close examination of the issue. How cohesive and stable were these states and societies in late 2010? And what have been the sources of, and challenges to cohesion after 2011?

This volume identifies and presents four region-wide challenges to state cohesion following the Arab Spring upheavals in 2010 and 2011. In the introductory chapter of this volume, Bruce Maddy-Weitzman and Asher Susser provide a historical overview of state cohesion in the modern Middle East. They

---

1. David A. Bell, "Inglorious Revolutions," *The National Interest*, January–February 2014.
2. Crane Brinton, *The Anatomy of Revolution* (New York: W.W. Norton, 1938).
3. Bell, "Inglorious Revolutions."
4. Henry A. Kissinger, *American Foreign Policy: Three Essays* (New York: W.W. Norton & Company, Inc., 1969), p. 81.

also explain how state cohesion has been affected by retreating secularismand the Islamist challenge to the state, which sets the stage for the book's four thematic issues. First, sectarianism, driven by the breakdown and polarization of state authority in Iraq and Syria, is undoubtedly a major component of political change in the region. Whether sectarianism is the cause or effect of evolving political processes in the region is the subject of much debate, but perhaps the argument is a bit like the question of the "chicken or the egg," and what is important is trying to understand the contours of the problem, and the similarities and differences across the region, rather than trying to identify a chain of causality. In Part I, Elisheva Machlis maps sectarianism's place in the Arab state, in the framework of nationalism and Islamism. The second thematic issue is the relationship between economy and regime stability. What can be extrapolated from the economic failures and successes across the region? How do we intrepret and understand economic change and performance? These are a few of the questions Paul Rivlin addresses in his chapter. Esther Webman examines the challenge *of*, as well as the challenge *to al-Qa'ida* in the Middle East. Whether it is a worldview, a brand or an organization, the impact of the Arab Spring upheavals on its position and ideology and its ability to exert influence on states and societies in the region following the political upheaval has been an important development. The fourth theme presented in this volume, is the emergence of Kurdish autonomy. Ofra Bengio examines the rise of the Kurdistan Regional Government (KRG) in Iraq and its impact on the states and borders of the region, while at the same time exploring the affect of Kurdish autonomy on the relations between Iraq, Syria, Turkey, and Iran. The KRG's growing autonomy and increasing sovereign independence will have a multi-dimensional impact that is difficult to fully assess at this stage; nevertheless, it is hard to overstate the challenge to existing state cohesion that a Kurdish autonomous entity presents to the region.

Ernest Gellner viewed states where cohesion was based on nationalism as being the repository of a legitimate national culture or identity. In other words, nationalism is most effective or legitimate where structure (the state) and culture (national identity) are aligned.[5] Sectarianism, economic instability, salafism, and Kurdish nationalism are all forces that appear to have gained more traction and momentum in recent years, in part, as a result of the breakdown of existing state cohesion and authority in the region. Social and religious schisms become matters of life and death in the absence of a unifying social and political principle. And "where political obligation follows racial, religious, or tribal lines, self-

---

5.  Ernest Gellner, *Culture, Identity, and Politics* (Cambridge: Cambridge University Press, 1987), pp. 8–9.

restraint breaks down. Domestic conflicts asssume the character of civil war."[6] Major political upheaval and the breakdown or deterioration of state or social cohesion have led to the erosion of state structures in some places (Iraq) and the dissolution in others (Sudan), yet, in other parts of the Middle East, the state endures, even in the case of attenuated social and political cohesion. Only in Sudan has the state officially broken apart. And in the case of Sudan, the split into two separate states occurred only after a long and uneven political process that evolved over many years. Therefore, examining the ongoing political processes and trends within each of the states of the Middle East remains an important part of identifying sources of social and political cohesion or disintegration.

It is difficult to generalize about the post-Arab Spring Middle East. In North Africa, a sub-region of the Middle East, Libya is sliding towards civil war, while neighboring Tunisia is showing signs of being able to make the hard choices necessary for political compromise and power sharing. In Algeria, the ossifying political leadership shows no interest in relinquishing power, while the Moroccan monarch appears practiced in the art of using limited political reform as a gesture to relieve popular pressure for greater participation in government. In the Arabian Peninsula, Yemen is facing the possibility of state dissolution and territorial fragmentation and stands in contrast to Saudi Arabia and Oman's questions regarding royal succession. The essays in this volume reflect this political diversity.

Part II of this volume contains essays addressing the volatile political dynamics in Syria (Eyal Zisser), Iraq (Ronen Zeidel), and Lebanon (Joel D. Parker). It also includes an essay on the attempts to implement socio-economic reform in Saudi Arabia (Brandon Friedman), and a recap of how the political upheaval in Yemen unfolded (Uzi Rabi). In Part III, Mira Tzoreff examines the historical position of the Copts in Egyptian society, and explains how they have been affected by the political upheaval in Egypt. Joyce Van de Bilt writes about Nasser "nostalgia" in post-Mubarak Egypt, explaining the politics of how Nasser is remembered in post-Mubarak and post-Morsi Egypt. Irit Back explains the dissolution of Sudan and the challenges facing South Sudan. In Part IV, Daniel Zisenwine provides an overview of the move towards power-sharing and compromise in Tunisia. Yehudit Ronen traces Libya's gradual slide towards lawlessness and war. Gideon Gera outlines Algeria's challenges, despite having avoided political upheaval. And C. Richard Pennell mines a unique body of sources to describe the patterns and human costs of political dissent in Morocco. In Part V, Menachem Klein paints a bleak picture of the state of the Palestinian national project, while Ephraim Lavie attempts to contextualize

---

6. Kissinger, p. 81.

the political apathy or indifference among Palestinian youth in the aftermath of the Arab Spring upheaval. In Part VI, Hay Eytan Yanarocak describes Recep Tayyip Erdoğan's evolving leadership in light of the Gezi Park protests in 2013, while Duygu Atlas examines recent developments in the Turkish state's political approach to its Kurds. Finally, Meir Litvak provides a historical overview of the Islamic Republic of Iran's cohesion since 1979.

What each of the essays in this volume share is the basic assumption that in order for political authority to be "legitimate," there must exist some kind of political obligation, a socio-political contract between state and society that depends on more than coercive power or some kind of personalized loyalty. The conclusions found in these essays further underscore Shimon Shamir's admonition, which was made in a different context some years ago, "to pay greater attention to cultural undercurrents, to study further structural continuities, and to bear in mind that in the world of real politics things are never what they seem to be, at least initially."[7]

This volume is the intellectual heir to the Moshe Dayan Center's 2006 anthology edited by Asher Susser, *Challenges to the Cohesion of the Arab State*. It is the product of the Center's ongoing effort to approach the post-Arab Spring Middle East with a scholarly lens. In the aftermath of the 2010–2011 upheavals, it seemed appropriate to revisit the questions posed in the 2006 volume: How are the states of the Middle East coping with challenges to their cohesion and stability? To what extent are they succeeding?[8] This volume of essays also addresses the potential for failure. Weakening territorial cohesion and the erosion of social-political solidarity have had consequences; the emergence of Kurdish autonomy and nascent statehood is just one example. This book represents the beginning and not the end of the Center's effort to ask questions and examine the political processes that led to, and resulted from, the Arab Spring upheavals beginning in late 2010. I trust that it will be a valuable resource for scholars and students alike.

***

The essays in this volume are the offspring of the Moshe Dayan Center's (MDC) researcher's forum, which met every other week throughout the 2012–2013 academic year. The book would not have happened without the dedicated efforts of the MDC's researchers, who are scholars and teachers of the region's history

---

7.  Shimon Shamir (ed.), *Egypt from Monarchy to Republic* (Boulder, CO: Westview Press, 1995).
8.  Asher Susser (ed.), *Challenges to the Cohesion of the Arab State* (Tel Aviv: The Moshe Dayan Center, Tel Aviv University), p. 16.

and politics. I am grateful for their hard work and contributions. This book also benefited from the participation of two distinguished guest contributors: Richard Pennell, of the University of Melbourne, and Menachem Klein, of Bar-Ilan University. I would also like to thank Brandon Friedman and Bruce Maddy-Weitzman for their editorial guidance and supervision of this project. This book is enriched by their perspectives. I would also like to thank Ruth Berber, David Friedman, Molly Lower, and Ben Mendales for their assistance with the book's preparation for publication. Marion Gliksberg, the MDC's librarian, patiently supports the MDC's research staff with her knowledge and assistance. Michael Barak and Michael Reshef are capable managers of the MDC's invaluable Arabic press archive. Elena Kuznetsov managed the book's publication with grace and patience; I am thankful for her hard work and capable hand. I would also like to acknowledge and thank the MDC's administrative staff for all of its vital and invaluable assistance. They keep the wheels on the tracks, and the MDC relies on their competence and devotion. This book is the product of a team effort, and the MDC is indebted to all.

Uzi Rabi
*Director, Moshe Dayan Center (MDC)*

# State Cohesion in the Middle East: Historical and Contemporary Perspectives

## Bruce Maddy-Weitzman and Asher Susser

The Middle Eastern territorial state came into being after a prolonged period of Westernization that resulted in the formation of mostly secular authoritarian regimes. Over time, the state's ability to bend the will of its citizens increased, and political stability in most countries was reinforced. But toward the end of the twentieth century and the first decade of the twenty-first, secularism gradually eroded, Islamic politics became considerably more popular, authoritarian regimes in the region were put on the defensive, and with the advent of the "Arab Spring," state cohesion has been seriously undermined in a number of countries.

### Stateness, Cohesion, and the Arab States

There is no single, uniform entity called the Arab state. The 22 members of the League of Arab States can be categorized according to a number of criteria, including regime type, ethnic and religious makeup, degree of "Arabness," and historical trajectories, and hence varying degrees of social cohesion. One may also distinguish them from one another according to their degree of "stateness," a concept promoted by J.P. Nettl, and often referred to in the writings of Gabriel Ben-Dor, and Joseph Kostiner.[1] "Stateness" is related to "cohesion." But like stateness, cohesion is an elusive term, for it includes vital social, economic, and institutional components. It does not just simply mean political stability.

In fact, the overall degree of cohesion plays a critical role in determining the degree of political stability in any particular state. It similarly determines whether a heightened degree of political instability or even a regime-toppling crisis might pose a threat to the very existence of the territorial state itself. Without trying to idealize Tunisia's situation or minimize its difficulties in any way, the country where the first spark of the Arab Spring protests was improbably lit stands at one end of the Arab spectrum as the one with the most reasonable chance of establishing functioning legitimate institutions that can ensure a critical mass of social and political pluralism. If achieved, this will, in turn, reinforce the legitimacy of the system and those chosen to lead it. The source of Tunisia's comparatively favorable prospects lies in the country's relatively high degree of social cohesion, not just referring to an immediate familial, tribal or religio-communal level, but also to a broader collective sense of self, captured by Ernest Gellner's pithy and insightful observation that Tunisians appeared to feel "quite at home in their own cultural skin."[2] Yemen and Libya, where tribalism is deep-rooted and stateness is extremely low, are at the other end of the spectrum; the post-'Ali Abdallah Salah and post-Qaddafi eras there, respectively, have rendered them as empty shells of formally sovereign entities, as competing tribal-oriented militias jockey for position, often violently.

There are vital social and economic components to measuring the degree of a state's cohesion, such as the authorities' capacity to collect taxes, deliver services, maintain social peace and security, and provide an overall vision or direction that would be considered legitimate by the majority of the population. Employing the terminology of Joel Migdal, one may think about whether these states are "strong" or "weak" in relation to their societies, i.e., whether states have the requisite degree of social control that enables them to overcome existing social forces resistant to centralizing policies aimed at transforming social and political realities to the state's benefit.

Migdal's ideal type is an entity which is both a strong state and a strong society, in which a healthy balance is maintained between the two. In his analysis of Egypt's land reform policies during the Nasser period, he concludes that for all of the changes introduced, Egypt's "society" won out over the "state," and that the state remained essentially weak, with limited capabilities.[3] Indeed, today's Egypt, while being the epitome of an entity with a high degree of "stateness," even to the point of being a "deep state," is nonetheless a "weak" state, unable to effectively address its deep-rooted social and economic problems, build viable and legitimate governing institutions, and assume its so-called "natural," self-defined role as the leader of the region and of the Arab world in particular.

Mention of the "Arab world" necessitates a discussion of the intricate, complex relationship between Arabness, Arabism, Arab nationalism and territorial nationalism. The grand narrative of Arab nationalism, which was propagated by Arab nationalists and accepted by generations of Westerners, was one that emphasized Western betrayal of war-time Arab allies, and the carving up of the "natural" Arab political space into unnatural territorial units which lacked the basis for social and political cohesion.

The pan-Arab movement, whose heyday was the 1950s and 1960s, but whose world view was formed earlier, championed this view, and used it as a weapon to de-legitimize the newly independent, narrowly based and weak regimes. But more and more scholars understand the limitations of this narrative, for it is more ideological than a reflection of what actually transpired. Israel Gershoni, Philip Khoury, and others have shown that there is not one Arab nationalist experience, but rather many experiences, as the modern Arab state system gradually emerged in the decades after the World War I.[4]

More than two decades ago, Ilya Harik poked major holes in the grand Arab nationalist narrative, arguing that a majority of the member states of the Arab League, from North Africa to the Gulf, acquired a considerable degree of legitimacy which predated the arrival of colonialism.[5] This was true regardless of the specific pre-modern regime types: the Ottoman Regencies of Tripoli, Tunis, and Algiers, were all run by military-bureaucratic oligarchies with only tenuous ties to Istanbul; the imam-chief system which prevailed in Morocco and Oman, in which religious and political legitimacy were invested in a single person; the Arabian chieftaincies of Najd and Hijaz; and 19th century dynastic Egypt and Maronite-dominated Mount Lebanon.

In all of these cases, important foundations had been laid for what would become modern states. It was only the Fertile Crescent, Harik noted, that lacked this long history of durable local centers and ruling elites. Given the Fertile Crescent/Levant's social, religious and ethnic fragmentation, it was only natural that Arabism, Arab nationalism, and pan-Arabism would develop there, providing a possible tool to overcome the "primordial" divisions and absence of independent political traditions.

Radical pan-Arabism was usually contrasted with territorial states, threatening the existing order by de-legitimizing local regimes. At one point, the decisive component of a fragmented Syrian elite even gave their country away for a brief period (1958-61) in the name of pan-Arabism. But Syria's subordination to Egypt under the banner of the United Arab Republic did not last, and thus began the gradual fall from grace of the pan-Arab doctrine, accelerated by the 1967 debacle.[6]

However, the dichotomy between integral pan-Arabism and the territorial state is only part of the story. Arab nationalism and the adherence to pan-Arab norms were also crucial in terms of state building and for the forging of cohesion.[7] As Malik Mufti has shown, this was true for Iraq and Syria where unionism was an effective defensive mechanism to ensure the respective Ba'thi regime's authoritarian hold on power.[8]

## Secularism, Authoritarianism, and the Territorial State

Despite the upheavals of the Arab Spring it would be premature to speak of the end of authoritarianism. But one can point to the fall of the totalitarian-like "*mukhabarat* state" of Ba'thist Iraq and the severe weakening of its Ba'thi twin in Syria ("fierce states," to use Nazih Ayubi's term).[9] In today's Arab states, and even in Iran, public space is increasingly contested and turbulent while Turkey's admittedly imperfect democracy has long stood apart from its Middle Eastern neighbors. Nearly all Middle Eastern states are being challenged to build workable institutions which can channel and manage social differences, and address underlying economic problems.

Questions are being raised regarding the appropriate guiding values of society, such as the exact mix of Arab identity, the degree of religiosity, the desired amount of openness to modernity and the extent of toleration of religious minorities and women, as well as other minorities including secular liberals and the youth of Facebook and Twitter. However precisely defined, this erosion of authoritarianism meant that one of the key forces that had contributed to the maintenance of a degree of cohesion in the Arab states has been seriously undermined, calling into question the stability and integrity of various countries.

In the Middle East of the nineteenth century, under the impact of the Western challenge, the Ottoman Empire and Egypt underwent a prolonged period of Western-style reform, which extended well into the twentieth century. European ideas reshaped the local discourse and gave rise to intensive intellectual ferment and debate. Secular liberalism challenged the centrality of religion in political life, eventually producing a headlong assault on tradition and the subsequent emergence of new forms of collective identity that gave preference to common language, territory, and cultural heritage over religion. European ideas and influence and the measured secularization of society went hand in hand with the creation of the Arab territorial state, while in Turkey's Kemalist Republic secularization was the leadership's explicit mantra.

But in recent generations, many of these processes have been arrested or even reversed. Western cultural influence and secularism have been in retreat for decades as religious revivalism has captured much of the popular imagination. Neo-traditionalism in its various manifestations such as political Islam, religious sectarianism, and tribalism have all resurfaced with great force in recent years, posing an unprecedented challenge to the secular-based ideas of the age of Westernizing reform, such as nationalism and in some cases, the territorial state itself. In the aftermath of the Arab Spring convulsions, which have reinforced these neo-traditionalist trends, some Arab states are presently facing what is possibly the most serious challenge of their entire century of existence.

For centuries, it was customary for the peoples of the Middle East to define themselves collectively not by the territory they inhabited nor by the language they spoke, but rather by their religious belief. The Muslim majority belonged to a community of believers (*ummat al-mu'minin*) who shared a common destiny with co-religionists who spoke different languages, and lived many hundreds or even thousands of miles away, more than they did with their Arabic, Turkish, Persian, Kurdish or Berber-speaking Jewish or Christian minority neighbors, with whom they shared the same city or town, somewhere in North Africa or the Fertile Crescent, and who similarly defined themselves by their faith.

The idea that people who spoke the same language and inhabited a clearly defined territory were a nation unto themselves, irrespective of their religion (at least in theory, even if in practice this was often not entirely so), was a European import to the Middle East. It was gradually introduced during the nineteenth century as an integral part of the process of Westernizing modernization and reform.[10]

Territorial nationalism, intimately linked to the post-enlightenment notion of self-determination, was an essentially secular idea. Those who espoused it postulated the inherent right of nations to determine their fate in this world by their own collective rational decision, as opposed to religious observance designed to secure their well-being in the next world through devout belief in God. Nationalism was about the sovereignty of man and not the sovereignty of God, and at least in the European experience, nationalist movements were very often built from the bottom up by revolutionary movements for whom collective self-determination went hand-in-hand with the establishment of representative, popularly elected institutions.

According to Israel Gershoni, nationalism in the Middle East, as in many other societies, was a "principal agent" for the introduction of Western modernity and progress, "forging a new and authentic collective identity, a 'new nation,' able to inculcate 'in its own way' a modern value system."[11] Focusing on language and territory (rather than on religion) as the dominant cohesive elements of society, nationalism became the main secularizing vehicle of politics in the Middle East of the twentieth century. Everywhere in the Muslim world, a process of consolidation of nation-states was in motion: in Egypt, and the successor states to the Ottoman Empire, the process of marginalizing religion had been underway for more than a century.[12]

Arabism, Egyptianism, and Turkish and Iranian nationalism demoted religion to a secondary role, as but one component of the peoples' cultural heritage. Their movements rested on two main pillars: the rejection of foreign control and the need for internal reform and cultural change. Referring to Arab movements, Immanuel Wallerstein wrote that "the future they envisaged was a modern one, by which they meant a secular one," and they "shared many of the premises of Kemalism."[13]

Kemalism itself was the natural outcome of a century of Ottoman reform — the innovations of the *Tanzimat*. The most revolutionary of all the reforms was the formal proclamation of equality of all Ottoman subjects before the law, first in the reforms of 1839, and then again in the decrees of 1856. The granting of equality was a radical departure from the very core of the *shari'a*, which guaranteed and enforced a legal system that had traditionally preserved and enforced Muslim superiority over all other tolerated, but not equal, religious communities. The Ottoman sultans had hitherto been more insistent than all their Muslim predecessors on the strict application of the *shari'a*.[14] The deviations of the Tanzimat were therefore all the more meaningful and had far-reaching implications as they slowly but surely eroded the supremacy of the *shari'a* in the Ottoman legal system.

Most importantly, secularizing reforms from the very outset were intimately related to both territorialism and authoritarianism. By proclaiming all equal before the law, Ottomans were all henceforth to be subject to a unified legal code, thus gradually abandoning the differential legal systems that applied to the various religious communities, with their autonomous court systems that enforced their own religious law. The same law was to apply equally to all Ottoman subjects in the entire territory of the Empire, thus establishing a territorialized legal system instead of the communal systems that had applied previously. This was a great step towards the territorialization of collective identity, first to Ottomanism and then, on a more lasting footing, to Turkish nationalism.

The reforms were hardly popular among Ottoman Muslims. To override long-standing Ottoman-Islamic traditions and to subdue the opposition of the widely supported and established classes, including the men of religion (*'ulama*) required the establishment of a more centralized and authoritarian state. The Tanzimat measures, as much as they were about reform, were also about the creation of a modern centralized state to implement the reforms, top-down, on a population that had hitherto treated any ideas or innovation of "infidel" origin with total disdain.[15]

The introduction of Western-inspired reforms led to an unprecedented intensive internal debate on Islamic modernism, in an effort to establish a synthesis between Islamic culture and civilization and Western thought. Leading Muslim intellectuals, such as Muhammad 'Abduh in Westernizing Egypt of the late nineteenth century, argued that there was no inherent contradiction between Islam and reason and science, or between Islam and democracy.

Though 'Abduh's style of Islamic reform "remained firmly anchored in the basic teachings of Islam about morality, society, and order," it set the stage in the early twentieth century for what P.J. Vatikiotis called the "stirrings of secular liberalism." 'Abduh inspired a generation of liberal-minded thinkers who sought rational and secular answers to the questions of Egypt's collective identity, political orientation, and socio-economic development, as opposed to those who still believed in the prescriptions of Islamic tradition. The Young Turks' ascent to power in Istanbul in 1908 added impetus to the secularizing trend.[16]

Concurrently, liberals in Egypt gained momentum and adopted the European secular notion of the nation-state instead of the basically religious concept of the *umma*. As far as they were concerned, Egyptian patriotism, "the allegiance and loyalty of individuals, irrespective of religious belief or community, to an 'Egyptian nation,' was now the guiding principle of political action instead of the supranational and universalist formula of Islamic and Pan-Islamic nationalism." As they formulated "a strictly Egyptian national consciousness," in a "territorially-defined nation state," they abandoned Islam "as a principal of political organization and action." As they decoupled the Egyptian nation from any Islamic identity, they simultaneously contributed to the general awareness "of the need to escape the bonds of traditionalism in favor of modern scientific knowledge."[17]

In the 1920s and 1930s, secular liberal intellectuals in Egypt placed special emphasis on the role of science and technology in the modern world. They proclaimed Western civilization as the highest stage of man's spiritual and material development, declared Islamic civilization and culture dead and useless, and advocated the adoption of Western civilization and culture without reservations as the only way for the advancement of their country.[18]

The secular liberals' promotion of Egyptian-ness and their concomitant attempt to identify a peculiarly Egyptian culture independent of either its Islamic or Christian heritage opened the way for a questioning by Egyptians of Islamic ideas, values and institutions. The promotion of Egyptian-ness was, therefore, "not only part of the nationalist wave, but also an integral dimension of the attack upon Islam and its values."[19]

Indeed, not only in Egypt but also in the newly founded states of Syria and Iraq, the Turkish Republic and Pahlavi Iran, the general nationalist tendency, whether territorial or pan-Arab, was secular in principle, defining the people by language and/or territory but not religion. The state, therefore, tended to formally ignore, deny or suppress sectarian and even ethnic differences (the Kurds in Iraq and Syria for example, not to mention Kemalist Turkey's branding of Kurds as "mountain Turks"), in the process of state-building and the assertion of centralized territorial control.

Throughout the region, the men of religion appeared momentarily to be "in full retreat before the forces of modern reform." But, to take Egypt as an example, the influence of the secular liberals on Egyptian society as a whole was not nearly as profound as it had been on the country's intellectual elite. The liberals had seriously "underestimated the political power inherent in the instinctive adherence of Egyptians to their Islamic heritage."[20]

Benedict Anderson has observed that in Western Europe, the eighteenth century marked "not only the dawn of the age of nationalism but the dusk of religious modes of thought," which were superseded by rationalist secularism.[21] In the Middle East, the late nineteenth and early twentieth centuries were indeed an era of profound ideological ferment and Islamic reform, as Western ideas, such as secularism and nationalism, dominated the local intellectual discourse. Nonetheless, the dawn of nationalism was never quite the dusk of religious modes of thought; rather, the two continued to compete with each other, experiencing different periods of relative success in the marketplace of ideas.

Arab nationalism was commonly and correctly understood as a secular idea. But it was not only that, and as the idea penetrated deeper into Arab Muslim societies, it became more associated with Islam. Indeed, as James Gelvin persuasively argues, Arab nationalism always had a populist stream, which was able to mobilize networks of lower classes with simple anti-foreigner, anti-occupation themes deploying Islamic symbols, such as in Syria in 1920 during Faysal's struggle or in the 1925 rebellion there against French rule. 'Izz al-Din al-Qassam's activities in Palestine in the 1930s was another of these early populist expressions and the Muslim Brotherhood in Egypt also would make no clear divide between Arab nationalism and Islam.[22]

## Secular Retreat and the Islamist Challenge to the State

Western theories of modernization regarding the newly emerging countries of the world tended to be linear, holding the expectation of the irrevocable decline of religion in society and politics as had been the case in the European experience of state formation and modernization. The idea of secularization as expounded upon in the works of the "trinity" of social theorists — Durkheim, Marx, and Weber — in which the decline of religious belief was "scientifically" forecasted, was widely accepted. State-sponsored secularism in the twentieth-century Middle East, however, failed to produce secular societies.[23] Though organized religion did decline, new religious movements with mass followings emerged. As ever, religion remained "a key marker of identity in Muslim societies."[24]

The decline of Arab nationalism was a momentous setback for the secularization process that had introduced nationalism in the first place. The post-1967 era witnessed two simultaneous but contradictory trends. On the one hand, the failing fortunes of pan-Arabism paved the way for the pragmatic acceptance of the colonially created Middle Eastern state order, the entrenchment of the territorial state and accompanying formulations of territorial nationalism, and the unapologetic pursuit of *raison d'état* by the various Arab states.

The conflict with Israel was all that was left to unite the Arab world and that did not last for very long, as Egypt departed from the Arab ranks in the late 1970s. The Iran-Iraq war dealt a further severe blow to tattered Arab norms, as Syria supported Iran against a fellow Arab state. Iraq's subsequent invasion of Kuwait in 1990 and the alliance of most Arab states with the US against Iraq was nothing less than an earthquake for the Arab region.[25]

The last semblance of meaningful collective Arab action came in 2002 with the issuing of the Arab Peace Initiative. Although it was born out of disagreement and compromise, with no mechanism to promote its implementation, it nonetheless still serves as a reference point of sorts for Arab-Israeli peacemaking.[26] The other, contradictory post-1967 trend was the filling of the ideological vacuum left by Arabism by the Islamist movements that challenged the incumbent regimes and sought to Islamize their respective states and societies.

Arab societies in the post-1967 era therefore generally tended to share, in varying degrees and with different orders of priority, a multidimensional set of identities. Egyptians, Jordanians, Palestinians, and Iraqis were the proud possessors of their respective territorial identities as they were also, at one and the same time, Arabs and Muslims, Christians, Sunnis, or Shi'is, and so on. In the new circumstances, it was the more secularist purveyors of existing territorial identities who competed with the Islamists. As for the pan-Arabists, they were increasingly marginalized after the two or three decades in which they had dominated their ideological competitors.

Secularism was in its origins a project of the state — first of the colonial state and then of its post-colonial successor. It was a Western import intended to support the ruling elites' long-term aim of modernization and development. Over the long run, the dislocations generated by rapid urbanization and changing cultural and socioeconomic relationships, coupled with increasing economic mismanagement and corruption, rising poverty, and income inequality undermined the legitimacy of Arab regimes, creating the impression that the modernization project was failing. These developments also reflected badly on secularism, as the post-colonial regimes were by and large openly secular-nationalist. The despotism and ruthless suppression instituted by these regimes were similarly associated with secularism — which increasingly began to appear as a handmaiden to repression.[27]

To be sure, the secularizing nationalist regimes of mid-century in countries like Egypt, Iraq, and Syria maintained the relevance of religion in public life by dabbling on occasion, for their own purposes, in Islamic politics. But overall, they effectively blocked the Islamists, who were crushed underfoot by military dictatorships. As Stephen Humphreys and others have contended, had "the nationalist regimes not bent every effort to controlling the resurgence of Islam ... it might well have swept the boards even by the mid-1950s."[28]

Indeed, for the Islamic fundamentalists, Arabism was not only the ultimate political oppressor but also an ideological adversary that had served as the "supreme manifestation of political secularism." The fundamentalists had pursued a tactical flirtation with pan-Arabism in its heyday, but when it met with ignominious defeat in the 1967 war with Israel, the final divorce from those who had thrust Islam onto the margins of politics and society was total.[29]

In Egypt, Islamists planned for the *jama'at Islamiyya* (the Islamist groups on campuses) to be the engine for the process whereby Egyptian society would be transformed from its *jahili* nature (that is, governed by unbelief) into a true Muslim society. In the eyes of *jama'at* ideologues, nationalism was but another form of Westernization through which infidels had penetrated the minds of the people. Thus, it was incumbent upon the *jama'at* to devote themselves to the revival of Islam and to fulfill their role as the "vanguard of the *umma*."[30]

But the Islamists had to contend with powerful regimes that fought to contain their impact. The Arab states were built top-down and in the Middle Eastern case the modern state was invariably ruled by some form of authoritarian regime that also guaranteed the cohesion of the institutional order through the use of varying degrees of force. As pan-Arabism waned from the 1960s onwards, more concerted and deliberate efforts were made by many of the Arab regimes to actively promote a sense of genuine territorial identity and consciousness, ostensibly overriding religious identities and bridging over longstanding sectarian, ethnic, or tribal fault lines. At long last, this seemed to be the entrenchment of Arab territorial states, enabling and legitimizing the unencumbered pursuit of their respective *raisons d'état*.

However, the decline of pan-Arabism and the loss of hope that it represented has left Arab regimes bereft of an important legitimizing tool. Arab nationalism as an expressive ideology[31] was not enough by itself. The regimes had to perform, and, as the Arab Human Development Reports (AHDR) have consistently shown, they have not delivered.[32] The reports highlighted many state shortcomings; the concept of "stalled" states and societies had already entered into the lexicon.[33] And when the spark was lit by a young, despairing unemployed Tunisian in December 2010, the resulting Arab Spring protests spread like wildfire.

According to some, the Arab nationalist idea was actually rejuvenated by the new media, and the uprisings created a newly meaningful regional bond, constituting a second "Arab awakening." Marc Lynch observed that "a radically new Arab political space" had been created by "a new generation of Arabs." They had "come of age watching al-Jazeera…connecting with each other through social media; and internalizing a new kind of pan-Arabist identity," as they shared complaints about their authoritarian leaders, their stalled economies, and their stagnant politics.[34]

However, this excitement, dominated by ideological yearnings and no little wishful thinking, was off the mark. As Stephen Humphreys had already noted, Arab nationalism was "even in its heyday, a new plant…with very shallow roots in the political tradition of [the] region."[35] Bernard Lewis agreed with Fouad Ajami's earlier evaluation that *raison d'état* among Arab states was triumphing over pan-Arabism.[36] Martin Kramer's erudite analysis of the rise and decline of Arab nationalism went even further, speaking of a case of "mistaken identity."[37] Taking the middle ground, one could argue that "being" Arab remains a meaningful category of collective identity for a majority of Arabic speakers, and most Arab states will remain as self-defined Arab states. At the same time, it has become less of a tool in their foreign policies, and at best is an implicit and not an explicit focus of domestic debates, and is folded into the debates about the role of Islam in political life and in the shaping of collective identity. Arab nationalism, therefore, has lost its role both as a platform for secular politics and as a cohesive force overriding more traditional forms of collective identity.

# Case Studies in Territorialist Cohesion and its Limitations

The retreat of secularism, the rise of Islamist politics, the resurgence of other neo-traditionalist forces, the advent of the Arab Spring, and the consequent erosion of authoritarianism have all had their varying effects on the cohesion of important Arab states.

In Egypt, after succeeding 'Abd al-Nasser in 1970, one of the first decisions made by Anwar Sadat was to change the name of the country from the "United Arab Republic" to the "Arab Republic of Egypt" (*Gumhuriyyat Misr al-'Arabiyya*). This was not about semantics, but a redirection of Egyptian politics. From its devotion to the Arab cause, so much so that under Nasser it had dropped "Egypt" from its name, Sadat was moving decisively towards an Egypt-first orientation. Indeed, in Arabic, "Egypt" (*Misr*) preceded the "Arab" in Egypt's new name. Clearly, it was in the service of Egypt's state interests that Sadat first went to war with Israel and then chose to make peace with it, without reference to the wishes of the Arab collective. Of all the Arab states, Egypt of the Nile was the most self-evident "natural" territorial state. Egypt was a separate, clearly defined political entity with a relatively homogeneous population and Egyptians had an authentic collective sense of belonging to the Egyptian state well before the advent of pan-Arabism.

But with the rise of Islamic politics, the regime made significant concessions to the Islamists. Especially under President Hosni Mubarak, the regime conceded much of the public space and public debate to the Islamists.

Moreover, in response to increasing popular religious sentiment, Mubarak resorted to religious legitimization considerably more than his predecessors, regularly seeking the endorsement of the religious establishment for his policies and actions.[38] Islamic sentiment in Egypt thus "eroded nationalism's secular expression." [39] More significantly, Islamic activists openly challenged Egyptian secular national solidarity and cohesion by assuming an ever more militant posture toward the country's Coptic Christian minority, some 10 percent of the population. The government invested little or no effort to deter the Islamists and the situation of the Coptic minority became steadily more precarious as they were exposed to increasing levels of intolerance and violence.[40]

With the advent of the Arab Spring and the overthrow of Mubarak in February 2011, the situation of the Copts deteriorated further. The rise to power of the Muslim Brotherhood, the political prominence of the even more radical Salafis, and the general chaotic decline of law and order, exposed the Copts to rising sectarian violence against individuals, churches, and other institutions. It was therefore not surprising that politics assumed a more blatantly sectarian character. In the various referenda and elections after the fall of Mubarak, the Copts generally voted against the Islamists. In the mass demonstrations that preceded the military coup that unseated President Mohammed Morsi in July 2013, Copts were noticeably present. Moreover, Naguib Sawiris, the Copt multi-millionaire media mogul was, by his own admission, instrumental in financing the *Tamarrud* movement that led the struggle to bring Morsi down. After the coup, the dispossessed Islamists singled out the Copts as targets for their anger and frustration. Copts faced a new wave of violence amidst accusations that they had conspired with the secularists and the military to unseat the legitimate and freely-elected government of Egypt. The Copts felt yet again that they were not receiving adequate protection, irrespective of the regime in power.[41] If sectarianism at the expense of national cohesion was becoming a fact of life in Egypt, in other more heterogeneous Arab states it had long been so.

Ba'thi Iraq (1968-2003) was the most extreme example of the phenomenon. In Saddam Hussein's "republic of fear," the ethnic or sectarian minorities, the Kurds and the Shi'is (the latter were a minority in the political, but not numerical sense), were crushed into submission by the "institutions of violence" of the Iraqi Ba'thi polity.[42] Cohesion in the name of Iraqi Arab nationalism and leadership of the Arab world with which neither Kurds (who were not Arabs) nor Shi'is (for whom Arab nationalism was just another version of Sunni domination) could identify, was no solution. Nor was Iraqiness, which was an illusory concoction thrust upon on the public from above. Neither of these could really become "the credo of all Iraqis."[43]

Saddam, through state sponsorship of historical theories, the arts and archaeology, endeavored "to foster a sense of national Iraqi uniqueness and pride through the creation of an intimate relationship between the people and the territorial pre-Islamic history" of Iraq.[44] But these "Babylon-Iraq" manipulations could not erase or even paper over the predominant sectarian identities within Iraq.[45]

After all, as Hazim Saghiya, the Lebanese author, columnist and editor for the London-based Arab daily *al-Hayat*, has argued, all the modern trappings of the Ba'thi regime were a mere pretext for sectarian Sunni domination of Iraqi society. Indeed, from the outset, the Iraqi national project had been a Sunni Arab one, giving short shrift to the rest of society. Of course, Saddam's regime took this to a whole new level. It was founded on the kinship values of family, relatives, and blood ties as they prevailed in the so-called Sunni Triangle (the area in Iraq between Baghdad in the East, Ramadi in the West, and Tikrit in the North), especially within the "Tikrit group" (*majmu'at Tikrit*) — that is, people from Saddam's hometown.[46] The real political foundations of the regime had nothing to do with Saddam's "Babylon-Iraq" invented historical manipulations.

But the iron-fisted grip of *majmu'at Tikrit* on Iraq began to loosen after Iraq's expulsion from Kuwait in early 1991. The Kurdish and Shi'i uprisings of the spring of 1991 were suppressed. But the regime could not prevent the de facto autonomy that was established, with US support, in the Kurdish region. After the fall of Saddam in 2003, the Kurdish Regional Government, though part of the new Iraqi federal structure, developed into a quasi-independent state in all but name, and achieved a level of stability and prosperity far above the rest of the country.

The toppling of Saddam was in fact the overthrow of the Sunnis who had been in control of Iraq for more than a millennium, from the Abbasids to the Ottomans and then in the British-constructed state of Iraq. The new post-Ba'thi Iraq was no longer defined as an Arab state but as a more decentralized Arab–Kurdish federation. The Kurds took their separate course, but the Arabs of Iraq remained deeply divided between Sunnis and Shi'is.

The US invasion of Iraq had swept away the "comforting fantasy" of a nonsectarian society. "For the first time in the modern history of Iraq, the Sunni Arabs were forced to confront the loss of their ascendant power *as a community*."[47] The empowerment of the Shi'i majority was an insufferable defeat for the Sunnis, who have essentially refused ever since to acquiesce in the new reality. Sunni disaffection is at the root of the on-again, off-again violent struggle, if not to say civil war in Iraq, ever since the US invasion, which has claimed the lives of many thousands on both sides.

There is even talk amongst Sunnis about the formation of a distinct region in Iraq that would be composed of the Sunni majority provinces, or alternatively of the possible secession of the western Sunni province of Anbar from Iraq.[48] Some in Jordan even speak of Anbar province being incorporated into the Hashemite

Kingdom. This may all be just so much empty conjecture, but the very fact that it takes place at all is indicative of a new reality in which the state order is being questioned as never before. Iraq's Christians, caught in the crossfire between Sunnis and Shi'is, have been harassed into massive flight. According to various reports, Iraq's Christian population of about one million has been depleted by more than half since the US invasion in 2003.[49] As Arab commentators constantly lamented, the ever-present "demon of sectarianism" (*ghul al-ta'ifiyya*) continued to bedevil Iraqi politics.[50]

Syria, like Iraq, has drifted towards fragmentation in recent years. Ba'thi Syria had always been deeply influenced by sectarian politics, and ever since the rise to power of the Ba'th in 1963, 'Alawi sectarian solidarity played an important role in regime stability — a fact never openly admitted by the men in power, but a fact just the same. As Hanna Batatu wrote many years ago about the regime in Syria: "[T]he ruling element consists at its core of a close kinship group which draws strength simultaneously, but in decreasing intensity, from a tribe, a sect-class, and an ecological-cultural division of the people." Ba'thi secularism was a vehicle for the sectarian domination of the 'Alawi minority, with the support of the countries' Christian and Druze communities, and for the political dispossession of the Sunni majority in the struggle for control of the modern Syrian state.[51]

The 'Alawis, who became "the lords of Syria,"[52] were from the most humble origins, constituting part of the downtrodden underclass of rural Syria for centuries. Service in the military, beginning from the time of the French Mandate, was their main avenue of social mobility, coupled with membership in the Ba'th party and the systematic marginalization of religion — a blessing for the 'Alawis, whose heterodoxical faith was a political and social liability.

Much like Ba'thi Baghdad, Damascus also remained committed in principle to pan-Arabism, but here too, a certain Syrian territorialism was fostered as of the mid-1970s, even if more slowly and less perceptibly than in Iraq. While Hafiz al-Asad officially remained faithful to the party's long-term vision of Arab unity, the Syrian leadership searched for a formula that would "muffle the cognitive dissonance between party ideals and political reality." As Egypt shifted away from the conflict with Israel, Syria was desperately in need of a new strategic alignment that would encompass Lebanon, Jordan, and the Palestinians. Thus, the old motif of Greater Syria was given a new lease on life by the Ba'thi regime, in service of Syria's *raison d'état*. In later years, it did not disappear and actually became part of Ba'thi political thinking, together with a more traditional pan-Arabism, coupled with notions of a more narrowly defined territorial nationalism based on Syria's existing borders.[53]

But as in Iraq, these formulations failed to overcome sectarian fault lines. Many in the Sunni majority community, particularly in the big cities, continued to regard the 'Alawis as socially inferior heretics, whose political dominance was unbearable. The failure of the regime's efforts to secure religious legitimacy for the 'Alawis[54] eventually resulted in the revolt of the more militant factions of the Muslim Brotherhood from 1976 to 1982. They were finally and ruthlessly suppressed, with the destruction of the last redoubt of the rebels in the northern city of Hama in February 1982. Hafiz al-Asad was unflinching in battle but magnanimous in victory, and from the mid-1980s he offered the former rebels a reconciliation of sorts, albeit on tough terms set by the regime.[55]

Syrian domestic stability was thus secured for the next three decades. However, under Bashar al-Asad, beginning in June 2000, Syria was never as effectively governed as it had been by his father. And with the arrival of the Arab Spring protests in March 2011, Syria progressively spun out of control, with disastrous humanitarian consequences. What began as a minor protest by disgruntled peasants and workers in Syria's rural backwater soon mushroomed into a full-scale sectarian civil war, the end of which is presently nowhere in sight.

The opposition in Syria is, needless to say, composed mainly of representatives of the Sunni majority. But not all Sunnis are firmly allied with the opposition and the regime still enjoys support among urban Sunnis, who have largely remained neutral and uncommitted. A myriad of Sunni organizations make up the bulk of the opposition, from the defectors from the Syrian Army who have formed the Free Syrian Army to the more radical Islamist organizations that have some form of affiliation with al-Qa'ida, such as *Jabhat al-Nusra li-Ahl al-Sham* or *al-Dawla al-Islamiyya fi al-Iraq wal-Sham* (ISIS). The names of these groups, and others, suggest that they do not even recognize the legitimacy of the Syrian state, referring only to Greater Syria (*al-Sham*) which includes Syria, Lebanon, Palestine, and Jordan.

In the meantime, Syria is no longer the unitary state it once was. It might recover if Asad wins in the end, and it could disintegrate if he does not, with a variety of partial and decentralized options in between. Presently the country is divided into a number of zones of control. The regime has lost control of the border area with Turkey, which is divided into two different zones, one in the northwest controlled by the rebels (in which Aleppo is still contested territory), and the other in the northeast controlled by Syria's long-marginalized, and newly assertive Kurds, much to the consternation of the Turks, who fear that the Syrian Kurdish region might soon merge with its Iraqi counterpart to create a larger, more powerful, de facto state.[56] The rebels also control much of the Jazira area in the east, including the towns of Raqqah and Dayr al-Zur. The regime still controls the capital Damascus (but not entirely), important sections of the border area with Lebanon, and the northwestern coastal area, which is predominantly 'Alawi territory.

With the regime challenged by a radical Islamist opposition, the other minorities, like the Druze and the Christians, have remained neutral. In the current circumstances, neutrality essentially meant siding with the regime, which seemed to be largely true of the Christians. Looking at the examples of Egypt and Iraq, they could only throw in their lot with the incumbent secular regime, considering their prospective fate with the possible advent of an Islamist regime and, in the meantime, growing Islamist influence in a country of declining law and order.

Chaos would mean less protection for the Christians and much greater exposure to the wrath of the Islamists. In the ongoing fighting, the Christians at times have felt they were being deliberately targeted by the opposition because of their ostensible support for the regime. This was true, for example, in the shelling by the rebels of Christian quarters in Damascus in November 2013,[57] or previously in the heavy fighting in Homs, when Christian quarters were reported to have been very badly damaged by the rebels and eventually evacuated.

In sum, the territorial identities that were cultivated by the regimes in Iraq and Syria have proved to have been very thin veneers. Behind the territorialist façade, the regimes in question were sectarian to the core. Just like *majmu'at Tikrit* in Iraq, the Syrian Ba'thi regime was dominated (though obviously not exclusively) by the Asads and their allies from the 'Alawi community, especially those of the Kalbiyya tribe to which the Asads belonged.[58] The intimate cohesion of these minorities in power was a source of great reliability and stability as long as they lasted, but once they lost their control, the sectarian genie was let out of the bottle. The oppressed and the oppressors changed places, as in Iraq, or fought it out, inconclusively so far, as in Syria.

By contrast, Jordan's relative cohesion in comparison to the other states of the Fertile Crescent has contributed to its surprisingly long-term stability. Its rather soft authoritarian regime has remained in power without change for nearly a century, effectively holding the country together despite major demographic transformations. No less an artificial creation than its neighbors, and many would argue even considerably more so, Jordan has had a much better political record.

Jordan is a homogenous society in religious terms, being more than 90 percent Sunni Muslim Arabs. Since 1948, it has become increasingly Palestinian, and Palestinians presently constitute a majority of just over 50 percent in Jordan of the East Bank alone, not taking into account the West Bank territory occupied by Israel since 1967. But as tense as relations are between Jordanians and Palestinians, the distinctions between them are latter day twentieth century ones: they are skin deep in comparison to the far more profound sectarian fault lines in the region that date back centuries.

Tribalism amongst Jordan's East Bankers is a strong and very relevant social marker, but tribalism in Jordan has been mobilized far more in the service of the state than against it. In fact, the Jordanian state has become their political patrimony. They have no other and they will fight to defend it. As in other countries in the region, the regime deliberately fostered a Jordanian territorial identity. As of the 1970s and 1980s, in the aftermath of the "Black September" civil war of 1970 between the Jordanian armed forces and the Palestine Liberation Organization, the regime consciously promoted a shared Jordanian historical heritage, especially as a counterweight to the Palestinian "Other."

But in Jordan, this was not just a top-down exercise, but a bottom-up one too, whereby the tribes actively adopted the Jordanian identity as their own to the extent that they have actually become the main standard-bearers of what can be termed Jordanianism. Some tribesman have been said to believe that tribalism is commensurate with Jordanianism, and that the state has become the representative and aegis of the "tribe of the Jordanians" versus "the tribe of the Palestinians."[59] In the state bureaucracy, dominated by East Bankers, tribal mores lead to the appointment of ever more loyal East Bankers and thus, what has become known as the "bedoucracy" continues to perpetuate itself.[60]

In recent years, however, an unprecedented crack has appeared in the edifice of the traditionally loyalist East Banker elite and among the rank and file of the regime's tribal base. For decades, regime stability rested on an unwritten social contract between the monarchy and the East Bankers, according to which the regime has enjoyed the unswerving loyalty of East Bankers in exchange for jobs and salaries and other forms of government largesse. Since "Black September", there has been an institutionalized functional cleavage between original East Bank Jordanians and their less trusted compatriots of Palestinian extraction.

A process of Jordanization (*ardanna*) was initiated in the early 1970s whereby Palestinians were systematically removed from positions of influence in the government bureaucracy and the security establishment. Ever since, East Bankers have held the bulk of government jobs and almost exclusively run the security services and the military, while Palestinians dominate the country's private sector. Tensions between Palestinians and original Jordanians are ever-present, as the former resent their exclusion from positions of political influence while the latter resent Palestinian affluence, which they increasingly feel has been gained unfairly at their expense.

Ever since the late 1980s, when Jordan sank into deep economic crisis, Jordan has been urged by the IMF and the World Bank to engage in neoliberal economic reforms — including the extensive privatization of state enterprises — designed to reduce government spending. These measures, partially adopted, have mainly hurt the loyalist East Banker constituency who, having lost government jobs, are forced into the swelling ranks of the unemployed and are generally in receipt of ever-decreasing government support. At the same time, the privatization of state enterprises has tended to further enrich Palestinian entrepreneurs, generating a sense among East Bankers that the regime is not holding up its end of their historical bargain. In recent years, condemnation of King 'Abdullah II (r. 2000–) has regularly been heard from within the inner sanctums of the East Banker elite.

While both the non-Islamist East Bankers and mainly Palestinian Islamists call for greater democratization, the East Bankers face a genuine dilemma on this issue. While they want more influence in determining how wealth and power are distributed in the kingdom, they are hardly interested in a democratization process that would almost certainly empower the Islamists and the Palestinians at their expense. Notwithstanding cracks in the edifice of the East Banker elite, the fractious opposition has yet to come up with a viable alternative to the status quo.

The Arab Spring had initially emboldened the Jordanian opposition, but the outcomes of the revolutions in countries like Egypt and Libya, and especially the bloodbath in Syria, were horrifying to most Jordanians. Even opponents of the monarchy tend to see "the Hashemite regime as the thing that holds [the country] all together."[61] The situation, therefore, remains manageable. As long as the unswerving loyalty of the security establishment lasts, the capacity of the regime to continue muddling through will depend more on its ability to deal effectively with the economy than on any other single factor, including the pace of political reform.

# Concluding Thoughts

In many of the Arab states, even in those where the regime remained in power, e.g. Jordan and Morocco, the Arab Spring resulted in the diminution of the notorious *haybat al-sulta* (the fear of government) as Arab publics were said to have overcome the "barrier of fear." That however did not necessarily result in a transition to democracy, but rather in the weakening of the highly centralized state. As traditions and institutions of functioning democracies were not in place, Islamism, sectarianism, and tribalism contributed towards illiberal governance or conflict, or both combined. In June 2013, in a radical reversal, the Egyptian military, in what was nothing other than a counter-revolutionary coup, acted to bring about the deliberate restoration of the old-fashioned military regime, albeit a new version of it. With the use of virtually unbridled force, the army has consciously reestablished the former *haybat al-sulta*. The eventual endgame, like just about everything else is unpredictable. But it is most likely to look far more authoritarian than the initial, rather fanciful, secular-liberal expectations of the so called Arab Spring.

Years before the Arab Spring, Egyptian political scientist Amr Hamzawy observed that Islamists did well in elections in various parts of the Arab world, from Egypt to Iraq, because they were "well embedded in the social fabric" of Arab societies. This ought to dampen, he wrote, "the dangerous illusion" that political openness in the region "will ultimately replace authoritarian regimes with secular forces" committed to Western-style liberal democracy. To invest hope in secularists, he argued, was to be completely detached from the realities of the current situation.[62]

Also long before the Arab Spring, Hassan Nafaa [Naf'a], a professor of political science at Cairo University, expressed his undisguised, but prescient, concern that throughout the Arab countries,

> a common denominator prevail[s]: overwhelming anxiety over the future of the Arab world... [over the danger that] the Arab order will collapse entirely and the whole region will fall into protracted chaos and bloodshed...[There was] the risk of comprehensive chaos and the fragmentation of the Arab world into rival sectarian entities... [Therefore] the most urgent task is to keep the existing states from shattering into even smaller entities founded upon narrow sectarian, ethnic or tribal affiliations... [and] to steer the Arab world out of its present era of darkness...[63]

What was previously suppressed by authoritarian regimes was now out in the open, with manifestations from tribal, ethnic, and sectarian competition and conflict to all-out civil war. It would therefore seem that for the foreseeable future a degree of authoritarianism would be necessary to maintain stability, and that a lack of stability could result in a further weakening of overall societal cohesion, which was never very strong in the first place. Fashioning genuine, durable cohesion in a situation of economic distress and chaotic efforts to democratize and build institutions was a herculean, and probably impossible task.

But democratization did not necessarily have to subvert the very existence of the state. In cases where there was a cohesive and determined minority movement that had reached a critical mass, and possessed a territorial core, like the Kurds in Iraq or the people of Southern Sudan, this was more likely. But, in fact, in both places the breakup was much more a function of war than of democracy, and so is the case elsewhere. Although ethno-national reassertion among North Africa's Berber populations is very much part of the picture in Morocco, Algeria, and Libya (and, further afield, in fragmented Mali), the Berber/Amazigh challenge in both Morocco and Algeria is peaceful, and thus not threatening to the existence of either state, while in Libya, Amazigh militancy can have only a limited impact in certain areas, owing to the small size of the community.[64]

Yemen and Libya are extreme cases of countries that might break up. Yemen is presently no more than a shell of a state, surviving, like Lebanon, and one might eventually witness the reconstitution of South Yemen as it had existed before the unification of 1990. Libya is very low in components of statehood. It has ineffective state institutions and is torn asunder by tribal identities and regional divisions between Tripolitania, Cyrenaica, and Fezzan that were thrust together in the creation of Libya by the Western allies in 1951. Its oil wealth is unequally distributed between the three provinces, very much in Cyrenaica's favor, another factor which may precipitate the dissolution of the state, as warring tribes and factions compete for control of the country's resources.

Syria's breakup, if it happens, will also be more a function of the war and the resultant collapse of a "fierce" state, than of democratization. The longer the war goes on, the more damage is done to the social fabric, although even in the worst case, Syria will probably survive in some form, with a Syrian Arab identity, heavily Sunni, with some formula for including Christians, Druze, anti-Asad 'Alawis, and perhaps Kurds (a less likely prospect as time passes). Interestingly, in June 2011 the Antalya Declaration of opposition groups declared their intent to establish a multi-ethnic state, not an Arab state, thus acknowledging the difficulties in holding the country together under the current formula.[65]

The picture is thus extraordinarily varied and fluid. But overall, state and societal cohesion appear to be an increasingly dear resource throughout the Middle East and North Africa.

# Notes

1. J. P. Nettl, "The state as a conceptual variable," *World Politics*, Vol. 20 (1968), pp. 559–592; Gabriel Ben-Dor, *State and Conflict in the Middle* East (NY: Praeger, 1983), Joseph Kostiner, "Solidarity in the Arab State: An Historical Perspective," in Asher Susser (ed.), *Challenges to the Cohesion of the Arab State* (Tel Aviv: The Moshe Dayan Center, 2008), pp. 21–39.
2. Ernest Gellner, "Cohesion and Identity: the Maghreb from Ibn Khaldun to Emile Durkheim," in *idem, Muslim Society* (Cambridge: Cambridge UP, 1983, paperback edition), p. 95.
3. Joel S. Migdal, *Strong Societies and Weak States* (Princeton, NJ: Princeton University Press, 1988), pp. 3–41, 181–205.
4. Israel Gershoni, "Rethinking the Formation of Arab Nationalism in the Middle East, 1920-1945: Old and New Narratives;" in James Jankowski and Israel Gershoni (eds.), *Rethinking Nationalism in the Arab Middle East* (NY: Columbia UP 1997), pp. 3–25;

Phillip Khoury, "The Paradoxical in Arab Nationalism: Interwar Syria Revisited," in *idem*, pp. 273–287.

5.  Ilya Harik,"The Origins of the Arab State System," in Giacomo Luciani (ed.), *The Arab State* (Berkeley, CA: University of California Press, 1990), pp. 1–28.

6.  Fouad Ajami, "The End of Pan-Arabism," *Foreign Affairs*, Vol. 52 (Winter 1978–1979), pp. 355–373.

7.  For instructive discussions on the value of Arabism in promoting territorial, state-centered nationalism, see Michael Barnett, *Dialogues in Arab Politics* (NY: Columbia UP, 1998); Cyrus Schayegh, "1958 Reconsidered: State Formation and the Cold War in the Early Postcolonial Arab Middle East," *International Journal of Middle East Studies*, Vol. 45, Issue 3 (August 2013), pp. 421–443; Christopher Phillips, *Everyday Arab Identity: The Daily Reproduction of the Arab World* (London: Routledge, 2013).

8.  Malik Mufti, *Sovereign Creations: Pan-Arabism and Political Order in Syria and Iraq* (Ithaca and London: Cornell University Press, 1996).

9.  Nazih N. Ayubi, *Over-stating the Arab State* (London, NY: I.B. Tauris, 1995).

10. Bernard Lewis, "The Map of the Middle East: A Guide for the Perplexed," *The American Scholar*, Vol. 58, Issue 1 (Winter 1989), pp. 19–38.

11. Israel Gershoni, "The Evolution of National Culture in Modern Egypt: Intellectual Formation and Social Diffusion, 1892–1945," *Poetics Today*, Vol. 13 (1992), p. 328.

12. P. J. Vatikiotis, *Islam and the State* (London: Routledge, 1987), p. 75.

13. Immanuel Wallerstein, "Islam, the West, and the World," *Journal of Islamic Studies*, Vol. 10, Issue 2 (1999), pp. 117–118.

14. Bernard Lewis, *The Emergence of Modern Turkey*, second edition (London: Oxford University Press, 1968), pp. 106–110.

15. *Ibid.*, pp. 89–105.

16. P. J. Vatikiotis, *The Modern History of Egypt* (London: Weidenfeld and Nicolson, 1969), pp. 204–208.

17. *Ibid.*, pp. 210, 219, 226, 234.

18. *Ibid.*, 303.

19. *Ibid.*, pp. 303, 308.

20. *Ibid.*, pp. 234, 304.

21. Benedict Anderson, *Imagined Communities: Reflections on the Origin and Spread of Nationalism*, revised ed. (London: Verso, 1991), p. 11.

22. James Gelvin, "The Social Origins of Popular Nationalism in Syria: Evidence for a New Framework," *International Journal of Middle East Studies*, Vol. 26, Issue 4 (November 1994), pp. 645–661; *idem*, "Arab Nationalism": Has a New Framework Emerged?", *International Journal of Middle East Studies*, Vol. 41, Issue 1 (February 2009), pp. 10–12.

23. Mansoor Moaddel, *Islamic Modernism, Nationalism, and Fundamentalism: Episode and Discourse* (Chicago: University of Chicago Press, 2005), pp. 339–340.

24. Nader Hashemi, *Islam, Secularism and Liberal Democracy: Toward a Democratic Theory for Muslim Societies* (New York: Oxford University Press, 2009), p. 135.

25. Amin al-Huwaydi, *Zilzal 'Asifa al-Sahra'a Watawabi'hu* (Cairo: Dar al-Shuruq, 1998).

26. Bruce Maddy-Weitzman, "Arabs vs. the Abdullah Plan", *Middle East Quarterly*, Vol. 17, Issue 3 (Summer 2010), pp. 3–12.

27. Hashemi, *Islam, Secularism and Liberal Democracy*, pp. 137–141.

28. R. Stephen Humphreys, *Between Memory and Desire: The Middle East in a Troubled Age* (University of California Press, 1999), p. 188; L. Carl Brown, *Religion and State; The Muslim Approach to Politics* (New York: Columbia University Press, 2000), p. 158.

29. Emmanuel Sivan, *Radical Islam: Medieval Theology and Modern Politics* (New Haven and London: Yale University Press, 1985), pp. 16–49.

30. Gilles Kepel, *Muslim Extremism in Egypt: The Prophet and Pharaoh*, trans. Jon Rothschild (Berkeley, CA: University of California Press, 1985), pp. 144–145, 152–153.

31. Clement Moore Henry, "On Theory and Practice Among Arabs," *World Politics*, Vol. 24 (1971), pp. 106–126.

32. See: http://www.arab-hdr.org.

33. E.g., Hamied Ansari, *Egypt: The Stalled Society* (Albany NY: SUNY Press, 1986).

34. Marc Lynch, *The Arab Uprising: The Unfinished Revolutions of the New Middle East* (New York: Public Affairs, 2012), p. 8.

35. Humphreys, p. 64.

36. Ajami, "The End of Pan-Arabism," and Bernard Lewis, *The Multiple Identities of the Middle East* (New York: Schoeken Books, 1998), p. 140, cited in Adeed Dawish, *Arab Nationalism in the Twentieth Century* (Princeton: Princeton University Press, 2003), pp. 10–11.

37. Martin Kramer, "Arab Nationalism: Mistaken Identity", *Daedalus*, Vol. 122, Issue 3 (Summer 1993), pp. 171–206.

38. Ami Ayalon, "Egypt's Quest for Cultural Orientation" (Tel Aviv University, Moshe Dayan Center, *Data and Analysis Series*, June 1999), pp. 39–40.

39. Asef Bayat, *Making Islam Democratic: Social Movements and the Post-Islamic Turn* (Stanford, CA: Stanford University Press, 2007), p. 165.

40. Ami Ayalon, "Egypt's Coptic Pandora's Box," in Ofra Bengio and Gabriel Ben-Dor (eds.), *Minorities and the State in the Arab World* (Boulder, CO: Lynne Rienner, 1999), p. 56.

41. Ben Hubbard and David D. Kirkpatrick, "Sudden Improvements in Egypt Suggest a Campaign to Undermine Morsi," *New York Times*, July 10, 2013; Sarah Lynch, "Egypt's Christians Under Attack since Morsi's Ouster," *USA Today*, August 15, 2013; Febe Armanios, "Egypt's Copts between Morsi and the Military," *The Cairo Review of Global Affairs*, September 2, 2013.

42. Kanan Makiya, *Republic of Fear: The Politics of Modern Iraq* (2nd edition, Berkeley, CA: University of California Press).

43. Ofra Bengio, "Iraq — From Failed Nation-State to Binational State?" in Asher Susser (ed.), *Challenges to the Cohesion of the Arab State* (Tel Aviv University, The Moshe Dayan Center, 2008), p. 67.

44. Amatzia Baram, "Territorial Nationalism in the Middle East," *Middle Eastern Studies*, Vol. 26, Issue 4 (October 1990), pp. 426–427.

45. Bengio, p. 64.

46. Hazim Saghiya, *Saddam Husayn: Aya Totalitariyya?* ["Saddam Husayn: Which totalitarianism?"], October 21, 2007, at www.iraqmemory.org/inp/view.asp?ID=837.
47. Ali Allawi, *The Occupation of Iraq: Winning the War, Losing the Peace* (New Haven and London: Yale University Press, 2007), p. 135 (emphasis in orginal).
48. Ahmad al-Moussawi, "Is Western Iraq Moving Toward Secession," *al-Akhbar* (Beirut), December 29, 2012 (http://english.al-akhbar.com/print/14522).
49. *France 24*, November 20, 2013 (http://www.france24.com/en).
50. Elie Shalhub, "Khulasat 'Iraqiyya" [The Essentials of Iraq], *al-Akhbar* (Beirut), October 14, 2009; see also "Al-'Iraq ba'd sit sanawat min al-ihtilal" [Iraq after six years since the occupation], editorial in *al-Quds al-'Arabi*, March 20, 2009.
51. Hanna Batatu, "Some Observations on the Social Roots of Syria's Ruling Military Group and the Causes for its Dominance," *Middle East Journal*, Vol. 35, Issue 3 (Summer 1981), p. 331.
52. Eyal Zisser, "The 'Alawis, Lords of Syria: From Ethnic Minority to Ruling Sect," in Bengio and Ben-Dor (eds.), *Minorities*, pp. 129–145.
53. Amatzia Baram, "Territorial Nationalism," pp. 433–438.
54. This notwithstanding the proclamation by Lebanese Shi'ite leader Imam Musa Sadr in 1973 that the Alawis were to be considered a legitimate branch of Shi'i Islam. Martin Kramer, "Syria's Alawis and Shi'isim," in *idem* (ed.), *Shi'ism, Resistance and Revolution* (Boulder, CO: Westview Press, 1987), pp. 246–252.
55. Eyal Zisser, *Faces of Syria: Society, Regime and State* (Tel Aviv: Hakibbutz Hameuhad, 2003), pp. 247–251 [Hebrew].
56. The Turks were said to be troubled by a reference made by Mas'ud Barzani, the President of Iraq's Kurdish Regional Government, to the Kurdish area in Syria as "western Kurdistan" (see Ted Galen Carpenter, "The Kurdish Issue Returns to Prominence," Aspen-Institute, November 28, 2013).
57. *Associated Press*, "Fear in Syrian Capital as Mortar Shells Rain Down," *Washington Post*, November 28, 2013.
58. Eyal Zisser, "The 'Alawis," in Bengio and Ben-Dor (eds.), *Minorities*, p. 135.
59. Schirin H. Fathi, *Jordan—An Invented Nation? Tribe State Dynamics and the Formation of National Identity* (Hamburg: Deutsches Orient-Institut, 1994), pp. 259, 264.
60. *Ibid.*, pp. 179–180; and Laurie Brand, "The Quest for Civil Society in Jordan," in Augustus R. Norton (ed.), *Civil Society in the Middle East* (Leiden: Brill, 1995), pp. 180, 184.
61. Shadi Hamid and Courtney Freer, "How Stable is Jordan? Abdullah's Half-hearted Reforms and the Challenge of the Arab Spring" (Brookings Doha Center, Policy Briefing, November 2011), p. 4.
62. Amr Hamzawy, "Islamists Re-awaken Religious Politics," *Al-Ahram Weekly*, December 29, 2005–January 4, 2006.
63. Hassan Nafaa, "Road to Salvation," *Al-Ahram Weekly*, May 3–9, 2007; see also Khalid al-Dakhil, *"Al-Harb 'ala 'Iraq: nihayat al-Ba'th, thum madha?"* ["The war against Iraq: The end of the Ba'th, then what?"], *al-Hayat*, March 23, 2003.

64. Bruce Maddy-Weitzman, "Arabization and its Discontents: The Rise of the Amazigh Movement in North Africa", *The Journal of the Middle East and Africa*, Vol. 3, Issue 2 (June–December 2012), pp. 109–135.
65. "The Final Declaration of the Syria Conference for Change in Antalya 02/06/2011," http://www.lccsyria.org/583 (last accessed on December 8, 2013).

# PART I
## Thematic Issues

# The Arab State between Sectarianism, Nationalism, and Islamism

## Elisheva Machlis

In December 2004, King Abdullah of Jordan warned of the threat from an emerging "Shi'a crescent" in the Middle East. In this well-known remark, Abdullah captured the fear of many Sunnis in the Arab milieu that the Shi'is would create a united front stretching from Iran across Iraq to Lebanon, and thereby undermine the historical Sunni hegemony over the region.[1] Similarly, in April 2006, Hosni Mubarak of Egypt declared that the Shi'is are more loyal to Iran than to the countries in which they reside.[2] In essence, these two important Arab leaders argued that the Shi'is have the desire, and perhaps the potential, to take over the Arab and Muslim worlds, following the empowerment of Shi'is in Iraq since 2003. Another dimension to this fear is the economic factor; the Shi'is reside in the oil-rich regions of a number of Arab states, including in Iraq, Saudi Arabia, and Bahrain.

The ascendance of Islamist-led movements following the "Arab Spring" uprisings added another layer to the growing concern over the rise of a new Shi'i power in the Middle East. Yet to what extent does the historical Sunni-Shi'i divide play a part in the geopolitical situation in the contemporary Middle East? Further, has the "Islamic Awakening" in the last decades strengthened this conflict? This chapter will explore these questions in the context of the Arab milieu with some references to Iran, focusing on the post-2003 period.

## The Rise of Sectarianism

Throughout most of the twentieth century, sectarian conflict appeared to be subsiding in the Arab world. Instead, ideologies, power struggles, national identities, and tribalism were the leading factors behind the Arab political system that developed over the course of the century. Yet since the 1980s, the historical schism between Sunnis and Shi'is has been thrust back onto the center stage of Middle East politics. This process began with the Islamic Revolution in Iran and continued through the Iran-Iraq war and the rise of jihadist movements in the

Middle East, movements which, following the Soviet invasion of Afghanistan, enjoyed Saudi support. This process reached its peak with the empowerment of Shi'is in Iraq in the aftermath of the US invasion of 2003.[3]

Iran's Islamic revolution had a clear universal message. Its main ideologues were engaged with the leading Western ideologies and ideologues of the time.[4] They mitigated their Shi'i affiliation, emphasising instead an affinity with third-world revolutionary causes, particularly anti-imperialism.[5] These revolutionaries projected a universal message of Islam and presented the Iranian revolution as a model for the entire Muslim world. However, while emphasizing an ecumenical worldview, Imam Khomeini's doctrine of *velayat-e faqih*, guardianship of the jurist, alienated Sunnis. This notion had some basis in Shi'ism yet was entirely foreign to Sunni thought, and posed a clear threat to existing regimes in the Arab world.[6] Because of this, the Islamic Revolution ultimately contributed to the rise of sectarianism more than to the spread of Islam's universal religious appeal.

The eight-year-long Iran-Iraq war that erupted in 1980 also strengthened the sectarian dimension of Middle East politics. Neither Iran nor Iraq tended to depict the war as a struggle between Sunnis and Shi'is. The Islamic Republic of Iran (IRI) presented the conflict as a battle between Islam and unbelief. It relied on Shi'i symbols of martyrdom to mobilize its population, yet did not champion a sectarian war.[7] Saddam Hussein, on the other hand, emphasized the Arab-Persian ethno-national rivalry. As the war dragged on to Iraq's disadvantage, Saddam also adopted an inclusive Islamic discourse in order to rally Iraq's large numbers of Shi'i troops behind his command and counter Khomeini's message.[8] Yet in the wider Arab and Muslim worlds, the war was perceived as a struggle between Sunni Arabs and the Shi'is of Iran, adding another layer to the ascendance of sectarianism in the region.

Beginning in the 1980s, sectarian conflict was intensified by the rise of jihadi movements in the Muslim world and Saudi support for this development, at least in its early period. Al-Qa'ida, which emerged in the late 1980s, combined a salafi call to return to the pristine Islam of the forefathers with the Wahhabi notion of *tawhid al-'ibada* (the unity of worship). Ibn 'Abd al-Wahhab (1703-1792) — the founder of the Wahhabi movement — argued that one cannot embrace Islam only by accepting the *shahada* (the Islamic declaration of faith), but by practicing a literalist and uncompromising monotheistic worldview. His call for the purification of Islam was accompanied by a campaign against manifestations of polytheism (*shirk*). Adherents of Wahhabi Islam directed their message against Shi'ism and Sufism, and called upon followers to fight these "unbelievers" until they accepted Wahhabism.[9] Al-Qa'ida, with its endorsement of these ideas, its broad network of jihadi fighters, and its extensive use of new media, provided an important platform for the propagation of this anti-Shi'i worldview.

The US-led invasion of Iraq in 2003 and resulting empowerment of the Shi'is added another factor to the rise of sectarianism in the region. This was the first time in the modern history of Iraq that the Shi'i majority took control of the country. In 2006, with the mounting losses inflicted by the Sunni insurgency, the new Shi'i-led government began reaching out to the now embattled and embittered Sunni Arab minority. In June 2006, Prime Minister Nuri al-Maliki announced a national reconciliation and dialogue project. One of the project's tasks was to review the ban against the participation of former Ba'th members in the new government, through the de-ba'thification process, which prevented many Sunnis from joining the Shi'i-led administration. Concurrently, from late 2006, Sunni tribal members who participated in the opposition movement began cooperating with the US forces in Iraq in order to eliminate the threat of Sunni extremism led by al-Qa'ida in Iraq. However, steps towards political integration of the Sunnis were slow and insufficient. Furthermore, Maliki, who garnered a second term in 2010, came under growing criticism from Sunnis in Iraq and elsewhere for implementing a sectarian policy.[10] Maliki may have been driven by a clear sectarian motive stemming from the desire to empower the Shi'is after years of political marginalization. Yet his policy also reflected the political culture in modern Iraq, which was controlled for decades by an authoritarian regime that favored a loyal cadre of associates. Perhaps Maliki, who strongly opposed the former regime, was actually the product of its political culture, and sectarianism was the result of this deeply entrenched tendency.

## The Emergence of Multiple Shi'i Identities

Political and religious developments beginning with the Islamic Revolution restored sectarianism to the political forefront of the Arab and Muslim worlds. Nevertheless, other factors mitigated the influence of the historical Sunni-Shi'i conflict on contemporary Middle East politics. These factors included mutual cross-sectarian elements, such as ethnicity, religion, and political interests, which at least in theory were able to provide a basis for cooperation between Sunnis and Shi'is in the region. For example, Arabism gained ground during the first half of the twentieth century and created a platform for cross-sectarian collaboration. In Iraq and Lebanon, which contain the largest numbers of Shi'a in the Arab world, proponents of Arabism included members of the embryonic Shi'i elite of politicians, businessmen, and intellectuals. They endorsed Arabism as a cultural identification, reflecting their own heritage as natives of the region.

In addition, they embraced its political dimension, supporting the causes of anti-imperialism and justice for the Palestinians. Some reformist members of the religious Shi'i elite also expressed an affinity with Arabism. Progressive elements among both the religious and the more secular Shi'i leaderships called for a dialogue with the Arab-Sunni world based on a mutual bond of Arabism, shared political interests, a joint struggle against the West and support for modern values of progress and rationality.[11]

However, during the second half of the twentieth century, the Shi'is of Iraq and Lebanon became disillusioned with the process of integration in these nation-states. In Lebanon, Imam Musa al-Sadr, the charismatic Iranian-born cleric, founded *Harakat al-Mahrumin* ("Movement of the Dispossessed") in 1974, contributing to the emergence of a new social conscience among the Shi'is. The party reflected a growing political awareness among Lebanon's developing Shi'i bourgeoisie, who began challenging the distribution of power and resources in Lebanon's political system. It was a protest movement that enjoyed mass support among the urban poor, the deprived peasants, and the budding Shi'i elite.

A similar focus on sectarian affiliation also occurred in Iraq during this period. In the late 1950s, the *Da'wa* party[12] was founded by a group of reform-minded Shi'i clerics against the backdrop of the rising threat of secularism and the growing attraction to communism within the community. It signaled a new Shi'i understanding that only separate political representation would safeguard their rights and preserve their cultural heritage.[13] While some Shi'is managed to penetrate the Iraqi administration, the state system as a whole was controlled by Sunnis from the years of the British Mandate, the monarchical decades and, after 1958, Iraq's revolutionary regimes.[14] By the 1970s, the Shi'is, with their separate political representation, were headed toward direct confrontation with Saddam's brutal and increasingly totalitarian rule. The *Da'wa* party, which in its early days represented a universal call to Islam, now began expressing a clear sectarian orientation.[15] The return of the historical Sunni-Shi'i fault line to contemporary Middle East politics was solidified in the following decade, beginning with the Iranian Islamic Revolution. Yet the re-emergence of sectarianism did not mean that the Arab Shi'is perceived themselves as a foreign element in the region, politically or culturally. Their inclination towards sectarianism resulted from disappointment with the Sunni-led nation-state, and not from their rejection of Arabism or Islam as shared identifications for both Shi'is and Sunnis living in the region.

Shi'i affinity with Arabism and nationalism can also be viewed by assessing Shi'i efforts to unite with members of their creed outside the boundaries of the nation-state and even beyond the Arab world. In the course of the twentieth century, Shi'i scholars in their diverse locations expanded the historical clerical networks that had developed through the Shi'i centers of learning in Najaf and Karbala. They also came to demonstrate an affinity with the new nation-states while endorsing diverse ideologies that transcended their sectarian identity. During this period, members of this community maintained a certain bond with their Shi'i heritage from religious, cultural, and/or social perspectives. Yet, they also defined themselves as loyal members of their nation-states and as Arabs, Muslims, or members of a particular political current, including communism, the Ba'th party, and other ideological affiliations.

Hence, sectarian affiliation was no longer an exclusive mark of identification for Shi'is in the region. As a whole, Shi'is living in the Arab world did not exercise efforts to unify the Shi'i world since they perceived themselves as members of particular Arab nation-states. Several examples demonstrate the lack of a pan-Shi'i strategy including the failure of Khomeini to export the Islamic revolution to the Shi'i-Arab world, and the particularist political interests and orientation of Hizballah with its growing focus on the Lebanese national arena.[16] Even in post-2003 Iraq, as the Shi'is obtained control of the state for the first time in the country's modern history, they did not unite behind one political front. Rather, the Shi'i political landscape was divided between various factions, including the *Da'wa* party, the Islamic Supreme Council in Iraq, followers of Muqtada al-Sadr, and secularists, each with a different vision regarding the future of Iraq.[17]

Another impediment to the unity of the Shi'i world has been the nature of clerical authority. Clerical leadership is diffused within a hierarchal religious elite linked through a myriad of scholarly networks, in which there are no clear guidelines enabling Shi'is to acknowledge one supreme leader. The method of studying in the Shi'i centers of Najaf and Karbala contributed to the entrenchment of this informal character of clerical authority, in which students were divided among multiple circles of learning and split along lines of ethnicity, nationality, and prominence. Within this decentralized leadership system, the ordinary believer was required to follow and emulate a particular *mujtahid*, or high-ranking jurist, known for his superior knowledge and piety.[18] To be sure, there were several leading clerics in the Shi'i milieu who obtained large followings that cut across national lines. Yet, given its multiple authorities, the Shi'i world was not unified. Thus, for example, while Iran was criticized in the Arab world for meddling in the revolt of Shi'is in Bahrain which erupted in February 2011, the population itself was divided in its allegiances. They followed a range of spiritual guides, including Ayatollah Khamenei, the Supreme Leader of Iran, Ayatollah Sistani in Iraq, and, in the past, the late Ayatollah Fadlallah of Lebanon, as well.

Nevertheless, an international Shi'i scholarly community, which had already existed prior to the twentieth century, expanded during this period. The development of transportation and communication networks strengthened this pan-Shi'i element but also opened these previously secluded communities to the wider Muslim world. Empowerment of the Shi'is in Iraq after 2003 bolstered connections between this community and its fellow believers in neighboring Iran through business, pilgrimage and scholarly ties. Yet, in the transition to the twenty-first century, Shi'is in their diverse locations upheld a variety of social, political, and ideological links — both sectarian and non-sectarian — within the boundaries of the nation-state and beyond.

Overall then, the Arab and Muslim worlds from the 1980s onwards witnessed a clear shift towards sectarianism. However, many among the Arab Shi'is themselves did not perceive their Shi'i affinity as the sole mark of their identity. Even Iraq under Maliki is a case in point. In the post-2003 period, Shi'i-led Iraq began cultivating strong connections with Iran, including ties with the main Shi'i political forces in the country and increasing the volume of trade with its neighbor. Baghdad did not feel a need to legitimize these political and economic ties by evoking a common Shi'i identity, which developed as the new Shi'i-led state also cooperated with the US. Yet, together with these official relations, some reports suggest that beneath the surface, there were more ties, including Iranian support for Iraq's Shi'i militias and the flow of arms through Iraq to the Asad regime in Syria. Nevertheless, together with its growing alliance with Tehran, Baghdad also sought to refurbish its ties with the Arab world. While many Arab countries are critical of Maliki's current sectarianism, they are also wary of losing whatever remaining influence they have over this important country. As a result, although Iraq remains marginal to the current Arab system, Arab states are gradually seeking to build bridges to Baghdad in order to counter its close relations with the Islamic Republic of Iran.[19] For its part, Iraq, while desiring close ties with Iran, is also interested in forging multiple bilateral connections, which serve its diverse interests in the Arab, Muslim, and Western worlds.

## Arab-Sunni Views of the Shi'i Question

Arab-Sunni approaches to the sectarian question are influenced by the character of individual countries and their dominant ideologies, political interests, relations with Iran, and the presence or absence of Shi'is. As a result, there is a range of attitudes towards the Shi'a among different parties in the Arab world, including *al-Qa'ida* and the Saudis' radical and uncompromising abhorrence of the creed, as well as pragmatic approaches, particularly among the small Gulf states. As will be delineated below, the Muslim Brotherhood's stand on this question balanced affinity with modernist Shi'is — on the promotion of political Islam, a universal reading of religion, and the joint struggle against the West — with a more traditional Sunni view insisting on the hegemony of the Sunni Muslim majority.

Within the anti-Shi'i camp, both al-Qa'ida and Saudi Arabia contributed to the intensification of sectarianism in the region. Yet even al-Qa'ida, with its radical ideology, has shown some willingness to prioritize its goals in order to serve particular interests. Thus, for example, there were indications that members of al-Qa'ida in Iraq were willing to compromise in the struggle against the Shi'a in order to fight the greater US enemy. There have also been unverified reports of cooperation between al-Qa'ida members and Iranian officials for the purpose of conducting a joint battle against the West.[20]

Saudi Arabia contributed more than any other power in the region to awakening the rift between Sunnis and Shi'is, beginning with its support for the Sunni jihadist forces in Afghanistan in the 1980s. More recently, Saudi Arabia helped quell the Shi'i revolt in Bahrain, as the leader of a joint Gulf Cooperation Council (GCC) force.[21] Besides its Wahhabi inclination, Saudi Arabia's approach to the Shi'is stems from its desire to lead the Muslim world, being the cradle of Islamic civilization and protector of the holiest shrines in Islam, Mecca and Medina. It perceives itself as the guardian of the Sunni world against the Shi'i forces of heresy. The differing political orientations of the Islamic Republic of Iran and the Saudi monarchy further sharpened the irreconcilable ideological struggle between these two countries.[22]

The existence of a Shi'i minority in Saudi Arabia added another dimension to the country's sectarian orientation. Shi'is living in Saudi Arabia are the most oppressed in the Arab-Sunni world, suffering from religious, judicial, and socio-political discrimination. Following the attacks of September 11, 2001, the Saudi establishment understood the need to curb the influence of radical Wahhabis in the kingdom. Nevertheless, the government did not want to clash with the Wahhabi establishment, due to its historical alliance with the House of Al Sa'ud.[23] The concentration of Shi'is in the oil-rich Eastern Province adds another dimension to Saudi suspicions towards this 'deviant minority'.

Shi'i communities exist in each of the other Gulf states. The approach of the smaller Gulf states to the sectarian question is linked to the existence of Shi'i minorities in their countries as well as to their geo-strategic position. Living under the constant threat of Iran's Islamic Republic and Saddam's Iraq, and also subordinated to Saudi Arabia, these small monarchical regimes — Kuwait, Bahrain, Qatar, the UAE, and Oman — tried to forge positive relations with the larger powers in the region while safeguarding their core alliance with the Sunni-Arab world and enjoying the protection of a US military presence.[24]

The position of the Shi'i minority in Kuwait is among the best in the Gulf region due to the pluralistic nature of the country's politics. On the other end of the spectrum is Bahrain, home to the largest concentration of Shi'is among the smaller Gulf states, who constitute approximately 70 percent of the population. They are ruled by the Sunni Al Khalifa family and suffer from socio-political discrimination. With his ascendance to power in 1999, Hamad bin Isa Al Khalifa, the current ruler of this autocratic regime, opened up the political system. He renewed the activities of the parliament, which was suspended in 1975, and began a dialogue with Shi'i opposition. Nevertheless, the Al Khalifa maintained overall control over policy; the Shi'is were also barred from the military.[25] The 2011 uprising in Bahrain stemmed from the local Shi'is' demand for greater democratization and equal rights. While identifying with the Islamic Republic's religious worldview, there is little support among the Shi'is for the Iranian model of *velayat-e faqih*, the guardianship of the jurist, since the Bahraini Shi'is' situation, goals, and relationship with the Sunnis stem first and foremost from particular conditions in Bahrain.[26] Nevertheless, from the Shah to the Islamic Republic, Iran has periodically laid claim to Bahrain, based on its control of this territory at different points in the past. There are also scholarly connections between the two communities dating back to the sixteenth century. Following the uprising in Bahrain in 2011, Gulf leaders pointed an accusing finger at Tehran, while the Islamic Republic voiced its growing concern for the plight of the local Shi'i community.

The Shi'i revolt in Bahrain altered the traditional balancing act of these mini-states in the Gulf. Given their obligation to assist a fellow GCC member, they were obliged to side with Bahrain's Sunni ruling family, the Al Khalifa, in its effort to crush the uprising of the Shi'i majority.[72] As these countries provided support for the Al Khalifa, the Gulf media presented a more complex picture. News outlets from the region blamed Iran for arousing sectarianism. There were also calls for all sides to avoid the sectarian card and there was even some criticism of Bahrain itself for its disregard of the socio-political demands of the Shi'is.[28] In other words, while sectarianism is on the rise in many places in the Middle East, public opinion makers in the region are also aware of the perils of the volatile situation and are seeking to restore calm on the basis of common political interests.

Besides Saudi Arabia and the Gulf states, another important player in this new power game, and particularly following the overthrow of Hosni Mubarak in February 2011, has been the Muslim Brotherhood. By and large, the Brotherhood's approach to the Shi'i question is pragmatic, although it is influenced by the salafi view of the supremacy of Sunni Arabs. This has created a duality in the movement's perception of Shi'is. Iran's close alliance with the

Palestinian Hamas, an offshoot of the Brotherhood, can be seen in the context of the Brotherhood's pragmatism. Iran provided Hamas with much needed financial and military assistance, in support of a common uncompromising animosity towards the West and Israel. Lately, there has been tension in this relationship due to Hamas' support for the Sunni insurgents in Syria, while Iran continues to back its ally, Bashar al-Asad.[29]

From an ideological perspective, the Muslim Brotherhood and the Islamic Republic shared a universal perception of religion, a revivalist tendency, a vision of political Islam, an anti-Western position, and a similar cultural worldview. However, their common all-encompassing Islamic outlook contrasted with the Muslim Brotherhood's fundamental salafi hostility towards the Shi'is. The Brotherhood's anti-Shi'i position stems from the salafis' glorification of the early period of Islam, which also marked the onset of the sectarian schism. One of the precursors to the modern salafi movement, Rashid Rida (1865-1935), emphasized his vocal support for the Wahhabi movement, yet also met with the spiritual leader of the Shi'is in Tyre, Lebanon.[30] Concurrently, some of these early twentieth century salafis put aside their hostility towards the Shi'is and joined forces in order to revive religion and fight foreign occupation and Western supremacy. For example, Hasan al-Banna (1906-1949), the founder of the Muslim Brotherhood, supported the cause of Muslim unity.[31] In al-Azhar itself there was a clear change in this important Sunni institution's view of Shi'ism. In 1959, Mahmud Shaltut, who was the Shaykh al-Azhar during these years, acknowledged Shi'ism as a fifth *madhhab* (school of Islamic law).[32]

During the second half of the twentieth century, while some Islamists continued to further Muslim unity, others championed an anti-Shi'i discourse. These divergent opinions in some cases reflected the actual presence or absence of Shi'is in the country. Thus, for example, the Muslim Brotherhood in Egypt tended to adopt a fairly moderate position towards the Shi'is since it did not need to deal with an actual Shi'i presence in the country. In this context, a noteworthy figure among the the Muslim Brotherhood of Egypt was the businessman Yusuf Mustafa Nada, who was involved in the movement for many years and acted as its foreign minister. Nada endorsed the notion of Shi'ism as a fifth *madhhab* and argued that this creed did not digress from the true principles of Islam. He even glorified the figure of 'Ali and members of his household, and attributed differences between Sunnis and Shi'is to politics rather than religion.[33]

Shaykh Yusuf al-Qaradawi, the well-known Sunni Egyptian preacher who resided in Qatar until 2011, and joined demonstrations in Cairo with the outburst of the popular revolt, exemplified efforts among the Brotherhood to promote reconciliation with the Shi'is. Al-Qaradawi emphasized that tolerance is the basis of Islam. He overtly rejected the Wahhabi notion of *tawhid al-'ibada*, in which only Muslims who practiced religion in accordance with the rigid and literalist understanding of this movement were accepted into Islam. In 2004, the influential Sunni leader established the International Society for Muslim Clerics that was designed for both Sunnis and Shi'is.[34] Yet, alongside this reconciliatory position, he also made some anti-Shi'i remarks that exemplified the Sunni fear of losing its hegemony in the region. Following the eruption of the Arab Spring protests, al-Qaradawi defended the popular uprising in Egypt while calling for the suppression of the riots in Bahrain.[35] Thus, while al-Qaradawi supported the notion of Muslim unity and even endorsed Shi'i jurisprudence, he nevertheless upheld the Sunni perception of supremacy within the *umma* (community) of Islam.

Mohammed Morsi, the former president of Egypt, elected in June 2012 and then removed from power by the military in July 2013, also served as an important barometer to evaluate Islamists' views of the Shi'a. Morsi, the chairman of the Freedom and Justice Party, which was founded by the Muslim Brotherhood in the wake of the 2011 Egyptian revolt, chose to make Saudi Arabia, a country that exemplifies radical Sunni sectarianism, the destination of his first foreign visit. Yet, this visit was not intended to provide support for Saudi Arabia's uncompromising Wahhabi worldview, nor was it expected to, given the ideological differences between Saudi Arabia and the Muslim Brotherhood. Viewed through the prism of Egypt's political and socio-economic interests, the visit was designed to assert Egypt's position in the Arab world and to draw foreign investment into the country's empty coffers.

Morsi's visit to Saudi Arabia was followed by his decision to participate in the conference of the Non-Aligned Movement in August 2012, which convened in Tehran. This move highlighted Morsi's pragmatic approach to foreign policy. It was the first visit of an Egyptian leader to Iran since the 1979 Islamic revolution, which led to a severing of relations between the two countries. Morsi's participation in the 2012 conference, the respect he was given by his Iranian hosts, and, particularly, his choice of words on the podium reflected a desire to delineate an independent foreign policy based on the country's complex interests, and not on a one-dimensional outlook, sectarian or otherwise.[36]

Egypt under the Muslim Brotherhood conducted a complex foreign policy, balancing the country's diverse interests in the Arab world with its interests in the broader Muslim milieu, including the Shi'i Iran, as well as the West. This marked a clear change from Mubarak's approach, which had led Egypt to be perceived by many as a Western satellite state. The Islamist regime in Egypt, like Iran, embraced a vision of political Islam. The two also championed the Palestinian issue. On the other hand, Morsi also had to take into consideration the diverse parties involved in Egypt's internal power game and particularly the military, due to its prominent place in Egyptian politics and society.

Egypt's military coup and the ousting of Morsī threw into question the newly established relations between Cairo and Tehran. The Islamic Republic, which had sought to lay claim to the Arab revolts as an "Islamic Awakening," lost an important stronghold of political Islam and a potential Sunni ally following the removal of the Islamist government in Egypt.[37] Furthermore, Saudi Arabia, which views Iran in the most dire terms, was quick to proclaim its support for the new military rulers in Egypt.[38] General 'Abd al-Fatah al-Sisi, Egypt's strongman, began a crackdown on Islamic militants operating out of the Sinai as tensions mounted between the military rulers in Egypt and the Hamas-led government in Gaza.[39]

Officials in the Islamic Republic strongly criticized Egypt's new military authorities, depicting the takeover as an anti-democratic foreign plot.[40] However, Hassan Rouhani, the newly elected president of Iran, expressed a more nuanced approach towards the military leaders in Egypt. Referring to the latest developments in Egypt, Iran's Rouhani declared, "We are against war and bloodshed among Muslims in any place in the world…."[41] His position reflected the problematic relationship that had emerged between the Islamic Republic and Egypt's now-deposed Islamist government as the two parties supported conflicting sides in the Syrian uprising. Iranian officials were also critical of Morsi's performance in the domestic arena and his continued relationship with Israel.[42] At the same time, Rouhani's ambiguous position towards Egypt's military leadership may also reflect his effort to reach out to the Arab world — and particularly to the Gulf states. There are signs that Rouhani's government is promoting a conciliatory approach towards the Gulf states manifested in contacts with Gulf officials.[43] He also nominated 'Ali Shamkhani as the Supreme National Security Council secretary — the first Iranian Arab to be appointed to such an influential position.[44]

While both Egypt and Iran are safeguarding their national interests, the popular revolt in Syria has assumed a clear sectarian character. There are reports suggesting that radical jihadi forces are taking over the Syrian insurgency, which is supported by Turkey, Saudi Arabia, and Qatar, while Asad's regime is backed by Iran and also, indirectly, Iraq. Still, the struggle in Syria is complex. Asad's Syria does not represent Shi'i Islam, as the secular regime relies on the narrow power base of the 'Alawis, considered by many Muslims to be a deviant sect. The relationship between the Islamic Republic and Asad's regime is, in essence, a strategic pact. Several Shi'i scholars had already pronounced the 'Alawi sect as a branch of Shi'i Islam, paving the way for the development of this close relationship, though Syrian-Iranian relations are not based on the Islamic factor. The two countries forged close ties following the Islamic revolution and during the Iran-Iraq war, in a period during which Iran had become isolated by much of the Arab world that supported Saddam Hussein's war effort and was wary of

Iran's effort to export its revolution. Syria's relations with Iraq were marked by hostility between two competing Ba'th parties, as Damascus found a partner in the Islamic Republic for their mutual resistance to the West.[45] Nevertheless, this Iran-Syria partnership, which has been reinvigorated by the current civil war in Syria, is not entirely based on sectarian affiliation.

Adding to this complexity, the opposition in Syria is an amalgamation of diverse factions operating from Syria and the diaspora. It includes Kurds, members of the Christian community, and even some former supporters of Asad's regime, although the Sunni Islamists appear to be setting the tone. At its heart, the Syrian conflict is a political, socio-economic, and religious protest by various groups who felt marginalized by Asad's authoritarian regime. At least in the early days of this insurgency, the rebellion was not driven exclusively by sectarian considerations.[46]

# Conclusion

Since the 1980s, the sectarian question has indeed returned to the center stage of Middle East politics and affects developments throughout the region. From the Sunni perspective, there is a widespread fear that the Shi'is are seeking to gain control of the Arab arena. Yet this concern is not anchored in the reality of the Shi'i world. Shi'is are divided between nation-states, and their sectarian affinity tends to be a core (though non-exclusive) mark of their identity. Alongside radical Sunni forces and their uncompromising anti-Shi'i view, there are many in the Sunni-Arab world who balance their sectarian affiliation with political interests and national goals in a pragmatic fashion. Gradually and carefully, they are willing to improve relations with the Shi'a while seeking to halt growing Shi'i influence in the region. There is a clear difference between Sunni traditional or conservative visions of Islam that adopt an uncompromising hostility towards Shi'ism, and more modern religious approaches that advance a more universal Islam incorporating both Sunnis and Shi'is. Consequently, following the Arab Spring, the rise of the Islamist trend with its modern revivalist agenda created a common ideological basis between Iran and countries like Egypt. At the same time, this relationship was constrained conflicting political considerations and divergent ideologies. Yet, the takeover of the military in Egypt and the rise of a moderate president in Iran point to the emergence of a more national discourse in both countries, which provides room for pragmatic considerations between Sunnis and Shi'is in the region.

Diverse factors played a part in the intensification of sectarianism in the region since the 1980s. The sectarian rift has been more prevalent in countries where there is competition between Sunnis and Shi'is over economic resources and political power. Moreover, the sectarian card has reappeared in the toolkit of various political forces in the region, in the context of heightened political and economic difficulties, and rapid social change. In the contemporary Middle East, the new geopolitical dynamics created by the Arab Spring complicate power-sharing efforts between Sunnis and Shi'is, and the outcome of these efforts remains to be seen. What is clear is that the sectarian dimension will continue to play a part in the volatile Arab and Middle East arenas, together with political interests, socio-economic factors, and a unifying Islamic foundation.

# Notes

1. See: "Iraq, Jordan See Threat to Election From Iran: Leaders Warn Against Forming Religious State," *Washington Post*, December 8, 2004.
2. See: "al-'Iraq wa-Iran tastankiran tashkik al-ra'is mubarak fi wala al-shi'a al-'arab," *al-'Arabiyya*, April 8, 2006.
3. On this idea, see: Vali Nasr, *The Shi'a Revival: How Conflicts within Islam Will Shape the Future* (New York: Norton, 2006).
4. For example, 'Ali Shari'ati engaged Western thought, Muslim modernism, and Islamic philosophy in his work. See: Elisheva Machlis, "Ali Shari'ati and the Notion of *tawhid*: Re-exploring the Question of God's Unity," *Die Welt des Islams*, Vol. 54, Issue 2 (2014); Shahrough Akhavi, "Shari'ati's Social Thought," in Nikki R. Keddie (ed.), *Religion and Politics in Iran* (New Haven: Yale University Press, 1983), pp. 125–144; Mehdi Abedi, "Ali Shariati: The Architect of the 1979 Islamic Revolution of Iran," *Iranian Studies*, Vol. 19, Issue 3–4 (Summer–Autumn, 1986), pp. 229–234; and Hamid Dabashi, *Theology of Discontent: The Ideological Foundation of the Islamic Revolution in Iran* (New York: New York University Press, 1993), pp. 102–146.
5. On these ideas, see: Farhang Rajaee, with a preface by Kenneth W. Thompson, *Islamic Values and World View: Khomeyni on Man, the State and International Politics, Volume XIII* (Lanham, New York, London: University Press of America, 1983), pp. 86–87; Ayatollah al-Khomayni, *al-Hukuma al-Islamiyya* (Beirut: Dar al-Tali'a lil-Taba 'a wa'l-Nashr, 1979), pp. 9–22; Ali Rahnema, *An Islamic Utopian: A Political Biography of Ali Shari'ati* (London: I.B. Tauris, 2000), pp. 359–360; Ali Mirsepassi, *Political Islam, Iran, and the Enlightenment: Philosophies of Hope and Despair* (Cambridge: Cambridge University Press, 2011), pp. 116–128; Farzin Vahdat, "Return to which Self?: Jalal Al-e Ahmad and the Discourse of Modernity," *Journal of Iranian Research and Analysis*, Vol. 16, No. 2 (November, 2000), pp. 55–71; Brad Hanson, "The Westoxication" of Iran: Depictions and Reactions of Behrangi, Al-e Ahmad, and Shari'ati," *International Journal of Middle Eastern Studies* (IJMES), Vol. 15 (1983), pp. 1–23.
6. See Bassam Tibi, "The Iranian Revolution and the Arabs: The Quest for Islamic Identity and the Search for an Islamic System of Government," *Arab Studies Quarterly*, Vol. 8, No.1 (1986), pp. 29–44; Emmanuel Sivan, "Sunni Radicalism in the

Middle East and the Iranian Revolution," *IJMES*, Vol. 21, No. 1 (Feb. 1989), pp. 1–30; 'Abd Allah Muhammad Gharib, *al-Khumayni bayna al-tatarruf wa'l-i'tidal* ([Cairo: s.n.], 1986); and Fathi 'Abd al-'Aziz, *al-Khumayni al-hal al-islami wa'l-badil* (Cairo: al-Mukhtar al-Islami, 1979).

7.  See: Roxanne Varzi, *Warring Souls: Youth, Media, and Martyrdom in Post-Revolution Iran* (Durham & London: Duke University Press, 2006), pp. 44–75.

8.  See: Ofra Bengio, *Saddam's Word: Political Discourse in Iraq* (Oxford & New York: Oxford University Press, 1998), pp. 139–145, 176–191.

9.  On the Wahhabi movement, see Abdulaziz H. Al-Fahad, "From Exclusivism to Accommodation: Doctrinal and Legal Evolution of Wahhabism," *New York University Law Review*, Vol. 79, No. 2 (May 2004), pp. 485–519; Michael Cook, "On the Origins of Wahhabism," *Journal of the Royal Asiatic Society*, Third Series, Vol. 2, No. 2 (July 1992), pp. 191–202; Hamid Algar, *Wahhabism: A Critical Essay* (Oneonta, NY: Islamic Publications International, 2002); Muhammad b. 'Abd al-Wahhab, *Majmu'at al-tawhid: al-ma'ruf bi-majmu'at al-tawhid al-najdiyya: majmu'at kutub wa-rasa'il* (Riyadh: al-Amana al-'amma lil-ihtifal bi-mi'at 'am 'ala ta'sis al-mamlaka, 1419 [1999]). See, also: Ayman al-Yassini, *Religion and State in the Kingdom of Saudi Arabia* (Boulder & London: Westview Press, 1985), pp. 26–29.

10. On these developments, see: David Ucko, "Militias, Tribes and Insurgents: The Challenge of Political Reintegration in Iraq," *Conflict, Security & Development*, Volume 8, Issue 3 (October 2008), pp. 341–372; Ronen Zeidel, "Sunni Discontent in Iraq: An Historical Perspective," in Amnon Cohen and Noga Efrati (eds)., *Post-Saddam Iraq: New Realities, Old Identities, Changing Patterns* (Brighton, Portland, Toronto: Sussex Academic Press, 2011), pp. 129–145.

11. See: Yitzhak Nakash, *The Shi'is of Iraq* (Princeton: Princeton University Press, 2003 edition), pp. 269–272; Orit Bashkin, *The Other Iraq: Pluralism and Culture in Hashemite Iraq* (Stanford: Stanford University Press, 2009), pp. 39, 128–129, 170–175; Elisheva Machlis, "A Shi'a Debate on Arabism: The Emergence of a Multiple Communal Membership," *British Journal of Middle Eastern Studies*, Vol. 40, Issue 2 (2013); Elisheva Machlis, "Shi'ism, Culture and Group Membership Amidst Social Change," *Bustan: The Middle East Book Review*, Vol. 4, Issue 1 (2013), pp. 17–32.

12. *Da'wa* means the "call to Islam."

13. See John Walbridge, "Muhammad-Baqir al-Sadr: The Search for New Foundations," in Linda S. Walbridge (ed.), *The Most Learned of the Shi'a: The Institution of the Marja' Taqlid* (Oxford & New York: Oxford University Press, 2001), pp. 131–139; Chibli Mallat, "Aspects of Shi'i Thought from the South of Lebanon," *Papers On Lebanon*, No. 7 (The Centre For Lebanese Studies); Chibli Mallat, *The Renewal of Islamic Law* (Cambridge University Press, 2003); Joyce N. Wiley, *The Islamic Movement of Iraqi Shi'is* (Boulder & London: Lynne Rienner Publishers, 1992).

14. Elie Kedourie, "The Iraqi Shi'is and Their Fate," in Martin Kramer (ed.), *Shi'ism, Resistance, and Revolution* (Boulder, Colorado: Westview Press, 1987), pp. 135–157.

15. Chibli Mallat, "Religious Militancy in Contemporary Iraq: Muhammad Baqer as-Sadr and the Sunni-Shia Paradigm," *Third World Quarterly*, Vol. 10, Issue 2 (1988), pp. 699–729; Rodger Shanahan, "Shi'a Political Development in Iraq: The Case of

the Islamic Da'wa Party," *Third World Quarterly*, Vol. 25, Issue 5 (2004), pp. 943–954; Amatzia Baram, "The Ruling Political Elite in Bathi Iraq, 1968–1986: The Changing Features of a Collective Profile," *IJMES*, Vol. 21, Issue 4 (Nov. 1989), pp. 447–493; Ofra Bengio, "Shi'is and Politics in Ba'thi Iraq," *Middle Eastern Studies*, Vol. 21, Issue 1 (Jan. 1985), pp. 1–14.

16. On this idea see, for example: Hassan Mneimneh,"The Arab Reception of Vilayat-e-Faqih: The Counter-Model of Muhammad Mahdi Shams al-Din," *Current Trends in Islamist Ideology*, Vol. 8 (2009), pp. 39–51; Roschanach Shaery-Eisenlohr, "Postrevolutionary Iran and Shi'i Lebanon: Contested Histories of Shi'i Transnationalism," *IJMES*, Vol. 39 (2007), pp. 271–289; Talib Aziz, "*Fadlallah and the Remaking of the Marja'iya*," in Linda S. Walbridge (ed.), *The Most Learned of the Shi'a: The Institution of the Marja' Taqlid* (Oxford: Oxford University Press, 2001), pp. 205–215; Shahrough Akhavi, "Contending Discourses in Shi'i Law on the Doctrine of *Wilayat al-Faqih*," *Iranian Studies*, Vol. 29, Issue 3-4 (1996), pp. 229–268; Talib Aziz, "Baqir al-Sadr's Quest for the Marja'iya," in Walbridge, *The Most Learned of the Shi'a*, pp. 140–148; Nizar Hamzeh, "Lebanon's Hizbullah: From Islamic Revolution to Parliamentary Accommodation," *Third World Quarterly* Vol. 14, Issue 2 (1993), pp. 321–337.

17. See: Liora Lukitz, "Shi'is in Post-Saddam Iraq: A Common Political Front, but Different Tactics?" in Amnon Cohen and Noga Efrati (eds)., *Post-Saddam Iraq*, pp. 53–103.

18. See Meir Litvak, *Shi'i Scholars of Nineteenth Century Iraq: The 'Ulama' of Najaf and Karbala'* (Cambridge: Cambridge University Press, 1998), pp. 4-11; Ahmad Kazemi Moussavi, "The Establishment of the Position of Marja'iyyat-i Taqlid in the Twelver-Shi'i Community," *Iranian Studies*, Vol. 18 (1985), pp. 35–50.

19. See Eldad J. Pardo, "Iran and Iraq: Between Opportunity and Threat," in *Post-Saddam Iraq*, pp. 212-42; Vali Nasr, "When the Shiites Rise," *Foreign Affairs* 85: 4 (July–August, 2006), pp. 58-74; Elie Podeh, "Iraq and the Arab System since the 2003 War: A Persistent Marginality" in Amnon Cohen and Noga Efrati (eds)., *Post-Saddam Iraq*, pp. 266–294. See, also: "Flow of Arms to Syria through Iraq Persists, to U.S. Dismay," *The New York Times*, December 1, 2012.

20. Vali Nasr, "Regional Implications of Shi'a Revival in Iraq," *The Washington Quarterly*, Vol. 27, Issue 3 (Summer 2004), pp. 7–24; Brian Fishman, "After Zarqawi: The Dilemmas and Future of al Qaeda in Iraq," *The Washington Quarterly*, Vol. 29, Issue 4 (Autumn 2006), pp. 19–32; Seth G. Jones, "Al Qaeda in Iran: Why Tehran is Accommodating the Terrorist Group," *Foreign Affairs*, January 29, 2012.

21. On these developments, see Geneive Abdo, "The New Sectarianism: The Arab Uprisings and the Rebirth of the Shi'a-Sunni Divide," *Analysis Paper: The Saban Center for Middle East Policy at Brookings*, No. 29 (April 2013); Mehran Kamrava, "The Arab Spring and the Saudi-Led Counterrevolution," *Orbis* (Winter 2012), pp. 96–104.

22. See Joseph Nevo, "Religion and National Identity in Saudi Arabia," *Middle Eastern Studies*, Vol. 34, Issue 3 (July, 1998), pp. 34–53. See also Shahram Akbarzadeh and

Kylie Connor, "The Organization of the Islamic Conference: Sharing an Illusion," *Middle East Policy*, Vol. 12, Issue 2 (Summer 2005), pp. 79–92.

23. Bruce Riedel and Bilal Y. Saab, "Al Qaeda's Third Front: Saudi Arabia," *Washington Quarterly*, Vol. 31, Issue 2 (Spring 2008), pp. 33–46; Michael Scott Doran, "The Saudi Paradox," *Foreign Affairs* (January-February 2004).

24. See: Kamrava, *The Arab Spring and the Saudi-Led Counterrevolution*. See, also: "Washington Presses UAE over Iran Trade," *Financial Times*, December 5, 2011.

25. See: Daniel Brumberg, "The Trap of Liberalized Autocracy," *Journal of Democracy*, Vol. 13, Issue 4 (October 2002), pp. 56–68; J. E. Peterson, "Bahrain: Reform, Promise and Reality," in Joshua Teitelbaum (ed.), *Political Liberalization in the Persian Gulf* (New York: Columbia University Press, 2009), pp. 157–185; Steven Wright, "Fixing the Kingdom: Political Evolution and Socio-Economic Challenges in Bahrain," *Occasional Paper: Center for International and Regional Studies at Georgetown University: School of Foreign Service in Qatar* (CIRS), Vol. 5 (2008), pp. 1–17.

26. On the Bahraini Shi'is' political views, see: Mahjoob Zweiri, "The Victory of al Wefaq: The Rise of Shiite Politics in Bahrain," *Research Paper: Research Institute for European and American Studies (RIEAS)*, Vol. 108 (April 2007), pp. 1–18. See also Fred H. Lawson, "Repertoires of Contention in Contemporary Bahrain," in Quintan Wiktorowicz (ed.), *Islamic Activism: A Social Movement Theory Approach* (Bloomington: Indiana University Press, 2004), pp. 89–111.

27. On these Shi'i Arab communities in the Gulf, see: Yitzhak Nakash, *Reaching for Power: The Shi'a in the Modern Arab World* (Princeton and Oxford: Princeton University Press, 2006); Graham E. Fuller and Rend Rahim Francke, *The Arab Shi'a: The Forgotten Muslims* (New York, N.Y. & Houndmills, Basingstoke, England: Palgrave 1999), pp. 119–202.

28. See, for example: "al-kuwayt shahadat akhar fusuliha: al-ta'fiyya fi al-waqi' al-'arabi... ma'rik bi-la muntasir," *al-Itihad*, April 3, 2013; Shi'at al-mintaqa wa'l-'aqliyyat fi zil al-rabi' al-'arabi, *al-Jazira*, October 25, 2011; "khututat zahirat al-sira' al-madhhabi fi'l 'iraq, *al-Sharq al-Awsat*, February 23, 2013; "al-bahrayn bayna al-qaradawi wa'l sistani, *al-Sharq al-Awsat*, March 20, 2011.

29. On the pragmatist element in the Brotherhood's operations, see: Sana Abed-Kotob, "The Accommodationists Speak: Goals and Strategies of the Muslim Brotherhood in Egypt," *IJMES*, Vol. 27 (1995), pp. 321–339. See, also: Rola El Husseini, "Hezbollah and the Axis of Refusal: Hamas, Iran and Syria," *Third World Quarterly*, Vol. 31, Issue 5 (2010), pp. 803–815.

30. On Rashid Rida's defense of the Wahhabis, see entry "Rashid Rida" in Encyclopaedia of Islam New Edition 8, pp. 446–448. On the other hand, Rashid Rida was in contact with the Shi'i reformist 'Abd al-Husayn Sharaf al-Din al-Musawi (1873-1957), the spiritual leader of the Shi'i community in Tyre at the time. See: Rainer Bruner, *Islamic Ecumenism in the 20<sup>th</sup> Century: The Azhar and Shiism between Rapprochement and Restraint*, translated from the German by Joseph Greenman (Leiden & Boston: Brill, 2004), pp. 57–58.

31. On the activities of this society, see: Brunner, *Islamic Ecumenism*, pp. 121–207. On the salafi movement, see: David Dean Commins, *Islamic Reform: Politics and Social*

*Change in Late Ottoman Syria* (New York & Oxford: Oxford University Press, 1990), pp. 124–144.

32. On this development, see: F. R. C. Bagley, "The Azhar and Shi'ism," *The Muslim World* 50 (April 1960); Hamid Enayat, *Modern Islamic Political Thought: The Response of the Shi'i and Sunnī Muslims to the Twentieth Century* (London: I.B. Tauris, 2005), pp. 48–50.

33. See "al-qiyadi al-bariz fi ikhwan al-muslimin (yusuf nada) yudafi'u 'an al-shi'a wa-yuhajimu muntaqadihim bi-shidda," *Shabakat Rasid al-'Akhbariyya*, February 20, 2009, http://www.montadaalquran.com/articles/readarticle.php?articleID=544.

34. On Qaradawi's thought, see: Samuel Helfont, *Yusuf al-Qaradawi: Islam and Modernity* (Tel Aviv University: The Moshe Dayan Center for Middle Eastern and African Studies, 2009).

35. "El-Qaradawi from Al-Azhar: Egyptian Revolution is Gift from God," *Ahram online (English edition)*, January 25, 2013; "Qaradawi says Bahrain's Revolution Sectarian," *al-Arabiya* (online English edition), March 19, 2011.

36. For Morsi's opening speech in the conference, see: www.youtube.com/watch?v=xLunVPL_Aos.

37. Elisheva Machlis, "Iran's Spin on the Arab Spring," *Iran Pulse*, November 13, 2011.

38. "Saudi King Backs Egypt's Military," *al-Jazeera*, August 17, 2013.

39. "Sinai Tribal Leader Rejects Gaza Buffer Zone," *al-Monitor*, September 9, 2013.

40. "Iran Condemns Violence in Egypt, Urges Respect for People's Demand," *Press TV*, July 14, 2013.

41. "Iran against War, Bloodshed among Muslims: Rohani," *Press TV*, July 13, 2013.

42. See "Morsi 'Confused Friends with Enemies,' Says Iranian Cleric," *Iran Pulse*, July 5, 2013.

43. See for example, "Iran, UAE Voice Hope for Closer Relations," *Press TV*, August 12, 2013; "What Message did Sultan Qaboos Convey to Iran?" *Iran Review*, August 29, 2013.

44. Shamkhani played an important role in improving Iran's relations with the Gulf in his former position as defense minister. See: "The 'Admiral' Heads Iran's National Security Council," *al-Monitor*, September 11, 2013.

45. Yvette Talhamy, "The *Fatwas* and the Nusayri/Alawis of Syria," *Middle Eastern Studies*, Vol. 46, Issue 2 (March 2010), pp. 174–194. See, also: El Husseini, *Hezbollah and the Axis of Refusal: Hamas, Iran and Syria*.

46. "Guide to the Syrian Opposition," *BBC online*, March 26, 2013. See, also: Joshua Landis and Joe Pace, "The Syrian Opposition," *The Washington Quarterly*, Vol. 30, Issue 1 (Winter, 2006-2007), pp. 45–68.

# State Cohesiveness, Regime Stability, and the Economy in the Arab World

## Paul Rivlin

This chapter examines the relationship between economics, regime stability and the cohesion of Arab states. First, it is necessary to define cohesion: Is it any more than the stability of the regime, or is it about the capacity of the regime to hold the state together and prevent regions from declaring independence and seceding from it? The main link between the cohesion of the state and the economy is via the nature and stability of the regime.

There are at least two types of Arab states: those that have a long history, a relatively homogenous population and unambiguous borders and those that are the creation of the colonial era. Egypt, Morocco, and Tunisia are examples of the first; Iraq, Syria, Lebanon, the Gulf Arab states, and Jordan are examples of the second. The second group is further divided into two groups: those with religiously or ethnically heterogeneous populations (Sunni versus Shi'a and/ or Arab versus non-Arab), and those with largely homogeneous ones (e.g. the smaller Gulf states, at least in terms of those who are actually citizens).

In economic terms, the Arab world can be divided into those states that are oil-rich and those that are not. The oil rich states are the Gulf Cooperation Council (GCC) members with high levels of oil income per head and homogenous populations.[1] These states were largely created by the British and the most powerful tribes in the area. Iraq is an exception (as are Libya and Algeria). It was created by the British with three different populations: Two are Sunni and one is Shi'a, while two are Arab and one is Kurdish. The country has two areas with oil fields, one in the predominantly Kurdish north and one in the Shi'a-dominated southeast. The British not only determined the borders but also chose the country's first ruler, Faisal, whom they imported from the Hijaz. In North Africa, there are two states with strong identities–Morocco and Tunisia–and two with weaker ones–Libya and Algeria. Libya was created out of the Italian colonies of Cyrenaica and Tripolitania and, since Qaddafi was ousted, has partly disintegrated into tribal sub-regions. Algeria is controlled by a military regime and escaped the "Arab Spring" largely because the memory of the bloody civil war during the 1990s is too painful and recent.

Egypt has a pre-Arab and pre-Muslim identity. Its borders are undisputed and its population is overwhelmingly Sunni. The Coptic minority feel themselves to be Egyptian and have never made separatist claims on the state.

In view of this, it is very significant that the Arab Spring began in the most cohesive states: Tunisia and Egypt. Furthermore, Tunisia was the most successful Arab economy outside the Gulf, proving that economic success was no guarantee against instability. In fact, modest economic success may have contributed to the overthrow of the Ben Ali and Mubarak regimes, as a result of a revolution of rising expectations.[2] This may also have been true in Syria, where economic developments played an important role in generating the current conflict. In Syria, faster economic growth was accompanied by drought and the adverse effects of economic policies that devastated the northeast of the country. There were winners — the urban class, close to the regime — and losers — the rural class, who had traditionally been the backbone of the regime.[3]

The benefits of growth were very unequally distributed in all Arab countries. In an autocratic system, the only way to achieve a change in distribution is by demonstrations, peaceful or violent, which is one of the main explanations for the Arab Spring.[4]

The underlying question is why economic performance has often been unsatisfactory and why, during a period when it was more satisfactory, unrest broke out, even leading to regime change in a number of countries. These questions are closely related because the pattern of economic growth was the factor causing unrest. This in turn was closely related to the nature of the regime. From this we get our first premise: politics determined the countries' economics. The link is both direct and indirect, via other factors such as religion and culture.

Is there any meaningful relationship between the cohesion of the state and its economic performance? Or does better economic performance increase the cohesiveness of the state? There are methodological problems that make it almost impossible to answer this type of question because so many other variables may explain cohesion and economic growth.[5]

There is literature on the economic history of the Middle East and other regions that does help to explain the weak economic performance of Arab states. This is somewhat interdisciplinary in that it looks at factors that economists usually consider exogenous and, as such, will also be of interest to non-economists. This literature helps us understand the role of political, cultural, and religious issues as well as economic ones.

# Geography

There are a number of schools of thought on the long-term causes of economic development. The first of these places emphasis on the role of geography. Human civilization developed in the river valleys of semi-tropical zones which Karl Wittfogel called "hydraulic societies." In the Middle East, the two major rivers are the Nile and the Euphrates. The civilizations that developed along their banks needed central authority to survive because they needed to control irrigation from the river to the lands around it and regulate life in the valleys. The first postal and secret police forces known were developed thousands of years ago in those regions. Geography thus dictated strong government that has been a central feature of the political economy of the Middle East ever since. The strong state preceded Islam in key regions in the Middle East.[6] The main feature of hydraulic societies was that the leaders had "despotic state power" while private owners or entrepreneurs were relatively weak. In a largely agricultural economy, the main resource, land, was owned by the state. It was therefore much stronger than the society, and one of the main ways in which the state maintained its strength was to attach itself to the society's main belief system or religion.

In regions where there was hydraulic despotism, those that might have contested the attempts of masters of hydraulic power from attaining absolute power failed to do so. They lacked "the proprietary and organizational strength that in Greek and Roman antiquity, as well as in Medieval Europe, bulwarked non-government forces of society."[7] In the hydraulic state, the government maintained a monopoly over fast transportation, which was interlocked with an intelligence system and thus became a formidable weapon of social control.[8]

The nature of the state also had very significant effects on the development of private property. Hydraulic states denied property owners or landowners the right to dispose of their property among their heirs at will. Their inheritance laws favored a more or less equal division of property in the estate of a deceased person, something that helped to fragment the ownership of wealth periodically. Islam retained these laws, and so the holders of family *waqf*s (religious endowments) kept their land undivided because they were ultimately to serve religious and charitable purposes. While the family *waqf* temporarily benefited the grantee and his descendants, it was neither a secure nor a free form of property. While less frequently singled out for confiscation than other kinds of property, the family *waqf*s might be seized if the state chose. The *waqf*s were taxed, and their beneficiaries were never able to consolidate their power through a nationwide political organization.[9] This contrasted with the signing in 1215 C.E. in England of the Magna Carta. The charter contained a clause that effectively recognized the right of the barons, as a group, to coerce the king. In thirteenth-century England, the barons were also ensuring the perpetuation of their property rights by primogeniture and entail.[10] The charter reflected a plurality of political power far greater than that prevailing in the Middle East at the time.

In the Middle East, the pre-Islamic inheritance was a strong one. In Egypt, the Pharaoh was a god or son of a god. In Mesopotamia, the pattern was more complex, but, in effect, the ruler had divine authority. In Islam, Mohammed was neither Allah nor his son: He was the Prophet. Although the caliphates were not theocracies, the caliph was strong enough to prevent the emergence of an Islamic religious institution separate from the state.[11]

Jeffrey Sachs has suggested that geography is the most important explanation of economic development.[12] The region has three significant geographical characteristics. First, it is largely a desert. This is in contrast to largely temperate Europe. The Middle East straddles Africa, Asia and Europe and is therefore a trading center. A third factor, which since the beginning of the twentieth century has been far more important, is the region's reserves of oil and gas that are the largest in the world. This has given it immense geopolitical importance.

Islam developed in the desert and those who spread it in the seventh and eighth centuries used technology developed in the region. Food production, camel transport, and other methods were suitable for North Africa and Central Asia. Early Islam also entered Europe but only held areas in the southern regions. The Ottomans, who had a temperate base in Anatolia, were more successful in the Balkans and in Central Europe. Temperate regions have emerged with major advantages for economic development. They had much more wood and coal, which were the main fuels. They also have climates that are less propitious for disease and more suitable for food production. The dependence of populations on limited or even single sources of water was much more prevalent in the Middle East than in Europe. This meant that the population in the Middle East was more exposed to water-borne infection. Making use of the advantages of colder climate regions required technological development: the development of metal ploughs for heavy earth and forest clearing as well as housing that could support the population in the cold. When these technologies became available, the advantages of the north began to outweigh those of the south that had sustained some of the earliest civilizations on earth. The Middle East had oil which Europe did not, but this did not bring economic development, for oil was not a source of energy prior to the twentieth century.

The boundary between Christianity and Islam shifted continuously since the emergence of Islam in the seventh century. The period of Arab expansion followed the death of the Prophet and the Ottoman expansion was from 1200 to

1500 C.E. Between 1500 and 1700, there was a stalemate between the Ottomans and Christian European powers, followed by European expansion until the collapse of the Ottoman Empire at the end of the World War I. According to Sachs, the reason for these changes was the balance of long-term demographic, geopolitical, and economic factors. Until about 900, the Middle East had a larger population than Europe and in line with its role as a trading center, was more urbanized. Between 900 and 1500, Europe's population expanded faster than that of the Middle East, as its agricultural technology came into play and the Middle East felt the constraints imposed by the desert. The same change occurred in urbanization as Europe overtook the Middle East in both the scale and number of urban settlements. Europe also gained from the expansion of its trade with India and the Far East, using trade routes via the Cape of Good Hope that circumvented the Middle East. Following the failure of its siege of Vienna in 1683, the Ottoman Empire began losing territory to European states. Europe began to benefit from the Industrial Revolution that left most of the Middle East behind, right up until present day. The Ottoman Empire lacked the resources to finance its military operations aimed at defending its frontier in Eastern Europe and maintaining internal order. It went into debt and ultimately went bankrupt while Europeans were its main creditors. This occurred despite numerous reforms designed to modernize the Empire, such as the *Tanzimat* (1839–1876). Egypt and other parts of the Empire were gradually taken over by the British or the French and were opened to international trade. The Western powers barely invested in the educational systems and thus denied these countries the skilled labor that they needed when they gained independence. The contrast with East Asia is dramatic. In 1970, 71.2 percent of the adult Arab population was illiterate, while in East Asia and the Pacific the share was 42.5 percent.[13]

## Factor Endowments

Closely related to the geography school is what may be called the factor endowments school. This suggests that different parts of the world attracted certain types of human capital because of their natural resource base. The differences between the pattern of development in North and South America can partly be explained by climatic, soil, and other geographic factors. These made Central America more suitable for plantation farming and the northern states of the US and Canada more suitable for grain farming. These products required different agricultural systems with different labor intensities and social organization.[14] Tropical areas were suited to labor intensive plantation production. More temperate areas required extensive cultivation with lower ratios of labor to land. Geography dictated the kind of agriculture that would be profitable and thus the human skills required. This dictated or influenced migration patterns (slaves were taken to the southern states of the US and the Caribbean region) while in the northern US states they were much less important. The factor endowments school shows that the natural resource base — mainly soils and climate — largely determined the nature of political institutions in particular regions. In the small-holder settlements that typified the northern states of the US and Canada, wealth and income were much more equally distributed than in slave societies in the south of the US, the Caribbean, and parts of South America. Wittfogel's work can also be understood in terms of factor endowments: geography determined institutions that in turn determined the pattern of economic development.

## Factor Endowments and Colonialism

The role of factor endowments has been extended to include the effects of historical processes, most notably colonialism. Large income gaps developed between different areas, and the factor endowments school suggests that this was the result of the institutions that were created in those areas. The areas that created legal and other systems to protect property rights were those that were able to industrialize. Central to their thesis is the role of European colonialists. Societies that had low death rates among European settlers were better able to transplant European institutions than those that had higher death rates.[15] Much depended on the country of origin of the settlers and the kind of institutions that they were transplanting. For example, a significant number of English settlers in New England emigrated in protest of the existing order in their country of origin. They wanted to create a new society; those that set up slave economies in the Caribbean had other things in mind. In the Middle East in the nineteenth and twentieth centuries, when Britain and France took over much of the Ottoman Empire, there was, with the exception of Algeria, no large movement of settlers into the newly conquered areas. There was, therefore, no serious attempt by the Western powers to implant Western institutions, although the Arab Enlightenment of the late nineteenth century tried to move in that direction.[16]

Late nineteenth century Egypt, like the southern states of the US, was a cotton producer. The cotton economy needed large numbers of cheap laborers supervised by relatively few skilled managers. Unlike the US, Egypt had an ancient civilization with a tradition of strong central government, something that continued despite changes in rulers (Arab, Mamluk, Ottoman, British, and

Egyptian). European colonial powers did not need to import slaves to work in Egypt; the labor force already existed and was organized. This limited the need for the British to impose new institutions on the country when they took control.

The Western powers exploited the Middle East for its natural resources and markets, its geography (e.g. the Suez Canal), and later for its oil. Oil led to the close relationship between leading Arabian tribes and the British. It explains the way in which states were created for them by the British and how oil revenues flowed into the coffers of the rulers, and from there to the state treasury. The political economy of the Gulf can only be understood if the role of oil is taken into account, which is a geographical factor. Sachs asserts that geographical factors are much more important in explaining the problems of economic development in the Middle East than cultural or religious ones. It is to these that we now turn.

# Culture

Culture has been defined as denoting the distinctive attitudes and actions that differentiate groups of people. Culture is the result of, and expressed through religion, language, institutions, and history. The attributes that make up culture change slowly, but they can and do change over time.[17] The founder of the culture school was Max Weber. He ascribed the Industrial Revolution to the dominance of Protestantism in northern Europe, where it began. Protestantism, especially its Calvinist version, defined and advocated a set of values that were conducive to business relations.[18] The Catholic areas of Europe industrialized later because the culture was less effective in encouraging work and savings. This view has been the subject of much controversy but has not been abandoned. David Landes and others have suggested that Islam was bad for economic development and implicitly make use of Weber's argument.

Landes claims that culture makes almost all the difference. Examining the economic success of the Chinese in East and South East Asia, the Lebanese in West Africa, Indians in East Africa and other expatriate minorities led Landes to conclude that the values and attitudes that these groups brought from their origins explained their business success. The lack of economic development of their home base at the time that they or their parents emigrated was due to institutions that prevented the economy from working effectively, and that was the incentive to emigrate.[19]

Culturally derived attitudes have a long legacy and evolve in complex ways. They can adapt, or partly adapt, to new circumstances and do not always replace older ones. Hence, Egypt's 1978-1982 Five Year development plan noted that

> more and more young people and workers perceive the contradictions of a socialist society which thinks with a capitalist mind, which takes from socialism and communism the concepts of public ownership, the dominance of the public sector, guaranteed employment, educations, services and social security, but neglects to take firm enforcement of civil authority or condemnation of the carelessness which decreases productivity. Similarly, the government has taken from capitalism the features of consumption and interclass mobility, the concept of the importance of the individual and of historical tradition. But it has not adopted from the capitalist system the stringency of market competition or the responsibility of the firm for quality control, upon which depends the success or failure of the firm. The end result is a society lacking discipline or supervision, distribution without production, promises without obligations, freedom without responsibility.[20]

While policies change over time, the way in which people think and behave does not necessarily do so at the same pace. Hence, in Egypt the government was expected to provide the benefits of socialism even as it was moving towards a more capitalist system. One of the influences on the way in which people think about society and the economy is religion, examined in the next section.

# Religion

Maxime Rodinson argued that Islam does not provide the explanation for economic problems in the Muslim world. The reason is that Islam has not been adopted in a comprehensive way, and choices have always been made as to what aspects of the faith to implement. Economic weakness was the result of material conditions that Muslims faced, a Marxist view but not exclusively so.[21] Marcus Nolan and Howard Pack, both orthodox economists, have also argued that Islam is not the cause of economic problems in the Arab World, largely because it has not been adopted and therefore does not act as a constraint. They surveyed econometric attempts to assess the influence of Islam on economic growth and concluded that it was not significant. They did, however, note that Islam may well have exerted negative, indirect influences. Islam, along with other factors, may have influenced the way in which institutions in the region developed and these may have negatively influenced economic growth.[22] Econometric studies, such as those surveyed by Nolan and Pack, are dismissed by Jean-Philippe Platteau. He points out that it is possible to identify factors that militate against economic growth in most religions. Furthermore, the effect of religion is hard to estimate because it is endogenous. Rather than preventing growth directly, a culture or religion may develop in a particular direction because of the lack of economic growth. It is almost impossible to find variables that influence culture or religion while not affecting economic growth. As a result, econometric tests based on cross-sectional analysis tell us little. The other major weakness of cross-sectional testing is that very crude measures are used because of the poor quality of the data available. Furthermore, Islam has never been homogenous and cannot as such be measured in a simplistic way.[23]

Eric Jones has said that Europe's experience of economic growth is the miracle that requires explanation. Those who view success as the factor that has to be explained imply that the lack of it is normal. Viewed historically, this is correct: Many societies existed with minimal economic progress for hundreds of years, and the Arab experience in the last fifty years should not be considered exceptional in this regard. One of the factors that he uses to explain Europe's success was that it consisted of many countries. These countries had to justify their existence, defend themselves against their neighbors, and compete economically. Europe could therefore be thought of as a much more decentralized system than the various Islamic empires, including the Ottoman one.[24] Charles Kindleberger noted how economic success or, to use his term, "primacy," moved from one country to another. Between the years 1500 to 1900, primacy moved from Italy to Portugal and Spain, to the Low Countries, to France, to Britain, to Germany, and then to the US and Japan.[25]

Timur Kuran rejected the idea that Islam, or the culture associated with it, was the sole or direct cause of weak economic performance; rather, it was the use made of Islam that had negative effects. Economic weaknesses were therefore due to political factors, but these were reinforced by unwillingness in Muslim society to encourage or engage in public discourse for fear that this might lead to disunity. Kuran stated that one way in which Islamic jurisprudence hindered economic growth was its emphasis on the need for unity. Muslim jurists did not want to do anything to encourage factionalism, and so they did not create or recognize the concept of incorporation, or what later became known as private companies or legal entities. Those services that had large set-up costs were supplied through the *waqf*, which was a form of unincorporated trust. It absorbed the resources that might have stimulated or called for incorporation and generated a constituency that had vested interests in its preservation. Muslim rulers also lacked incentives to make changes in the direction of incorporation while private merchants were unable to generate sufficient political power to reform the legal system until modern times.[26] In addition to the problems of incorporation, Islamic inheritance laws were based on detailed specifications in the Qur'an, making them hard to challenge. These laws were designed to protect the family and meant that assets had to be divided upon death between surviving family members. This led to the division of land, when it was inheritable, as well as businesses and other assets. This was true until the reforms of the nineteenth century.[27] The fact that the Islamic legal system was changed in the nineteenth century suggests that culture can be changed if the legal system is considered part of culture. It requires powerful interest groups to make it happen, which is a political matter.

Kuran suggests that preference falsification helps to explain the weakness of economic development in the Islamic world. When people refrain from expressing their views (in particular, their desire for change), they make it easier for existing structures to continue. They refrain because of fear of punishment if they call for change. This may be because the state will act against them or because public opinion is hostile and they may be threatened by individuals or groups. Islam may not be the obstacle to change, but conservative views, put forward in the name of Islam, may be durable because of public affection for Islam and therefore make it dangerous to propose change. Preference falsification corrupts public debate by extinguishing it: if new ideas are never expressed, then society's new members never hear them. This further reinforces the status quo. If sufficiently large numbers of people fear the consequences of expressing dissenting ideas, then the resulting social pressure will keep others from speaking honestly. This will cause preference falsification to spread and an equilibrium will be established in which the status quo will be reinforced by the lack of opposing ideas. This equilibrium could and did last for generations. Preference falsification was not only due to fear of the regime but also to the identity of the regime and Islam.[28]

Avner Greif noted that in the early Muslim world, legitimacy resulted from being a close companion of the Prophet. Later, legitimacy derived from maintaining a strict or pure interpretation of Islam. The Muslim jurist al-Mawardi stated that a caliph should not be obeyed if he contradicted Islam. Hundreds of years later, adherence to *shari'a* (Islamic law) remained a source of legitimacy. The constitution of the Egyptian monarchy, established in 1922, declared *shari'a* to be a source of law. In 1971, the constitution of the Arab Republic of Egypt declared it to be a socialist and democratic state and that *shari'a* was the principle source of legislation. In Europe, by way of contrast, legitimacy increasingly derived from the state and corporations. In the late medieval period, the church in Europe lost its bid to become the ultimate source of legitimacy governing economic, social and political affairs. Unlike Islam, it was not there at the foundation of what became Europe's polity. Christianity came to the Roman Empire, which had its own laws and traditions of secular conduct. Christianity had to fight for its place, resulting in conflicts, splits, and wars, but also in greater pluralism of thought and institutions.[29]

There is, according to Kuran, a two-way relationship between cultural and material factors, which rejects absolutist explanations that either culture or materialistic factors are the sole explanations for the region's woes. Rodinson showed how the Islamic ban on interest was rarely obeyed and suggested that this was proof of the insignificance of cultural-religious factors in the economic development of the Islamic world. By implication, materialistic factors were the explanation in Rodinson and other Marxist works. By contrast, Kuran suggests that Islam did have a negative influence because of indirect effects on long-term economic development, even though its precepts were often ignored. As a result of the restrictions on incorporation and the nature of inheritance laws, the Middle East failed to create companies of significant size. This restricted the level scale of economic activity within the region and also left it unable to compete with European joint stock companies. Over time these factors had cumulative negative effects and resulted in poor growth performance. The loss of competitiveness was not only the result of these organizational factors — it was also due to the lack of technological, educational, and even military power.[30]

Platteau, uses historical rather than econometric analysis and concludes that Islam was the handmaiden of politics. Religion was not the cause of economic failure in the Middle East; rather, it was the use made of religion that was the problem. In his words, there is a "complex interaction and feedback between culture and institutional change." In Western Europe, institutional and ideological changes reinforced each other in ways that were beneficial for economic development. In the Islamic world, economic development and social progress were hindered by despotism and the lack of a revolutionary idea that would attract enough people to successfully insist on political change.[31]

Both Douglass North and Deepak Lal suggest that societies can continue for hundreds of years in what economists call "sub-optimal equilibria" with institutions that maintain stability but prevent growth largely because it suits key interest groups. [32]In the Middle East, the most important of these was the state, which was able to carry on underperforming because other sections of society were weak. It was these key interest groups that pushed for change elsewhere. Most obvious was the political weakness of the middle class.

# Institutions

One of the most interesting attempts to evaluate the effects of institutions on economic development was carried out by Greif. He compared the ways in which European and Middle East traders performed in the late Middle Ages and found that European culture encouraged impersonal trade while Middle Eastern culture encouraged trade between members of extended families or closely connected communities. The two groups were in competition and the Europeans won out gradually coming to dominate Mediterranean trade.[33] The social organization of the late medieval Middle East traders resembled modern collectivist societies while that of the late medieval Europeans resembled modern individualist ones. The Middle East traders (including Jews, who had absorbed the dominant Islamic cultural values of the region in which they lived) considered themselves members of the same people. Their loyalty was to the *umma* and their membership meant that they were mutually responsible for each other. The fact that the group examined by Greif was made up of Jews who had moved from Iraq to Tunisia reinforced this. They "retained social ties that enabled them to transmit information that enabled them to maintain collectivist equilibrium." The collectivist culture encouraged them to retain business affiliations within this network.[34]

The Middle East traders made great efforts to share information so as to maintain their trading network. Their primary concern was to discover if any of them, acting as an agent, had tricked another and thus caused him a loss. The knowledge that dishonest practice would be revealed to the community was a strong incentive to behave honestly. Remaining honest was a way of staying in business, because in most circumstances it would not pay to cheat.[35]

European Christians, who were represented by Genoese traders in Greif's work, had an individualistic culture. They maintained as much secrecy about their business relations as they could; they did not restrict their choice of agents to members of their family or others with whom they had personal connections. In the absence of a network that would inform them of an agent's misconduct, they were forced to develop impersonal systems of enforcement, the most important of which was the legal system. This was, over time, to prove invaluable for the development of trade and the economy. The difference in values played a role in determining institutions that in turn influenced economic development over hundreds of years. How did cultural differences manifest themselves in the way trading was carried out? Apart from the development of legal systems, the Genoese developed bills-of-lading as a method of documenting obligations and transactions; the Middle East traders did not. The Genoese were more likely than the Middle Eastern traders to be economically upwardly mobile, to experience greater division of labor and to develop the legal system. These developments would have profound, long-term economic consequences. The belief system generated institutions that permitted economic growth. Either the absence of these institutions, or their weakness, was a cause of economic problems in the Middle East.[36] Ghislaine Lydon noted that Islamic law placed much greater emphasis on verbal rather than written documentation, despite the Muslim emphasis on literacy and the advances of the Golden Age. The lack of faith that Islamic courts had in written documentation may well have prevented the growth of joint stock companies and other commercial developments.[37] In this connection, the unwillingness of the Ottoman authorities to permit the use of printing until the eighteen century should be noted.[38]

## Long-Term Stagnation

Douglass North has examined how institutions are created and how they develop. Institutions are, from an economic point of view, limits that men create in order to organize economic and social activity, and to maintain order and reduce uncertainty. There are formal institutions and informal ones. The evolution of institutions is incremental.[39] Hundreds of years can pass without sufficient change occurring to permit economic development. One well-documented example of institutional stability blocking social and economic development was the persistence of the caste system in India.

Deepak Lal explains the endurance of the caste system, which lasted for a thousand years until the twentieth century, in the following way[40]: the ancient Hindus tried to overcome a series of chronic social and economic problems by creating a unique institution, the caste system. In order to retain manpower in agriculture and prevent the population from being conscripted into armies or forcefully removed for other purposes, the caste system was developed. It in effect made it impossible for people to leave the villages or change professions. Despite the fact that, or perhaps because, India was divided into many warring factions, the caste system provided a vital element of stability and a steady supply of agricultural labor. In the harsh environment dominated by the monsoon, agriculture was thus maintained throughout the country despite the ravages of war. Lal called this the "Hindu Equilibrium."

## The Middle Class

The economic and political weakness of the Arab middle class has been a key feature in the development of the region over hundreds of years. Charles Issawi noted the difference between the large-scale political influence of the Hansa merchants of Northern Europe between the thirteenth and sixteenth centuries and the limited influence of the Karimi merchants of the Indian Ocean area between the twelfth and sixteenth centuries.[41] To be sure, there have been exceptions, the most obvious of which is Lebanon. Of the countries examined in Issawi's book, Egypt during the period of Taalat Harb in the early decades of the twentieth century, Morocco, and Syria provide temporary partial examples. Bent Hansen showed how sections of the bourgeoisie planned to change Egypt's economy by introducing modern industry, banking, and other services. They were a small group and faced opposition from the landowning elite (although they had their origins in that group) and from others. The fact that a significant number of them were foreigners weakened them politically at a time of rising nationalism. This group was expelled from the country after the revolution of 1952 with the loss of their skills, capital, and international connections.[42] Hansen also stated that large and middle-sized landowners who were subject to expropriation of their assets after the 1952 revolution were not merely a feudal class who prevented progress, but were entrepreneurial. Their destruction may have been harmful to agriculture, economic growth, and even to the distribution of income.[43]

In Morocco, a group of prominent families, who had their origins in Fez, played a dominant role in the economy. They could be called the old elite because of their long-standing connections to the sultan's court. Using these connections, they were able to gain monopolies over the import and export of certain goods and won public procurement contracts. In the late 1980s, a new group rose to prominence, taking advantages of the liberalization of the economy. This group pushed for the end of the traditional privileges that had been granted to the "Fez elite"; they also demanded reform of business practices and called for Morocco to adopt international standards in taxation and regulation.

Meanwhile, the merchants of Aleppo, in Syria, invested in mechanizing agriculture. The sharecropping system provided peasants with incentives to work in estates, and landlords had incentives to invest in physical capital. Much of this was brought to a halt by Syria's membership in the United Arab Republic with Egypt in 1958. This was followed by the implementation of agrarian reforms that were the result of political rather than economic factors. In 1961, a group of conservative business leaders together with members of the armed forces staged a military coup resulting in the denationalization of a number of companies, raising the ceiling on land ownership. In 1963, however, the Ba'th staged a coup and the nationalization program was renewed.[44]

The failure to generate a significant middle class in the Arab world contrasts strongly with Europe, especially west and northwest Europe. In the development of late medieval Europe, the structures that substituted for an effective state were not tribal or family-based. In the cities of northern Italy and in other urban centers where commerce developed, the main social institutions were self-governed, interest-based organizations set up to benefit their members. The most famous of these were the guilds. Private institutions were the hallmark of the expansion of trade.[45]

The rise of the European cities between the tenth to twelfth centuries was the result of a breakdown of the feudal order in rural areas and a desire to move to areas where people could improve their lot. The towns provided this space: the environment was more innovative and less controlled than in the countryside. Not only peasants but also lesser feudal nobility, merchants, and craftsmen migrated to the towns. Following long political struggles and with big differences between Italy, Germany, England, and Eastern Europe, the towns became centers of power of the triumphant bourgeoisie. This had major economic implications. The new class had new patterns of consumption and the income to fund them. Given the hostility of the rural, feudal world, the urban population felt the need for new types of organization. In the feudal system, organization was vertical from the king to the lord, vassal, and serf. In the towns, a horizontal system emerged among equal citizens. The guilds were the most important. The towns became the source of radical changes in values, relations, administration, education, production, and trade that were to transform the economy of Europe.[46] The middle class was at the center of this process.

In contrast, Muslim society was based on tribes, families, and clans. Corporations did not emerge, nor were they recognized as legal entities. Merchants and guilds could not intervene in the political process to advance their interests. There was no urban autonomy in the Muslim world comparable to that among the cities and city-states of Europe. Society was not organized along corporate lines to represent the interests of classes or particular groups. As has been said, there was very little contact between the traders and the government. Traders preferred it that way because governments were so venal. As trade was discouraged by the laws governing incorporation, over time the social standing of the merchant class deteriorated. This facilitated the spread of anti-mercantile ideologies that in turn made it harder for merchants to obtain legal changes that would encourage trade.[47]

# Conclusions

Given that these factors, originating hundreds of years ago, cannot be quantified, how far do they provide an explanation for the current state of Arab economies? Greif gives a number of reasons why they do. As the division of labor is a condition for long-term economic growth, institutions that provide formal enforcement of exchange make economic development possible. Individualism reinforces these institutions, enabling the economy to capture efficiency gains. Individualism also reduces social pressure to conform to social norms, and corporations are better able to mobilize resources and diversify risks than families. This encourages risk-taking, initiative, and organizational and technological changes. Corporations set up to further the interests of their owners are institutionally dynamic: those that succeed continue and flourish, while those that do not disappear.[48]

In the 1970s and 1980s, as state-owned sectors of the economy buckled under the strains of over-employment and low productivity, governments had to find other ways to generate revenues. In most Arab states, they turned to the private sector and encouraged its expansion. Permission was given to private sector entrepreneurs to operate with or within sectors run by the state. In a situation in which resources were scarce and the government played a central role in controlling the economy, rent-seeking became an important activity.

Yahya Sadowski analyzed the relationship between businessmen and government bureaucrats in the liberalization of Egyptian agriculture in the 1980s. Each side felt that the other was indispensable. Businessmen gained influence through political parties and lobbies to such an extent that they could not be ignored.[49] Concurrently, there was a rise in the size of the middle class, stemming from changes in state policy, most notably the shift away from public sector domination of the economy towards a liberalized system. Both Marxists and liberals have claimed that these new forces have captured the state. An alternative view was that new forces were created by economic policy change.[50] For example, the near-collapse of the landowning class resulted in economic losses not only because of the effects on agriculture but also because landowners were among those investing in industry.[51]

It is significant that the regimes that came to power with the end of Western colonialism in the middle of the twentieth century generally weakened the political and economic position of middle classes still further. This was true in all the countries that experienced Arab socialism, nationalized assets and expelled and/or expropriated the assets of minority populations. Insofar as entrepreneurship was associated with the middle class, the weakness of the latter had negative effects on the economy. In political terms, it meant that one of the forces that might have challenged the ruling elites did not exist on a scale that would provide a threat or alternative source of leadership. In many respects, the regimes that rule in the Arab world today continue a tradition of centralization that has existed in the region for hundreds, if not thousands, of years.

Policies favoring economic growth are likely when class conflict and ethnic tensions are absent. When the middle class has a large share of the national income and there is a high degree of ethnic harmony, then a middle class consensus can exist. When there is a middle class consensus, better institutions emerge, making faster and more stable economic growth more likely. According to Easterly, middle class consensus explained the difference between North and South America's development and helps to explain development successes and failures elsewhere.[52]

The fundamental and long term weaknesses in economic and political development that have been analyzed above came to a head in the events known as the Arab Spring. This has so far resulted in the fall of four leaders and the partial collapse or total collapse of the regimes that they headed. Conflict continues in Libya, Syria, and Yemen. The reasons for the protests were different in each country, although all included the call for freedom. Behind the revolt in these countries and the pressures for change in Bahrain, Jordan, and Morocco are economic as well as political factors. One contributing factor to the call for change in the Arab world was that authoritarian rule had not produced the promised economic transformation, or at least not enough economic transformation.[53] While there was economic growth in Mubarak's Egypt and Ben Ali's Tunisia, it was accompanied by very unequal distributions of income, high poverty rates, and massive corruption.

How did these rulers manage to control their societies for so long and accumulate so much wealth? Ayubi's explanation was that for hundreds of years the state in the Middle East was strong and society was weak.[54] This prevailed into the twenty first century: not only was society weak and the *mukhabarat* ("secret police") state "fierce," but the later increased its power at the expense of the former. In Egypt, Nasser, Sadat, and Mubarak all acted against political parties that had their origins in Egypt's relatively democratic period from the 1930s to the 1950s. The military regime tried to monopolize power in a way that left democratic forces very weak. The economic system that they created placed the state in the center. The private sector was emasculated in the 1950s and 1960s and has remained deeply dependent on the state ever since, despite many years of economic liberalization. Not only the private sector, but the society as a whole, became dependent on the state.

Among the factors that have created tensions in recent years are demographic pressures, the role of rents, the impact of colonialism and the reaction to it, the legacy of Arab socialism (huge employment in the public sector) and finally the impact of economic policies implemented under the framework of the "Washington Consensus." This required countries to stabilize their economies, liberalize foreign trade, and increase the role of market forces in exchange for financial assistance.

More generally, the absolute size of the population in all Arab states has increased even though in recent years growth rates have slowed. In 1970, the Arab population was 122 million. By 2005 it had more than tripled to over

300 million and in 2015 it has been forecast at 385 million. The population of working age has grown much faster: from 64 million in 1970 to 164 million in 2000 and a forecast of 240 million in 2015. The fact that the share of those of working age in the total population has increased from 52 percent in 1970 to 54 percent in 2000 and a forecast of 62 percent means that there are more shoulders to carry the burden of looking after the young and old.[55] But that assumes that there is work for them and that assumption is false. Unemployment has, in fact, increased and among the consequences have been poverty and income inequality. Demographic transition means more young people coming onto the labor market but the economy has not growing fast enough to absorb them. This has major political implications and the role of young people in the revolts in Tunisia and Egypt has been a key factor in their success.

The weakness of the productive system — industry, agriculture, and services — in the Arab world is closely related to the role of rents. There are several kinds of rents: the first is income from natural resources, primarily oil and gas. The second is foreign aid. Emigrant remittances are also rents in that they are not earned inside the economy. What all these sources of income have in common is that they are largely not earned as a result of work in the economy. The most dramatic example is oil: a barrel of crude oil costs as little as $10 to drill out of the ground in Eastern Saudi Arabia and Iraq, but it sells for up to $100. This means that 90 percent of the proceeds are rental.

The three main schools of thought reviewed here all contain useful explanations, but it is the institutional school that is the most powerful. Perhaps the most dramatic proof of the power of institutions is the economic development of Germany and Korea, two countries that were politically divided and rent asunder by war. There were no significant geographic differences between East and West Germany (except that West Germany had a larger area and population). Prior to their division, North Korea had more industry than the South and there too, geography cannot provide a significant explanation. Furthermore, in both cases the people and their culture (including religion) were the same. The differences between East and West Germany and between North and South Korea were political and economic, and were the result of differences in institutions. Within forty years, those differences generated huge gaps in economic performance.[56]

In the Arab world, the long history of Ottoman rule adversely affected the way in which the region developed. British and French rule after the World War I did little to change things, and the limited democracy that developed in parts of the region between the 1930s and 1950s was crushed by a series of military coups. As a result, few of the economic and political institutions needed for economic growth developed. The key institution is "inclusiveness": the involvement of people in the economic and political system. "The ability of economic institutions to harness the potential of inclusive markets, encourage technological innovation, invest in people and mobilize the talents and skills of a large number of individuals critical for economic growth."[57] The Arab Spring was a dramatic demonstration of the absence of inclusiveness in the political and economic systems across the Middle East and North Africa.

# Notes

1. The states include: Bahrain, Kuwait, Oman, Qatar, the United Arab Emirates, and Saudi Arabia.
2. Randall Kuhn, "On the Role of Human Development in the Arab Spring," *Population and Development Review*, Vol. 38, No. 4, pp. 644–683.
3. Paul Rivlin, "Behind the Tensions in Syria: The Socio-Economic Dimensions," *Tel Aviv Notes*, The Moshe Dayan Center, 2011, Vol. 5, Special edition, No. 6, http://www.dayan.org/sites/default/files/TA_Notes_RIVLIN_Syria_MAR30_11[1].pdf.
4. *Idem*, "Behind the Tensions in Syria: The Socio-Economic Dimensions," *Tel Aviv Notes*, The Moshe Dayan Center, 2011, Vol. 5, Special edition, No. 6, http://www.dayan.org/sites/default/files/TA_Notes_RIVLIN_Syria_MAR30_11[1].pdf.
5. *Idem*, "Arab Economies in the Twenty First Century," 2009, p. 51 and Jean-Philippe Platteau, "Religion, Politics and Development: Lessons from the Lands of Islam," Economic Research Forum working paper no. 434, 2008, http://www.erf.org.eg/CMS/uploads/pdf/1221388605_434.pdf.
6. Karl Wittfogel, *Oriental Despotism: A Comparative Study of Total Power* (New Haven and London: Yale University Press, 1957), p. 49.
7. *Ibid.*, pp. 55–57.
8. *Ibid.*, pp. 84–85
9. *Ibid.*, pp. 84–86.
10. *Ibid.*, p. 84
11. *Ibid.*, pp. 93–97.
12. Jeffrey Sachs, "Long Term Perspectives in the Economic Development of the Middle East," *Riv'on le-Kalkala*, Vol. 48, No. 3, October 2001 [Hebrew] (Tel Aviv: Am Oved, 2001), pp. 417–440.
13. UNESCO, Education for All: Global Monitoring Report Paris UNESCO, 2006, http://www.unesco.org/education/GMR2006/full/chapt7_eng.pdf. p. 166.
14. Stanley L. Engerman and Kenneth L. Sokoloff, "Factor Endowments, Inequality, and Paths of Development among New World Economies," National Bureau of Economic Research Working Paper no. 9259, October 2002.
15. *Ibid.*
16. Albert Hourani, *Arabic Thought in the Liberal Age, 1789–1939* (London: Oxford University Press, 1962), pp. 183–184, 267–268.

17. Peter Temin, "Is Culture Kosher?" *Journal of Economic History*, Vol. 57, No. 2 (June 1997), pp. 267–282.
18. David Landes, *The Wealth and Poverty of Nations* (New York: W.W. Norton, 1999), Chapters 4 and 12.
19. *Idem*, "Culture Makes Almost All the Difference," in Lawrence E. Harrision and Samuel P. Huntington (eds.), *Culture Matters* (New York: Basic Books, 2000), pp. 2–13.
20. Quoted in Khalid Ikram, *The Egyptian Economy, 1952–2000: Performance, Policies and Issues* (London and New York: Routledge, 2006), p. 50.
21. Maxime Rodinson, *Islam and Capitalism* (London: Allen Lane, 1974 edition), pp. 76–117.
22. Marcus Nolan and Howard Pack, *The Arab Economies in a Changing World* (Washington DC: The Peterson Institute, 2007), p. 144.
23. Jean-Philippe Platteau, "Religion, Politics and Development: Lessons from the Lands of Islam," *Journal of Economic Behavior and Organisation,* 2008, Vol. 68 (2), pp. 321–351.
24. Eric L. Jones, *The European Miracle: Environments, Economies and the Geopolitics in the History of Europe and Asia* (Cambridge: Cambridge University Press, 1988).
25. Charles P. Kindleberger, *World Economic Primacy: 1500 to 1900* (New York, Oxford: Oxford University Press, 1996).
26. Timur Kuran, "The Absence of the Corporation in Islamic Law: Origins and Perspectives," CLEO Research Paper Series C04-16 Law and Economics Research Paper, No. 04-21, 2006; and *idem*, "Islam and Underdevelopment: An Old Puzzle Revisited," *Journal of Institutional and Theoretical Economics*, Vol. 153 (1997), J.C.B. Mohr (Paul Siebert), pp. 41–71.
27. *Idem*, "The Islamic Commercial Crisis: Institutional Roots of Economic Under-development in the Middle East," *Journal of Economic History,* Vol. 63, No. 2 (June 2003), pp. 414–446.
28. *Idem*, "Islam and Underdevelopment: An Old Puzzle Revisited".
29. Avner Greif, *Institutions and the Path to the Modern Economy* (Cambridge: Cambridge University Press, 2006), pp. 149–150.
30. Timur Kuran, "Explaining the Economic Trajectories of Civilizations: Musings on the Systemic Approach," 2007, <www.usc.edu/schools/college/crcc/private/ierc/conference_registration/papers/Kuran.pdf>.
31. Platteau, "Religion, Politics and Development: Lessons from the Lands of Islam."
32. Douglass North, *Institutions, Institutional Change and Economic Performance* (Cambridge: Cambridge University Press, 1990); Deepak Lal, *The Hindu Equilibrium: Cultural Stability and Economic Stagnation, India c1500-AD 1980* (Oxford: Clarendon Press, 1988), pp. 309–315.
33. Avner Greif, "On the Social Foundations and Historical Development of Institutions that Facilitate Impersonal Exchange: From the Community Responsibility System to Individual Legal Responsibility in Pre-modern Europe," Stanford University, Working Paper, 1997, <http://econpapers.repec.org/paper/wopstanec/97016.htm>.
34. *Idem, Institutions and the Path to the Modern Economy*, pp. 309–310.
35. *Ibid.*, pp. 62–70.

36. *Idem*, "Cultural Beliefs and the Organization of Society: A Historical and Theoretical Reflection on Collectivist and Individualist Society", *The Journal of Political Economy*, Volume 102, Issue 5 (October, 1994), pp. 912–950, quote from p. 923.

37. Ghislaine Lydon, "A 'Paper Economy of Faith' without Faith in Paper: A Contribution to Understanding the Roots of Islamic Institutional Stagnation," 2007, http://www.usc.edu/schools/college/crcc/private/ierc/conference_registration/papers/Lydon2.pdf, pp. 1, 31.

38. Metin M. Cosgel, Thomas J. Miceli and Jared Rubin, "The Political Economy of Mass Printing, Revolt and Technological Change in the Ottoman Empire," *The Journal of Comparative Economics*, Vo. 49, Issue 3, August 2012, pp. 357–371.

39. North, *passim*.

40. Lal, *passim*.

41. Charles Issawi, "The Adaptation of Islam to Contemporary Economic Realities", in Charles Issawi, *The Middle East Economy: Decline and Recovery* (Princeton: Markus Wiener Publishers, 1995), p. 192.

42. Bent Hansen, *Egypt and Turkey: The Political Economy of Poverty, Equity and Growth* (Oxford: Oxford University Press, 1991), p. 534.

43. Robert Springborg, "The Arab Bourgeoisie: A Revisionist Interpretation," *Arab Studies Quarterly*, Vol. 15, no. 1, Winter 1993, pp. 13–39.

44. *Ibid.*

45. Avner Greif, *Institutions and the Path to the Modern Economy: Lessons from Medieval Trade* (Cambridge: Cambridge University Press, 2006), pp. 388–394 and Francis Fukuyama, *The Origins of Political Order* (London: Profile Books, 2011), pp. 227–241.

46. Carlo M. Cippola, *Before the Industrial Revolution* (London: Routledge, 1993), pp. 117–122.

47. Kuran, "The Islamic Commercial Crisis: Institutional Roots of Economic Underdevelopment in the Middle East", p. 39.

48. Greif, Institutions and the Path to the Modern Economy: Lessons from Medieval Trade, p. 398.

49. Yahya Sadowski, *Political Vegetables* (Washington D.C.: Brookings Institutions, 1991), p. 139.

50. Alan Richards and John Waterbury, *A Political Economy of the Middle East* (Boulder, Colorado: Westview Press, 1996), p. 34.

51. *Ibid.*, p. 403.

52. William Easterly, "The Middle Class Consensus and Economic Development", *Journal of Economic Growth*, Vol. 6, No. 4, December 2001, pp. 317–336.

53. Robert Kaplan, "The Good Autocrat," *The National Interest*, July–August 2011, pp. 1–5.

54. Nazih N. Ayubi, *Over-stating the Arab State* (London, New York: I.B. Tauris, 1995).

55. Paul Rivlin, *Arab Economies in the Twenty-First Century* (New York: Cambridge University Press, 2009), pp. 8–9.

56. Daron Acemoglu and James A. Robinson, *Why Nations Fail* (New York: Crown Publishers, 2012), pp. 48–49.

57. *Ibid.*, p. 79.

# Al-Qa'ida and the "Arab Spring": Constraints and Opportunities

## Esther Webman

Elated by the killing of Usama Bin Ladin on May 1, 2011, Saudi journalist Muhammad bin 'Ali al-Mahmud boasted that

> we live between two times, reflecting two extremely contradicting choices: The time of the deceased terrorist (Bin Ladin) and the Abu 'Azizi[1] time. The first time is fading away, and the second time is rising. The first time suffered a total failure, while the second time highly succeeded... It was clearly the masses that eventually determined the choice and implemented a real achievement, which directly affect their daily reality and shrinking away from the utopian promises hung on the hollowness of the sick fundamentalist imagination.[2]

Mahmud was confident that the "Arab Spring," in conjunction with the death of the symbol of religious fanaticism, would put an end to Bin Ladinism and terrorism in the Arab world, which in his opinion was already in decline.

Since the mid-1990s, the assessment that al-Qa'ida and Islamist movements were in crisis and on the wane has been widespread among Muslim intellectuals and commentators, as well as Western scholars of political Islam.[3] They have argued that Islamist movements failed to adjust their messages to the changing political conditions and to consolidate themselves as a reliable popular force. According to this argument, they were divided in their goals and strategies, which split them into endless factions and damaged their effectiveness, and despite their intensified social involvement, they were not able to translate it into political power. The very success of the Islamic revival, said Olivier Roy, led to the de-politicization of Islam; namely, it distanced Islamists from political centers.[4]

Developments in the wake of the uprisings in the Middle East that led to the ascension to power of Islamist movements in a number of countries challenged those claims. This article focuses on one stream of the Islamist movement–al-Qa'ida and its offshoots. It seeks to assess its present state, the impact of Bin Ladin's death and years of war on its activities, and its reaction to the Arab Spring. It contends that al-Qa'ida, like other fundamentalist movements, is a dynamic organization, which wittingly or unwittingly, shapes and reshapes itself in response to external circumstances, time, and place. Although the organization has been dealt severe physical and moral blows since September 11, 2001, it has made a number of adaptions in order to survive, while maintaining an ideology and message that still appeal to various Muslim circles. The article also contends that the Arab Spring posed new challenges to al-Qa'ida but also afforded it unprecedented opportunities that turned the organization, its affiliates, and those inspired by it into a potent threat to failed and failing states already suffering from low levels of cohesion, and to the stability of ungoverned regions in the Middle East and North Africa.

# Al-Qa'ida in Shambles

From documents seized during the raid of the US Special Operations forces on his hideout in the Pakistani town of Abbottabad, Bin Ladin seemed to emerge as a very pessimistic person. In his speech at the Woodrow Wilson Center on April 30, 2012, marking the first anniversary of Bin Ladin's killing, Assistant to the President for Homeland Security and Counterterrorism John Brennan revealed that Bin Ladin was disappointed that his most skilled and experienced commanders had been killed and that the members of his organization were on the run. He was worried about the rise of inexperienced leaders that "would lead to the repeat of mistakes," his isolation and bad communication with subordinates and affiliates, and especially the organization's tarnished reputation. He apparently confessed to "disaster after disaster," and "agreed that 'a large portion' of Muslims around the world 'have lost their trust' in al-Qa'ida."[5]

Indeed, al-Qa'ida of 2013 is not al-Qa'ida on the eve of September 11, 2001. Then, it acted as a centralized, hierarchical organization that considered options and targets of operation, on the basis of their cost, available squads, and the expected damages. Due to the 'War on Terror' launched by the West, many of its senior leaders were killed and its members scattered in the Afghani-Pakistani mountains. The central command's operational control was undermined, and the organization lost much of its power and luster, as well as its international momentum. Most of its initiatives to carry out operations in the West had been foiled. The organization was in chaos, and in order to remain relevant it had to cooperate with other militant groups, turning into more of an ideological movement providing tactical and strategic assistance.

Bin Ladin was aware of the changes that his organization was experiencing. He regarded al-Qa'ida's transformation into an "ideological umbrella" for a network of independent organizations as harmful to his original vision and message, and leading to terrorist activities in Muslim countries that were causing Muslim civilian casualties. He wanted to lead reforms in order to stop the bloodshed against Muslims and to re-prioritize the fight against Americans. He was critical of al-Shabab in Somalia for its inflexible interpretation of Islamic law, and refused to officially recognize it as an al-Qa'ida affiliate. He was also urged by some members to reconsider the issue of *takfir* (excommunication of fellow Muslims, which labels them unbelievers liable to be killed) and to take a clear position on its interpretation to avoid being seen as rigid and narrow-minded.[6]

Analyzing the decline of al-Qa'ida, the Combating Terrorism Center at West Point, the United States Military Academy, published a research report in December 2010, in which it pointed to two categories of endogenous problems plaguing al-Qa'ida and the jihadi movement in general: internal divisions, and "the fault lines dividing the jihad movement from other Muslim and Islamist actors."[7] The internal divisions revolved around crucial issues pertinent to the strategy of struggle, such as what should be the focus of activity: the near enemy, i.e., Muslim regimes; or the far enemy, the United States and its western allies; and the issue of *takfir*, which alienated fellow Muslims. There were also rifts between pragmatists and doctrinarians, between Arab and non-Arab members, and between al-Qa'ida's central command and local affiliates. But despite the constraints of these divisions, they also leave a degree of flexibility in defining goals and choosing modes of operation by enabling them to consider all possible options. Being part and parcel of the Islamist current, al-Qa'ida shares with them the same basic tenets and hostility toward the West and Israel, yet also competes with them. Nor does it enjoy the broad social base and financial resources of the Muslim Brotherhood, Hizballah, or Hamas. Sometimes, however, it enjoys the underdog status.

The demise of Bin Ladin, whose stature had diminished over the years, dealt a serious blow to the organization, and Bin Ladin's successor, Ayman al-Zawahiri, has not succeeded thus far in filling the gap that Bin Ladin left behind. The formal announcement of Zawahiri as Bin Ladin's successor took place on June 16, 2011, and concluded a six-week period of the organization's initial re-adjustment after Bin Ladin's death. Zawahiri, a former leader of the Egyptian Jihad group, had been Bin Ladin's second-in-command since the establishment of the World Islamic Front for Jihad against the Jews and the Crusaders in February 1998, and yet his appointment as Bin Ladin's successor could not be taken for granted, and exposed the organization's internal divisions and disagreements.

Examining the multitude of Arab reactions to Bin Ladin's death in the immediate aftermath provides an illuminating glimpse of the attitudes towards him and his organization among various factions within Arab societies. Reactions ranged from anger to joy, promises of revenge to hopes for the end of terrorism, belief that Bin Ladinism was alive and kicking to the conviction that the culture of death was gone forever. This polarity reflects two conflicting agendas that have been seeking change in Arab societies, but in opposite directions and by opposite means: One agenda has been propagated by Islamists and their followers, and the other by their opponents who reject their worldview and methods and draw comfort from the Arab Spring.

Among Islamists, Bin Ladin was a *mujahid* (holy warrior), a hero and a martyr who sacrificed his life following the path of God, and his death was perceived as an aggression against every Muslim Arab. They conducted prayer sermons in Yemen, Kuwait, Sudan, Somalia, Algeria, Mauritania, and even in Tahrir Square in Cairo. In Gaza, Hamas Prime Minister Isma'il Haniyya condemned the killing and eulogized Bin Ladin as a *mujahid*. Movements affiliated with al-Qa'ida, such as AQAP (Al-Qa'ida in the Arabian Peninsula), ISI (Islamic State in Iraq), AQIM (Al-Qa'ida in the Islamic Maghreb), and *al-Shabab al-Mujahidin* in Somalia, mourned Bin Ladin and vowed to avenge his death, urging their members to kill Americans and carry out one-man jihad operations. The death of the leader does not mean the death of the ideology of jihad, they claimed. On the contrary, it serves as an incentive to accelerate the fight against the infidels, which is a personal duty incumbent upon every Muslim until Judgment Day. Usama Bin Ladin is "a phenomenon of resistance of the downtrodden on earth," according to the leading Sunni Islamist ideologue, Shaykh Yusuf al-Qaradawi, or "an idea of resistance against tyranny" that will continue to spread and will never die, as Fayiz Abu Shamala wrote in the Hamas daily *Filastin*.[8] Moreover, it will create thousands of Bin Ladins. "Every mother will want to give birth now to a Shaykh Usama Bin Ladin," declared Anjem Choudary, British spokesman for the Islamist group Islam4UK and former member of the defunct *al-Muhajiroun* group.[9]

Yet despite these manifestations of sympathy, several commentators criticized Bin Ladin's worldview in Islamist papers, casting doubts on his achievements and admitting that he had lost popular support. Terrorism against innocent people harmed the perception of jihad in Islam and contradicted Islamic values, they contended. Moreover, they called upon Salafi-jihadist movements to revisit their policies in view of the apparent success of the alternative, peaceful and democratic means used to bring about change during the initial Arab Spring protests.[10]

Indeed, the largely peaceful revolutions in Tunisia and Egypt that toppled the old regimes were quickly trumpted by the Islamists' opponents and some analysts as the ultimate proof that the Arab publics rejected Islamist ideology and methods. This was the leitmotif in most of their commentaries. A survey conducted by the Pew Research Center's Global Attitudes Project in six Arab and Muslim countries in 2011 clearly showed that support for Bin Ladin and for al-Qa'ida since 2003 had largely eroded.[11] The organization "has long been structurally weak and moribund," and its death knell is the rejection of its "ignorant fanaticism" by Muslim youths, claimed the liberal Egyptian academic and commentator 'Abd al-Mun'im Sa'id.[12] "The movement for change that the region is witnessing has marginalized such narrow-minded groups," wrote 'Ali Ibrahim. Bin Ladin was no more than an icon in recent years, he said, and his end was inevitable one way or another. Bin Ladin's operations did not serve Islam and in fact most of his victims were Arabs and Muslims. His death converged with the collapse of the old Arab regime, of which he was a part, marking a victory over terrorism and extremism.[13]

## Prioritizing and Redefining Goals

"As a structured entity al-Qa'ida is clearly less formidable than before, and even as a more fluid movement it has lost momentum. But it endures as an idea and sense of mission."[14] In his book *The Al Qaeda Factor: Plots Against the West*,[15] Mitchell Silber, director of intelligence analysis for the New York City Police Department, analyzed 16 perpetrated or foiled plots against the West from 1993 to 2009 in order to assess the role of the "al-Qa'ida core" in "global jihadist plots." He argues that the organization has demonstrated flexibility and ability to adapt to changing circumstances. With the American occupation of Iraq, Bin Ladin changed his tactics and began forming al-Qa'ida branches that relied on local recruits instead of exporting his trained fighters–a strategy that resulted in a privatization process, of sorts, of the organization. In a similar manner, the organization founded branches in Yemen and in the Maghreb, which consisted mainly of local organizations that operate against existing regimes. The weakening of the Saudi Jihad network due to the regime's tough and successful security policies strengthened the Yemeni branch and led to the unification of the two branches in 2009.

Three factors challenged the ability of the organization to function:
1. A lack of financial resources — Bin Ladin had invested a huge amount of his personal wealth and managed to raise money from wealthy Muslims in the Gulf, but since his death, al-Qa'ida has encountered problems raising comparable resources;
2. A shortage of experienced commanders because many of them had been killed during the war in Afghanistan, and others fled to the Middle East and North Africa; and

3. The Arab Spring which posed the greatest test to its ideology.
The Arab Spring challenged the ideology of all Islamist streams and forced them
to adjust themselves to the new circumstances. The uprisings across the region
exposed the weakness and indeed meaninglessness of the idea of al-Qa'ida in
the eyes of many Arabs and Muslims. Incomplete as they are, they have made
"both the means and the rationale of the *jihadi* network look even more obsolete
than they were before," claimed Palestinian scholar Khaled Hroub.[16] Hassan
Mneimneh, an expert on extremism and insurgency in the Arab and Muslim
worlds, had maintained:

> Three decades since the onset of the anti-Soviet Afghan jihad and the
> emergence of a Jihadist *internationale*, more than two decades after
> the Saudi monarchy had sought western protection against the loud
> objections of the Jihadists, and the almost decade after the Jihadist 'raids'
> of September 11, 2001, meant to ignite the millennial confrontation with
> the usurpers of the rights of the *umma*, Jihadist mobilization in Arab and
> Muslim societies has still not managed to ignite a revolution."[17]

Al-Qa'ida was caught by surprise by the Arab Spring like everyone else.
Its attitude toward the revolutions was initially ambivalent. After all, they
constituted a tacit rejection of al-Qa'ida ideology; nevertheless, they succeeded
in realizing the goal that al-Qa'ida had sought. The Arab Spring presented a
model of regime change that was a blow to the theory that jihad is the only
way for toppling autocratic Arab regimes. Eventually, however, al-Qa'ida
supported the demonstrators and, once the success of Islamist parties became
apparent, even tried to claim credit for some of this success. Zawahiri broadcast
an appeal to the Egyptian people on January 29, 2011, calling upon all Islamist
movements to unite and anticipating the return of all Jihadi Islamists who
had left Egypt in order to fulfill a comprehensive Islamic revolution. In other
appeals, he encouraged opposition to the Syrian regime and warned against
relying on the West. He urged Syrians to unite and rise above sectarian
affiliations to bring down President Bashar al-Asad and to thwart what he said
were US plans to set up a client state in Syria to safeguard Israel's security.[18]

In May 2012, al-Qa'ida's most prominent ideologue, Mustafa Setmariam Nasar,
a.k.a. Abu Mus'ab al-Suri, who was released from the Syrian prison in December
2011, redefined the strategy, the goals, and targets of global Jihadism. Speaking
via AQAP's electronic mouthpiece, *Inspire*, he reiterated his views, expressed
in his 1,600-page book, "A Call to a Global Islamic Resistance," published on
the Internet in 2005, shortly before being captured in Pakistan and transferred
to Syria. Al-Suri declared Western and Jewish interests to be the main target of
the global jihadist struggle, and individual jihad as the primary course of action.

"The Islamic *umma*," he said,

> is vast, and so are the arenas in which targets and interests of the invader enemy are present. It is furthermore impossible for all the youth who want to participate in the Resistance to travel to the arenas of [open] confrontation. It is even unlikely that such Fronts should emerge in the foreseeable future. Hence, our method should therefore be to guide the Muslim who wants to participate and resist, to operate where he is, or where he is able to be present in a natural way. We should advise him to pursue his everyday life in a natural way, and to pursue jihad and Resistance in secrecy and alone, or with a small cell of trustworthy people, who form an independent unit for Resistance and for individual jihad.[19]

The priority arenas for this struggle, he said, stretched from Pakistan and South East Asia, through the Middle East and North Africa to European countries allied with America and "the heart of America." The goal of the operations was

> to inflict as many human and material losses as possible upon the interests of America and her allies, and to make them feel that the Resistance has been transformed into a phenomenon of popular uprising against them.[20]

Among these targets are "places where Jews are gathered, their leading personalities and institutions in Europe, avoiding places of worship and synagogues."[21]

This redefinition of goals and targets was a response to al-Qa'ida's state of weakness. Yet it also marked a return to the original ideological platform issued by Bin Ladin in February 1998 and seems to coincide with Bin Ladin's views reflected in the documents seized after his death. It marked a shift in the organization's locus of activity from the "near enemy," corrupt regimes in Arab countries, to the "far enemy," the West and the Jews. Bin Ladin's reliance on individual Muslims living in the West, who were familiar with its culture and pursued "everyday life in a natural way," seems to guide al-Suri as well in his instructions to potential al-Qa'ida-inspired individuals. With both ideological guidance and practical training readily available online, the threat of homegrown terrorism is on the rise, especially in the West.[22] Muhammad Merah's attack on French soldiers and Jewish school children in Toulouse in March 2012 is a glaring example of this development.

Therefore, the idea of al-Qa'ida remains potent, despite its weaknesses and failures, and "Bin Ladenism is still a source of inspiration for the militants fighting from Afghanistan to Yemen and from Iraq to Palestine," as Pakistani journalist Hamid Mir asserted.[23] A third generation of al-Qa'ida is growing fast, according to veteran US policy Bruce Riedel: the first generation was the original band of *mujahidin* in Afghanistan created by Bin Ladin in the 1990s; the second surfaced after 9/11 when the group re-emerged in Pakistan, Iraq, and then across the Muslim world; and the third appeared following Bin Ladin's death and the "Arab Awakening."[24]

Al-Qa'ida "has devolved into an expanded, diffuse network of affiliates, allies, and ideological adherents," and formed a loose coalition of the top tier organizations that include AQAP, AQIM, *al-Shabab*, *Tehreek-e-Taliban* (TTP), and *Lashkar-e-Taiba* (LeT), among others. The next tier of organizations operate in the ungoverned spaces of the Sahel in West Africa in regions of Mauritania, Mali, Algeria and Niger. These locations not only serve as radicalization incubators or logistical hubs, but constitute the biggest challenge to the cohesiveness of the states they are operating in.[25]

## Accelerating the Instability and Disintegration of Troubled Areas

"The Arab Spring, with its 'peaceful' revolutions in Egypt and Tunisia, and its violent revolutions in Yemen, Libya and Syria, has proved a boon for the Salafist movement," wrote 'Abd al-Mun'im Sa'id, warning of the marked and dangerous rise in armed Salafist groups in Arab societies. Sa'id, who was optimistic in the first few months of the revolution, and believed that the Arab Spring would usher a new era for Middle Eastern societies, had become disillusioned by the course of events. When the state was strong, he explained,

> the Salafis created their bases under a cloak of piety and religious observance. As the authority of the state weakened due to the winds of the Arab Spring, they formed political parties that sought to seize control through democratic means to be discarded once they were in power. Where the authority of state was totally absent, they would turn to armed violence against the state and society.[26]

Most of the pan-Islamist movements, first and foremost the apolitical Salafist stream, have forsaken, particularly in the wake of the Arab Spring, their transnational agenda, opting instead for a national one. Even the Egyptian jihadist movements, such al-Jama'a al-Islamiyya and the Egyptian Jihad, formed parties to run for the parliamentary elections in November 2011 and January 2012. Since those movements chose the political path in the framework of the nation-state, they temporarily shelved jihadism, while maintaining their ultimate goal of establishing one united Islamic *umma*. Aware of the prevailing public mood in Egypt and other Arab societies, al-Qa'ida did not condemn this trend although it was critical of it.

Traditionally, Middle Eastern and North African states suffered state weakness and instability due to a number of factors,

> including the unrepresentative and unpopular nature of the ruling political institutions, the lack of a cohesive and unitary citizenship discourse, the failure to provide social and political goods to all citizens, and the difficulties in preventing the proliferation of non-state armed groups and alternative pockets of authority within the country's territory.[27]

Al-Qa'ida-affiliated groups, whose pan-Islamist worldview and basic rejection of nationalism are inimical to the concept of the nation-state, exacerbated this weakness. If in the 1990s al-Qa'ida ceased its subversive activities against corrupt Arab regimes and targeted the West, the pendulum of the global jihad movement is swinging back again in the wake of the Arab Spring. Al-Qa'ida and its affiliates have since focused the majority of their activities against national governments while leaving the global arena to individual initiatives, mainly Muslims and converts to Islam living in the West and inspired by its worldview.

Al-Qa'ida-affiliated groups have exploited the Arab revolutions to create operational bases across the Arab world. They have expanded their activities in weak and failed states, such as Yemen and Libya, states where civil war erupted, such as Syria, and even in states that experienced a peaceful transition to Islamist regimes, such as Egypt and Tunisia. AQAP-affiliated militants in Yemen, *Ansar al-Shari'a* in Libya, *Jabhat al-Nusra* in Syria, and *al-Jihad wal-Tawhid* and *Ansar Bayt al-Maqdis* in Sinai, allied themselves with local Sunni or tribal militants, aggravating sectarian divisions and further undermining the stability and cohesion of these states.

Striving to remain relevant and reinforce his authority over the organization's affiliated groups, Ayman al-Zawahiri has continued to publicly express his views on current developments. In May 2013, he intervened to resolve a dispute between the emir of *Jabhat al-Nusra*, Abu Muhammad al-Julani, and the emir of ISI, Abu Bakr al-Baghdadi, who announced the merger of the two groups earlier in April, claiming that the Front is "merely an extension and part of the Islamic State of Iraq." Julani had reportedly rejected Baghdadi's move and reaffirmed his oath of allegiance to Zawahiri directly, although he previously operated in the ISI. In a letter issued on May 23, 2013 and publicized two weeks later, Zawahiri ruled against the merger, called on members of both groups to refrain from infighting, and named Abu Khalid al-Suri, a local Syrian commander and a longtime al-Qa'ida operative released from a Syrian prison in the wake of the rebellion, as a personal emissary "to oversee the implementation" of the accord.[28] On the occasion of the 46th anniversary of the June 1967 war, he released an audio message posted on July 31, 2013, refuting allegations that al-Qa'ida was attempting to hijack the revolutions in order to appoint its own people as the Muslims' rulers, and denouncing Hizballah for its support to Asad as Iran's proxy.[29]

The removal of Mohammed Morsi, the first Egyptian Islamist president, on July 3, 2013 as a result of mass protests and military intervention, gave Zawahiri another opportunity to voice his views and reiterate his belief in jihad as the only way for regime change. Morsi's ousting, he stated, provided proof that Islamic rule cannot be established through democracy, and he urged his followers to abandon the ballot box in favor of armed resistance. He also criticized Islamists for losing power and not uniting to implement *shari'a*. In concluding, he declared defiantly that

> the battle isn't over, it has just started...the Islamic nation should offer victims and sacrifices to achieve what it wants and restore power from the corrupt authority governing Egypt." [30]

In early August 2013, a heightened terror alert was prompted by an intercepted conference call between Zawahiri, AQAP's leader Nasir al-Wuhayshi, and about 19 other people spread across the Middle East and Africa, and appeared to challenge one of the assumptions of this chapter that al-Qa'ida's core in Afghanistan does not control its affiliates, which basically decide on their independent operations. Hinting at a potential attack at American and western targets, the communication led to the closure of nearly two-dozen US embassies and consulates for a few days.[31] Was this an indication of an evolution of al-Qa'ida into a new phase, showing that it is now more cohesive and centralized than it had previously been? The content of the call has not been revealed, but according to published reports, they discussed in vague terms plans for a pending attack.[32] It would be safe to assume that Zawahiri was urging the various local commanders to intensify their activities against American and western targets without providing any specific operational guidance. He was obviously seeking to secure their allegiance to him, and establish his authority among the affiliates by conferring on them titles and tasks, thus creating some kind of symbolic internal hierarchy and discipline to avoid chaos. Zawahiri's position might have been improved since his appointment after the death of Bin Ladin but he remained far from having control over the disparate and diffuse operations of al-Qa'ida-affiliated or -inspired groups and individuals. Yet, these attempts confirm the postulation here that the organization adapts and evolves in response to external circumstances and developments. Moreover, the Arab Spring afforded al-Qa'ida new and unprecedented opportunities that turned the organization, its affiliates, and those inspired by it, into a newly potent threat to the cohesion and stability of the Middle East and North Africa.

# Notes

1. The Tunisian Mohammed Bouazizi, whose self-immolation prompted the Tunisian uprising in December 2010.
2. *Al-Riyad*, May 12, 2011, http://www.alriyadh.com/2011/05/12/article 631801.html.
3. Esther Webman, "The Polarization and Radicalization of Political Islam," in Bruce Maddy-Weitzman (ed.), *Middle East Contemporary Survey*, Vol. XXII, 1998 (Boulder, Colorado: Westview, 2001), pp. 128–129; *Idem*, "The Undiminished Threat of Political Islam," in *idem* (ed.), *Middle East Contemporary Survey*, XXIV 2000 (Tel Aviv: Tel Aviv University, 2002), pp. 91–92.
4. Olivier Roy, "Post-Islamic Revolution," February 2011, http://www.europeaninstitute. org/February-2011/qpost-islamic-revolutionq-events-in-egypt-analyzed-by-french-expert-on-political-islam.html; *Le Monde*, February 14, 2011, http://www.lemonde. fr/idees/article/2011/02/12/revolution-post-islamiste_1478858_3232.html.
5. Transcript of Remarks by John O. Brennan, "The Ethics and the Efficacy of the President's Counterterrorism Strategy," April 30, 2012, http://www.wilsoncenter.org/ event/the-efficacy-and-ethics-us-counterterrorism-strategy.
6. Robin Sincox, "Analyzing the Bin Laden Documents," *World Affairs Journal*, May–June 2012, http://www.worldaffairsjournal.org.
7. Assaf Moghadam and Brian Fishman (eds.), "Self-Inflicted Wounds: Debates and Divisions within al-Qa'ida and its Periphery" (Combating Terrorism Center at West Point), December 16, 2010, www.ctc.usma.edu.
8. *Filastin*, May 3, 2011.
9. An offspring of Hizb U-Tahrir founded in Britian in 1996 by Syrian fugitive Shaykh Omar Bakri Muhammad.
10. See for example: Al-Quds al-'Arabi, May 8, 2011, http://www.alquds.co.uk/index. asp?fname=data\2011\05\05-08\08qpt995.htm; *Al-Sharq al-Awsat*, May 10, 2011, http://www.asharq-e.com/print.asm?artid=id25125.
11. "Osama bin Laden Largely Discredited Among Muslim Publics in Recent Years," Pew Research Global Attitudes Project, May 2, 2011, http://www.pewglobal. org/2011/05/02/osama-bin-laden-largely-discredited-among-muslim-publics-in-recent-years/.
12. *Al-Ahram Weekly*, May 19, 2011.
13. *Al-Sharq al-Awsat*, May 4, 2011.
14. Paul Rogers, "Syria, Iraq, and al-Qaida's opportunity," *Open Democracy*, April, 26, 2012, http://www.opendemocracy.net.

15. Mitchell D. Silber, *The Al Qaeda Factor: Plots Against the West* (Philadelphia: University of Pennsylvania Press, 2012).

16. Khaled Hroub, "The Arab revolutions and al-Qaida," Open Democracy, May 23, 2011, http://www.opendemocracy.net/khaled-hroub/arab-revolutions-and-al-qaida.

17. Hasan Mneimneh, "The Spring of a New Political Salafism?" *Current Trends in Islamist Ideology*, Vol. 12 (October 19, 2011).

18. *The Guardian*, February 12, 2012; *Irish Times*, June 6, 2013.

19. *Inspire*, Vol. 8, May 2, 2012, www.ict.org.il/NewsCommentaries/Commentaries/.../2/Default.aspx.

20. *Ibid.*

21. *Inspire*, 9, May 2, 2012, www.ict.org.il/NewsCommentaries/Commentaries/.../2/Default.aspx. See also Esther Webman, "Al-Qa'ida Redefines Its Goals in the Wake of the Arab Spring," *Tel Aviv Notes*, Vol. 6, No. 23, December 10, 2012.

22. Rohan Gunaratna, "New Terror Threats in 2012," *National Interest*, January 20, 2012.

23. *The News* (Pakistan), April 30, 2012, MEMRI, special dispatch 4684, May 1, 2012.

24. *Al-Monitor*, January 24, 2013, http://www.al-monitor.com/pulse/originals/2013/01/al-qaeda-new-generation-arab-spring.html.

25. Silber, *The Al Qaeda Factor*, pp. 295–297.

26. 'Abd al-Mun'im Sa'id, *Al-Ahram Weekly*, October 4, 2012.

27. Yoel Guzansky and Benedetta Berti, "Instability and State Weakness: The 'Post-Revolutionary' Challenge in the Arab World," Tel Aviv Notes, Volume 6, Number 15, August 9, 2012.

28. *The Long War Journal*, June 10, 2013, http://www.longwarjournal.org/archives/2013/06/analysis_alleged_let.php#ixzz2bq4kJZGX; *Al-Jazeera*, June 9, 2013, http://m.aljazeera.com/story/2013699425657 882.

29. MEMRI Jihad News, July 31, 2013, http://www.memrijttm.org/content/en/blog_personal.htm?id=6818&param=GJN.

30. *AP*, August 3, 2013, http://abcnews.go.com/International/wireStory/al-qaida-leader-egypts-morsi-abandoned-jihad-19860482; *Daily News*, August 6, 2013.

31. *The Daily Beast*, August 7, 2013, http://www.thedailybeast.com/articles/2013/08/07/al-qaeda-conference-call-intercepted-by-u-s-officials-sparked-alerts.html; *Christian Science Monitor*, August 9, 2013, http://www.csmonitor.com/World/Backchannels/2013/0809/Al-Qaeda-s-conference-call-and-claims-that-the-group-is-on-the-rise.

32. According to the reports, he promoted Wuhayshi to "al-Mas'ul al-'Amm," giving him operational control of al-Qa'ida's many affiliates throughout the Muslim world.

# From Victims to Victors: The Kurdish Challenge to the State in the Middle East

## Ofra Bengio

For the greater part of the twentieth century, the political system in the Middle East was governed by the notion of the nation-state. In that system, there was very little room for minority ethnic groups, which struggled to maintain their identity in the face of the ruling "Turkish", "Persian" and "Arab" nation-states. This was especially true for Kurds, whose core territorial living space span four countries: Turkey, Iran, Iraq, and Syria. At the same time, however, the Kurds of these four countries gradually developed the concept of "Greater Kurdistan", creating a sub-system of their own which posed a challenge to the established order and dominant paradigm.

This essay presents four interrelated arguments. First, the legitimacy of the existing nation-states of the Fertile Crescent/Mesopotamian region had substantially eroded by the turn of the twenty-first century. Second, the emerging pan-Kurdish regional sub-system was both an important cause and major consequence of this erosion. Third, ties between different Kurdish regions had always existed, albeit often quietly and largely hidden from view. Fourth, by the beginning of the twenty-first century, trans-border Kurdish nationalism had reached a critical mass, posing a threat to the existing state system.

## The Terminological Debate

In the leading scholarly literature about the Kurds in the twentieth century, they were always referred to as a minority. According to scholars, there are many different types of minorities, including ethnic, religious, political, compact, and diffused. The Kurds may fit the description of an ethnic, religious, and compact minority.[1] In practice, however, neither the Kurds themselves nor the states in which they live were comfortable with the minority label. Kurdish nationalists argue that Kurdish-speakers constitute a nation of some 30 million people, living in a homeland the size of the state of Iraq, making them the fourth largest nation in the Middle East, and thus cannot be considered a minority. For their part, ruling elites have been reluctant to use this term because they insisted on the subsuming of Kurdish identity within the "national" fabric, be it Turkish, Arab or Persian. Interestingly, in the Lausanne treaty of 1923, Turkey recognized Jews and Christians as minorities and allowed them to use their own languages, but denied that right to the Kurds, in line with the older Ottoman practice of recognizing religious *millets* but not ones which included fellow Muslims.[2]

Nor is the nation-state concept, as has been applied in the Middle East, palatable to the Kurds. The Westphalian system of sovereign states began to develop in Europe in the seventeenth century, and crystallized more fully along nation-state lines during the nineteenth century. This concept was applied in the Middle East after World War I, and elites in the newly formed entities applied it to solidify their rule. But for the Kurds, this development signified an existential threat: unlike in Western democracies, the national-territorial states which emerged in the Middle East lacked basic democratic norms, institutions governed by the rule of law, and the requisite civil society organizations that together could place a check on executive power and enable their heterogeneous societies to cohere under a single legitimate political framework. Consequently the new states sought to liquidate the very identity of the Kurds and to assimilate them by way of Arabization, Turkification, or Persianization

The Kurds may be classified as a "non-state nation." As such, they are the largest nation in the Middle East, and perhaps the entire world, without a state of their own. Historically, the utmost that they ever achieved was the establishment of semi-autonomous principalities under the Ottoman Empire between the sixteenth and mid-nineteenth centuries.[3] Even after that, they retained a measure of social and cultural autonomy. Hence, the formation of new nation-states in the twentieth century constituted a severe regression for the Kurds. Even scholars tended to ignore them in favor of the narrative of the newly established nation-states: the two most glaring examples are Majid Khadduri's *Independent Iraq* (1960) and Bernard Lewis's *The Emergence of Modern Turkey* (1965), each of which devoted a mere page to the Kurds.[4]

In recent years, a new category has entered the lexicon of international relations, namely "an unrecognized state."[5] At present, there are 20 such de facto states in the world, ones which lack international recognition or are essentially states within existing states.[6] The Kurdistan Regional Government in Iraq (KRG) is one such de facto state.

# The Burden of the Twentieth Century

The fragmentation of the Kurdish communities notwithstanding, they remained mutually influential upon one another, albeit subtly, and at times tacitly, creating a synergic effect on the overall Kurdish sub-system. Developments in one region would shift the Kurdish center of gravity accordingly, while affecting other areas. For example, the Kurdish war in Iraq in 1974-1975 contributed to the rise of the PKK in Turkey in 1978. During the Iran-Iraq War (1980-1988), anti-regime Kurdish activities unfolded first in Iran, then in Iraq, and finally in Turkey. The 2003 Gulf War and the strengthening of the KRG in northern Iraq triggered the Kurdish uprising in Syria in 2004 and energized the PKK's activities after a five year hiatus. Similarly, the establishment of a Kurdish autonomous region in Syria in 2012 energized the Kurdish national movement in Turkey.

Another factor that should be taken into account is internal migration between the different parts of Kurdistan, a phenomenon caused mainly by wars, but which had an important impact on trans-border activities and contributed to the crystallization of the Kurdish national movement.[7] Such waves of migration took place in the 1920s from Turkey to Syria after the collapse of the Kurdish uprising in Turkey, in the 1940s from Iraq to Iran, and in 1975 from Iraq to Iran following the Kurdish defeat in Iraq. Another wave took place at the end of the Iran-Iraq War from Iraq to Turkey, in 1991 from Iraq to Iran at the end of the Gulf war and renewed Kurdish uprising in Iraq, and from 2011 onwards from Syria to the KRG. Migration to countries beyond the Middle East has also played an important role in Kurdish nation-building and in bringing the voice of the Kurds to the outside world.[8] Of late there is a growing tendency among the Kurds in the diaspora to return back to Kurdistan, especially to the KRG, in order to contribute to nation-building there. Indeed, Cemil Bayik, a leader of the political wing of the PKK, recently called on Kurds who had migrated to Europe or had been forced by the Turkish government to migrate to Turkish metropolitan areas to return to their villages for, as he put it, the Kurds' "ancient land is waiting for us."[9]

The change in the Kurds' fortunes began in the final decades of the twentieth century and has since gathered further momentum. The causes of this change included the collapse of the Soviet Union and the legitimization granted by the international community to the establishment of new states in its former territories; the three Gulf wars (1980–1988, 1991, 2003), resulting in the alteration of the regional balance of power; the increasing salience and legitimation in international affairs of the values of multi-culturalism and ethno-nationalism; and, most importantly, the so-called "Arab Spring" upheaval which began at the end of 2010 and has continued to reverberate through the region, including Turkey, a non-Arab democratic country. Capping all these developments was the withdrawal of American forces from Iraq at the end of 2011 and the resulting power vacuum. Taken together, these developments combined to significantly weaken the existing nation-states while empowering non-state nations in their drive to achieve independence. The first successful example of this trend was South Sudan, which attained independence in July 2011.

The Kurds are currently experiencing a national awakening and a "Pan" movement resembling that experienced by Arabs a century ago. The four parts of Kurdistan resemble a system of inter-connecting vessels, notwithstanding their distinct historical experiences, varying socio-economic and political systems, and particular political goals. Indeed, each Kurdish zone has in large part been shaped by the political system of the particular state to which it was attached. As with the Arab nationalist discourse, Kurdish nationalists speak of their struggle to liberate themselves from colonialism, but in their case, the colonialists are not the Great Powers of the West but the independent, post-Empire and post-colonial states in which they live. As Ismet Sherif Vanly, a leading Kurdish nationalist, declared in 1993:

> The Kurdish people do no longer accept to be the last colonized and the most oppressed people on earth. Whatever might be the price, they are decided to pursue their patriotic struggle to get rid of colonialism and racism, and to have a place of their own in the sun. Their way is the path of democracy in the Near East. For the Kurds, it does not matter whether their colonizer is white or brown, Muslim or Christian. Theirs is the desire to live better, in a free and democratic Kurdistan…[10]

For his part Abdullah Öcalan, the leader of the PKK, formulated the issue of colonialism as follows:

> In political terms, Kurdistan is under the rule of four colonialist states that are tied to imperialism. Each state, in the light of its interests and the interests of international monopolies, plays the central role in developing colonialism in the part it keeps under its rule.[11]

Clearly, the conceptualization of the role of the state as a colonizing entity gives a new twist to Kurd-state relations, one that seeks to legitimize the drive for independence exactly as the Arab states had done when they struggled to liberate themselves from Western domination.

## The Rise of a Kurdish Subsystem

One of the most important indications for the existence of a Kurdish subsystem can be found in the evolving Kurdish discourse. In this emerging new discourse, Kurdistan is portrayed as one unit divided into four parts: north Kurdistan (*bakur*) corresponding to the Kurdish region in Turkey, south Kurdistan (*bashur*) to that in Iraq,[12] east Kurdistan *(rojhelat)* to that in Iran, and west Kurdistan *(rojava)* to that in Syria. This lexicon has become so widespread among the Kurds that even in Turkey, where the very word Kurdistan had been a taboo for many decades, the term *bakur* began to be circulated openly. Thus, for example, the Kurdish conference held in July 2013 in Diyarbakir, the central city of that region in Turkey, carried the following title: "North *(bakur)* Kurdistan unity and solution conference."[13] In fact, the Kurdish discourse at the beginning of the twentieth century also employed this holistic terminology.[14] It was only after the official division of the Kurdish-populated region into four countries took place, and the campaigns for the assimilation and denial had been initiated, that more partial and fragmented concepts of Kurdistan took root, even among the Kurds themselves. By contrast, official state discourse employed opposing, state-centric terminology to denote the same geographical regions: Turkey's Kurdish region was referred to as the southeast *(güneydoğu)*, and that of Iraq as the north *(shimal)*.[15]

Another new trend in the Kurdish discourse has been the circulation of the vision of a Kurdish confederation that would comprise all four parts of Kurdistan. Öcalan is the architect of this new vision, after having abandoned the idea of an independent Kurdistan. According to this conceptualization, the Kurds would be part of a large Kurdish confederation while enjoying a democratic autonomy within existing states, which would not have to modify their borders.[16] These ideas have become widespread among Öcalan's supporters in Turkey and the diaspora as well as in the Democratic Union Party (*Partiya Yekitiya Demokrat*, PYD) which is a Syrian offshoot of the PKK. The new media, which enabled an unprecedented development of trans-border interactions, brought these ideas to other parts of Kurdistan as well. The idea of a Kurdish confederation, with all its inherent ambiguity, is supposed to assuage the anxieties of the states that are fearful of Kurdish separatism. In the KRG, however, there is no great enthusiasm for the confederation idea. The Kurds in Iraq are already part of a federal system with Baghdad, and are maneuvering away from it towards independence.

There are signs of an emerging sub-system on the political level as well. First of all, the KRG in Iraq functions at one and the same time as a quasi-state and as a political center for the other parts of Kurdistan, as well as for Kurds in the diaspora. This dynamic has fostered jealousy and rivalry between the KRG and the Kurdish region of Turkey, and between the KRG and the emerging Kurdish autonomous entity in Syria. Still, Kurds everywhere look upon the KRG with great pride and view it as a model for emulation. For many, the KRG also provides a safe haven from persecution and hardships in their own countries. In the last two years, approximately 200,000 Kurds from Syria have found refuge there[17]. According to *Al-Monitor* they were even granted Iraqi civil status by the Kurdish authorities.[18] The KRG has also become a center for conferences and meetings of Kurds from other core Kurdish regions and beyond, as well as a magnet for Kurds arriving to consult with the KRG authorities, and even forge common policies.[19] The latest example of such cooperation took place in the context of the Turkish-Kurdish peace process that began in early 2013. Not only did KRG president Mas'ud Barzani play an important role in brokering the agreement between the Turkish government and the PKK, but Barzani and the KRG agreed to allow the PKK forces to relocate to territory under its control. This move was strongly opposed by the authorities in Baghdad, which regarded it as a blatant infringement on Iraqi state sovereignty. Moreover, the movement of PKK forces into the KRG's territory is likely to increase the trans-border activity in this part of the Kurdish subsystem and grant the KRG another bargaining chip *vis-à-vis* Turkey as well.

An emerging Kurdish sub-system is also manifesting itself in the military-security sphere. The KRG has transformed its formerly guerrilla force, the *peshmerga*, into a conventional army with some 200,000 soldiers[20] and heavy weapons, including "a large fleet of Russian-made warplanes left from the Saddam era"[21] as well as tanks that were taken as booty from the wars of 1991 and 2003. Furthermore, the KRG has been providing bases for Kurdish guerrilla forces operating in the three other parts of Greater Kurdistan, including not only the PKK but also the Party of Free Life of Kurdistan (*Partiya Jiyana Azad a Kurdistane*, PJAK) and other groupings from Iran, and an umbrella organization, the Kurdish National Council (KNC) from Syria. The KRG has of late even begun training Syrian Kurds with a view to sending them to the Kurdish autonomous region in Syria. Confirming the existence of a training camp for Syrian Kurds, Barzani stated that "a good number of the young Kurds who fled have been trained."[22] This caused friction between the PYD and the KRG but it also indicated that the borders between all parts of Kurdistan were now quite porous, and that the KRG is determined to exert influence in other parts of Greater Kurdistan.

The Kurdish collective identity has also received a significant boost in recent years, through the rapid expansion of the Kurdish language. Outlawed by the Kurds' host states for the greater part of the twentieth century, Kurdish has begun to flourish in an unprecedented manner, thus becoming a source of unity for all Kurds. This is true notwithstanding the reality of linguistic heterogeneity and the fact that there are three main dialects, Kurmanji, Sorani, and Zaza, and three different scripts — Arabic, Latin, and Cyrillic. In the KRG's territory, Kurdish is the official language. In Turkey, where linguistic repression may have been the harshest, the use of Kurdish has been sanctioned and even included the opening of a Kurdish-language television channel, TRT6. One cannot emphasize enough this development, because for the Kurds the most important symbol of nationhood is the Kurdish language alongside the historical territory of Kurdistan.[23] The Kurds also have common symbols, such as the yellow color in the midst of their flags, symbolizing the sun; a common anthem and a common ethos built around the epos of *Mem u Zin* that was written by Ahmed Xani at the end of the seventeenth century.

On the organizational level, there is now an all-Kurdish umbrella organization based in Brussels whose main task is to promote Kurdish interests. The Kurdistan National Congress (*Kongra Netewiya Kurdistan*, KNK) is a coalition of Kurdish organizations from across Europe whose main purpose, according to its website, is "to lobby national governments, the EU, the UN and other international organizations [and] raise awareness of the situation in Kurdistan through the media and in public forums…[24] Its intense lobbying campaign is contributing to the Europeanization of the Kurdish issue.

## The Kurdish Spring in the Regional Context

Parallel to the so-called Arab Spring, there has also been a "Kurdish spring", albeit a quieter one, which encompasses much of Greater Kurdistan. The common denominator between the four Kurdish regions has been the effort to undermine the ideological basis of the nation-states in which they reside, and to demand various forms of self-determination such as broad autonomy, federation with the mother state or confederation between all parts of Kurdistan.

A brief comparison between the Kurdish and Arab popular movements highlights several important differences. Whereas popular Arab movements challenged the existing political order in their countries, Kurdish movements challenged the fundamentals of their countries' national identities and territorial integrity.

Furthermore, unlike the Arab states that experienced revolutionary uprisings, political Islam has not struck deep roots in Kurdish societies. For example, in the KRG the Islamic parties won only 16 percent of the vote in the most recent elections in September 2013.[25] Also, while the uprisings in the Arab states caused severe fissures in their societies, in the Kurdish case there has been a growing trend toward unity, notwithstanding the existing rivalries and competition between the Kurdish regions and among the Kurds within each region. Similarly, in the Kurdish case, the diaspora has been playing a crucial role in bringing the Kurdish cause to the attention of the world, while there has been no such role for Arab diasporas.[26] The differing roles of the new media in the Arab and Turkish "springs" should also be noted. Whereas the new media played an important role in the eruption of the Arab uprisings, it played a crucial "pan" role in articulating and disseminating the very essence of the Kurdish national identity project. Finally, the role of Kurdish women in politics has become much more prominent than that of Arab women in the aftermath of the upheavals in their countries. For example, whereas in Egypt the percentage of women in the post–Hosni Mubarak parliament was reduced from 12 to 2 percent,[27] in the KRG, of the 111 current parliamentarians, 30 percent are women.[28] The political role of Kurdish women in Kurdistan in Turkey and in Syria is even more prominent than in the KRG. For instance, all of the political and military structures of the PKK and PYD have women co-chairs, who carry out their work alongside men.

## Multiple Challenges to the Nation-State

The Kurds have presented their states of residence with several major challenges: the growing trans-border cooperation between Kurds, the contagious effect of the developments in one part of Kurdistan spreading to the others, and the solidification of Kurdish national movements throughout Greater Kurdistan. In addition, a new generation of young Kurdish scholars has started to reclaim Kurdish studies and to spread a counter-narrative to that of the nation-state.[29] Another cause for concern to the central authorities in Ankara, Tehran, Baghdad and Damascus is the younger Kurdish generation as a whole, whose Kurdish consciousness is much more developed than the earlier ones, due in no small part to their exposure to social media platforms. It appears unwilling to accept a continuation of the second rate status traditionally accorded them by state authorities and is much more outspoken regarding Kurdish demands.

The Kurdish challenge to the cohesion of existing states encompasses not only Iraq and Syria, whose cohesion was weak from the very start, but Turkey and Iran as well, which are comparatively stronger and more cohesive entities. At the same time, the nature, degree, and scope of the Kurdish challenge varies from one state to another. In Turkey, the very fabric of Turkish society is being called into question. Furthermore, a Kurdish "parallel state" seems to be developing steadily.[30] In Syria, the autonomous region which the Kurds have carved out for themselves appears likely to follow the KRG's model, especially as there is no end to Syria's civil war in sight. Indeed, the longer the war lasts the greater the chance that the Kurds will carve out substantial autonomy. As for the Kurds in Iran, although they appear more docile than the Kurds of the other regions, there are distinct rumblings just below the surface. Kurds in Iran are essentially engaged in a religio-political clash with the state, having been doubly victimized by the Islamic Republic of Iran both as Sunnis and as Kurds. No less important is that they have had a long history of struggle against the state, pre-dating the 1979 Islamic Revolution. Moreover, it is in Iran where the short-lived Kurdish Mahabad Republic was established in early 1946.[31] The Iranian Kurdish opposition is now calling for the dismantling of the Islamic state and the establishment of a federated system, as in Iraq.

As for the Kurds of Iraq, they pose a profound challenge to the cohesion and territorial integrity of the Iraqi state, and hence they constitute the vanguard and model of emulation for all the other Kurdish regions. What were the internal, regional, and international circumstances that had facilitated this turn of events? First, at the end of World War I, Great Britain encouraged Kurdish nationalism in the Vilayet of Mosul which was populated by a Kurdish majority. However, Britain forsook this project very quickly: in 1925, it was behind the decision to annex the Mosul vilayet to the state of Iraq. Still, this decision did not extinguish Kurdish proto-nationalism, quite the contrary. In fact, as Sherko Kirmanj demonstrates in his recent book, Arab and Kurdish identities developed in parallel since the establishment of the Iraqi state in 1920.[32]

The second crucial factor is the weakness of the Iraqi state and its inability to assert its control over the Kurdish region except for short periods of time, and only by using brute force. One could argue that the same was true for Syria, which was as weak as Iraq. However, the Kurds of Iraq have several advantages over their brethren in Syria. Their percentage of the general population is much higher, the territory that they inhabit is much larger, and they live in the high mountains, which make it hard for outsiders to rule them.

Currently, the KRG has all the trappings of a state. In fact, it fulfills the criteria stipulated by the 1933 Montevideo Convention on the Rights and Duties of States: (a) a permanent population; (b) a defined territory; (c) a government; and (d) the capacity to enter into relations with the other states. As to the first criterion, there are over 5 million Kurds living in the KRG. There are also minorities such as Christians, Turkmen, and Yezidis, whom the KRG vows to grant equal treatment and not to forcibly assimilate them. In terms of territory, the KRG rules three governorates, with the Iraqi government's agreement — Irbil, Dhok, and Sulaymaniyya. However, Irbil and Baghdad have been in dispute over the disputed territories around Kirkuk that are rich in oil and gas. This bone of contention may turn out to be the main trigger for separation, violent or otherwise. The Kurdish part of Iraq is much better governed than the Arab ruled areas, and the KRG is stable and has flourished economically. Democratization is also proceeding at a faster pace in the KRG than in the Arab areas of Iraq. In fact, as a rule, non-recognized entities seek to improve democratic norms as a strategy in order to enhance their chances for gaining international recognition and preserve their de facto independent status.[33]

# On Balance: The Kurds' Strong and Weak Points

The juxtaposition of regional upheaval with the sweeping changes in the Kurdish subsystem has produced a new geopolitical map in which existing nation-states are being weakened and ethno-national actors are strengthened. In Iraq, the notion of a unified and centralized Iraqi Arab nation-state is a thing of the past and in its stead there are now two de facto states: Kurdistan and Arab Iraq. In Syria, the war is still raging but one thing is certain: the Kurds of Syria, who had been the least visible group of all the Kurdish communities in the region, put themselves on the map within a short period of time following the outbreak of the Syrian rebellion in March 2011. It seems, therefore, that the autonomy which they have carved out for themselves may well prove to be enduring, whether or not the Ba'th regime remains in power. As for the Kurds of Turkey, they are now in the middle of a peace process with the AKP government. In the meantime, they have established a parallel state in areas where the writ of the central government is quite weak. They too will certainly continue to challenge the existing hegemonic notion of the nation-state which denied their collective existence. The Kurds of Iran, while ostensibly submissive, are in fact being deeply influenced by developments in other parts of Greater Kurdistan, and have called for the downfall of the Islamic government and demanded a federated system of government.

An additional shift has occurred in the relationship between the four Middle East states where Kurds reside in large numbers and the Kurdish subsystem. While in the past, two or more of the states could forge alliances among themselves with a view to containing Kurdish opposition movements, after the upheavals of recent years they no longer seem able to do so. The change in the geopolitical map is so sweeping that the Kurds are no longer the common denominator for promoting regional cooperation between states. Rather, the contrary is true. Turkey, for example, has opted to ally itself with Iraqi Kurdistan at the expense of the Iraqi state. Iran is so furious about the Turkish-Kurdish peace process that it is ready to support the PKK if only it decides to stop the process.[34] Turkey's decision to stand against the Asad regime enabled both the PKK in Turkey and the PYD in Syria to be strengthened significantly, so much so that they forced Ankara to initiate the peace process with the PKK and to turn to the KRG for help in pacifying the Kurdish communities in Turkey and Syria.

As important as the Kurds' achievements of the last decade have been, the existing states may try to exploit certain Kurdish weaknesses in the hope of riding out the storm. First, there is no one goal that unites all Kurds. Furthermore, the various goals of the Kurdish movements keep changing. For example, the KDP has been fluctuating between the pursuit of autonomy, federation, and independence. Likewise, the PKK shifted its goal from independence to democratic autonomy. Another problem is the strong rivalry between what one may call Barzanism and Öcalanism over the leadership of the Pan-Kurdish movement. Lastly, the Kurds still lack sustained international support, and the US, in particular, continues to adhere to the illusory concept of the territorial integrity of one of the region's failed states, namely Iraq.

At bottom, it is the Kurds who have now set the agenda in the region of Greater Kurdistan and threaten the cohesiveness of existing nation-states there. These states' twentieth century fears are fast becoming twenty-first century realities.

# Notes

1.  Gabriel Ben Dor, "Minorities in the Middle East: Theory and Practice" in Ofra Bengio and Gabriel Ben Dor (eds.), *Minorities and the State in the Arab World* (Boulder: Lynne Rienner, 1999), pp. 1–30; The religious criterion holds mainly for Iran, where Sunni Kurds live in a Shi'i ruled state.
2.  Kemal Kirisci and Gareth Winrow, *The Kurdish Question and Turkey* (Frank Cass Publishers: London, 1997), pp. 44–45.
3.  Janet Klein, *The Margins Of Empire: Kurdish Militias in the Ottoman Tribal Zone* (Stanford: Stanford University Press, 2011), pp. 52–60.
4.  Majid Khadduri, *Independent Iraq* (London: Oxford University Press, 1960), pp. 60–61; Bernard Lewis, *The Emergence of Modern Turkey* (London: Oxford University Press, 1965), pp. 260–261.
5.  Nina Caspersen and Gareth Stansfield (eds.), *Unrecognized States in the International System*, (Routledge: London, 2011).
6.  Nina Caspersen and Gareth Stansfield, "Introduction", in *Ibid.*, pp. 1–8.
7.  In 1975, 50,000 Kurds moved to Turkey and in 1988, 65,000 did the same. Martin van Bruinessen, "Transnational Aspects of the Kurdish Question," Working paper, Robert Schuman Centre for Advanced Studies, European University Institute, Florence, 2000.
8.  Ofra Bengio and Bruce Maddy-Weitzman, "Mobilized Diasporas: Kurdish and Berber Movements in Comparative Perspective," *Kurdish Studies*, Vol. 1, Issue 1 (October 2013).
9.  ANF-NEWS Desk, July 8, 2013. Bayik maintained that one third of the Kurdish people in Turkey were displaced during the 1960s. http://www.mesop.de/2013/07/08/cemil-bayik-about-the-resettlement-of-ancient-land-in-modern-times-will-young-kurds-from-europe-really-go-back-to-their-ancient-soil/.
10. Quoted in David Romano, *The Kurdish National Movement: Opportunity, Mobilization and Identity*, (Cambridge: Cambridge University Press, 2006), p. 132.
11. Cengiz Gunes, *The Kurdish National Movement in Turkey: From Protest to Resistance* (Routledge: New York, 2012), p. 84.

12. The term "South Kurdish Confederation" was used by the British in 1918 when they attempted to install a pro-British government, headed by Shaykh Mahmud Barzinja, in parts of Kurdistan. Wadie Jwaideh, *The Kurdish National Movement: Its Origin and Development*, (Syracuse: Syracuse University Press, 2006), pp. 160–170.

13. Kurdpress, July 11, 2013. http://kurdpress.com/En/NSite/FullStory/News/?Id=4803#Title=Diyarbakir conference announces demands from government.

14. *Jiyan* (newspaper, 1926–1936), Mustafa Shawqi, *Kurdistan*, year 1, no. 1.

15. In October 2013 Barzani prohibited the use of the term "Northern Iraq" in the KRG.Haber7.com, quoting Yeni Safak, October 23, 2013, http://www.haber7.com/ortadogu/haber/1087312-barzani-kuzey-iraki-yasakladi (accessed, 27 October 2013).

16. *Hurriyet Daily News*, April 8, 2013, http://www.hurriyetdailynews.com/pkk-leader-reiterates-kurdish-confederation-as-stateless-solution-.aspx?pageID=238&nid=44479

17. KRG.org, September 12, 2013, http://web.krg.org/a/d.aspx?l=12&a=48957.

18. *Al-Monitor*, June 26, 2013, http://www.al-monitor.com/pulse/originals/2013/06/kurdistan-region-abnormal-population-growth.html.

19. On July 22, 2013, for example, Barzani convened an all-Kurdish conference in Irbil, with the participation of 39 Kurdish parties from all parts of Kurdistan as well as the Diaspora. *Nefel*, July, 23, 2013, http://www.nefel.com/articles/article_detail.asp?RubricNr=1&ArticleNr=7683#.UfDpfx9BSkw.

20. *Kurdnet*, January 17, 2011, http://www.ekurd.net/mismas/articles/misc2011/1/state4537.htm.

21. *Press TV*, April 29, 2012, http://www.presstv.com/detail/238746.html.

22. Al-Jazeera, July 23, 2012, http://m.aljazeera.com/SE/201272393251722498.

23. Martin van Bruinessen, "Transnational Aspects of the Kurdish Question," Working paper, Robert Schuman Centre for Advanced Studies, European University Institute, Florence, 2000.

24. http://peaceinkurdistancampaign.wordpress.com/resources/kurdish-national-congress-knk/.

25. Musings on Iraq, October 9, 2013, KRG.org, September 12, 2013, http://web.krg.org/a/d.aspx?l=12&a= (accessed October 24, 2013).

26. For an excellent discussion of the Kurdish diaspora, see Khalid Khayati, *From Victim Diaspora to Transborder Citizenship? Diaspora Formation and Transnational Relations among Kurds in France and Sweden* (Linköping Studies in Arts and Science No. 435, Linköping University, Department of Social and Welfare StudiesLinköping 2008).

27. *Reuters*, March 3, 2012.

28. *AKnews*, February 8, 2012, http://www.aknews.com/en/aknews/4/288834/. Nevertheless this compares positively with the Iraqi cabinet (see above).

29. To mention jut a few: Khalid Khayati, *From Victim Diaspora to Transborder Citizenship?* (Linköping, 2008); Abbas Vali, *Kurds and the State in Iran: The Making of Kurdish Identity* (London: I.B. Tauris, 2011); Aram Rafaat, "The Kurdish and Iraqi Counter-Quest for Nationhood and the Transformation of Iraqi Kurdistan into a Quasi-State" (Ph.D. Dissertation, University of Adelaide, 2012); Cengiz Gunes, *The Kurdish National Identity in Turkey: From Protest to Resistance* (London: Routledge, 2012); Sherko Kirmanj, *Identity and Nation in Iraq* (Boulder: Lynne Rienner, 2013).

30. *International Crisis Group — Europe Report*, N° 222, 30 November 2012), p. 3.

31. Abbas Vali, *Kurds and the State in Iran: The Making of Kurdish Identity* (London: I.B. Tauris, 2011), pp. 49–81.

32. Sherko Kirmanj, *Identity and Nation in Iraq* (Boulder: Lynne Rienner, 2013).

33. Nina Caspersen, "States without sovereignty" in Nina Caspersen and Gareth Stansfield (eds.), *Unrecognized States in the International System*, (Routledge: London, 2011), p. 77.

34. Lara Vergnaud, *Middle East*, May 9, 2013, http://blogs.blouinnews.com/ blouinbeatworld/2013/05/09/iraq-rejects-pkk-withdrawal-but-lacks-leverage/.

# PART II
## The Fertile Crescent and Arabia

# Syria: Between Dar'a and Suwayda: Communities and State in the Shadow of the Syrian Revolution

## Eyal Zisser

In March 2011, the fires of protest and rebellion that had toppled Tunisia's and Egypt's long-ruling autocratic presidents reached Syria. The initial flare-ups first occurred in several small towns and cities in the south, but soon spread all over the country. At first, the protests were limited and local in character: the participants were almost exclusively Sunni peasants from rural and peripheral areas, hungry for bread and change. Gradually, thanks in no small measure to the iron fist that the Syrian regime raised against its opponents, the protest turned into a broad popular uprising, and ultimately into a bloody civil war, and even a war of jihad, with no end in sight.[1]

As is so often the case in conflict zones where savage incidents occur daily, the enormous dimensions of the human tragedy that has struck Syria has had a brutalizing effect on the Syrian public. Several of these incidents, however local and limited in scope, deserve attention because they are indicative of the breadth and depth of the ongoing civil war. They can also help one to sketch the face of Syrian society, with its various communities, camps, and factions, in the shadow of the civil war. And perhaps most importantly, they may provide an indication of what will occur in the country on the "day after" the insurrection ends, whether in victory or defeat.

A report of one such incident in southern Syria appeared at the end of May 2011 in the Lebanese newspaper *al-Akhbar*:

> On Sunday, 27 May 2011, armed men kidnapped 13 policemen and their driver, residents of the Suwayda province, as they were on their way to work. In retaliation, residents of Suwayda kidnapped 240 villagers from the Dar'a province. In the wake of the incident, the dignitaries of the two provinces began to hold negotiations, and after a couple of days of discussions they reached a compromise, to which the representatives of the Syrian government also gave their approval. On 30 May 2011, in the afternoon, the kidnapped men were exchanged, and it was agreed that no one would harm peaceful citizens any more. The two sides also reached an agreement stating that everything possible should be done to prevent

the outbreak of a civil war between the "plain" ("Plain of *Hawran*") and the "mountain" (*Jabal Hawran*), because such a war would help no one, embitter the lives of the residents, and endanger the territorial integrity of the Syrian state.[2]

On the face of it, this incident was exceedingly minor: a quarrel between neighbors such as have often been known in the Syrian lands (*Bilad al-Sham*) since time immemorial, one which ended without blood being shed. However, there was much more to it. The two sets of neighbors involved were from different religious communities: the Druze of the Suwayda province on Jabal Hawran (also known as *Jabal Druze*, i.e. the Druze Mountain), and the Sunnis of the Hawran plain, with the city of Dar'a at its center. Thus, the May 2011 incident was more than simply a neighbors' quarrel. At its core was the rising tension between the Druze and Sunni communities of the Hawran who found themselves on opposite sides in the Syrian revolution. The Sunnis of Dar'a support the uprising; indeed, they were the ones who first raised the flag of rebellion against the Ba'th regime in Damascus. The Druze of Jabal Hawran, on the other hand, have remained loyal to the regime and refused to join the revolt against it. Although the policemen were kidnapped because they were serving in the regime, and not because they were Druze, the episode had an inter-communal dimension to it as well.

This relatively mild incident of May 2011 is quite instructive, because it was an early expression of the inter-communal dimension of the Syrian revolution and civil war that over time has become more and more prominent. By now, inter-communal differences have come to represent a serious threat to the delicate fabric of the Syrian entity, where interwoven confessional groups managed to coexist in relative harmony for hundreds of years.

The events in Hawran can be viewed as a reflection of what is happening all over Syria. On the one hand, there is growing tension between the various communal groups, while on the other hand, one can discern a desire to maintain coexistence in the shadow of war. This desire indicates that people recognize the demographic, geographical, economic, and other constraints that shape their lives. Each community is secluding itself to some extent in the living space it has occupied for centuries. However, each is also aware that on the "day after" it will be compelled to come out of its shell and seek a way to negotiate with whatever regime will be installed in Damascus. The main issue of the negotiations will, of course, be the reconstruction of the Syrian state's institutions and the reintegration of its religious and ethnic communities into the state framework, and the underlying identity of the Syrian state. The outcome may well be something different from what was in the past, and is likely to be based on the balance of power that will emerge from the outcome of the battles now being fought.

# Syria and the Communal Question

For many years, the "communal question," that is, the divisiveness and fragmentation that characterized Syrian society because of its communal makeup, was perceived as the source of the state's weakness and the basis of the political instability that prevailed there, particularly during the first quarter-century of Syrian independence. However, following the rise to power of the Asad dynasty in November 1970, it seemed as if the Syrian state had learned how to successfully cope with the "communal question," and that the state had succeeded in accommodating its various confessional groups. They all seemed to have been united into a relatively cohesive political entity with common interests, and perhaps even with a common Arab, Syrian territorial, and secular identity, capable of bonding them together. The Ba'th revolution of 8 March 1963 seemed to be an important step toward ensuring the survival and durability of the Syrian state thanks to, paradoxically, its decisive alteration of the existing political and socio-economic order. For hundreds of years, an urban Sunni Muslim elite had dominated the political, social, and economic life of *bilad al-Sham*. The 1963 revolution constituted its replacement by a coalition of rising political and social forces that had emerged from the downtrodden and deprived sectors of Syrian society, particularly among members of the minority communities living mostly in rural and peripheral areas. At the heart of the new order stood a coalition of forces:

1. Members of the 'Alawi community, or at least the portion that was close to the Asad family. The 'Alawis (12% of the total population in Syria) were a dominant factor in the coalition; they ensured its cohesion and continued existence thanks to the relative advantage conferred by their preeminence among the officer corps and their own internal solidarity.
2. Members of the Sunni Muslim community who came from the rural and peripheral areas of the country (nearly half of the Sunni population in Syria, i.e. 30% out of the 60% of Syria's total population);
3. Members of other minority communities, including Christians (13% of the total population), Druze (5%), and Isma'ilis (1%), and even the Kurds (10%). These groups viewed 'Alawi dominance in Syria as a factor guaranteeing their own status, and even their personal and economic security.
4. An additional group that was gradually absorbed into the ruling coalition, even if only as a junior and marginal partner — the Sunni Muslim economic elite, based mainly in Damascus, which was smart enough to take advantage of the policies of greater economic and even

political openness adopted by the Asad regime, tentatively at first, and then more substantially at the beginning of the 1990s.[3]

This, then, was the array of forces that supported the Asad regime from its inception, up until the upheavals that began in March 2011. This support, or at least the belief that the continuation of Ba'th rule was Syria's best option, manifested itself during the years of the Islamic insurgency against the regime (1976-1982). During this period, the rural regions were generally quiet, as was Damascus. The insurgency was confined to several of the large towns in the north of the country, first to Aleppo and its surroundings, and afterwards, to Hama, scene of the infamous 1982 massacre.[4]

## The Hawran Region under the Rule of the Asad Dynasty

The Hawran region's integration into the texture of Syrian life, and particularly its integration into the government's bureaucracy, Ba'th Party institutions, and the security and military apparatuses, served as a clear example of the success of Hafiz al-Asad's regime in dealing with the "communal question." It also provided an example of the regime's ability to overcome Syria's deep-rooted class and regional divisions. Asad integrated the oft-rebellious region into his regime by placing many Dar'a and Jabal Druze natives in senior positions. For example, Vice President Faruq al-Shar' hails from Dar'a, Deputy Foreign Minister Faysal al-Miqdad is from the village of Ghussun, near Dar'a, Prime Minister Wa'il Nadir al-Halqi is native to the small town of Jasim, near Dar'a, and Rustum Ghazalah, who heads one of Syria's security apparatuses, comes from the small town of Hirbat Ghazzalah, near Dar'a. Jabal Druze natives also found their way into leading positions in the Ba'th regime, e.g. the various members of the Atrash clan who were appointed to ministerial positions in various Syrian governments and to high posts in the Ba'th Party's leadership institutions. Druze also hold senior positions in the upper ranks of the military.[5]

## The Roots of the Syrian Revolution

However, with the passage of time, and especially from the beginning of the 2000s, the more inclusive, representative character and orientation of the Syrian regime declined. It even seemed as if the ruling elites had turned their back on the Sunni population in the villages and peripheral areas that had until then been its own flesh and blood. The main reason was a social and economic crisis caused by a number of interlocking factors. One fundamental development was the dramatic growth of the Syrian population during the 1970s and 1980s, during which Syria had one of the highest rates of natural increase in the world (3.5-3.8%). As a result, Syrian society became not only very young — more than 60% are below 16 years old — but also poorer, with most of its 20-40 year-olds unemployed and without hope for a better future. During the second half of the new century's first decade, Syria experienced one of the worst droughts the state had ever known. Its impact was felt most intensely in the Jazira region of northeastern Syria and in the south, especially in the Hawran region and its center, Dar'a. In addition, these regions were adversely affected by the government's economic policies, which aimed at changing the character of the Syrian economy from a rigid, state-controlled system to a "social market economy." The aim was to open Syria to the world economy, encourage foreign investment, and promote activity in the domestic private sector as well. Consequently, the regime managed to preserve its image of strength and solidity, but its actual base of support was considerably narrowed, as the authorities lost the broad popular support that it had previously enjoyed among the Sunni village and periphery populations.[6] Previously submerged communal and religious tension between the 'Alawis and Sunnis added to the growing rift between the Ba'th regime in Damascus and members of the Sunni community living in the rural and peripheral areas.

## Revolution in the Hawran

The outbreak of the Syrian revolution disrupted the relative harmony that had characterized Sunni-Druze relations in the Hawran region in recent decades: the communal genie was let out of its bottle, reviving the divisive and fragmenting forces that had always characterized Syrian society. Unlike in the past (1925-1927),[7] however, it was the city of Dar'a and the Sunni villages in its surrounding hinterland that raised the flag of rebellion, not Jabal Druze.

At the beginning of March 2011, fifteen teenagers were arrested in the city of Dar'a for painting anti-regime graffiti on the walls of a local school. It is likely that the youths acted under the inspiration of the "Arab Spring" protests that were then at their height in several Arab states. At first, appeals to the authorities by family members and relatives to release the detainees were turned down. Then, when the teenagers were finally released, it turned out that they had been tortured during their detention.[8] All of this served to inflame passions in Dar'a. Hence, the first demonstrations that broke out in the city on March 18,

2011, at the end of Friday prayers in the mosques, were much more vigorous than parallel demonstrations held elsewhere in the country. Several thousand people took part in the protest held near the city's main mosque, 'Umar Ibn al-Walid. Matters quickly got out of control, as the demonstrators began to attack public and government buildings, including the offices of the governor and the headquarters of the province's Ba'th Party branch. Two demonstrators were killed in clashes with the security forces, and three more the next day during the funeral processions for the victims. From then on, Syria has known no peace.[9] During the following weeks, protests continued in Dar'a and spread to nearby towns and villages, and the regime deployed military units to Dar'a to suppress the unrest. However, the disturbances in Dar'a had lit the spark for a country-wide revolt, and the original demonstrators were replaced by armed groups that actively fought Syrian army forces and even imposed their authority over towns and villages throughout the region. The fight over Dar'a turned into a fight for control of the main roads linking Damascus and Amman, which the Syrian regime perceived as strategic lifeline for its survival. Regime forces succeeded in maintaining control over the center of Dar'a and the military installations in the city and its surroundings, as well as keeping the main roads open, although not entirely secure. The rural areas generally fell into the hands of the rebels, who also managed to breach the border with Jordan. Hundreds of thousands of residents of the Dar'a province fled to Jordan, where they found shelter either with relatives or in refugee camps. The traffic also ran in the other direction: volunteers, aid and weapons all flowed into Syria from Jordan, often under the half-closed eyes of the Jordanian authorities.[10]

The neighboring Suwayda province has remained quiet throughout the uprising. Some Druze individuals did raise their voices in support of the revolution. However, these were mainly intellectuals residing in Damascus, persons who had been long been cut off from the situation in the Druze community living in the Jabal Druze area. A few voices calling for support for the rebels in Syria were also heard in the Druze villages under Israeli rule on the Golan Heights. However, most of the Golan population preferred to remain silent, which implied continued support for the Asad regime. In Lebanon as well, Druze leader Walid Junblatt was an exception among its Druze citizens when he raised his voice against the Syrian regime.[11]

During 2012, the Syrian revolution spread toward Damascus. In a major terror attack on July 18, 2012, several of the regime's top security officials were killed, including Minister of Defense Da'ud 'Abdallah Rajiha, a member of the Greek Orthodox community, and his deputy, Asaf Shawkat, brother-in-law of President Bashar al-Asad. From this point onwards, rebels were to be found right in the heart of the capital. The spread of the war to the neighborhoods surrounding the center of the city, and especially in the southern and eastern approaches, together with the chaos already prevalent throughout the country, added a large Druze population to the circle of parties injured by the violence. These included tens of thousands of Druze who had migrated to Damascus over the years as part of the process of their integration into the state institutions and military and security apparatuses. The newcomers had settled mostly in the Jaramana neighborhood in the southern part of Damascus, near the international airport. Now, even though there were no reports of attacks on the Druze population of the city or of confrontations between the Druze and the rebels, many left and returned to their ancestral homes on Jabal Druze.[12]

As the fighting escalated and became increasingly brutal, a backlash undermined the delicate balance between the residents of Dar'a and Suwayda, particularly as the religious dimension to the struggle became increasingly salient. New players entered the scene, jihadi fighters streaming into Syria from all over the Arab and Muslim world. These foreign volunteers, joined by native Syrians, served as the basis for the al-Nusra Front ("Support Front for the People of Syria; *Jabhat an-Nus'ra li-Ahl al-Sham*), which became the local branch of al-Qa'ida in Iraq (known there as the Islamic State of Iraq; *al-Dawla al-Islamiyya fi al-'Iraq*). In April 2013, the Iraqi branch separated from the Syrian one and began operating independently as the Islamic State in Iraq and Syria (*al-Dawla al-Islamiyya fi al-'Iraq wal-Sham*). Other radical religious groups arose as well, e.g. the radical Salafi group known as the Syrian Islamic Front, and the Syrian Islamic Liberation Front, which is identified with the Syrian Muslim Brotherhood. Some of these, especially the adherents of the Al-Nusra Front and the Islamic State, have no loyalty or connection whatsoever to the Syrian state entity, that is, to Syria's territorial integrity or its national identity. These radical groups hold a simplistic religious view, based on the crude idea of jihad against the supposedly heretical regime in Damascus and the communities supporting it, as part of the effort to bring about the establishment of an Islamic emirate stretching over the whole Arab East — Iraq, Syria, Lebanon, Palestine, and Jordan.[13] Their aggressiveness led them to attack not only 'Alawis and Christians but Druze as well, as evidenced by an Islamic legal ruling published in the name of the adherents of the al-Nusra Front on April 2, 2013, according to which the monotheistic Druze are heretics who should be killed.[14]

This situation led to a further deepening of the tension in southern Syria, as an April 2, 2013 press report about an incident in Dar'a testifies:

> The escalation occurred following the appointment of a new commander of the Al-Nusra Front in the Dar'a region. His followers began attacking police and army checkpoint in the Dar'a region. They kidnapped a group of 21 Druze. Among those taken hostage was a well-known cleric, Shaykh

Abu Khaled Jamal 'Izz al-Din.... A short time later Al-Nusra Front men
attacked an army checkpoint in an area manned by men from Suwayda
serving in the Popular Committees *(al-Lijan al-Sha'biyya)* (a local militia
established by the regime). The men from the checkpoint managed to kill
six of the attackers and capture two of them. The Al-Nusra Front now
demanded that the bodies of its casualties and its men being held captive
be handed over to it, and only then would it release the Druze it had
kidnapped. In response, the Druze kidnapped 14 villagers from the Dar'a
province. The Druze leader, Shaykh Abu Wa'il Hamad al-Hannawi...
succeeded in reaching a compromise with them, in the framework of
which the bodies of the six al-Nusra Front casualties were handed over
to the organization and the 14 Dar'a villagers who had been kidnapped
were released. However, the al-Nusra Front people did not release, as
part of the exchange, the 21 Druze hostages they held, and even denied
that these men were being held by them.[15]

Concurrently, disturbances broke out in the Qunaytra province on the Golan
Heights opposite the ceasefire line with Israel. Most of the residents of the region
are Sunnis. However, several Druze villages are also located in the northern
section of the region. The rebels, mainly men of the Free Syrian Army, gained
control of the rural areas in Qunaytra province, and in particular, the territories
near the border with Israel. They were careful for the most part not to harm the
Druze. Men of the al-Nusra Front attacked the residents of the Druze village
of Khadar several times. The attacks on Khadar agitated the Druze in Israel,
and their leader, Shaykh Muwafak Tarif, even declared that the Israeli Druze
would come to the aid of their brethren if attacks upon them continued.[16] At the
same time it was reported that Israel had opened channels of communication
with the Druze population on the Syrian side of the Golan Heights, alongside
the contacts Israel had already cultivated with groups of rebels active in the
Qunaytra province, as part of its efforts to prepare itself for the possibility that
the Syrian regime might lose all control over the Golan Heights.[17]

However, despite the tendency toward escalation of hostilities between
the Sunni majority and the minority communities of Syria, both sides have
manifested a clear desire not to cross the line that was likely to drag the country
into an even more brutal civil war. This tendency has been apparent not only
among the Sunnis of the Dar'a province, but also among the Druze, who show a
desire not to push matters beyond the current status quo. To be sure, the Druze
have not severed their ties with the regime, but at the same time they have
refrained from sacrificing themselves for it and from doing any more than what
is demanded of them. They continue to serve in the governmental bureaucracy
and in the army and security apparatuses. At most, they have also been willing

to be drafted into the local militias established by the regime, e.g. the Popular Committees *(al-Lijan al-Sha'biyya)* or the Homeland Defense Units *(Quwat al-Difa' al-Watani)*. These bodies are based on supporters of the regime, but the Druze set conditions for their participation, namely, limiting their activities to Jabal Druze and to the defense of its residents.[18]

# Syria's other communities

### The 'Alawis

Clearly, Syria's various communal groups differ in the degree to which they are loyal to the regime and willing to volunteer to defend it. Not surprisingly, many 'Alawis volunteered enthusiastically to fight on the government's side, as the core the regime is based on their community, they are identified with it, and they have more invested in it than the other groups. Hence, the regime's survival is bound up with their communal well-being, for they would most likely pay a heavy price if the regime should fall. These considerations find expression in the extensive 'Alawi enlistment in the Popular Committees and the Homeland Defense Army, both of which operate even in areas beyond those inhabited by the 'Alawis.

Not surprisingly as well, many 'Alawis have fallen victim to communal-based violence. Sunni rebels, particularly fighters belonging to the various radical Islamist organizations, have slaughtered 'Alawi villagers on numerous occasions. However, the converse — 'Alawi militias slaughtering their Sunni neighbors — has also been true. Thus, numerous stories of communal massacres have become part of the blood-soaked history of the Syrian civil war. At times, it even seemed as if regime forces were carrying out ethnic cleansing among the Sunni population living in areas with large 'Alawi populations, for example the town of al-Qusayr and its surroundings, which fell into the hands of the regime in June 2013 after heavy fighting, and the village of al-Bayda in the Tartus province, which the regime took control of on May 2, 2012. According to the Syrian opposition, the government's aim was to ensure its control in these key areas, which could become the basis for a largely 'Alawi canton, spreading from Damascus through Homs to the 'Alawi region and the Syrian coast.[19]

### The Christians

The biggest losers in the Syrian civil war are the Christians, an economically well-established community living mostly in urban areas, where they constitute a minority among a large Sunni majority. They are divided into a number of denominations, not bereft of rivalries, and have no tradition of bellicosity. All this made them a conspicuous target for ordinary criminals but also, ultimately, targets of the radical Islamist groups, who began attacking churches and clergymen, as well as Christian businesses and businessmen. Some Christians did join the anti-regime protests, but these were mainly intellectuals active outside the borders of Syria. They included, among others, Michel Kilo (born 1940, a Greek Orthodox Christian writer and human rights activist, one of Syria's leading opposition thinkers) and George Sabra. For several weeks in 2013, Sabra, also a Greek Orthodox Christian, served as acting president of the Syrian National Coalition, an umbrella organization of the Syrian opposition based in Turkey. However, it seems that most Syrian Christians remain loyal to the regime, like their neighbors, the upper middle class Sunnis, who reside in the big cities.[20]

In this regard, it is worth mentioning the warning issued in September 2011 by the Maronite Patriarch of Antioch (Lebanon), Cardinal Bishara Boutros al-Ra'i, during a meeting with then-President of France, Nikolas Sarkozy:

> We must give a chance to reforms in Syria and understand that Bashar is just an "unfortunate man" who is unable to perform miracles. We are not forgetting what this regime did to us, and in no way are we standing by its side. But we are concerned about what might happen here if this regime falls. Our foremost obligation is to defend the Christian community, since the changes taking place in the Arab world, and especially in Syria, could lead to genocide of the Christians instead of democracy.[21]

The Patriarch's statement is particularly noteworthy, since it was expressed by the head of the Maronite Church, an institution well-known for its historic hostility to the Ba'th regime in Syria.

## The Kurds

Syria's Kurds remained on the fence for quite a long period, refusing either to come out against the regime or to support it. This changed following the major rebel attack in the heart of Damascus on July 18, 2012, in which a number of senior regime security officials were killed. The brazen and successful attack seemed to signal the imminent fall of Bashar al-Asad's regime. Sensing this, the Kurds cast aside their restraint and moved to carve out a degree of autonomy in the areas they inhabited, which they call Western Kurdistan. At the same time, they left the door open for dialogue, and even limited cooperation, with both the government and the rebels.

This approach was conditioned by their historical memory of what they had suffered under the heavy hand of the Ba'th regime, but even more, of what they had suffered in the pre-Ba'th era under Sunni-led governments. For example, in

November 1962, one of the pre-Ba'th Syrian governments deprived hundreds of thousands of Kurds in the Jazira region of their citizenship.[22]

The areas inhabited by large numbers of Kurds, the Jazira region and northern Syria, are also inhabited by Arabs, some of whom are organized according to tribal frameworks. After the revolt broke out and regime forces began to withdraw from these areas, confrontations ensued between local Kurds and Arabs over control of the territory, and especially over the large grain storage facilities and oil fields located there. These confrontations became sharper because of the presence of radical Islamic movements. Al-Nusra and the Islamic State set the tone, with the support of local Arab tribes inclined to cooperate with them Not surprisingly, Islamists oppose the Kurds' efforts to gain control, and even some degree of autonomy, in these regions.[23]

# Conclusions

Several broad conclusions can be drawn from the picture outlined above.

First, the Syrian civil war is assuming ever increasing ethnic, sectarian, and religious features that will have an additional deleterious effect on relations between the Sunni majority and the minority communities. The great majority of the Sunnis have come out against the Asad regime, while the minorities, apart from the Kurds' related actions, have refrained from joining the ranks of the rebellion, and in effect continue to support the regime.

Second, Druze support for the regime finds expression in a number of ways. Thus, Druze serving in the government bureaucracy, the army, and security forces continue to report to work, Druze soldiers return to their bases from their leaves of absence, and young Druze continue to report to the army induction centers for enlistment as required by Syrian law. On the other hand, the Druze refuse to volunteer to sacrifice themselves in the service of the regime or to fight for it outside the territory of Jabal Druze.

Third, minority communities concentrated in their traditional regions have tended to confine themselves there, for safety's sake. In many cases, fellow-members of their communal groups have been compelled to move into these areas because of the deteriorating security situation in their previous places of residence. The 'Alawi, Druze and Kurdish communities will undoubtedly be helped in their struggle for survival by the fact that they live in areas in which they constitute the majority of the population.

Fourth, there are no signs of a trend towards the detachment of most of the various communities from the Syrian state. There are no signs of separatist sentiments among the Druze, Christians or 'Alawis that could grow into the desire for a completely independent identity based upon ethno-communal markers. This stands in contrast to Syria's Kurds, who have begun cultivating an ethno-national foundation that binds together the Kurds of Syria, Iraq, and Turkey.

Fifth, the trend towards to religious extremism among the rebels and the appearance of radical religious movements, some of which have no roots in Syria, add a previously non-existent dimension to the struggle over the country's identity. Such religious extremism poses a profound threat to the delicate and already damaged fabric of coexistence that has existed among Syria's various ethno-confessional communities.

The incident with which this chapter opened, involving the Sunnis of the Dar'a province and the Druze of the Suwayda province on Jabal Druze, peoples who have coexisted peacefully, side by side, for many decades, is indicative of the course of developments since the conflict began. The built-in, yet subdued tensions that normally existed between the various communities increased sharply as time passed, and hostilities took on an ever more sectarian coloration, particularly as the prominence of radical Islamists in the rebellion grew.

On the other hand, the Druze, and the 'Alawis as well, are communities with deep roots, traditions of bellicosity, and the capability of delivering severe blows to their enemies. Jabal Druze has been the fortress of the region's Druze community from time immemorial. Knowing this, the rebellious Sunni population of the Dar'a province feels compelled to preserve their coexistence with the Druze, despite the accumulating tension that surfaces from time to time. The Sunnis' restraint is understood and accepted by the groups composing the Free Syrian Army, but, of course, less so by the adherents of the al-Qa'ida-oriented Al-Nusra Front.

On the face of it, the current collapse of the Syrian state structure has led to the fading of the Syrian dream of creating a "state of all its communities," that is, a state in which the various communities live together after having become amalgamated in the Ba'th crucible into a unified political entity. This entity was supposed to have a common Arab, Syrian territorial, and secular national identity. Its inhabitants were to have shared interests, a main part of which would be the maintenance of an administrative and government system in which members of the various communities would be integrated and, in practice, in control. The very existence of this body politic was supposed to provide stability and ensure the prosperity of its members. At present, this dream is fading. Nevertheless, the members of the minority communities who stand at the base of the present regime, constituting a coalition of minorities, together with a portion of the Sunni partners in this coalition, remain loyal to it.

The ways that Syria's various communities — the Sunnis and Druze in the Hawran, the Kurds and Arabs in al-Jazira, and even the 'Alawis and Sunnis along the Syrian coast — are conducting themselves during these tumultuous, blood-soaked years provides an indication of what the Syria of the future might look like. No matter who rules in Damascus, each community is likely to tend to withdraw into itself in areas where it constitutes the dominant population, and defend itself from there. From this position of strength they will negotiate with the central government and with their possibly hostile neighbors as well. If this projection proves to be correct, then the collapse of the present Syrian regime, if it were to occur, would not necessarily result in complete chaos. It is quite possible that from the ruins of the present regime, an updated political system will emerge, based on the formula "Syria as a state for all its communities." This updated structure will probably be ruled by a coalition of minorities, and in practice, by the 'Alawis.

# Notes

1.  For more on the Syrian uprising, see: Fouad Ajami, *The Syrian Rebellion* (Stanford: Stanford University, 2012); David W. Lesch, *The Fall of the House of Assad* (New Haven: Yale University Press, 2012). On the human tragedy in Syria see *Ha'aretz*, May 23, 2013; see also an interview with former Syrian Deputy Prime Minister for Economic Affairs, 'Abdallah al-Dardari, *Associated Press*, May 19, 2013.

2.  See *al-Akhbar* (Beirut), May 31, 2011, http://www.al-akhbar.com.

3.  See Hanna Batatu, *Syria's Peasantry, the Descendants of its Lesser Rural Notables, and Their Politics* (Princeton, New Jersey: Princeton University Press, 1999). For more on Syrian society since the Ba'th revolution, see: Raymond A. Hinnebusch, *Authoritarian Power and State Formation in Ba'thist Syria, Army, Party, and Peasant* (Boulder, Colorado: Westview Press, 1990).

4.  See Umar F. Abd-Allah, *The Islamic Struggle in Syria* (Berkeley: Mizan Press, 1983); see also: Raphael Lefevre, *Ashes of Hama, the Muslim Brotherhood in Syria* (London: Hurst, 2013).

5.  One of the commanders of a division in the Syrian army is a Druze, while twelve commanders are 'Alawis, and only a few are Sunnis. See Batatu, *Syria's Peasantry*, and Eyal Zisser, *Faces of Syria* (Tel Aviv: Hakibbutz Hameuchad, 2003) [Hebrew], pp. 145–150.

6.  For more on the socio-economic roots of the Syrian revolution see Eyal Zisser, "The Renewal of the "Struggle for Syria": The Rise and Fall of the Ba'th Party," *Sharqiyya* (fall 2011), pp. 21–29. See also EIU (Economist Intelligence Unit), *Syria — Country Report*, April 2011.

7.  For more on the Druze revolt see Michael Provence, *The Great Syrian Revolt And the Rise of Arab Nationalism* (Austin: University of Texas Press, 2005).

8.  Ajami, pp. 172–180.

9.  *Ibid.*, pp. 180–185. See also *al-Jazeera TV*, March 18 & 19, 2011, http://www.aljazeera.net/portal.

10. See *al-'Arabiyya TV*, April 19 &22, 2011, http://www.alarabiya.net/ar.htm; *al-Nahar* (Beirut), May 5, 2012, http://www.annahar.com; *al-Hayat* (London), May 25, 2013, http://alhayat.com; *al-Sharq al-Awsat* (London), May 27, 2013, http://www.aawsat.com.

11. For the background to Junblat's animosity towards the Asad regime, see Eyal Zisser, *Blood in the Cedars: From the Lebanese Civil War to the Second Lebanon War* (Tel Aviv: Hakibbutz Hameuchad, 2009) [Hebrew], pp. 74–75.

12. See *al-Akhbar* (Beirut), May 31, 2011, http://www.al-akhbar.com; *All4syria*, May 25, July 19, November 11, 2012, http://all4syria.info.

13. See Aron Lund, "Holy Warriors, A field Guide to Syria's Jihadi Groups." *Argument,* October 15, 2012. See also, BBC Guide to the Syrian opposition: http://www.bbc.co.uk/news/world-middle-east. See also: Stephen Starr, "The West's dilemma: Who is the official opposition in Syria?", *The Globe and Mail* (Toronto), April 10, 2013. For more see: Thomas Pierret, *Religion and state in Syria, The Sunni Ulama from Coup to Revolution* (Cambridge: Cambridge University Press, 2013).

14. *Al-Sharq al-Awsat* (London), April 2, 2013, http://www.aawsat.com.

15. See *al-Akhbar* (Beirut), May 31, 2011, http://www.al-akhbar.com.

16. *Ha'aretz*, March 31, 2013, http://www.haaretz.co.il, *Ma'ariv*, April 2, 2013, http://www.nrg.co.il.

17. See for example *Ha'aretz*, December 20, 2012, http://www.haaretz.co.il.

18. For a detailed report on the Druze resistance to regime blandishments to more actively join the war on its behalf, see: *al-Khalij* (UAE), May 31, 2013, http://www.alkhaleej.co.ae.

19. For more on ethnic cleansing in Syria see: Joshua Landis' *Syria Comment* blog, http://www.joshualandis.com/blog.

20. See Syrian intellectual 'Amar 'Abd al-Hamid's blog *Syrian Revolution Digest*, syrianrevolutiondigest.com. See also the official website of the Syria National Coalition, http://www.etilaf.org/.

21. *The New York Times*, September 27, 2011.

22. For more on the Kurds in Syria, see: Jordi Tejel, *Syria's Kurds, History, Politics and Society* (New York: Routledge, 2009).

23. See for example *al-Safir* (Beirut), August 3, September 19, 2013, http://www.assafir.com; *All4syria*, July 30, August 2, 2013, http://all4syria.info.

# From Deba'thification to "Justice and Accountability": Iraqi Reform in a Wider Context

## Ronen Zeidel

The Arabic term for Deba'thification is *Ijtithath al-Ba'th*, namely "uprooting the Ba'th party." The name denotes a process with much wider implications than the purge of individuals from state service. While the formerly all-powerful Ba'th Party is no longer a functioning political organization in Iraq and as most of its senior members have been either executed or jailed, there have been problems carrying out the removal of middle- and lower-ranking Ba'thists working in government ministries. An issue in Iraq's sectarian-charged politics, Deba'thification was occasionally used for political purposes, especially by the current (summer 2014) Prime Minister Nuri al-Maliki.

This study begins with a brief presentation of the bureaucratic and procedural history of Deba'thification,[1] and then discusses its consequences and repercussions for Iraqi culture and collective identity. There is an ongoing debate regarding the heritage of the Ba'th and the lessons to be drawn from the recent past. Some Iraqi intellectuals have argued that Deba'thification was conducted solely on political and bureaucratic grounds, treating the Ba'th merely as a political party and an institution. Nothing would be accomplished, they claimed, without an accompanying rejection of the Ba'thi spirit and ideology, replacing it with a liberal and democratic spirit. This study treats both of these aspects of Deba'thification, providing a broader context for the contentious political and cultural struggle to refashion the post-Saddam Iraqi state.

The Ba'th party ruled Iraq for 35 years (1968-2003) and established a totalitarian dictatorship in which the party controlled almost every part of the country down to the smallest villages. It was a hierarchical party with a pyramidal structure, ranging from the smallest unit — the "cell" — to the "Regional Command" (*al-Qiyada al-Qutriyya*). There were several ranks of membership in the party; some were preliminary ranks before attaining the full membership (*'Udw 'Amil*). In addition, there were many more candidates for membership and potential collaborators. Consequently, before 2003 it was almost impossible to estimate the actual number of members in the Ba'th party. In a secret meeting of the leadership held in 1989, senior Ba'thists claimed that the number of "supporters, collaborators and members of the party" ranged from between 1.5 and 2 million. Joseph Sassoon provides a Ba'th party document from late 2002 in which the total number of members was given as 3.99 million, including 223,000 "active members" and over 50,000 division, section and branch members.[2] The numbers may have dropped after the Shi'i and Kurdish revolts in 1991, which followed the Gulf war in which many party members were slain. However, as will be explained later, the differences in the party ranks would become significant after 2003. Also important was the distinction between the party and state apparatuses: though the party ruled the state, it maintained its distinctiveness from the state apparatus so that senior officials in the state service would not necessarily be senior party members. Promotion within the two apparatuses was often run on different lines.

Prior to the US invasion of Iraq in 2003, US officials worked with leading Iraqi expatriates to plan the country's Deba'thification after the war. From the American side, the issue was handled by the Pentagon, which worked with Ahmad Chalabi, the leader of the Iraqi National Congress (INC), one of the main secular Iraqi opposition groups. Not having access to Ba'th party files which would have enabled them to estimate the number of members and determine their identities, Pentagon representatives could only establish a broad set of principles for Deba'thification. Therefore, on the eve of the occupation, there was no detailed US policy on Deba'thification. At that stage, in addition to the general principle that the Ba'th Party should be eradicated in Iraq, it was also decided that every Ba'th party member from the level of *firqa* (group) and up should be purged. The *firqa* is the second-lowest level in the organization of the Ba'th party, corresponding to a neighborhood or department; members of *firqa* were low-ranking Ba'thists. It was estimated that this move would affect tens of thousands of Iraqis,[3] but not much attention was given to the roles they had been playing in the civil administration. Shortly after the occupation of Iraq, the Pentagon seized a Ba'thi archive containing many thousands of personnel files of party members and handed it over to Chalabi. This was apparently the initial source material that the committee later used in the process of implementing Deba'thification.[4]

The High National Commission for Deba'thification (HNCD), headed by Chalabi and Director-General, Mith'al al-Alusi, officially came into being in September 2003. It was licensed to "blacklist" all prominent members of the previous state service, from the level of director-general and up, regardless of their rank in Ba'th party files, as well as members of the four upper ranks of the party, regardless of their civil service position. Those affected were purged from their jobs and not given pensions.[5] At the same time, L. Paul Bremer, the Head of the Coalition Provisional Authority, decreed the dissolution of the Iraqi armed forces and certain other organizations such as the Republican and Special Republican Guard. Under Bremer (July 2003-mid-2004), the US allowed the Iraqis to carry out the purge without thinking much about the consequences, such as the opportunity for personal vendettas or the collateral damage to the state apparatus.[6]

Estimates of the total number of those expelled from public service range between 60,000 and 200,000 civilians, 400,000 soldiers in the army and approximately 100,000 members of the security services.[7] Again, the lack of credible information poses difficulties: in a 2006 interview, 'Ali al-Lami,[8] a member of the HNCD committee, disclosed that no more than 100,000 out of a million Ba'this in Iraq were affected by Deba'thification.[9] It is not clear whether all the files were stored in one archive, certainly the committee was understaffed to deal with a million files. Therefore, already in 2005, the committee exonerated lower-ranking Ba'this. Al-Lami claimed that 80 percent of the files were those of lower ranking members of *firqa* (party group) who were allowed to return to their jobs, but banned from "leadership roles."[10] Salam 'Aboud claims that prior to 2005, the committee exonerated 8034 members of *firqa* in the provincial administration and 7784 in the ministries.[11] Therefore, the principle of exonerating lower ranking Ba'this, the large majority of party members in Iraq, was already established before the law of "Justice and Accountability" revised the policies of Deba'thification in 2008.

The rather careless work of the commission came under increasing criticism during the months after its establishment. In April 2004, Bremer, who had belatedly come to understand the fatal consequences of his policy, called for a halt to the work of the commission and actually opened the gate for a return of senior officers to the Iraqi army.[12] Yet there was almost no ministry in which employees could be sure that they would maintain their posts. Some of the ministries in which employees were under constant threat of Deba'thification were crucial to the functioning of the new government, such as the ministries of interior and education. The ministry of oil, the showcase of "The New Iraq," was notorious for purging able functionaries simply because they were registered as party members. From 2005, the US called for a "national reconciliation" that would include ex-Ba'this as well.[13] This shift in American policy regarding Deba'thification endured right up until the complete withdrawal of American forces in December 2011.

Article 7 of the new Iraqi constitution, approved by a referendum in October 2005, states that "the Saddamist Ba'th in Iraq and its symbols, under any name whatsoever, shall be prohibited" and provides that "this shall be regulated by law." This is the only specific reference to a party in the constitution and the definition of the ban is extensive.[14] This is the legal ground for Deba'thification and later was referred to in order to ban electoral candidates.[15]

In January 2008, after months of deliberations, the Iraqi Parliament passed the "Justice and Accountability" law (*al-Muhasaba wal-'Adala*), which modified the practice of Deba'thification, more or less according to the principles of International Transitional Justice and common practice in Iraq to that date. On the one hand, the law did not decrease the number of Ba'thi candidates to purge: it allowed members of the command of a *firqa* to be reintegrated into the workforce. On the other hand, the law acknowledged, for the first time, "personal responsibility" as a mitigating factor for collaboration with the former regime. "Instrumental membership" in the Ba'th was forgiven: there was an understanding that in a totalitarian system, many people were coerced into joining the party and in other cases, joined it to access some privileges and not out of genuine ideological conviction.[16] This is the first purely Iraqi law on Deba'thification and the commission in charge of it was placed under the Prime Minister's authority. Following the approval of the new law, the commission published, on a daily basis, long lists in the press of previously "blacklisted" Ba'this who were now reinstated.[17]

But the same law was also a double-edged sword: "personal responsibility" could be used to prevent officials for serving, even though they had not held senior Ba'th posts. The most famous case involved the prominent Sunni politician, Salih al-Mutlak, before the general elections of 2010. Officially, Mutlak was a lower ranking member of the Ba'th, who claimed to have abandoned the party in the late 1970s. However, he maintained very close relations with Saddam and his family until 2003. This was used against him in 2010 and the crisis was resolved only after American mediation efforts.[18] Eventually, he would become Maliki's first deputy. This, together with less known cases from the provinces,[19] demonstrated to many that Deba'thification was targeted solely against the Sunnis, an allegation that the committee denied. However, a problematic aspect of the committee's work was that it also banned "those who promoted Ba'thist ideas," and not only formal members of the party, without defining what these ideas were.[20] Thus, a law that was supposed to resolve sectarian problems, and adopted as a consequence of a national dialogue between Sunnis and Shi'is, was used for political purposes and perceived as a tool of the Shi'i prime minister to carry out a sectarian vendetta against his Sunni political rivals.

In April 2013, with unrest in the Sunni provinces and a recent rapprochement between al-Maliki and Mutlak in the background, the latter declared that a special committee of the Iraqi cabinet had decided to modify the 2008 law. According to Mutlak, members of *firqa* would be allowed into governmental service and those who had served in the Ba'thi militia *Fida'yun Saddam* would be given pensions. Furthermore, a final archive with all the names included in the law would be compiled by the end of 2013; after that date, no more names would be added to the list. However, the modifications still had to be approved by the Iraqi cabinet and parliament. Mutlak's announcement, as well as the approaching provincial elections on April 20, prompted a stormy response from Shi'i opponents, especially the Sadrist Block and the Fadhila party, that included demonstrations and fiery declarations. They warned against the reinstatement of "tens of thousands" of Ba'this into positions of leadership and also alluded to the symbolic date of the cabinet meeting that had approved the measure, April 7: the day of the establishment of the Ba'th. However, not all Shi'i members of the governing coalition were against the changes: 'Amar al-Hakim, the head of the Islamic Supreme Council in Iraq (ISCI), an important Shi'a actor, expressed his support, while members of al-Maliki's "State of Law" party branded the protest "propaganda for the elections" and denied that Ba'this would return to leading positions. Overall, this episode highlights the extent of the political tensions around Deba'thification and the fears that it arouses, but also that a significant part of the Shi'i coalition is continuing the trend of mitigating the practices of Deba'thification.[21]

The two government ministries most affected by Deba'thification were the education and interior ministries. According to al-Lami, most of those who were exonerated by the committee before 2008 were teachers: the total number of teachers investigated was 18,000, of which 11,000 were allowed to continue working.[22] Teachers were coerced into joining the Ba'th party as a basic precondition for employment and promotion. Mass exoneration acknowledged the diluted "personal responsibility" of those teachers and implied that with a changed curriculum, teachers could be re-employed.

The situation was more complicated with the ministry of interior. The Ba'thists there included security officers, torturers, executioners and interrogators of the previous regime. This ministry is considered the most important and sensitive in the Iraqi cabinet and, since 2005, had become a Shi'i stronghold. For some time after the 2010 elections and the establishment of the second al-Maliki government, the head position at the ministry was vacant and Nuri al-Maliki served as acting interior minister. Only in June 2011 did he nominate 'Adnan al-Asadi, a member of his "State of Law" party, for the post.[23] Nevertheless, the ministry was not entirely cleansed. As of early 2008 there were about 7,000 low-level members of the former secret police still serving in the security apparatus.[24] Not all were low-ranking; Salam 'Aboud mentioned five high-ranking officers that were still employed, among them the commander of intelligence of the special forces, an extremely sensitive position dealing with terrorist activities.[25] The ministry's personnel were accused of not preventing major terrorist attacks in Baghdad. Furthermore, according to Amir al-Khuzaa'i, the "State of Law" minister of national reconciliation, the Ba'th was behind a "conspiracy" to topple the regime following the US withdrawal in December 2011.[26] The new regime may have intended to use the experience of former Ba'th-affiliated employees, but in filling those sensitive positions (officers in the ministry of interior in charge of combating terrorism) they were also not beyond suspicion. The sight of Ba'thists in the ministry of interior and the return of officers from Saddam's army to public service may have shaken the still unstable Iraqi regime and rekindled the fear of "conspiracies," real or perceived.

The trials of the most prominent members of the Iraqi leadership are an overlooked aspect of Deba'thification. Between 2004-2010, almost all members of the Iraqi civil, party, and military leadership under Saddam were put on trial, accused of major human rights violations by an all-Iraqi tribunal. A significant number of these former officials were executed; most of those who avoided the death penalty were given very long prison terms. The trials were broadcast on Iraqi TV (Saddam's trial was also broadcast by other Arab channels) and provided the victims with an opportunity to confront their tormentors. These trials also provided the Iraqis an opportunity to come to terms with their past. However, the social impact was not as dramatic as the 1961 trial of Nazi German official Adolph Eichmann in Israel, or the Nuremberg trials of 1945-46 of senior Nazi officials. They did not set new legal norms as did the Nuremberg trials, or attract world attention as the Eichmann trial did. Apparently, they did not even change local attitudes toward the victims of their crimes, as the Eichmann trial did in Israel.

Ultimately, unlike similar processes in Germany and Japan, where there was a process of demilitarization (the military leaders responsible for Japan's involvement in World War II were judged as well), Deba'thification was not imposed by foreigners. It was an expression of genuine feelings of revenge, as well as of the new regime's need to assert itself. The process, which generated a lively internal debate in Iraq, was essentially a top-down attempt to "refine" popular hostility to the Ba'th by directing it toward bureaucratic avenues or trials. In general, this policy was relatively successful and so far incidents of violence against Ba'thists have been few.

Politically, Deba'thification buried the party as an actor in Iraqi politics. The trials and the purges brought about a complete change in the ruling elite, equivalent to the change in the Iraqi elite fostered by the 1958 revolution that toppled the monarchical regime. All the members of the top ranks of the previous regime are either dead or behind bars (or are elderly and infirm). The only "survivors," 'Izzat Ibrahim al-Duri and Muhammad Yunis al-Ahmad, are exiles in Damascus at the mercy of the Syrian regime, which has handed other exiles over to the Iraqi regime. Furthermore, the complex situation in Syria casts a shadow over their stay there.

But how committed is the current Iraqi leadership to including the Ba'this in a national reconciliation? Officially, the Maliki government takes a very tough stance against former Ba'this, in line with the constitution. The minister of national reconciliation stated that his ministry tries to involve every party in the political process "except al-Qa'ida and the Ba'th."[27] He even implied that the prime minister is tougher than he is on that issue. This did not mean, however, that individual former Ba'this who managed to establish good personal relations with the prime minister would be banned from serving the government and state. Moreover, organizations of Ba'this took part in covert negotiations that preceded the end of the so-called "Iraqi Resistance" in 2008.

## Deba'thification of the Ba'thi Heritage

In some aspects, there is a clash between official policy and popular sentiment. The Iraqi flag was changed. The official calendar includes anti-Ba'th commemoration days such as *"Anfal"* (commemorating the 1988 genocide against the Kurds), the *"Intifada"* (the 1991 Shi'i revolt against Saddam in the South) and "Mass Graves," whereas the Ba'thi "Martyr's Day," commemorating the fallen soldiers of Iraq's wars, was removed and not replaced by another date.[28] April 9th, marking the fall of Baghdad to US forces in 2003, has been proclaimed an official holiday.[29] Whereas the Saddam statue in Baghdad's Firdaws Square was brought down by the Americans, other statues all over the country were toppled by Iraqis themselves. The belated demolition of the gigantic "Victory Arch," one of the iconic emblems of the former regime, began in 2007. However, not all the iconic Ba'thi monuments were equally treated. Monuments, especially colossal ones, seem to have a life of their own: when word circulated that the government was considering the demolition of the "Martyr's Monument" (*Nasb al-Shahid*), some Iraqis expressed their indignation.[30] "Army Day" ceremonies are still held near the monument of the "Unknown Soldier."[31] In February 2010, the *al-Wahda* ("Unity") monument in Baghdad was sabotaged. The monument, two huge concrete blocks melting into one another, symbolizing the "unity" between Saddam and his people, was in the Sunni quarter of Mansur. The attack generated a lively debate regarding the heritage of the Ba'th. Ordinary people who lived near the monument declared to a television reporter that "these things are meant to stay after we pass away."[32] Intellectuals interviewed by a different TV channel also claimed that the monuments should be left to preserve, "for better or worse," the memory of the Ba'th period.[33]

# Literature

Out of seventy-four novels written and published in Iraq after 2003, fifty deal with the Ba'th period (1968-2003). There is no revisionism of the Ba'th years, despite the current harsh reality in Iraq: the period is portrayed in very dark colors by all the writers. Such an approach was emotional, lacking any attempt at selecting positive aspects from that harsh period that could serve as raw material for constructing a new national narrative.

This trend is noticeable among young Iraqi novelists based in Baghdad, aptly named "the Generation of Loss" (*Jil al-Diya'*). In his novel "The Flies and the Emerald" (*Al-Dhubab wal-Zumurud*), published in Baghdad in 2011, 'Abd al-Karim al-'Ubeidi describes the precarious existence of a group of educated young men in 1990s Basra, suffering from the regime's repression. The regime is depicted as degrading human beings to the level of flies; the novel concludes with the narrator reaching the point of feeling that he is "nothing." More than a novel, this is in fact a manifesto of a new generation that experienced the devastation brought by the Ba'thi vision of nationalism. The novel calls for a radical change of that vision. One of the main characters, a protagonist, dreams about having Israeli citizenship. The book was praised by Iraqi reviewers, albeit more for its anti-Ba'thism than for its "pro-Israeli" contents.[34]

In another novel, "Lost in Hafir al-Batin" (*Diya' fi Hafr al-Batin*), 'Ubeidi recounts his personal experiences as a soldier in the Kuwait war. He describes his alienation from life in Iraq and even radicalizes his opinions on the deformed Ba'thi versions of values such as "nation," "homeland," and "patriotism." Thus, he compares the American and later the Saudi prisoner-of-war (POW) camps favorably with his experience of returning to Iraq.[35] He finds a portion of an Iraqi newspaper in one of the abandoned outposts which describes "fighting for the Arab nation against the Zionists-Imperialist camp" and wipes his bottom with it.[36] His basic feeling throughout the ordeal that continued following his unhappy return to Iraq is of someone who does not belong (*la Muntami*).[37] The novel was a success in Iraq and even turned into a television series.

The rejection of national values is characteristic in other novels, as well. In Nassif Filk's "Khidr Qad and the Olive-Colored Age" (*Khidr Qad wal-'Asr al-Zaytuni*),[38] nothing is sacred for the hero: religion, ideology, homeland or nation. The key point in his life is when he is on a high mountain, on the border with Iran; there he strips himself of the "symbols of subordination," the military uniform and beret. Then he establishes, alone, "his nation" and later he gives himself, willingly, to the Iranians.

In other more conventional novels about the Ba'th period, one can detect outstanding qualities in the main characters. One of them is perseverance. In Taha Hamid al-Shabib's "Kerosene" (*Maqamat al-Kirosin*),[39] Ahmad and

Hamama spent most of their childhood in a Ba'thi prison. Hamama was born in prison. They lost their mothers in those prisons and were raised by other female inmates. Yet somehow they survive and reach April 2003. When Baghdad falls, they are not happy and insist on "liberating" their own town themselves. Hamama, an assertive woman in a conservative society, is the closest thing in Iraqi literature to the feminine emblem of the French revolution in Delacroix's painting. When they storm the Ba'th party offices in that town, she washes the blood-stained Iraqi flag, climbs the roof, and waves it. Later, when the offices are confiscated by one of the new parties, she demonstratively takes the flag down. In another novel by al-Shabib, "Buried Alive" (Wa'd),[40] set in the period 1958-1963, the hero, Jassim, a simple-minded youth who pretends to be a military officer, survives the onslaught of that period while preserving his good nature and courage But even these novels do not make use of these positive lessons from the Ba'th period for building a better Iraq. The narratives rotate between these figures and a kind of a determinist vision of an apocalyptic future. In "Kerosene," the odor of kerosene is frequently mentioned as a constant reminder that a fire is on the way. In another novel by Filk, "The Maggot's Eye" ('Ayn al-Dud),[41] it is the maggot which spreads like a plague. In both cases, the writers use kerosene and the maggot not only as destructive but also purifying devices. Only after total destruction, according to their message, will the country be able to embark on a new path.

The new writers rejected an older version of nationalism without constructing a new one. The lack of an alternative version of Iraqi nationalism in a period of national upheaval and distress, when many Iraqis may have felt the urge to redefine their identity, allowed some Ba'thi writers, notably Maysalun Hadi and 'Abd al-Khaliq al-Rikabi, to maintain their prominent status by "reinventing" themselves as Iraqi patriots and constantly expressing the suffering of the Iraqi people. Both writers, who started their careers under the Ba'th, wrote about both the Ba'th period and the US occupation. In the first period, they concentrated on the 1990s, focusing on the plight of the people under the internationally-imposed sanctions instead of writing about Ba'thi terror. Obviously, after 2003 it became easier for those writers to play the strings of anti-American Iraqi patriotism. Implicit expressions of Ba'thism can be traced in novels criticizing the US occupation, the current regime, and the current situation.[42]

Occasionally, novelists suggest a new way forward for Iraqi nationalism, as 'Ali Badr does in "The Lanterns of Jerusalem" (Masabih Urushalim).[43] The novel, which concerns the Palestinian American academic Edward Said's return to Jerusalem, is a polemic discussing the relative merits of wider pan-Arab nationalism vis-à-vis Iraqi nationalism. The author decisively supports pan-Arabism and suggests that Said, whose character represents the Western intellectual, the Arab, and the victim, is the champion of that nationalism. This, according to the author, would divest Arab nationalism of its previous useless militarist rhetoric and defeat the Zionists via cultural means. As could be envisioned, Badr did not succeed to convince the Iraqi intellectual milieu to turn its back on Iraqi nationalism and adopt an anti-Zionist Saidian version of pan-Arab nationalism. A more realistic endeavor was Nizar 'Abd al-Sattar's novel "The Americans in my House" (al-Amrikan fi Bayti).[44] Writing about Mosul under the US occupation, Sattar describes a city and a country in which nothing will be as it was before. The hero finds himself alone in Mosul and dedicates his time, as a consolation, to protecting cultural life in a city facing mounting fanaticism. The novel is about the love of culture and the connection to a specific place. The writer uses the city's glorious past as the backbone of a collective and individual identity. The book was a success in Iraq, and, in 2010, the author was awarded Iraq's most prestigious literary prize.[45]

A leading liberal intellectual in Baghdad pointed out two contradictory tendencies in Iraqi public and intellectual life today. Many, led by Maliki and his supporters, employ a political discourse based on the perpetual vilification of the Ba'th and Ba'thi oppression; hence, according to this intellectual, they "don't want Saddam to die." By contrast, he and like-minded people have tried to fully understand the evils of the Ba'th period and only after that bury the Ba'th, Saddam, and what another intellectual, Haydar Sa'id, termed "the culture of the national state" (Hadarat al-Dawla al-Wataniyya).[46] Theirs is a radical attempt to recognize and understand not only the atrocities of the Ba'th, but also its tenets, as well as the legacy of previous regimes that enabled these horrors. Pillars of the Ba'thi worldview included a forced homogenization of a very heterogeneous state, totalitarianism, militarism and the militarization of society, the persecution of minorities, rejection of pluralism, the constant search for external foes, a chauvinistic version of pan-Arabism, and anti-Zionism. This Deba'thification also includes a revision of the national narrative of Iraqi history, a deep commitment to multiculturalism and plurality, a constructive dialogue with Kurdish nationalism, and even a reappraisal of Iraqi policy toward Israel. Only in this way, according to adherents of this approach, can Iraq achieve true reconciliation and construct a national identity on a more solid basis, leading to a better future.

# Conclusion

Almost ten years after the US occupation of Iraq, the process of Deba'thification had registered some major achievements, mainly in the political sphere. Almost all of the senior Ba'thi leaders stood trial; some were executed and others were sentenced to long terms in prison. The Ba'th party was eliminated as a political factor and its ideology discredited. The governmental apparatus that constructed Iraq's "Republic of Fear"[47] was dismantled. Significantly, Deba'thification was a genuine expression of feelings among the majority of Iraqis and was not, as some claim, imposed by the Americans, as had been done in Germany and Japan after World War II. In fact, the Americans have been trying, since 2004, to mitigate vengeful and overenthusiastic Deba'thification and promote "national reconciliation" in its stead.

In other spheres the record is more complicated. At the individual level, it was not possible to purge the entire state apparatus of all Ba'this and even before the backlash against Deba'thification in 2008, most were exonerated, *de facto*. This exoneration was done without exerting serious effort to promote national reconciliation, and the result is that many personal accounts are left unsettled and only a semblance of justice was given to the victims. Another major obstacle was that Deba'thification was perceived as a "sectarian" issue in which only Sunnis were to pay the price. With the consolidation of a de facto authoritarian regime under Prime Minister Nuri al-Maliki, and especially after 2009, Deba'thification sometimes served to eliminate Maliki's political rivals.

Iraqi intellectuals continue to cope with the material, spiritual, and psychological heritage of 35 years of Ba'thi rule. They face difficult questions such as what to do with the memories of wars. Should Ba'thi monuments be left standing? How should lingering traumas be addressed? How can the culture of repression and almost inborn fear instilled by the Ba'th in every Iraqi be eradicated? And finally, how can a future be built from this terrible past? Should it be forgotten or remembered? If the past is to be remembered, what should be commemorated? If it is to be effaced, how is that to be done? It is probably too early to expect solutions, but at this stage intellectuals generally reject and negate the Ba'th period. While many write about it, some liberal intellectuals are trying to construct a "culture based on oblivion" or, in other words, to forget the Ba'th. In Iraqi novels about that period, one notices outstanding qualities of individuals, especially perseverance and assertiveness. The problem is that these qualities are not used by the intellectuals as raw material for fashioning a vision for a new Iraq. Instead, their vision alternates between the rejection of "Ba'thi" values, such as "Homeland" and "Patriotism," and a very pessimistic or even apocalyptic view of the future. Many look at the current reality in a determinist way, trying to understand if there is something unique in Iraqi history that has caused it so much misery.

Some Iraqi intellectuals are looking to Germany in their search for a model of an" oblivion based culture," not aware that Germans are constantly reminded of their past. Iraq, Germany, and Japan have each had to face the heritage of an evil regime of its making. Whereas the German and Japanese regimes inflicted terror on other populations, as well as their own, the Ba'th in Iraq mainly terrorized the Iraqi population. Moreover, Germany and Japan each had a solid national identity that was not compromised by the execution of senior leaders and the mass exoneration of low-ranking officials. Between 1945 and 1952, hundreds of thousands of Japanese were dismissed from their jobs without recourse by the Americans as part of the "White and Red" purges and the economic plan that was known as the "Dodge Line," yet Japan remained calm and later emerged as a democratic society with an advanced economy. By contrast, the Iraqi national project rested from the outset on shaky foundations, which have been fundamentally altered since 2003. In a way, the Iraqi experience is more self-directed, with relatively little interference from the occupier, and more reminiscent of the experiences of ex-East Germany and some other countries of the former Soviet Bloc or, in the Third World, that of South Africa and Rwanda. Finally, the Americans had a more active role in the denazification of Germany and the demilitarization of Japan than in the Deba'thification of Iraq. They were under the impression that, contrary to Japan and Germany, this was not necessary in Iraq.

For the time being, the underlying tension in Deba'thification continues to be the struggle between the eruption of popular emotions of revenge and the top-down effort to refine, contain, and channel them. It remains to be seen how long this situation will persist, and whether time will blunt painful memories or whether one monolithic system, the Ba'th regime, will be substituted with another: an authoritarian regime, based on violent sectarianism and political Islam.

# Notes

1. The subject is covered in detail by Fanny Lafourcade, "The National Iraqi Leadership 2003-7 and the Deba'thification Issue: The Fragmentation of the Iraqi Polity about its Immediate Past", paper presented in the conference "Writing the History of Iraq," Geneva, Switzerland, November 2008.

2. Ronen Zeidel, "The Iraqi Ba'th party 1948-1995: Personal and Organizational Aspects," M.A Thesis (University of Haifa, June 1997) [in Hebrew], pp.176–177. Joseph Sassoon, *Saddam Hussein's Ba'th Party: Inside an Authoritarian Regime* (Cambridge: Cambridge University Press, 2012), pp. 52, 286. There are countless stories about how people were forced to join the Ba'th, sometimes without even knowing that they did so. The following story is an example: in the early 1970s teachers in schools announced the establishment of a sports club. Registration required that the students fill out forms. The students were given blank forms and had to sign them. Later, and without the students' knowledge, a text proclaiming that the signatory joined the Ba'th was added by the teachers. Not all the signatories were accepted for the sports club and party membership. However, the signed forms were kept in party headquarters to

pressure the signatories in the future by claiming that they were party members who defected, a capital crime under the Ba'th. Hussein al-Sakkaf, *Kobinhajin Muthalath al-Mawt* ("Copenhagen: 'The Triangle of Death'", Cairo: Mirit, 2007), pp. 126–127.

3. The Ba'th party document in Sassoon's book has the number of 45,537 division members. Sassoon, p. 286.

4. Amatzia Baram, interview with author, October 15, 2012.

5. Lafourcade, 2008.

6. Baram, interview.

7. Lafourcade, 2008.

8. Later, al-Lami became the head of the committee for "Justice and Accountability." In May 2011, he was gunned down and killed.

9. *Al-Hayat*, May 17, 2006.

10. *Ibid.*

11. Salam 'Aboud, *Man Yasna' al-Diktatur* ("Who Produces the Dictator?", Cologne: Al-Jamal, 2008), p. 313.

12. Lafourcade, 2008.

13. Baram, interview, 2012.

14. For the Iraqi constitution of 2005, see: www.niqash.org/constitutions.

15. Mirvat Adwan, "Commission Defends Election Ban," *Niqash*, January 26, 2010, http://www.niqash.org/articles/?id=2593.

16. David Baran, *Vivre la tyrannie et lui suivre: L'Irak en transition* (Mille et une nuits; 2004), pp. 27–36.

17. For the text of the law see: www.gjpi.org/…/law no.10 on accountability.

18. Saad Saloum, Al-Hurra TV, February 3, 2010. On al-Mutlak see: an interview with Salih al-Mutlak on al-'Iraqiya TV, March 12, 2006.

19. For example: 'Abdulla, Salem, "Wrongful Dismissal: Sacked Ninawa Judges Won't Be Government 'Tools,'" *Niqash,* September 9, 2012, http://www.niqash.org/articles/?id=3121.

20. Saad Saloum, 2010.

21. "Al-hakuma tanhi faqrat al-makhbar as-suri wa-taqr qanoun 'aqarat masou'li an-nitham as-sabaq" *Azzaman.com*, April 7, 2013, http://www.azzaman.com/?p=30862. Hamza Mustafa, "Shurka' lilmaliki fi altahaluf a-shi'i yiti'ahadun b'ifshel ta'adilet 'ajtatheth al-ba'ath,'" *Ash-shar Al-awsat*, April 9, 2013; http://www.aawsat.com/details.asp?section=4&article=723913&issueno=12551#.UXO9i6KBl3I.

22. *Al-Hayat*, 21 September 2008.

23. www.niqash.org, posted 5.7.2011.

24. Kim Gamel, *Associated Press*, "New Iraq Law Lets Baathists Reclaim Jobs", February 3, 2008.

25. 'Aboud, *Man Yasna' al-Diktatur*, pp. 309–310.

26. Mustafa Habib, "Iraq's Reconciliation Minister on Negotiating with Militias, Saddam Hussein and Libya", *Niqash*, Nov. 10, 2011; http://www.niqash.org/articles/?id=2936.

27. *Ibid.*

28. Ronen Zeidel, Amatzia Baram, and Achim Rohde, "Between the Cemetery and the Monument of the Unknown Soldier: Commemoration of the Fallen Soldiers in Iraq from 1958 to 2010," in F. Pannewick and Leslie Tramontini (eds.), *Conflicting Narratives: War, Violence and Memory in Iraqi Culture*, Stefan Milich (Wiesbaden: Reichert Verlag, 2011), pp. 109–125.

29. Elie Podeh, *The Politics of National Celebrations in the Arab World* (Cambridge: Cambridge University Press, 2011), pp. 160–168.

30. This monument, a split dome, had become a Baghdadi icon over the years. The opposition of many to its demolition can be explained by its sheer beauty as well as by its being a monument to Iraq's fallen soldiers. The fact that it was built by Saddam and associated with its regime was put aside in this case. However, for the regime the idea of destroying this monument was certainly in line with the wider aspects of Deba'thification.

31. Zeidel, Baram, and Rohde, p. 120.

32. Al-Sharqiya TV, February 1, 2010.

33. Al-Hurra Iraq, February 3, 2010.

34. 'Abd al-Karim al-'Ubeidi, *Al-Dhubab wal-Zumurud* ("The Flies and the Emerald", Baghdad: Mesopotamia, 2011). For more on al-'Ubeidi, see: Ronen Zeidel, "Writing about the Other: Israel in Recent Iraqi Novels", *Arabica*, Vol. 60, Issue 6 (2013), pp. 778–794.

35. Al-'Ubeidi, *Diya' fi Hafr al-Batin* ("Lost in Hafir al-Batin", Baghdad: Masarat, 2008), p. 388.

36. *Ibid.*, p. 201.

37. *Ibid.*, p. 45.

38. Nassif Filk, *Khidr Qad wal-'Asr al-Zaytuni* ("Khidr Qad and the Olive-Colored Age", Baghdad: Dar al-Sabah), 2007. "Olive Colored Age" is an Iraqi slang for the Ba'th period, after the khaki uniform worn by the Ba'this.

39. Taha Hamid al-Shabib, *Maqamat al-Kirosin* ("Kerosene", Amman: Fidaat, 2nd edition, 2008).

40. Taha Hamid Al-Shabib, *Wa'd* ("Buried Alive", Amman: Fidaat, 2010).

41. Nassif Filk, *'Ayn al-Dud* ("The Maggot's Eye", Cologne: al-Jamal, 2010).

42. For an article on Hadi, see Ronen Zeidel, "Iraqi Nationalism in the Novels of Maysalun Hadi," in *Middle East Journal* (forthcoming). For books by Maysalun Hadi on the 1990s, see Maysalun Hadi, *Yawaqit al-Ard* ("The Sapphires of the Earth", Amman: Dar al-Shuruq 2001); *al-'Uyun al-Suwad* ("The Black Eyes", Amman: Dar al-Shuruq, 2002); *al-Hudud al-Bariya* ("The Land Borders", Beirut: al-Mu'asasa al-'Arabiya 2004); *Nubu'at Firawn* ("Pharaoh's Prophecy", Beirut: al-Mu'asasa al-'Arabiya 2007). For books by Hadi on post-2003 Iraq see: Maysalun Hadi, *Hulm Wardi Fatih al-Lawn* ("Light Rosy Dream", Beirut: al-Mu'asasa al-'Arabiya, 2009); *Shay al-Arus* ("The Bride's Tea", Amman: Dar al-Shuruq, 2010). Al-Rikabi's books include: 'Abd al-Khaliq al-Rikabi, *Sifr al-Sarmadiyya* ("The Book of Eternity", Beirut: al-Mu'asasa al-'Arabiya, 2005); al-Rikabi, *Atras al-Aklam* ("The Files of Speech", Beirut: al-Mu'asasa al-'Arabiya, 2009).

43. 'Ali Badr, *Masabih Urushalim* ("The Lanterns of Jerusalem", Beirut: al-Mu'asasa al-'Arabiya, 2006). A discussion of that novel in Zeidel, "Writing about the Other."

44. Nizar 'Abd al-Sattar, *Al-Amrikan fi Bayti* ("The Americans in My House", Beirut: al-Mu'asasa al-'Arabiya,2011 ).

45. http://alnoor.se/article.asp?id=67923 accessed January 30, 2012.

46. Confidential interview with an influential Iraqi intellectual, February 2013; Haydar Sa'id, *Siyasat al-Ramz: 'An Nihayat Thaqafat al-Dawla al-Wataniya fi al-'Iraq* ("The Policy of the Symbol: On the End of the Culture of the National State in Iraq", Beirut: al-Mu'asasa al-'Arabiya, 2009).

47. Kanan Makiya, *The Republic of Fear* (Berkeley, CA: University of California Press, 1998, updated edition).

# Lebanon in Crisis:
# The Specter of Sectarian Strife

## Joel D. Parker

Lebanon faces a potentially transformative crisis due to local responses to the Syrian civil war. In the two years since the rebellion against the regime of Bashar al-Asad broke out in March 2011, more than one million refugees are estimated to have fled from Syria into Lebanon.[1] The neighboring war and the influx of traumatized refugees have exacerbated ongoing sectarian tension in Lebanon, where locals fear that the full brunt of the increasingly Sunni-Shi'i war in Syria may soon become a daily reality. The Syrian civil war broke out just over two decades after the end of the Lebanese civil war (1975-1990) and less than a decade after the 2005 withdrawal of Syrian forces from Lebanon. While it began as an internal affair in Syria, it has drawn in volatile elements of Lebanese society, notably when the embattled Syrian regime called upon Sheikh Hassan Nasrallah, the top cleric of the militarized Shi'i party Hizballah ("Party of God"), to join directly in the fighting. Hizballah's direct involvement gave a significant tactical boost to the Syrian regime.[2] Moreover, it has rocked the fragile balance of power inside Lebanon and sparked religious tension among the populace, despite the aversion of Lebanese elites to renewed civil strife.

Lebanon's current caretaker coalition government, in power since April 2013, is composed of several Shi'i, Christian, and Druze-led parties, and is scheduled to oversee general elections in 2014. The minority opposition in parliament that includes a Sunni-Christian alliance, the so-called "March 14 Alliance," and which was formed after the assassination of former prime minister Rafiq al-Hariri in 2005, has condemned Hizballah's direct involvement in Syria's civil war.[3] However, the moderate Sunni-led Future Movement, which heads the March 14 Alliance, has found that its reluctance to actively support the Syrian rebels has left political space for more radical Sunni movements to take symbolic steps against supporters of Hizballah. The use of violence as a symbol can be seen as a way for new groups, unconnected to the political elite in Lebanon to gain what the French social philosopher Pierre Bourdieu called "cultural capital."[4] Sheikh Ahmad al-Asir and his radical Sunni followers based in Sidon provide the most prominent example of this phenomenon, which has led to violent clashes with the official Lebanese security forces, driving Sheikh Assir into hiding.[5]

Cultural capital and the use of popular rhetoric is also a tool in the repertoire of the Muslim clergy of Hizballah, while traditional elites and veteran politicians in Lebanon, often termed zu'ama' ("strongmen"), are notorious for their reliance less on cultural output than on traditional social hierarchies to retain their supporters' loyalty. Hizballah also employs vast patronage networks, funded by illicit trafficking and supported by Iran and Syria, as well as local partners. In addition, the militant Shi'i organization has acquired over 60,000 rockets since 2006, and according to Western and Israeli intelligence reports, may be seeking weapons of mass destruction from Syria or Iran.[6] No other organization in Lebanon, including the official state security forces, can claim such military power and deeply felt social influence, which is concentrated in Shi'a-majority areas of the country. Yet, since their involvement in Syria's civil war, factional splits have emerged within the Shi'i community. Harsh critics of Hizballah's intervention in Syria include the ousted former head of Hizballah, Sobhi al-Tufayli.[7] The existence of such voices, despite the lack of real power to back them up, is changing the traditional way of doing politics in Lebanon, a point that needs to be brought into proper historical perspective.

The larger picture of Lebanese history shows that sectarian strife in the past has tended to be part of elite power struggles and the fight to maintain a traditional fiefdom by a quasi-feudal "lord."[8] The Ottoman and French mandate periods inform the pre-state history of Lebanon and its unique "confessional" political system based on proportional representation, dating from the last official census of 1932. The nature of the Lebanese civil war (1975-1990) and its conclusion are largely responsible for the "militia politics" that underlie the contemporary Lebanese predicament. More recently, Shi'i-Sunni rivalries have emerged in the midst of the Syrian civil war. This chapter examines how and whether new forms of cultural capital may undermine traditional patron-client relationships, and their potential implications on the Sunni-Shi'i divide.

Recent socio-economic problems have increasingly put pressure on the Lebanese state, its confessional political system, and the middle class. For instance, the influx of refugees and sectarian violence fueled by the Syrian civil war serve as new sources of frustration for young educated workers who fear what might happen to their employment prospects if Lebanon were viewed by outsiders as a state in crisis. Many of the elite politicians, as well as a large number of the urban public, want to keep up the façade that Lebanon is not, in fact, in a state of crisis, and they use mainstream media forums to disseminate popular images of a prospering country. By contrast, many young people have expressed disillusionment with the country's situation and turned towards militant groups, such as that of Sheik Asir, who succeeded in attracting one of Lebanon's most popular male singers into his salafi group.[9] In between the wholehearted embrace and the wholehearted rejection of the elite-promoted image of a problem-free Lebanon, young people have emerged in the last few years since the Hariri assassination who are unhappy with the traditional Lebanese politics of the *zu'ama'*. They often use social media to express opinions that dissent from those of the elites, for instance, by calling for democratic reforms or pointing out instances of official abuse of power. In the long run, the young educated class's development of a more open and critical political culture that goes beyond traditional patron-client relations may be as important as maintaining the security situation and economic equilibrium is in the short run.[10]

# A Brief Overview of Lebanon's Political Composition before 1975

For centuries, Lebanon has been a center for global commerce and a contact point for the West, in addition to being a refuge for Middle East minorities. Although Egypt was the target of Napoleon's campaign in 1798, marking for many historians the start of the "modernization" project of the Middle East, the Levant had experienced European influence in the region ever since the Crusader period (1099-1291). Over the past millennia, the rocky hills of Lebanon became a refuge for Maronite Christians, Shi'i Muslims, and their distant heterodoxical offshoots, the Druze and 'Alawis. The refugees tended to form insular communities in which warrior leaders of small agricultural communities often struggled for dominance. By contrast, the coastal towns of Tyre, Sidon, Beirut, and Tripoli remained more cosmopolitan and tended to be populated by mainstream Sunni and Christian merchants who had ties to urban centers in the interior, including Mosul, Damascus, Baghdad and Aleppo.[11]

This unusual mixture of religious heterodoxy, protected by geography and *zu'ama'*, was both a blessing and a curse for the local populations: the blessing was a relatively dynamic economy in times of peace, but the curse was that the distribution of wealth and opportunity was often filtered through both local and distant patronage networks. This issue came to the fore when the Maronite elites rose to power in the late 18th century. Various inter-communal struggles and differences between Ottoman, Egyptian, and European powers contributed to a series of increasingly violent clashes from 1840 to 1860 between the previously powerful Druze *zu'ama'* and newly empowered Maronite strongmen. Samir al-Khalaf and other Lebanese historians have pointed out that, in addition to inter-communal fighting, much of the violence of this period was related to peasant uprisings around Mount Lebanon, which broke the ranks of the Maronite zu'ama' and led to violent suppression of the peasantry by the elites of both sects. Notably, the Christian clergy gained an independent role in some cases during the peasant uprisings, either mediating between powerful lords and the peasants, or by leading the peasants directly by advancing their claims against the zu'ama'.[12]

Concurrently, the Maronite elites of Lebanon successfully lobbied for greater European involvement to counter local forces and push the Ottoman government to protect Christians in urban centers where violence had turned sectarian. This trend reached a peak in 1920, with the French-Maronite alliance that created the expanded boundaries of modern Lebanon, within the emerging French Mandate over Syria and Lebanon. However, the Mandate, and the administrative separation of Lebanon from Damascus, came against the wishes of the Sunni-majority inhabitants of Damascus, Beirut and other urban centers. Their acceptance of the new reality would come only gradually.[13]

During the French mandatory period, as Elizabeth Thompson points out, the relatively open intellectual atmosphere of Beirut occurred as the French authorities in Lebanon relied on a diverse array of private charities, enterprises, and missionaries to administer the Mandate on a tight budget. The privatization of schools and hospitals was mixed with Mandate-authorized public works projects, which enabled Lebanon to balance the competing interests of the elites and the new intellectual bourgeoisie with the paternalistic nature of the French mission.[14] In Syria, by contrast, there was resistance to both missionary activity and French-sponsored projects, forcing the French, especially after the Druze Revolt of 1925-1927, to rely on urban notables who would cooperate on their terms. Under the French authorities, nationalist movements, particularly paramilitary youth movements, were formed in the major cities in the 1930s; but, in contrast to secular nationalist movements in Europe, most of the youth movements in Syria and Lebanon fell back on religious categories, even when under the guise of Syrian, Arab, or Lebanese nationalisms.

Despite the relatively liberal and welcoming atmosphere of Beirut compared to Damascus, local Lebanese politics often seemed to reflect the intra-elite conflicts of one za'im against another. For instance, the National Pact of 1943 ensured that Lebanon would have a Christian president, a Sunni prime minister, and a Shi'i Muslim speaker of the Chamber of Deputies. Lebanon, following the 1926 constitution, was and remained a republic upon gaining independence from the French authorities in 1943. The nature of the "National Pact" was a compromise between Christians and Sunni Muslims whereby the Christian representatives struck a closed-door deal with the Sunni notables stating they would not seek French intervention as long as the Sunnis would work to maintain Lebanese independence from Syria or other Arab countries.[15]

To be sure, the National Pact was never a formula for genuine national unity, as expressed by the clever slogan of a well-known Lebanese journalist, George Naccashe: "Deux négations ne font pas une nation" ("Two negations don't make a nation"), which referred to the fact that the National Pact was an agreement of two negative affirmations: The Sunnis agreed not to seek to merge Lebanon with any Arab state, while the Maronites agreed not to seek direct European intervention in Lebanese affairs.[16] Thus, the Pact seemed to be already on the verge of collapse by July 1958, when the US Marines landed in Lebanon upon the invitation of embattled President Camille Chamoun, in line with the Eisenhower Doctrine, following the outbreak of violence between Maronite Christians and Sunnis within the larger context of the ascendance of pan-Arabism championed by Egyptian president Gamal 'Abd al-Nasser.[17] Maronite President Camille Chamoun and Sunni Prime Minister Rashid Karami had deeply opposing views regarding the West and Gamal 'Abd al-Nasser. Chamoun and his allies were accused of rigging the 1957 elections to rid parliament of his opponents so Chamoun could have a second term. The situation quickly deteriorated, as elites of each sect prepared for a worsening of the factional violence spreading across the country. When the Iraqi monarchy was overthrown in July 1958 and replaced by radical Arab nationalists, Gamal 'Abd al-Nasser's supporters cheered — and the US and Chamoun himself feared — that Chamoun would be next. The US intervention placed enough pressure to force the elites to compromise and call off their rapidly-formed militias. Still, Lebanon had been on the brink of a deep precipice, as nearly 4,000 people had died in the violence and the economy had suffered a major blow.[18]

## The Legacy of the Lebanese Civil War

The failure of 'Abd al-Nasser and the Syrian Ba'th regime in the 1967 Six-Day War sent shock waves throughout the Middle East, including Lebanon, where elites had managed to keep Lebanon out of the fighting. The period between the 1967 and the 1973 Arab-Israeli wars sparked intense debates there. George Habash, a Palestinian refugee and militant left-wing Christian intellectual, represented a new kind of figure in Lebanese politics, whereas other Christian elites tended to be conservative and non-militant. Habash expressed his views thusly in mid-1976:

> We feel that the reactionary, bourgeois, confessional regime has collapsed and that the Lebanese national movement would make a big mistake if it allowed this regime to be resurrected and reconstructed on a reformist

basis. The Lebanese National Movement has a chance to insist on a new Lebanon — a democratic, nationalist, secular Lebanon.[19]

Fouad Ajami, an eminent Shi'i Lebanese-born American scholar, follows Habash's quote in *The Arab Predicament* with the sentence, "But the old Lebanon, although transformed, survived the civil war."[20]

Ajami's statement, published nine years before the Ta'if Agreement in 1990 which effectively marked the end of the civil war, was prescient. While the sons of "Sheikh" Pierre Gemayel, Rafiq al-Hariri, and Kamal Junblatt all assumed high-profile public roles in recent years, a number of factors underscore the "transformed" nature of the elite system of "old Lebanon." For instance, the Shi'i community, while not entirely ignored in the 1943 National Pact, was often marginalized as a political force until the civil war. Also, the rebuilding efforts in many urban areas reinforced the traditionally vibrant commercial spirit of the Lebanese coastal towns. Many of the younger generation emerged from the civil war with a desire to transform the old system of *zu'ama'*, whereby strongmen relied on loyal militias to gain leverage against rivals both within their own community and in other communities. Yet the Ta'if Agreement, signed in Saudi Arabia, reinforced the sectarian nature of the Lebanese political system and, despite giving lip-service to a future post-sectarian system, only slightly adjusted the National Pact of 1943, reflecting the increase in the Muslim population. In recent years, the *zu'ama'* have returned to prominence, with Western and conservative Gulf States' support. Instead of advocating inter-sectarian violence, they are calling for calm and co-existence — in other words, they fear an all-out war with Syrian- and Iranian-backed Hizballah.

## Hizballah: New Allies and New Opponents

When Syrian dictator Hafiz al-Asad (president from 1970 to 2000) decided to intervene on behalf of the Christian Maronites against the Palestinian militias in 1976, the Lebanese Shi'a gradually took on an instrumental role. They adopted the mantle of a resistance militia in southern Lebanon while simultaneously facilitating Asad's mission in the northern and eastern parts of the country. Inspired by the 1979 Iranian Revolution, Hizballah was only one of several movements among the Shi'i population. While Hizballah represented a reaction against the Lebanese left's radical secular nationalist and socialist tendencies, it also expressed frustration with the elite system of "sectarian privileges." Hizballah viewed the old system as "a fundamentally oppressive structure that no reform or patchwork improvement would do any good and that must be changed from the roots."[21] Yet Hizballah's rise to power was achieved only with

Iranian and Syrian help, providing arms and concealing various aspects of its global operations.[22] Iran and Syria even manipulated the image of Hizballah during the 2006 confrontation with Israel by treating the wounded in Syria in order to lower casualty numbers.[23] These moves provided the necessary cover to gain popular support,[24] which enabled Hizballah to enter electoral politics.

Certainly no democratic movement, Hizballah intended to manipulate the political system through threats of violence that included assassinations and the mere presence of its armed wing. The current political balance in Lebanon emerged in the wake of the assassination of Rafiq al-Hariri in February 2005 and the subsequent withdrawal of Syrian forces from Lebanon. The two March alliances were formed during the following month of protests and counter-protests. On the one hand, the March 14 Alliance, composed mainly of the Christian-oriented Kataeb (Phalanges) Party of Pierre Gamayel and the Sunni-based Future Movement of Sa'd al-Hariri, Rafiq's son, condemned the Syrian presence and desired a complete break from Syrian and Iranian influence. On the other hand, the March 8th Alliance was led by the Shi'i parties, namely, Hizballah and Amal ("Hope"), another Shi'i party that emerged during the Lebanese Civil War (1975–1990). Amal cleverly demanded a Syrian departure in 2005 but simultaneously called for ongoing friendship and ties with Iran and Syria. The March 8th Alliance was joined the following year by Michel Aoun, the self-made christian politician and former "General," head of the Lebanese Armed Forces during the civil war, who returned from exile at the time of the Syrian exit from Lebanon. From 2006 to 2008, the March 8th Alliance caused headaches for the March 14th-led government, and in May 2008 Hizballah's forces caused the collapse of the March 14th government; sat on the sidelines and Hariri's Future Movement opted not to confront Hizballah, allowing the Shi'i group to virtually take over western Beirut.[25]

In early 2006, Aoun signed an agreement with Hizballah and Amal, the other dominant Shi'i party, despite his anti-Syrian role in the late 1990s.[26] This alliance was tested in the summer war with Israel, sparked by a Hizballah ambush and kidnapping of two soldiers inside Israel. The kidnapping led to massive destruction and loss of lives, yet the Aoun-Nasrallah alliance endured; furthermore, the status of Nasrallah and even the Shi'i faith received a boost throughout Lebanon and Syria. In the three years after the war, there were many reports of conversions to the Shi'i creed, particularly from members of heterodox Muslim groups, and Iran promoted new religious centers throughout Syria and Lebanon.[27] These also served to increase Iranian influence in both countries, as Iran has been using Shi'i religious sites as bases to advance its political, military, and economic interests in the Levant since the early 1980s.[28]

The pro-Syrian Christian-Shi'i alliance (March 8) contends that the anti-Syrian Christian-Sunni alliance (March 14) is anti-Shi'a, backed by Saudi

Arabia, and transmits Islamist political messages from outside Lebanon.[29] There is evidence of the alleged Saudi backing since the late Rafiq al-Hariri initially came to Lebanon as a representative of Saudi interests and was a Saudi-Lebanese citizen.[30] In 2013, when the Saudis perceived that Michel Aoun had grown distant from Hizballah, they quickly arranged a meeting to discuss these matters. However, despite assurances that the Saudi-Aoun meetings would continue, there has been no indication of the March 8 Alliance's weakening, if indeed the Saudis tried to bring that about.[31]

When moderate Sunni Lebanese politicians such as Sa'd al-Hariri have expressed moral support for the Syrian rebel movement, they have little ability to follow through on their statements. Okab Sakr is a rare Shi'i member of the "Lebanon First" bloc of Hariri's Future Movement, and an outspoken critic of Hizballah and Aoun. He has denounced the *shabiha*, or pro-Asad militias in Syria, which he compared indirectly to Hizballah in 2012, and suggested closing the border to prevent fighters from crossing between the two countries.[32] In mid-2012, certain Western media outlets and pro-Shi'i news organizations, such as *al-Akhbar* and *al-Manar*, reported that Sakr was playing an intermediary role between the Saudis and the Free Syrian Army a coordination office in Istanbul.[33] Such reports are dubious, though plausible, and bear the traditional charge by Hizballah that all of its critics and opponents are involved in secret operations funded by the Saudis.

The often vague and abstract nature of Future Movement leaders' support for the Syrian revolt thus creates the impression that the only genuine supporters of the predominantly Sunni-led insurgency in Syria are the grassroots Islamist groups, particularly in the Lebanese coastal cities of Sidon and Tripoli. Even Sa'd al-Hariri himself, who is said to have fled Lebanon for fear of assassination, communicates with his constituency primarily through social media.[34] Moreover, the loss of economic and political power by the elite opponents of Hizballah has made it more difficult for them to carry on with traditional patron-client relations among the urban Sunni constituents of the Future Movement. This has led to the rise of fringe Islamist groups, some of which have popular support while others appear to be more isolated.

The radical Palestinian-refugee-led Sunni Islamist movement that may have ties to al-Qa'ida, Fatah al-Islam,[35] created enormous difficulties for the Future Movement. The fringe militant group incurred the wrath of the Lebanese security forces, directed against the refugee camp outside Tripoli, Nahr al-Bared, following bus bombings in 2007, which led to a clash that killed dozens. Subsequently, Syria argued that a car bombing of a Damascus *mukhabarat* ("secret police") facility that killed 17 civilians in September 2008 was carried out by ten members of Fatah al-Islam.[36] However, despite headlines reporting that Fatah al-Islam fighters were dying in combat in Syria,[37] their significance in the broader Lebanese political system seems to be very limited.

In striking contrast to the patronage politics of the veteran politicians, the rise of Sheikh Asir in Sidon demonstrates a new trend that has been brought on almost entirely by the uprising in Syria, which began in March 2011. Asir has gained enormous fame — and loathing — for his publicity stunts, including a ski trip with his Islamist followers and a mass beach trip, pictures of which went viral among Lebanese and Arab viewers. He does not fit into the mold of a "terrorist" and is often pictured merely having fun riding a bicycle or eating ice cream with young people. Indeed, his father is Sunni and his mother is Shi'i. The oldest of five, he was raised in a family of musicians and artists and supported Hizballah in his youth for some time.[38] The radical sheikh has even gained the loyal support of the famous Lebanese singer Fadel Shaker. Shaker has appeared prominently in the Sheikh's demonstrations since early 2012, and had to flee from hiding with him in the June stand-off with the Lebanese security forces, in which at least 17 soldiers were reportedly killed.[39]

The phenomenon of Sheikh Asir's meteoric rise and fall, as well as the way he sparked the ire of virtually all mainstream Lebanese voices, shows that nearly all of the elite patrons in Lebanese society dislike and fear his influence. Hizballah, however, does not have time to engage directly with such relatively small movements as it carries out its costly war with the Iranian and Syrian regime forces. As in 2006, Hizballah is fighting a propaganda war while it carries out military actions. For instance, the Shi'i organization refused to give counts of how many of its soldiers were "martyred" in Syria for the first few months of its involvement. Eventually, however, as high ranking members lost their lives, bodies were brought back to Lebanon for dramatic funerals. Later, a Hizballah graveyard was found in Syria, giving rise to the notion that perhaps many more fighters were dying than Hizballah was even telling its own supporters.[40]

# The Political Status Quo, Middle Class Reform, and the Refugee Burden

Despite the fact that Lebanon has been and will continue to be exposed to powerful interests in the Middle East and in the world, the periods of major civil strife have often been sparked and sustained primarily by internal divisions and frustrations inherent in the structure of the Lebanese political system. This is the general consensus of historians looking back at the Christian-Druze fighting of the 1840-1861 period, and it is an important aspect of the 1975-1990 civil war. Although the specifics of the alliances are extremely complex, and often contradictory, the fact remains that the Lebanese elites have always tried to survive as elites. They might fight each other, or make tactical alliances, but they tend to have the overarching goal of social and cultural continuity. The rise of Hizballah came as a result of popular militia opposition to the traditional elites, and today the Shi'i groups and their Christian allies dominate the old guard of the Hariri-Gemayel alliance. Yet this dominance has not completely broken the elite network and there are many points of interconnected interests; for instance, both the March 8 and the March 14 groups do not want to see the collapse of the Lebanese economy.

The Syrian civil war, then, despite bearing directly on the political system of Lebanon and creating cross-border fighting from both directions, does not currently present great opportunities for Lebanese social or political forces. Although wealth is unequally distributed outside the major cities, the middle class has been driving anti-sectarian moves and will most likely not give up the comforts of daily life in order to participate in the kind of desperate territorial wrangling going on in Syria. While the close proximity of Sunni and 'Alawi populations in Tripoli has proved troublesome at times, the Lebanese police and the official army have no interest in allowing what ultimately will be seen as persecution of the tiny 'Alawi minority. Furthermore, the Lebanese political system, as volatile as it may seem on the surface, has developed a widely held distaste for sectarian violence, as evidenced by the universal condemnation by local political leaders of all stripes following the tit-for-tat bombings in southern Beirut and Tripoli in August 2013.[41]

The Syrian regime no longer has the same influence over Lebanese affairs that it had before 2011 due to the intensity of the civil war that preoccupies the regime with its own survival, above all else. Although Asad's forces and their Iranian allies can call on Hizballah to join the fight in Syria, not all Lebanese Shi'a are in favor of Hizballah's participation. Moreover, Hassan Nasrallah has lost much prestige in the last three years among Sunni and Christian Arabs who admired his stand against Israel in 2006. Confrontation with Israel is still possible in the coming years since Hizballah has the ability to greatly damage Israeli morale by targeting major cities with tens of thousands of rockets. It would probably boost Hizballah's image to achieve a victory against Israel under favorable circumstances, but it could also backfire and give Israel an excuse to cause great damage to southern Lebanon.

One the other hand, Lebanon may see internal upheavals unrelated to external powers, based instead on the globally restive middle class as witnessed in Egypt, Brazil, China, and elsewhere. Recently, for instance, the feminist civil society group Nasawiya was attacked by security guards of the *za'im* Nadim Gemayel (of the Phalanges Party family, part of the March 14 Alliance). When his partisan media reported a distorted story of the events, the young feminists posted videos and pictures of the incident on Facebook and Twitter. Their images forced Nadim Gemayel to admit that his guards had broken the law, though he stopped short of an apology.[42] There are numerous similar examples, showing that there could be a revival at some point of the anti-sectarian and anti-corruption campaign that emerged in early 2011. Whether or not a broadly secular movement emerges, there is a tendency in Lebanon to see local events through a predominantly local lens. In much of the reporting about Sheikh Asir and his famous follower Fadel Shaker, Lebanese onlookers tended to perceive that the momentum of the movement derived not from the Syrian civil war or a regional *Salafi* sponsor, but rather from the motivation of these individuals to find authenticity in the face of local falsehoods generated by the *zu'ama'-*controlled media and popular culture.

It remains to be seen whether Lebanon can shield itself from the effects of the Syrian civil war given the entrance of Hizballah into the fray and the arrival of hundreds of thousands of refugees. Yet for the near future, the Lebanese security forces, and even the majority of the March 14 opposition, will probably seek to contain the spillover and rely on patronage politics as much as possible. Some reforms may be implemented in the media or capital markets to keep the liberal tradition going. They will probably not be wide-reaching, however, unless there is a dramatic change in the power balance between Hizballah and the radical Sunni groups. That, of course, could occur in the event of another major confrontation between Hizballah and Israel of the same or greater magnitude as the July 2006 confrontation. Barring such a conflagration, which could have a devastating effect on society, the National Pact and the Ta'if Agreement, are likely to survive. But in the long term, if chaos continues in Syria, Lebanese society may bear even greater costs than it has to date.

# Notes

1. International Crisis Group, "Too Close for Comfort Syrians in Lebanon," *Middle East Report*, No. 141, May 13, 2013. http://www.crisisgroup.org/~/media/Files/Middle%20East%20North%20Africa/Iraq%20Syria%20Lebanon/Lebanon/141-too-close-for-comfort-syrians-in-lebanon.pdf.

2. Paul Shinkman, "12K Hizballah Fighters Turning Tide in Syria, Top General Says," *US News and World Report*, May 30, 2013.

3. Thomas al-Bashri, "Hariri: Hizballah Dragging Lebanon into the Abyss," *The Daily Star*, June 14, 2013.

4. Sulfikar Amir, "Symbolic Power in a Technocratic Regime: The Reign of B.J. Habibie in New Order Indonesia," *SOJOURN: Journal of Social Issues in Southeast Asia*, Vol. 22, No. 1, 2007, pp. 83–106.

5. "Lebanon charges Assir, 37 others over Abra clashes," *The Daily Star*, July 4, 2013.

6. Joseph Federman, "Israel vows to keep weapons from Hizballah," *Associated Press*, July 14, 2013.

7. Laure Stephan, "Sobhi al-Toufayli, fondateur du Hizballah, affiche sa dissidence," *Le Monde*, March 29, 2013. Zvi Barel, "Nasrallah fights uphill battle for Assad," *Ha'aretz*, June 2, 2013.

8. Samir Khalaf, *Lebanon's Predicament* (NY: Columbia University Press, 1987), pp. 73–101.

9. An Al-Monitor Correspondent in Beirut for Al-Monitor Lebanon Pulse, "What Happened to Fadel Shaker?", *Al-Monitor*, July 4, 2013. http://www.al-monitor.com/pulse/originals/2013/07/fadel-shaker-lebanon-sidon-ahmad-assir.html.

10. *Global Security*, Lebanese Corruption, June 4, 2013, http://www.globalsecurity.org/military/world/lebanon/corruption.htm.

11. Kamal Dib, *Warlords and Merchants: The Lebanese Business and Political Establishment* (London: Ithaca Press, 2004, 2006, paperback), pp. 11–59.

12. Samir Khalaf, *Lebanon's Predicament*, pp. 22–44, 73–101; also Usama Makdisi, "Reconstructing the Nation-State: The Modernity of Sectarianism in Lebanon," *Middle East Report*, No. 200, July-September, 1996.

13. Patrick Seale, *The Struggle for Arab Independence: Riad al-Sulh* (NY: Cambridge University Press, 2010).

14. Elizabeth Thompson, *Colonial Citizens* (NY: Columbia University Press, 2000).

15. Akram al-Hawrani, *Mudhakkirat Akram al-Hawrani* (Cairo: Al-Nasher, 2000), Vol. 1, pp. 282–284.

16. Dib, *Warlords and Merchants*, p. 102, fn. 16.

17. Alasdair Sousi, "Legacy of US 1958 Invasion," *Aljazeera*, July 15, 2013, http://www.aljazeera.com/indepth/features/2013/07/201371411160525538.html.

18. Dib, *Merchants and Warlords*, pp. 83–89.

19. Fouad Ajami, *The Arab Predicament* (NY: Cambridge University Press, 1981), p. 145.

20. *Ibid.*, p. 146.

21. Rodger Shanahan, *The Shi'a of Lebanon: Clans, Parties and Clerics* (London: Tauris Academic Studies, 2005), p. 115.

22. Benjamin Weinthal, "Analysis: the rise of Hezbollah in Africa," *Jerusalem Post*, July 11, 2013.

23. Con Coughlin, "Iran is compensating families of Hezbollah dead," *Daily Telegraph*, August 4, 2006.

24. Neil MacFarquhar, "Tide of Arab Opinion Turns to Support for Hizballah," *New York Times*, July 28, 2006.

25. Robert F. Worth and Nada Bakri, "Hezbollah Seizes Swath of Beirut from US-Backed Lebanon Government," *New York Times*, May 19, 2008.

26. Ibrahim al-Amin, "From Aoun Activist to Nasrallah," *al-Akhbar*, July 15, 2013.

27. Khalid Sindawi, "The Shiite Turn in Syria," *Current Trends in Islamist Ideology*, Hudson Institute, Vol. 8, pp. 82–107.

28. Net Temko, "Iranian tourists in Syria: a sign of political coziness," *Christian Science Monitor*, February 24, 1984.

29. Israel Elad-Alman, "The Sunni-Shia Conversion Controversy," *Current Trends in Islamist Ideology*, Vol. 5, Hudson Institute, 2007, pp. 1–11.

30. Dib, *Warlords and Merchants*, pp. 294–300.

31. Marlene Khalifa, "Saudi Arabia's Lebanon Policy Takes a New Twist," *Al-Monitor*, July 4, 2013; originally published in Arabic in Lebanon's *al-Safir*, July 3, http://www.assafir.com/Article.aspx?EditionID=2502&ChannelID=60323&ArticleID=306#.Ue-8YI1mii1.

32. "Okab Sakr: A *shabih* slaughters in Syria, and a *shabih* threatens Lebanon, which will close the border," *An-Nahar*, December 23, 2012 [Arabic].

33. Rania Abouzeid, "Syria's Secular and Islamist Rebels: Who are the Saudis and the Qataris arming?", *Time*, September 18, 2012.

34. Andrew Kirkby, "The Lebanese Sunnis: A Community in Disarray," *Journal of Defense and Studies & Resource Management*, January 16, 2013.

35. Rebecca Bloom, "Lebanon: Fatah al-Islam," *Council of Foreign Relations*, backgrounder, June 8, 2007.

36. Thomas Pierret, *Religion and the State in Syria: the Sunni Ulama from Coup to Revolution* (NY: Cambridge University Press, 2013), pp. 212–213.

37. See for instance, Aryn Baker and Rami Aysha, "Lebanon's Most Wanted Terrorist Blows Himself up in Syria," *Yalibnan*, April 23, 2012.

38. Dana Moukhalati, "Breaking down Ahmad al-Assir: the man behind the beard," *al-Arabiya*, June 25, 2013.

39. Anonymous reporter from Beirut for *al-Monitor*, "What happened to Fadel Shaker?" July 3, 2013.

40. "A Syrian National found the graves of hundreds of Hizballah militants in Syria," *CNN Arabic*, 24 July, 2013.

41. See for example, "Beirut Blast Generates Wide Condemnation," *The Daily Star*, August 15, 1013; "Lebanese Officials Condemn Tripoli Blasts: All Blasts Have Same Murderer," *al-Manar*, August 23, 2013.

42. Maria Abi Habib, "Lebanese activists turn to Facebook and Twitter for defense," *Wall Street Journal Blogs*, July 2, 2013, http://blogs.wsj.com/middleeast/2013/07/02/lebanese-activists-turn-to-facebook-and-twitter-for-defense/.

# The Imperative of Saudi Reform: Conspiracy or Necessity?

## Brandon Friedman

Salman al-'Awdah, an important Saudi religious scholar, drawing on the thought of the Islamist modernist Muhammad 'Abduh and the Third World revolutionary Frantz Fanon, observed that Egypt's 2011 uprising was, in part, the result of a tyranny of decision-making and deprivation and neglect of the Egyptian public.[1]

Saudi Arabia's King 'Abdullah bin 'Abd al-'Aziz used billions of oil generated wealth to manage the domestic shockwaves generated by the "Arab Spring" uprisings. After witnessing the collapse of Zine al-'Abidin Ben 'Ali's regime in Tunisia followed by the deposition of Egyptian president Hosni Mubarak's regime during the first two months of 2011, 'Abdullah distributed $10.7 billion in social welfare to Saudi citizens. State employees were given a 15 percent pay raise, and funds were made available for housing, studying abroad, and social security. The regime also announced that unemployed Saudis would be paid 2,000 Saudi rials (approximately $535) per month for up to one year. At the end of February 2011, the Saudi authorities announced an additional $26 billion in social spending, and in March they added an additional $93 billion in distributive spending.[2]

Riyadh's mammoth precautionary handouts in 2011 were not fueled by paranoia alone. Saudi Arabia suffers from many of the same demographic trends that exist in Tunisia and Egypt, as well as elsewhere in the Arab world: 80 percent of Saudi Arabia's approximately 28 million people are under 40 years of age and 15 percent are under 15 years of age. Its population is expected to grow to 33 million in the next 10 years.[3] The Saudi regime recognizes it needs to make structural changes to its economy in order to create jobs for its rapidly expanding youthful population.

Unlike in the past, when Saudi kings announced elaborate programs of reform and then abandoned them when the crisis passed,[4] today there are important structural reasons that suggest the king is serious about reform. During the 2011 uprisings, the Al Sa'ud dynasty demonstrated that it has enough cash on hand *today* to buy-off domestic unrest and, if need be, to call on loyal security services to forcibly suppress it, as it did during the Shi'i unrest in the Eastern Province in 2011 and 2012.[5] Its first quarter cash reserves in 2012 were

$560.8 billion. But what really worries the king and senior princes of the Saud family is *tomorrow*: the possibility that in the medium-to-long term it will not have enough cash on hand to appease domestic discontent. Important changes in the supply-side of world energy markets during the past two years, as well as steadily increasing Saudi energy consumption, may cut into the enormous oil revenues and profits the Saudis have enjoyed during the past decade. There are also some that believe that Saudi oil reserves are diminishing and that, in the long-term, the Saudi regime will not be able to continue relying exclusively on its oil-wealth to support its population.[6]

Therefore, the ruling Saudi princes believe that the best way to ensure the cohesion of the Saudi state is to implement a top-down program of economic diversification that will create desirable jobs for its youthful population. The key to sustaining this program of economic diversification will be the ability to attract the foreign direct investment that is necessary to create such private-sector jobs. To that end, the king has committed to implementing legal reforms intended to make the kingdom's legal system more transparent and business-friendly. The king has also placed great emphasis on education reform in order to ensure that Saudi youth are equipped to compete for new private-sector jobs.

In other words, if these trends in the world's energy markets hold, the future of the Saudi state is likely to hinge on the regime's ability to implement fundamental changes to its education and legal systems. These proposed changes have been, and will be, hotly contested and debated by a powerful and ideologically diverse class of religious scholars that currently administer the key institutions that govern the kingdom's education and legal systems.

To be sure, the ruling family needs to implement top-down structural reform to secure its power and wealth. The growing youth demographic in the kingdom means there will be greater pressure for socio-economic change emanating from below. These two trends are starting from opposite poles on the Saudi political spectrum but appear to be moving towards one another.[7] Nevertheless, any program of government reform will have to be reconciled to a large religious class that forms the strongest segment of organized Saudi civil society. Simultaneous change from the top-down and the bottom-up suggests political culture in the kingdom may be changing. Change from the bottom-up is notoriously difficult to quantify and assess, but a more vocal and politically active younger generation may mean that, in the long-term, the Al Sa'ud will have to find a way to accommodate the increasing number of young people who would like to participate in the kingdom's political life.

Any change, whether top-down or bottom-up, will occur slowly, much too slowly for some young Saudis (particularly for the Shi'i minority of the Eastern Province, and for Saudi women), and perhaps too slowly for the West, as well.

But, if managed and executed properly, this change may provide the Saudi dynasty with the means to avoid the "tyranny of despotism" that Salman al-'Awdah, referring to Fanon's work, described as "not only a political system but a political and social culture that is produced and distributed to everybody."[8]

# The Urgency of Economic Diversification: Jobs

In 2009, the US surpassed Russia as the world's largest natural gas producer and by 2020 may displace Saudi Arabia as the world's largest oil producer. The shale energy revolution is expected to transform the US from a net natural gas importer to a net natural gas exporter by 2020, and reduce its dependence on oil imports from 60 percent in 2005 to 34 percent in 2019.[9] The US Energy Information Administration noted that "the rapid growth of US shale oil production in recent years, [is] a development that has the potential to change the structure of oil markets worldwide."[10] According to an International Monetary Fund (IMF) study, a sharp and sustained decline in oil prices ($30 per barrel or more) beginning in 2013 would create current account deficits in Saudi Arabia by 2017.[11]

The second factor that may negatively affect future Saudi oil revenue is its own rising consumption. Saudi oil and gas consumption has been growing at seven percent per year.[12] During the past thirty years, the Saudi population has more than doubled, from a little over 13 million in 1985 to more than 28 million people today. As the population has increased, its demand for energy has also jumped exponentially. Saudis consume twice the global average in oil relative to their economic output. On a per capita basis, the Saudis consume more oil than even the United States. Of the approximately 10 million barrels per day the kingdom produces, Saudis consume roughly a quarter of it.[13] It is reasonable to expect that this figure will increase, particularly as women, who constitute 45 percent of the population, move closer to winning the legal right to drive and join the work force in much greater numbers. Saudi Aramco's CEO Khalid al-Falih warned that rising domestic energy consumption in Saudi Arabia could result in the loss of 3 million barrels per day of crude oil exports by the end of the decade.[14]

Therefore, with less oil to export and a likely substantial increase in global supply, Saudi Arabia may have to adjust to diminishing oil revenues. As an important Chatham House report observed,

> the need to diversify the economy and create jobs is paramount. If this is not done fast enough — and the signs are it is not — the subsequent fiscal squeeze would have serious political consequences.[15]

Some critics believe the social consequences of oil dependency have already arrived. Journalist Karen House reports that unemployment among 20–24 year-old Saudi men is 39 percent, while, overall, 45.5 percent of all women are unemployed and 30 percent of all men. House argues that Saudi Arabia

> is a society in which all too many men do not want to work at jobs for which they are qualified; in which women by and large aren't allowed to work; and in which, as a result, most of the work is done by foreigners... who compose the majority of the labor force [estimated to be 8.5 million].[16]

Saudi Arabia is planning to spend $76 billion in 2013 and $397 billion in the next ten years on infrastructure projects. Today, the construction industry accounts for 3.5 million jobs across the kingdom, and 45 percent of the private sector workforce.[17] However, in the past, many of the construction jobs have gone to foreign laborers. The kingdom's new construction and development projects are labor intensive and designed to put young Saudis to work in the short-term, as well as to address a real need: Saudi Arabia is also expanding its industrial economy for the medium-to-long term, and it will need infrastructure to support such industry. The projects include new roads, railways, and urban transportation systems. There is a program to expand its airports, as well as to invest in building new water, sewage treatment, and electricity plants. And there are also plans to extend telecommunications and information technology (IT) infrastructure and build four new million new homes.[18]

Saudi Arabia is also attempting to leverage its downstream oil production by expanding in related industries such as petrochemicals and its derivative products. Jubail Industrial City in the Eastern Province is the largest petrochemical center in the world. In the early 1980s, Western media heaped scorn on this Saudi industrial initiative, but today it produces nearly seven percent of the world's petro-chemical products. In 2004, the government-appointed Royal Commission (RC) initiated a Jubail II master plan intended to double the city's industrial output. The cost of infrastructure expansion alone for Jubail II is $3.8 billion. The centerpieces of Jubail II are Satorp, a $14 billion refinery joint-venture between Saudi Aramco and the French oil company, Total, and Sadara, a $20 billion petrochemical joint-venture of Saudi Aramco and the US company, Dow Chemical, for plastics and specialty chemicals.

Jubail II is following Jubail I's recipe for success, which was building world-class infrastructure to attract foreign investment. The government is hoping that Jubail II will attract $56 billion in foreign direct investment. And, most importantly, the government hopes that Saudis will be able to fill some of the 55,000 industrial jobs that Jubail II is expected to create. In order to equip Saudis with the necessary skills, the new industrial complex will include three institutions of higher learning: Jubail Industrial College, Jubail University College, and Jubail Technical Institute. Construction jobs are also being created to expand the residential capacity of the city. It is currently home to 100,000 persons, with plans to expand to 300,000 residents by 2030.[19]

Eighty-five kilometers north of Jubail, the government is also building Ras al-Khair Industrial City for minerals and metals-based industries in order to take advantage of Saudi Arabia's large phosphate and bauxite deposits in the far north of the kingdom. Bechtel is building one of the world's largest greenfield (a project in an undeveloped area) aluminum smelters to service a joint venture between Ma'aden (Saudi Arabian Mining Company) and Alcoa. The city is expected to open in 2016.[20]

These industrial facilities presently represent 290 industries and foreign investment worth $110 billion. They generate more than 10 percent of the kingdom's non-oil GDP, and account for more than 85 percent of its non-oil exports.[21] Jubail, together with the Yanbu' Industrial City (another downstream industrial refinery complex located in Medina Province on the opposite side of the kingdom), have a combined population of 300,000, employ more than 175,000 workers in 600 factories, and are educating 70,000 future workers. The government's investment has been designed to attract foreign investment and ultimately employ employ young Saudis in skilled jobs. However, this ambition is being undermined by two primary obstacles to foreign investment: 1) the kingdom's opaque legal system; and, 2) the lack of a properly educated and trained work force. Therefore, the Saudis' ability to successfully diversify their economy and create jobs will likely depend on their ability to implement legal and education reform.

## Legal Reform: Will Saudi law be codified?

A major obstacle to increased foreign investment in the Saudi economy is its unique legal system based on *shari'a* law. In most Arab states, Islamic law maintains a strong influence that is mostly limited to matters related to family law and inheritance. In other areas, and in particular commercial and contract law, judges issue rulings largely on the basis of legislated texts and codes. In Saudi Arabia, judges rule on personal interpretation of the Islamic legal tradition, rooted in the *Qur'an* and the *Sunna* (the actions and sayings of the Prophet Muhammad recorded in a reliable chain of record, or *hadith*). While there are many large volumes of Islamic jurisprudence, there is no place where rulings are written down in any authoritative or binding form. Nathan Brown has rightly noted that religious scholars feel they should not be bound by whatever rulers have decreed to be the authoritative version of that tradition… [and that] each judge should have direct and unmediated access to the sources of law and the full range of jurisprudential debates rather than to have them redacted and imposed by a person or committee, no matter how powerful or learned.[22]

However, this means that legal decisions are often unpredictable. In the world of international business, commerce and finance, this is considered a source of business liability and risk, and, in general, foreign capital seeks stability and avoids risk. The lack of transparency and the absence of a binding corpus of legal precedent that governs and rationalizes law has meant that Saudi Arabia is losing foreign investment it needs to diversify its economy and create jobs.

Saudi Arabia's laws are governed by the principle of *siyasa shar'iyya* ("governance in accordance with *shari'a*"). This arrangement divides governance between religious-scholars, who address matters of "private" law and rule on these issues based on a personal interpretation of Islamic jurisprudence (*fiqh*), and the king, who addresses matters of "public" law that concern the collective interest of the public. This functional division of labor is often referred to by scholars as the pact between House of Al Sa'ud and the House of Al Shaykh (the descendants of Muhammad ibn 'Abd al-Wahhab, the eighteenth-century founder of what is commonly known as the Wahhabi movement, a strict interpretation of Islam's monotheism that constitutes official Islam in Saudi Arabia).[23] This union of secular and religious authority in Saudi Arabia has been aptly characterized as a "theo-monarchy."[24] The dual nature of the *siyasa shar'iyya* principle of governance is mutually reinforcing: The king issues laws on matters of collective interest (*maslaha*) that rely on Islamic jurisprudence for their legitimacy, and the religious scholars are dependent on the king for his ability to enforce their rulings on matters of private law.[25] Yet while decisions made by the king on matters of public interest are issued as royal decrees that are well-documented statutes (*nizams*) supplementing Islamic jurisprudence, the fiqh itself has remained uncodified. Because commercial matters are governed by fiqh, the lack of transparency caused by the absence of documented codification greatly increases the cost of doing business for both foreign and domestic businesses. Addressing this issue has been at the heart of the king's $2.8 billion program for legal restructuring and reform, which was decreed in October 2007.[26]

Among the salient aspects of the announced reforms, the king replaced the Supreme Judiciary Council with a Supreme Court, and recommended that it establish a web site to begin publishing Islamic legal rulings, or *fatawa* (sing., *fatwa*), and that these rulings — and only these rulings — should be recognized and used by religious scholars as precedent.[27] Critics of the king's plan have maintained that executing the legal reforms are an imaginary proposition, because even if billions of riyals were spent on a physical overhaul of the courthouses and reorganization of the system, it would still be a mere sugar-coating as long as the ideological underpinnings of the system remained untouched. Nevertheless, it seems that rather than challenge the underlying religious foundation of the legal system, the king has simply defined the end goal (codification of legal precedent and new specialty technical courts with properly educated judges) and is going to allow the religious class to battle it out amongst themselves, leaving it to the religious establishment to bring the administration of Islamic jurisprudence into line with the royal decree.

The large Wahhabi religious class in Saudi Arabia is not uniform or ideologically static. While there are only approximately 1,000 official *'ulama*, there are an estimated 18,000 prayer leaders or imams. Some guess that the total number of people belonging to their ranks approaches 80,000. The small group of powerful religious figures who constitute the "religious establishment" are the most important faction. These several dozen religious figures control the Board of Senior *'Ulama* (BSU), the Permanent Committee for Scientific Research and Legal Opinion (CRLO), the Grand Mufti's office, the Supreme Council of Islamic Affairs, and the Council for Islamic Mission and Guidance. Religious scholars also control the Ministry of Pilgrimage and Endowments, the Commission for Promotion of Virtue and the Prevention of Vice (that employs the morality police, or *mutawwi'in*), the Muslim World League (which spreads the Wahhabi doctrine abroad), the Higher Council of Qadis (judges), the muftis of the Grand Mosques in Mecca and Medina, and the Education Ministry.[28]

The *'ulama* of the religious establishment have been ideologically challenged by four groups of non-official religious scholars, some of whom exert considerable influence. The first, *al-Sahwa al-Islamiyya* ("Islamic Awakening") came to the fore in the aftermath of the 1991 Gulf War, when Salman al-'Awdah and Safar al-Hawali, two of the movements' charismatic leaders, were outspoken critics of King Fahd for inviting US troops into the kingdom for its defense. They were also staunch supporters of al-Qa'ida during that period. They were imprisoned in 1994 and then released several years later, and have since worked within the parameters of the Saudi system to advocate their ideas. Al-'Awdah is one of the most popular religious leaders in the kingdom, and Ibrahim al-Sikran and Yusuf al-Ahmad are two other increasingly popular Sahwaeen religious scholars.[29] The second group is the *wasatiyyun* (literally, "those of the middle way") or *'aqlaniyyun* ("rationalists"), a group of former Sahwa shaykhs who try to use independent reasoning (*ijtihad*) to bridge the gap between religious texts and the world as it is. 'Abdalaziz al-Qasim, Hasan al-Maliki, and 'Abdallah al-Hamid, are three prominent members of this group.[30] Al-Qasim works for a prominent international legal firm, and the regime has turned to him on several occasions in recent years for assistance in crafting legal solutions to sensitive issues.[31] The third non-official group are the *takfiri*[32] religious leaders who inspired the militants who carried out a series of terrorist attacks in the kingdom between 2003 and 2007. The most prominent of this group were Nasir al-Fahad, 'Ali al-Khudayri, and Ahmad al-Khalidi.[33] The fourth group that has opposed some of the religious establishment's rulings is a somewhat amorphous group of popular imams who use the internet and television to propagate their own Islamic rulings. Sulayman bin Ahmad al-Duwish, a populist preacher who attacked the decision to permit gender-mixing at the new co-educational King 'Abdullah University of Science and Technology (KAUST), is an example of this growing group of self-appointed religious authorities.[34]

Dutch scholar Roel Meijer has argued that because "there is no constitution and no clearly defined policy for reform...There seems to be an ideological power vacuum in which the state allows liberals and conservatives to slug it out."[35] It would seem that the king *has* defined his parameters for reform in terms of the basic structure and functionality (to include codification and precedent) of the legal system, while permitting the non-establishment *'ulama* to engage in a certain amount of ideological conflict in order to arrive at a natural consensus amongst themselves on issues of Islamic jurisprudence. To the extent the king feels compelled to weigh in on the debate, he usually does so indirectly through the establishment *'ulama,* or through an oblique public pronouncement. In this fashion, the king has avoided direct confrontation with the religious class and preserved his legitimacy founded on the dual nature of governance expressed in the principle of *siyasa shar'iyya.*

What remains to be seen is how fast the king's legal reforms will move forward to meet Saudi Arabia's growing need for more foreign investment. In May 2012, a draft program for the codification of kingdom's *shari'a* courts was submitted by the Board of Senior *'Ulama.*[36] In July 2013, it was reported that the Board of Grievances, one of the highest courts that hears cases related to business disputes, has started to publish its judgments.[37] Further, the Council of Ministers approved a new arbitration law in April 2012 that was intended to provide businesses with a more convenient recourse for resolving disputes.[38] This is a positive step towards bringing the kingdom's commercial procedures in line with those that govern the other members of the World Trade Organization. But critics of the new law contend that arbitration rulings under the new Saudi law can still be overturned if a religious scholar rules the arbitration decision is in violation of *shari'a.*

A key aim of King 'Abdullah's legal reforms was to create a more business-friendly investor climate by creating independent commercial courts, with accompanying appeals tribunals, in order to make commercial contract enforcement faster and more transparent. Yet, in 2012, a legal expert lamented that five years after the king's October 2007 decree, steps toward establishing commercial courts have been insufficient. He said that

> the delay in setting up commercial courts causes immense loss to both Saudi and foreign investors. The investors, who need immediate attention to a dispute, are forced to file their cases at a general court where they must wait several months for their hearing...such moves will cause considerable delay and while the investments are lying idle the company may suspend its activities and bank accounts...a final judgment will only be issued two or three years later.[39]

## Saudization and Education Reform

The debate surrounding the Saudization of employment in the kingdom links the issues of state cohesion, job creation and education reform. Saudization forces foreign companies to employ a certain percentage of Saudi workers, depending on the industry. It also forces foreign companies receiving military contracts to invest 40 percent of the value of the contract in the kingdom. Yet Education Minister Prince Faisal bin 'Abdullah,[40] the king's nephew and son-in-law, recognizes that such state-driven policies make the Saudi economy less globally competitive and can only be a temporary measure.

A real solution, according to Faisal, involves developing the economy, preparing the Saudi labor force, and implementing investment projects in a way that creates demand driven, rather than state mandated job opportunities.[41] However, 'Abdul Rahman Al-Zamil, the president of the Riyadh Chamber of Commerce and Industry, insisted that Saudi Arabia could not survive without Saudization. He said foreign contractors must purchase locally made goods, and that government maintenance contracts were another key to creating jobs for Saudi citizens. The urgency of the Saudization issue manifested itself throughout 2013. After a seven month amnesty for the kingdom's millions of foreign workers ended on November 5th, the Ministry of Interior began deporting thousands of illegal workers.[42] During the amnesty period, one million foreign workers left Saudi Arabia and four million registered for legal status. Many of the remaining illegal workers who were apprehended and deported were from Ethiopia and Yemen. The Yemeni press reported that more than 70,000 Yemeni workers were expelled from Saudi Arabia following the end of the amnesty, and that the local police ended up fighting running street battles with laborers in the poorer parts of Riyadh, resulting in the deaths of at least two Ethiopian workers.[43]

If the Saudi regime's path to consolidating its political power is to diversify the economy so that it can create jobs for its citizens in the medium to long term, its ability to successfully implement education reform will be an important barometer for its success. Karen House has noted that currently Saudi Arabia has an "unproductive economy with widespread unemployment, [one that] is importing labor to perform functions its own citizens are neither educated nor enterprising enough to perform." Saudis received only 9 percent of 2.2 million private sector jobs created in Saudi Arabia between 2002 and 2009. According to House, the government recognizes that "Saudis aren't qualified for the jobs they want and refuse the jobs for which they are qualified."[44]

Saudi officials also seem to understand that it must do more than create desirable jobs. It must also create an education system that will produce young Saudi minds capable of generating scientific and technological innovation and commercial ventures to leverage them. However, Saudi university students have historically showed a strong preference against studying science and technology. In the 1990s, one-fourth of all Saudi university students were enrolled in universities that emphasized programs in Islamic Studies.[45] In 2004, only nine percent of Saudi university graduates had majored in science or technology fields, as compared to 19 percent in Bahrain, 29 percent in Iraq, 25 percent in Jordan, 22 percent in Lebanon, and 19 percent in Morocco.[46] The government has launched a "Horizon" (*Afaq*) program that is designed to reform Saudi higher education. The goal is to reorient Saudi universities away from the traditional emphasis on memorization and repetition in religious studies and instead stress scientific innovation and commercial creativity.

At the institutional level, the state has focused on building universities that train Saudis for specific technocratic professions. Yet there are still no tangible signs the government is taking steps to create an environment that will nurture critical thinking. Between 2005 and 2010, Saudi Arabia created twelve public universities, consisting of colleges that focus entirely on applied sciences. These institutions offer programs in various disciplines, but all of them are related to professional studies, e.g. medicine, where a college might offers programs in dentistry, pharmacy, applied medical sciences, and nursing. These new institutions also offer programs in engineering, computer science, and business technologies.

The Saudi higher education success stories have been King Fahd University for Petroleum and Minerals (KFUPM) in the Eastern Province, which the current king has sought to replicate with the new co-educational King 'Abdullah University for Science and Technology (KAUST). What is intended to be the "MIT" (Massachusetts Institute of Technology) of Saudi Arabia opened in September 2009, and was built in three years at a cost of $3-4 billion. It is located away from its religious critics in Thuwal, near Jidda, along the Red Sea coast. The king has also resisted relentless pressure from the religious establishment to forbid gender-mixing in the classrooms at KAUST. Yet it is not clear how these institutions will imbue their students with skills that foster innovation, creativity, and business entrepreneurship. While both KFUPM and KAUST emphasize science and technology and are geared toward preparing students for research and practice in related fields, it remains to be seen if a technocratic curriculum alone can impart the intangible skills necessary to foster organic economic growth.

The state's emphasis on creating these model universities that emphasize science and technology also appears to be an attempt to circumvent the religious authorities, who maintain control over the Saudi education system. In his book *Awakening Islam*, Stephane Lacroix describes how the Saudi education system was turned over to Muslim Brotherhood ideologues fleeing 'Abdel Nasser in the 1950s and 1960s.[47] Radical Islamic thinkers like Sayyid Qutb influenced a new generation of Saudi neo-*salafi* religious educators who still exercise a great deal of formal and informal influence and control throughout the Saudi education system, particularly in primary and secondary schools. This institutional resistance to education reform has been so powerful that the state has created a public-private partnership called *Tatweer* ("Development") that is intended to circumvent institutional obstacles and create an alternative or parallel educational infrastructure that will deliver the government's vision, rather than a neo-*salafi* vision of Saudi education.

There are very good reasons for the Saudi government to create a parallel education system that risks drawing the ire of the religious officials by undermining their grip on education. Saudi youth are falling far behind by any reasonable statistical measures:

> In 2007, standardized tests were administered to a sample of 8th-grade students in the Kingdom and a host of other countries to assess proficiency in mathematics and science. In mathematics, Saudi Arabia reached rank 48 among 48 countries. The performance gap was substantial in comparison with many countries; for instance, while only 18 percent of Saudi students managed to achieve at least the lowest benchmark for the mathematics test, in Egypt 47 percent of the tested pupils reached that benchmark and in Malaysia 82 percent did. In particular, the Kingdom ranked lower than a number of countries that spend significantly less on education per pupil than Saudi Arabia, like Jordan, Syria, and Tunisia. The science test was slightly better for the Kingdom, as Saudi Arabia ranked 43 out of 48 countries. Still, the gap as compared to countries like Jordan, Malaysia and Egypt was substantial.[48]

These figures suggest that Saudi Arabia is not doing a good enough job creating the human raw material necessary to transition from an oil economy to a knowledge-based economy. It will not be able to lift Saudi employment from 25 percent to the OECD average of 70 percent in the near future unless it can find a way to begin giving its children the skills they need in primary and secondary school.

The state's emphasis on economic diversification and job creation in the near term has led the king to be much more demanding regarding higher education reform. The king's vision for the future can be seen in the fact that law schools have been opened to women despite the fact that women are still not permitted to appear in courts as lawyers. In 2006, women began enrolling in the law school at Riyadh's Prince Sultan University. The king also invested as much as $8 billion in building the beautifully designed all-women's Princess Nora Bint 'Abdulrahman University in Riyadh. The investment is commensurate with demand. Women consist of 60 percent of all university graduates each year. This highlights the biggest weak link in the government's plan to use foreign investment to create desirable and growth generating jobs for Saudis. Only 12 percent of the Saudi labor force is female. In other words, there is a huge segment of Saudi society that is not contributing to its economy. This issue must be resolved if Saudi Arabia is going to transform its political economy from one of state-dependent distribution to one of growth-oriented private production.

The severity of the challenge can be seen in a recent episode in which Muhammad al-Shunnar, a conservative religious figure, initiated a heated debate on Twitter, a microblogging social media site, by posting a picture of a women's marathon at Princess Nora Bint Abdulrahman University and describing it "as a conspiracy to Westernize women in the Kingdom."[49] Despite the fact that participants in the race were exclusively women and no men were allowed to attend, religious critics viewed the event as part of a conspiracy to contaminate and westernize Saudi-Islamic culture. If the state's initiatives to ease women's participation in the economy receive similar popular resistance at each baby step, then short- and medium-term Saudi political cohesion and economic growth will be strained and precarious, at best.

## The Imperative of Integrating Women into the Work Force

In the public sphere, men and women in Saudi Arabia inhabit separate and parallel worlds. Even in the religious sphere, women have a separate space that is organized and led by their own female religious authorities.[50] Gender segregation, and the religious controversy surrounding the question of gender-mixing in public spaces, is an important issue for the state, for two reasons: it creates social and political unrest that generates ill-will from both sides towards the ruling elites and, more importantly, it places restrictions on women's ability to efficiently participate in growing the economy.

The government's strategy toward gender-mixing (*ikhtilat*) has been similar to its approach on codifying the law: it appears to be allowing the various groups of religious scholars time and space to conduct a war of ideas that will ultimately affirm and legitimize a regime-friendly consensus on the issue. The tacit expectation is that a consensus will bridge the gap between the desire to protect religio-cultural norms of the kingdom and the socio-economic imperative of having full participation of women in the economy.

King 'Abdullah's decision to decree 30 women appointments to the state's Consultative Council (*majlis al-shura*) was an appropriate illustration of the king's desire to see women more integrated into the kingdom's workforce. Nevertheless, it was also indicative of the "one-step forward, a half-step back" approach to top-down socio-political reform in general, and women's issues in particular.[51] Two of the appointments were members of the royal family: Princess Sara bint Faisal bin 'Abd al-'Aziz (a daughter of King Faisal, r. 1964–1975) and Princess Moudi bint Khalid bin 'Abd al-'Aziz (a daughter of King Khalid, r. 1975–1982). The other 28 women are highly accomplished professionals, and include a leading pediatrician from the Eastern Province (Dr. Nuhad M. al-Jishi), a doctor in experimental physics (Ferdous S. al-Saleh), and a former undersecretary general of the United Nations (Thoraya A. Obaid). Despite the royal appointments that provided women with an active voice in the Saudi government, the story was not a total victory for women. It was stipulated that male and female members of the Council should be separated during the course of carrying out their duties, even using separate entrances for entering and leaving the *majlis* meeting hall. And while the women were to be sitting in the same hall with the men, they would be sitting in separate areas.

Established in 1992, the Consultative Council's primary function is to serve as a policy debate forum. Its 150 members are all appointed by the king. They review and comment on proposed government legislation, treaties and programs. Perhaps the Council's most important function is to draft the kingdom's five-year development plans, which are the basis for the government's annual budgets. The Council can also summon government officials for questioning and, since 2005, has the authority to propose new laws and amend existing statutes. The Council's importance has grown under 'Abdullah and its role in the Saudi decision-making process is not entirely insignificant.

The pro-royal media argued that the king's decision to appoint women to the Council was based on "approved Islamic doctrine," yet despite avoiding a move towards gender-mixing, the royal decree was met with resistance from certain elements of the Saudi religious class. On January 15, "dozens" of Saudi religious officials took to the streets and silently gathered in front of the Royal *Diwan* in a demonstration against the new edict. The group of clerics who participated in the demonstration drafted a petition outlining their grievances. The two most significant points were their objections to (1) allowing women to participate in sports, referring in particular to the first-ever participation of two female Saudis athletes in the 2012 Summer Olympics in London; and (2) "Normalization of gender mixing in society through encouraging women's employment in different fields [such as] retail, manufacturing, restaurants, law firms and other businesses, as well as allowing women to join the Shura Council and boards of public organizations and delegations."[52]

It is worth noting that a number of prominent conservative Saudi women have also spoken out against the group of women appointed to the Council, not because they are women, but because of their overly liberal views. Nawal al-Eid, a female preacher and academic at Princess Norah University, wrote in *al-Hayat* that the government is promoting the "demands of the minority that are rejected by the majority of Saudi women" and "many have wished that those specialized in *shari'a* law would be included in the council, as they represent the majority of Saudi women."[53]

Nora Alarifi Pharaon points out that for many Islamist adherents in Saudi Arabia, the West is not only a "cultural invader" bringing estrangement, but also a threat to the divine order, which "relies on a clearly defined gender-based cosmology." In the eyes of Islamist women like Nawal al-Eid, "women are oppressed precisely because they try to be 'equal' to men and are, therefore, put in unnatural settings and unfair settings that denigrate them and take away their dignity and integrity as women." In the eyes of Islamic feminists, Western feminism's demand for total equality of the sexes is unduly burdensome and unjust.[54] Be that as it may, the mobilization of dozens of women on October 26, who quietly defied the law and got behind the wheel of a car to protest for the right to drive, was another symbol of an increasingly large segment of Saudi women who are seeking greater gender equity and empowerment.[55]

The large amount of domestic and international publicity generated by the women's protests and the lack of any substantial state crackdown in response, suggests that the royal elites are tacitly behind empowering women, and for good reason. Saudi policymakers have come to realize that educated Saudi women are an increasingly underutilized section of the labor force. However, the state has not translated this recognition into forceful or urgent policy initiatives. If the state wants to create a more skilled labor force, stabilize population growth, increase household income and expand the tax base, it will have to more actively create an acceptable environment for women to participate in the economy, without being ostracized or persecuted by the more religious conservative elements of Saudi society.

However, it seems likely the state will only take small, tentative steps in the direction of women's empowerment in the short term, making incremental institutional adjustments in the direction of gender equity and simultaneously encouraging and quietly prodding the religious establishment to accept new, more gender-inclusive social norms. This process is likely to unfold across a generation and may not be fast enough to propel the economy forward at the rate that Saudi Arabia's evolving demographics seem to demand.

## Economic Diversification in a Changing Political Culture

In late December 2012, a year after the Arab uprisings had erupted across the region, Khalid al-Dakhil, a political sociologist, who wrote an important study on the social origins of the Wahhabi movement, and an important Saudi intellectual, wrote a series of provocative columns that appeared to be addressed to Saudi authorities and attempted to come to terms with meaning of the previous year's tumultuous events for the Saudi state and Saudi society. He tried to capture the sense of change the uprisings represented for both ruler and ruled. He asked,

> What will do in the face of this historical trend that pushes and imposes itself? Are you ready for the fact that what happened to the countries of the Spring may get to you one way or another or affect you in one way or another? Or do you think you are safe from all the implications of what is happening? In both cases, have you taken precautions to face either?[56]

Al-Dakhil claimed that whether one was for or against "the Spring," it created a new historic baseline, and there was no turning back. He argued that the post-uprisings public discourse on Twitter, which 33 percent of all Saudis regularly use, indicated a change in the popular mood in Saudi Arabia, which reflected the people's "attitudes, opinions, and demands on social, political, economic and even religious issues." He said that the widening gap between public opinion and traditional media meant that there was a widening gap between the government and the people.[57]

Al-Dakhil argued that the Saudi rulers had to recognize that the one-way direction of rule from the ruler to his people was desirable more than fifty years ago, when the kingdom was established, but circumstances had changed, and the ruler-ruled relationship should change accordingly. He claimed that political and constitutional reform were necessary: "If fixing the system before 'the Spring' became the demand of the Arab world, it became an unavoidable regional reality after 'the Spring.'" In what seemed like a subtle allusion to the harsh discrimination against the Shi'i in the kingdom, who are sometimes conveniently viewed as an Iranian fifth column, al-Dakhil called on the state to "put the rights of the people before the requirements of foreign relations." He wrote that "synchronized economic and political reform is the only option for the Kingdom to cope with the requirements at this stage." More specifically, he urged the state to reduce bureaucratic growth, stop recycling high-ranking older elite officials, expand the powers of the Shura Council until it is gradually converted into an elected legislature, and diversify the economy.[58]

In his final column, al-Dakhil observed that King 'Abdullah's decisions to reform the judiciary, set up the "Allegiance Council" as an institution to legally manage royal succession and appoint women to the Shura Council represented "a quantum leap in the life of society, as well as the development of the state." However, Al-Dakhil pointed out that "to be responsible, it is necessary to be free." He observed that through the enactment of laws and regulations,

> the state puts the citizen in a position of responsibility, and then gives the citizen the freedom to act...With such, the citizen senses his responsibility, his personality grows, his vision matures, and his is able to solidify this responsibility because he is involved in the formulation of the system, its application, its commitment.[59]

Al Dakhil's argument for individual freedom of choice was a subtle critique of the inherited political processes that had been in place between 1932 and 'Abdullah's October 2007 legal reforms, and reflected the popular sentiment among more liberal Saudis.

For al-Dakhil, a change in the popular mood meant political culture in Saudi Arabia was changing too. And, according to him, the impact of the changing political culture would translate into changes in the regional map, as well as changes "in the concept of the Arab state itself:"

> If the concept of the Arab state is changing, the Saudi state cannot afford to be separated from it because it is part of the Arab political and cultural fabric itself and is influenced by it and should affect it. Saudi Arabia is qualified to hold the reins of vulnerability [during this sensitive period] and take the initiative to influence. The question is: how should this be?[60]

For now, Saudi Arabia's ruling elites are still relying on financial cooption and coercion to manage dissent.[61] They still have the surplus oil wealth to make it work. In the medium to long term, they appear to have chosen a path of economic diversification that will demand real reform in the spheres of education and law. Another barometer for successful socio-economic reform will be the state's ability to empower women. These changes will test the dynasty's grip on power, and bring it into increasing conflict with a diverse religious class that is resistant to change. The future of the Saudi dynasty will depend on its ability to continue to find allies among the religious scholars while navigating a socially acceptable path to economic diversification that satisfies the twin demands of its people for socio-economic well-being and cultural authenticity. Yet change is a slippery slope. It usually begets more change and the Al Sa'ud may find it harder and harder to resist the calls from Khalid al-Dakhil and others for more substantial and swifter political reform.

# Notes

1. Salman al-'Awdah, *Asilat al-Thawra* ["Questions of the Revolution"] (Riyadh: Islam Foundation Today, 1433/2012), p. 189.
2. *The Banker*, "Saudi Arabia — Banking — An enviable position," May 1, 2013.
3. Riad Abu-Manneh and Wisam Sirhan, *Building*, October 14, 2013.
4. Sarah Yizraeli, *Politics and Society in Saudi Arabia: The Crucial Years of Development 1960–1982* (New York: Columbia University Press, 2012), pp. 104–117.
5. A detailed analysis of the Shi'i unrest in Saudi Arabia is beyond the scope of this essay. For a critical treatment of the events, see Toby Matthiesen, "A Saudi Spring? The Shi'a Protest Movement in the Eastern Province 2011–2012, *The Middle East Journal*, Vol. 66, No. 4 (Autumn 2012), pp. 628–659.
6. Perhaps the most radical expression of this hypothesis is Matthew Simmons, *Twilight in the Desert: The Coming Saudi Oil Shock and the World Economy* (New Jersey: John Wiley & Sons, 2005). For a more optimistic attitude towards energy markets and production, see: Daniel Yergin, *The Quest: Energy, Security, and the Remaking of the Modern World* (New York: Penguin Press, 2011).
7. Frank E. Vogel, "Shari'a in the Politics of Saudi Arabia," *The Review of Faith & International Affairs*, Vol. 10, Issue 4 (2012), pp. 18–27.
8. Al-'Awdah, p. 190.
9. Erica S. Downs, "Implications of the U.S. Shale Revolution for China", *Brookings Institution*, November 8, 2013.
10. U.S. Energy Information Administration, "International Energy Outlook 2013," July 2013, p. 3.
11. International Monetary Fund, "Economic Prospects and Policy Challenges for the GCC Countries," October 2012, pp. 12–13.
12. Glada Lahn and Paul Stevens, "Burning Oil to Keep Cool: The Hidden Energy Crisis in Saudi Arabia," Chatham House, The Royal Institute of International Affairs, December 1, 2011, p. 2.

13. Yitzhak Gal, "Arab Use of Energy: Oil out, Renewable Energy in," *Iqtisadi*, September 15, 2013; Arjun Sreekumar, "Is Saudi Arabia Losing Its Importance in the Oil Market?" *The Motley Fool*, April 21, 2013.

14. U.S. Energy Information Administration, "Saudi Arabia Country Brief," February 26, 2013, p. 2.

15. Lahn and Stevens, p. 3.

16. Karen House, *On Saudi Arabia* (New York: Alfred A. Knopf, 2012), pp. 141, 158.

17. "Saudi Arabia major player in the world water market," *Mubasher*, October 3, 2013.

18. Abu-Manneh and Sirhan, October 14, 2013.

19. "Jubail — a growing industrial behemoth," *The Gulf*, October 2013.

20. *Ibid.*

21. *Ibid.*

22. Nathan J. Brown, "Why won't Saudi Arabia write down its laws?", *ForeignPolicy.com*, January 23, 2012.

23. For the most comprehensive English-language analysis of the king's recent legal reforms, see: Ziad A. Al-Sudairy, "The Constitutional Appeal of Shari'a in a Modernizing Saudi State," *Middle East Law and Governance*, Vol. 2, Issue 1 (2010), pp. 1–16.

24. Muhammad Al-Atawneh, "Is Saudi Arabia a Theocracy? Religion and Governance in Contemporary Saudi Arabia," *Middle Eastern Studies*, Vol. 45, Issue 5, pp. 721–737.

25. Frank E. Vogel, "Shari'a in the Politics of Saudi Arabia," *The Review of Faith & International Affairs*, Vol. 10, Issue 4 (2012), pp. 18–19.

26. Royal Decree M/78-19/09/1428H, see: Joseph A. Kechichian, *Legal and Political Reforms in Sa'udi Arabia* (London and New York: Routledge, 2013), p. 27.

27. Kechichian, p. 31.

28. *Ibid.*, pp. 31–33.

29. Stephane Lacroix, "Is Saudi Arabia Immune?," *Journal of Democracy*, Vol. 22, No. 4 (2011), p. 56.

30. Kechichian, pp. 35–36.

31. Al-Sudairy, pp. 1–16.

32. The term "takfiri" refers to "takfir," the act of declaring a Muslim an unbeliever, which makes it acceptable to takfiris to punish that unbeliever with death.

33. Kechichian, p. 36.

34. Roel Meijer, "Reform in Saudi Arabia: The Gender Segregation Debate," *Middle East Policy*, Vol. 17, Issue 4 (Winter 2010), pp. 80–100.

35. *Ibid.*

36. *Arab News*, May 6, 2012.

37. "Saudi court publishes rulings for first time," *Arab News*, July 17, 2013.

38. "Arbitration laws still considered weak, ineffective in Kingdom," *Arab News*, June 8, 2013.

39. "Delay in establishment of commercial courts harmful," *Arab News*, August 25, 2012.

40. Khalid al-Faisal replaced Faisal bin 'Abdullah as education minister on December 22, 2013. Faisal is reported to have asked to have been replaced. While Faisal is the king's

son-in-law, Khalid al-Faisal, who served as the governor of Mecca since 2007, is a more senior prince. See: *Asharq al-Awsat*, December 22, 2013.

41. P.K. Abdul Ghafour, "Saudization is not the solution," *Arab News*, October 1, 2013.

42. *Asharq al-Awsat*, November 6, 2013.

43. Ali Ibrahim Al-Moshki, *Yemen Times*, November 19, 2013; "Go home, but who will replace you?," *The Economist*, November 16, 2013.

44. House, pp. 162.

45. Gwenn Okruhlik, "Empowering Civility through Nationalism: Reformist Islam and Belonging in Saudi Arabia," in Robert W. Hefner (ed.), *Remaking Muslim Politics: Pluralism, Contestation, Democratization* (Princeton, N.J.: Princeton University Press, 2005), p. 195.

46. Paul Rivlin, *Arab Economies in the Twenty-First Century* (Cambridge University Press, 2009), p. 224.

47. Stephane Lacroix, *Awakening Islam: The Politics of Religious Dissent in Contemporary Saudi Arabia* (Cambridge, Massachusetts: Harvard University Press, 2011).

48. Giacomo Corneo, "Stakeholding as a New Development Strategy for Saudi Arabia," p. 4.

49. Laura Bashraheel, "Yet another debate about women," *Saudi Gazette*, November 7, 2013.

50. Amelie Le Renard, "From Quranic Circles to the Internet: Gender Segregation and the Rise of Female Preachers in Saudi Arabia," in Masooda Bano and Hilary Kalmbach (eds.), *Women, Leadership, and Mosques: Changes in Contemporary Islamic Authority* (Boston and Leiden: Brill, 2012), p. 120.

51. The following four paragraphs are based on Brandon Friedman, "The Saudi Kingdom in Transition: Women Appointed to the *Majlis*," *Tel Aviv Notes*, Vol. 7, No. 2, January 28, 2013.

52. Ahmad al-Omran, *Riyadh Bureau*, January 20, 2013.

53. As reported by Ahmad al-Omran, "Saudi Conservative Women Feel Marginalized by Shura Council Snub," *Al Monitor*, January 23, 2013.

54. Nora Alarifi Pharaon, "Saudi Women and the Muslim State in the Twenty-First Century," *Sex Roles*, Vol. 51, No. 5–6 (September 2004), pp. 356–357.

55. Ben Hubbard, "Saudi Women Rise Up, Quietly, and Slide Into the Driver's Seat," *The New York Times*, October 26, 2013.

56. Khalid al-Dakhil, "Saudi writer wonders how long the Kingdom will "isolate" itself from the Arab Spring," *Arab News*, December 17, 2012.

57. *Ibid.*

58. *Idem*, "What awaits the Kingdom after the 'Arab Spring'?," *Arab News*, December 24, 2012.

59. *Idem*, "A Big Step with Confusing Provisions," *Arab News*, January 14, 2013.

60. Khalid al-Dakhil, "Saudi writer wonders how long the kingdom will "isolate" itself from the Arab Spring," *Arab News*, December 17, 2012.

61. Joshua Teitlebaum, "Saudi Arabia Faces a Changing Middle East," *Middle East Review of International Affairs* (MERIA), Vol. 15, No. 3 (September 2011), pp. 76–96.

# "The Arab Spring": The Struggle for Yemen's Future

## Uzi Rabi

In hindsight, the 33-year rule of Yemen's autocratic president 'Ali 'Abdallah Salih was destined to end prematurely. Even before the "Arab Spring" uprising began in Yemen, his government's legitimacy was being challenged by the Huthi rebellion in the north, the secessionist Free South Movement (*al-janub al-hurr* or *al-hirak*), and al-Qa'ida in the Arabian Peninsula (AQAP), seemingly everywhere. The eruption of protests in Yemen's major cities in January 2011 quickly morphed into yet another challenge to Salih's authority. The protests were an unforeseen, game-changing phenomenon in Yemeni politics that turned former Salih allies into open rivals. The ensuing chaos in 2011 led to large swaths of Yemen coming under the de facto control of various non-government entities. As a result of these unexpected developments, Yemen, like Afghanistan and Somalia before it, appeared headed towards the list of failed states.[1]

## Maydan al-Taghyir ("Change Square")

Inspired by the ouster of Tunisia's president Zayn al-'Abidin Ben 'Ali on January 14, 2011, thousands of Yemeni protesters took to the streets in the capital, San'a. Many were under the age of 30. The protests were organized by the Joint Meeting Parties (JMP), a coalition of opposition parties in Yemen's parliament, the most important of which were the Islamist *al-Islah* party and the Yemeni Socialist Party. Tawakul Kirman — a journalist, women's rights activist and, for a time, member of *al-Islah* — was a leading figure in the first few days of the protests. She had called for the initial protests in San'a, and was briefly detained by security forces. Her detention in January 2011 provoked more demonstrations in the major cities of Yemen, which likely explained her release two days later.[2]

The General People's Congress made a poorly timed proposal to change the constitution, in January 2011, which fueled the protests and precipitated a crisis. The proposal would have eliminated presidential term limits, allowing Salih to remain in power after his latest term expired in 2013.[3] It was also well known at the time that Salih had been grooming his son Ahmad to be his successor, despite objections from other powerful figures in the government. Less than two months after the term-limits proposal was made, Salih pledged to his people that he would not seek another term and that Ahmad 'Abdallah Salih would not succeed him as president. Nevertheless, the protesters did not back away from their demand that Salih step down immediately. On February 3, an estimated 20,000 protestors marched in San'a. Change Square (*maydan al-taghyir*), near San'a University, became the hub of the anti-regime demonstrators.

In the early days of the demonstrations, protestors were met by riot police using tear gas and batons. But as it became clear that the protesters had no intention of giving in, the government began using more violence. On February 23, two students were shot dead and another 21 were wounded by pro-government gunmen wearing civilian clothing.[4] This violence foreshadowed even greater carnage that would take place in San'a less than one month later.

At the end of February 2011, 'Ali 'Abdallah Salih suggested forming a national unity government according to the Yemeni constitution in order to prevent the country from descending into chaos. The opposition, however, refused this offer and reiterated their demand for Salih's resignation. In the streets of San'a, the protests continued as demonstrators gathered for the "Friday of Defiance" (*jum'at al-thibat*), using the slogan "Here we are to plant the seeds of the freedom tree."[5]

In a speech delivered before an audience that included high-ranking *'ulama* members of the religious establishment, Salih blamed the opposition for being unwilling to cooperate in forming a national unity government. He emphasized that Yemen belonged to the *umma* (community of Muslim believers).[6] Nevertheless, his statements failed to resonate with the opposition and the protesters.

## A Turning Point

On March 18, 2011, the ranks of protesters in San'a had swelled to approximately 100,000. In the late afternoon, this large crowd was fired upon by uniformed security personnel and plain-clothed gunmen perched on the city's rooftops. By the end of this massacre, 52 people had been killed and hundreds were wounded. The number of casualties was larger than the combined total of protest-related deaths until that day. The government was widely blamed but denied any responsibility. Salih spoke of the victims as "martyrs of democracy."[7] He subsequently fired his entire cabinet, but asked them to remain until a replacement cabinet could be assembled.[8]

The March 18 violence was a turning point in the uprising against Salih. Government and military figures began defecting to the opposition and demanding Salih's resignation.[9] Yemen's ambassador to the UN, 'Abdallah al-

Sa'id, quit on March 20, along with four other government ministers and seven foreign ambassadors.[10] The events of March 18 gave pre-existing rivals the opportunity to openly challenge Salih's legitimacy to an unprecedented extent.

Salih's well-known plans to have his son Ahmad succeed him had already angered rivals, such as General 'Ali Muhsin al-Ahmar, who saw himself as a suitable successor to Salih.[11] Other notable opponents included Shaykh Hamid al-Ahmar and his brother, Shaykh Sadiq (not related to 'Ali Muhsin al-Ahmar) — prominent shaykhs of the Hashid tribal confederation, which included Salih's tribe, the Sanhan. Hamid was also a founding member of the Islamist opposition *al-Islah* party. During the 2006 presidential election campaign, Hamid al-Ahmar had been an outspoken critic of Salih. In a 2009 interview on *al-Jazeera*, he had even called for Salih's resignation.[12] The consensus among Yemen's elites in recent years was that the Sanhan tribe was taking a greater and greater share of a shrinking pie. Men like Muhsin al-Ahmar, and the shaykhs Hamid and Sadiq, were alienated by Salih's plans to consolidate his family's power. When the first protests erupted in January 2011, some supporters of Salih blamed the al-Ahmar family for orchestrating the unrest. It had even been reported that Hamid al-Ahmar paid for food to be brought to protesters camped in San'a's Change Square.[13]

From 1978 to 2012, President Salih had maintained power through a patrimonial system of corruption.[14] The most trusted officials, such as relatives or fellow members of the Sanhan tribal grouping, were given the most sensitive positions involving security and defense. Other allies were both enriched — and held in check — by crony capitalism. This system ensured that no serious threats to Salih emerged within the government. Not only were potential rivals co-opted and brought into Salih's ruling circle, they could easily be subject to campaigns of intimidation or have their privileges revoked if they stepped out of line. But this patrimonial system could not mitigate widespread grassroots opposition. Indeed, the government's failure to handle the Free South Movement, which became active in early 2007, foreshadowed its ineffectiveness in dealing with the Arab Spring.

On March 21, General 'Ali Muhsin al-Ahmar dispatched forces under his command to protect antigovernment protesters in the capital.[15] Ten more senior military commanders also resigned. At the protesters' encampment at San'a University, a rally was held in which former soldiers and policemen took turns announcing their resignations and denouncing the regime. Sadiq al-Ahmar also called on Salih to step down. His brother Hussein had resigned from the government a month earlier. The prospect of a civil war loomed ever larger as tanks belonging to Muhsin al-Ahmar's First Armored Division faced off against those of the loyalist Republican Guard in the Yemeni capital. Al-Ahmar's forces were concentrated around San'a University to protect the protesters, while Salih's forces were centered near the presidential palace and the ministry of defense.

The government's preoccupation with anti-regime protestors clashed with US interests, namely, the struggle against al-Qa'ida in the Arabian Peninsula (AQAP). Although it had been reported that the US supported a peaceful transfer of power during the initial stages of the protests, after March 18, US officials began quietly signaling to their regional allies and the media off the record that Salih's hold on power was untenable and that in the interest of stability he should step down.[16]

The violence against protesters on March 18 decisively eliminated any remaining legitimacy of Salih's rule in the eyes of a vast majority of the population. It also provided popular cover for Salih's rivals like 'Ali Muhsin al-Ahmar and Sadiq al-Ahmar to openly call on the president to resign. The patrimonial system of co-opting potential rivals could not endure such widespread and total condemnation of the regime. With both strong domestic and foreign opposition, Salih's days in power were numbered.

## Gulf States Intervene

In April, the Gulf Cooperation Council (GCC) — consisting of Bahrain, Kuwait, Oman, Qatar, Saudi Arabia, and the United Arab Emirates — began efforts to negotiate a peaceful transition of power in Yemen. Salih was invited to a conference in Riyadh along with the leaders of the Joint Meeting Parties (JMP), a coalition of Yemen's opposition parties. The basic principles of the deal, which came to be known as the Gulf Initiative, were widely circulated before they were officially made public on April 7.[17] Salih was to transfer the powers of the presidency to Vice President 'Abd Rabbu Mansur Hadi. Simultaneously, a coalition government led by the JMP would be put in place, and new elections for both the presidency and parliament would be held two months after the deal went into effect. Last but not least, the Gulf Initiative stipulated that Salih and his relatives would be immune from future prosecution.

While Salih's government made statements that were apparently receptive to the Gulf Initiative, indicating that Salih would "positively embrace" a compromise, in a speech to a crowd of supporters on April 8, Salih explicitly attacked the prime minister of Qatar for meddling in Yemen's domestic affairs. Earlier in the week, Qatar's prime minister had told the media that the GCC wanted Salih gone. Salih seized on this, accusing the GCC of attempting a coup against him.[18] The opposition's reaction to the Gulf Initiative was also mixed. The leaders of the JMP accepted the deal, but the grassroots opposition rejected immunity for Salih and his relatives. The Gulf Initiative in effect exposed a political rift between the anti-establishment protesters and the opposition parliamentarians of the JMP, who wanted Salih out of power, but did not want the revolutionary upheaval called for by the grassroots organizations.[19] Some protesters were also suspicious of the Gulf Initiative because they believed the GCC states were among the region's repressive regimes. Many protesters even viewed Salih as a shill for the Saudis.[20]

Salih's defiance continued through April. He praised the Gulf Initiative while simultaneously insisting that he would not step down until the scheduled end of his term in 2013. These mixed signals aroused the cynicism of the protesters. A statement from the grassroots Youth Revolutionary Council read: "This is the 12th time this month 'Ali [Salih] has told us he is ready to quit, yet he is still here. His promises are worthless to us now. This is political jockeying, nothing else." It was mistakenly reported on April 23 that Salih had signed off on the Gulf Initiative. But yet again, on May 2, Salih backed away from signing the agreement at the last moment.

## Reemergence of Old Rivalries

The first reported clash between Muhsin al-Ahmar's soldiers and the Republican Guard, which at the time was loyal to Salih, was on April 13, 2011, when Republican Guard soldiers seized a checkpoint manned by soldiers of the First Armored Division north of San'a. One opposition soldier was reported to have been killed, and six wounded.[21] The two sides traded fire again on May 12, again in San'a, when al-Ahmar's men came to the aid of protesters who were being fired upon by loyalist forces.[22] These firefights would pale in comparison, however, to the violence that would break out one week later between Salih's loyalist forces and armed Hashid tribesmen.

The struggle between the al-Ahmar family and Salih illustrates how the Arab Spring in Yemen was not only a struggle between the masses and the elites, but also between elites themselves. The al-Ahmar family (to which Gen. Muhsin al-Ahmar is not related) has been the paramount family of shaykhs that lead the Hashid tribal confederation. As previously mentioned, the confederation included Salih's own tribe, the Sanhan. Hailing from the Amran Province north of San'a, the patriarch of the al-Ahmar family was 'Abdallah bin Husayn al-Ahmar until his death in 2007. Even though he was one of the founders of the opposition, al-Islah, 'Abdallah al-Ahmar and President Salih were political allies throughout much of Salih's rule. From 1993 until his death, 'Abdallah was speaker of parliament. Most of his ten surviving sons continued to be active in Yemeni politics.

Tension between the Salih and al-Ahmar families had grown in the years leading up to the Arab Spring. Among the al-Ahmar brothers, the most outspoken critic of President Salih was Hamid al-Ahmar. In a 2010 interview with *al-Jazeera*, Hamid repeated his call for Salih to resign, accusing him of running the state like a family business, even going so far as to accuse Salih of committing high treason.[23] Indeed, well before the events of May 2011, there was an Arabic pun going around in reference to the rivalry "between the two *Bayt* al-Ahmars...." The play on words refers to Shaykh 'Abdallah's surname and the president's home village, *Bayt* al-Ahmar."[24]

Another brother, Hussein al-Ahmar, was a member of Salih's General People's Congress party before he defected to the opposition in February, weeks before the wave of defections that followed the March 18 killings. When announcing his resignation to a crowd of supporters in the Hashid heartland of Amran Province, Hussein called for the overthrow of the regime.[25]

The inevitable clash between the regime and armed tribesmen loyal to the al-Ahmar family came in late May, after the third time that Salih backed out of signing the Gulf Initiative. On May 22, in a televised signing ceremony at the presidential palace in San'a, members of Salih's General People's Congress signed the document, but Salih conspicuously did not. The event was meant to be a face-saving spectacle for Salih, who insisted on opposition leaders being present to sign the agreement. The opposition leaders had signed the document the previous evening on May 21. Since they refused to attend, Salih refused to sign. In his remarks on state television, Salih made a statement that was representative of his strategy to deal with the mounting crisis, which was to convince Yemenis and the world that he was the only alternative to civil war and chaos: "If they [the opposition leaders] don't bow, and want to take the country into a civil war, let them be responsible for it and for the blood that was shed and that will be shed if they insist on their stupidity," he said.[26] At this point, the GCC announced that it was halting its efforts at mediation.

On May 23, heavy fighting erupted between soldiers loyal to Salih and approximately 500 gunmen loyal to Sadiq al-Ahmar. The fighting was concentrated around al-Ahmar's residence in San'a as well as several government ministry buildings. Both sides used heavy weapons, including artillery and mortars. The interior ministry and al-Ahmar's residential compound were shelled. Both sides accused each other of being the first to fire, and opposition leaders claimed that Salih was intentionally trying to provoke a civil war in order to remain in power.[27] After several days of fighting and dozens of casualties, Hashid gunmen claimed to have taken over the interior ministry building, the headquarters of the state-run television station and Yemen Airways.[28] Fighting had also spread beyond the capital by May 26, with Hashid tribesmen engaging

Republican Guard forces. Thousands of fighters were trying to reach the capital while Salih's soldiers attempted to stop them.[29] A truce established on May 27 had broken down by May 31. Throughout much of this period, 'Ali Muhsin al-Ahmar's First Armored Division remained neutral. Most of the fighting was concentrated in the Hasaba District in the northeastern part of San'a.

## Losing the Periphery

The elite units of Yemen's military were meant to defend the regime as much as Yemen itself. With the regime facing unprecedented challenges to its authority, the military units that were still loyal to Salih were concentrated against the forces of Sadiq al-Ahmar, mainly in and around San'a.

On May 27, militants belonging to an Islamist militant group called *Ansar al-Shari'a* ("Supporters of Islamic Law") seized control of the town of Zinjibar, the capital of Abyan Province. This was the most alarming indication up to that point that al-Qa'ida-affiliated groups were filling the vacuum left by the shrinking presence of Salih's government outside of the major cities. Perhaps due to US pressure, the Yemeni air force and some ground forces did confront Ansar al-Shari'a, but the town was only brought back under government control after nearly two months of continuous fighting, by which time many of the town's 54,000 inhabitants had fled.[30] By contrast, the evolving crisis in the northern province of Sa'da went unresolved.

Since 2005, the Huthi insurgency in the northern Sa'da province had been growing into a serious threat to the territorial integrity of the Yemeni state. Prior to the Arab Spring, two of the forces most often deployed to suppress the Huthis were Muhsin al-Ahmar's First Armored Division and Hashid tribal militias loyal to Sadiq al-Ahmar. With both of Salih's former allies now confronting his forces in the capital, the Huthis finally saw an opportunity to exert their control over the northern province near the Saudi border. Two days after Muhsin al-Ahmar defected, on March 20, 2011, Sa'da came under de facto control of the Huthis. The insurgency installed its own governor, cementing its control in the province.[31]

## The Fall of Salih

On June 3, shortly after Friday prayers, an explosion at the entrance to the mosque in the presidential compound claimed the lives of eleven guards. Salih and six senior officials were wounded. [32] Initial reports described Salih's injuries as light,[33] but when he was flown to Riyadh for medical treatment on June 5, it became clear that Salih was gravely injured. Although the al-Ahmars never claimed responsibility for the attack, they were the immediate target of blame and heavy fighting resumed in the capital.

The remainder of 2011 witnessed additional instances of AQAP taking over towns, the Huthi consolidation of Sa'da Province, and a stalemate in San'a between loyalist forces, anti-government Hashid tribesmen, and Muhsin al-Ahmar's First Armored Division. There would not be any additional dramatic political realignment to match that which followed the March 18 shootings. In early June, when Salih was flown to Riyadh for medical treatment, anti-government protestors rejoiced in the belief that Salih would not return. However, in September, Salih surprised many when he returned to Yemen, as defiant as ever. Although Salih's return prompted a temporary surge in violence in the capital, he eventually acquiesced to the Gulf Initiative on November 23. On January 22, 2012, Salih left Yemen for medical treatment in the US He returned in February to be present when Vice President Mansur Hadi was officially sworn in as Yemen's new president on February 25, 2012.[34]

Although Salih's tenure as president of Yemen finally came to an end, his family's enduring influence over the government, especially among the most well-trained, well-equipped units of Yemen's military, suggests that the Salih family will continue to play an influential role in the expected transfer of power from the GPC to a post-Salih coalition government. Meanwhile, it remains to be seen whether Yemen's post-Salih government will be able to reverse the erosion of state authority in the face of the Huthis, the *Hirak*, and al-Qa'ida in the Arabian Peninsula (AQAP).

# Post-Salih Yemen

As of December 2013, Yemen's future as a viable, unitary state remained in doubt. The Huthis maintained firm control over Sa'da, Zinjibar was in the hands of al-Qa'ida, and fighting in San'a continued to rage between Yemen's tribal militias forces, which were no longer kept under control by Salih's iron fist. Part of the challenge of understanding of dynamic of post-Salih Yemen is predicting how old tribal alliances will interact with the new emerging political players. For decades, Salih cleverly balanced the interests of his political rivals to maximize his control of the state. But when the entire spectrum of Yemen's opposition succeeded in toppling the regime, the delicate balance of interests that had been carefully maintained quickly unraveled. The uprising in Yemen brought starkly different visions for Yemen's future into focus, resulting in a perfect storm that eventually toppled the Salih regime.

The American factor must be considered when trying to discern what is driving the reconfiguration of alliances in Yemen. Since September 2011, the frequency of American drone strikes under the auspices of the CIA significantly increased.[35] The American involvement was principally focused on neutralizing al-Qa'ida in the Arabian Peninsula. While American drone strikes succeeded in killing top AQAP leader Anwar al-'Awlaki in late 2011, the unmanned aerial bombings have resulted in a high number of civilian casualties, which some believed has counterproductively pushed Yemeni tribesmen towards an alliance with al-Qa'ida affiliated groups and away from any potential cooperation with the regime.[36] More generally, American hesitance and inconsistency towards other conflicts in the region have fostered a growing perception among Yemen's tribal elites that America may no longer serve as a viable patron, further strengthening the appeal of AQAP's virulent anti-American zeal.

For Yemen's tribesmen, the motivation to join AQAP stems not from a desire to turn Yemen into an Islamic state, but from a desire to avenge the deaths of their fallen. "'I would fight even the devil to exact revenge for my nephew,'" said former Yemeni soldier Abu Bakr 'Idrus, who deserted in response to the death of his nephew from an American strike.[37] 'Idrus insisted that his newfound sympathy for AQAP was due to hatred of the United States, and not al-Qa'ida's Islamist agenda. Similarly, in the north, religious disputes were secondary to tribalism. Late 2013 saw an uptick in fighting between Shi'i Huthis and Sunni salafis in Sa'da Province, in and around the city of Dammaj.[38] Militants on both sides claimed that religion had less to do with the conflict than tribal feuds that had reemerged since the fall of Salih. The Hadi government was ineffective in extending its control to the north and mediating a ceasefire.

Throughout the period of instability that has gripped Yemen since the Arab Spring protests spread to San'a, a reemergence of pre-modern tribal alliances has complicated the political landscape. Perhaps more so than in any other state affected by the recent upheavals, pre-modern, even pre-Islamic, tribal affiliations have provided the strong undercurrent shaping the course of events in post-Salih Yemen. While the young protestors at Change Square certainly played their role in bringing down the regime, much older fault lines have since been exposed among Yemen's political elites, providing the fuel that continues to propel the ongoing conflicts. The territorial integrity of the Yemeni state remains in doubt. As the era of nationalist ideology fades, the future of Yemen depends strongly on how primordial tribal forces interact in the new political landscape that has emerged since the fall of 'Ali 'Abdallah Salih.

*Special thanks to my research assistant Jordan Sokolic for gathering material and contributing to this article.*

# Notes

1. For analysis on some of the definitions of a failed state, see: Robert Rotberg, *When States Fail: Causes and Consequences* (Princeton: Princeton University Press, 2003) and Fund for Peace, "Failed States Index" available: www.fundforpeace.org/global/?q=fsi.

2. Kirman would later go on to receive the 2011 Nobel Peace Prize with two other women's rights activists. Kirman was among those protesting against Salih even before the Arab uprisings. To a large extent, she acted under the auspices of a movement of which she was one of the founders, named *sahafiyyat bila hudud* ("Female Journalists with no Boundaries"). See: *Al-Sharq al-Awsat*, October 8, 2011.

3. "US Objects to GPC Constitutional Amendments", Nationalyemen.com, January 3, 2011, http://nationalyemen.com/2011/01/03/us-objects-to-gpc-constitutional-amendments/.

4. Tom Finn, "Yemeni protestors shot dead at Sana'a University," *The Guardian*, February 23, 2011, http://www.guardian.co.uk/world/2011/feb/23/yemen-protesters-shot-dead-university.

5. *Al-Sharq al-Awsat*, April 8, 2011.

6. *Al-Sharq al-Awsat*, March 1, 2011.

7. Tom Finn, "45 protestors killed in Yemen," *The Guardian*, March 18, 2011, http://www.guardian.co.uk/world/2011/mar/18/yemen-police-massacre-45-protesters.

8. Laura Kasinof, "Yemen's president said to have fired cabinet," *The New York Yimes*, March 20, 2011, http://www.nytimes.com/2011/03/21/world/middleeast/21yemen.html?scp=648&sq=Yemen&st=nyt.

9. *Al-Sharq al-Awsat*, March 23, 2011.

10. Tom Finn, "Yemen military commanders join opposition as tanks take to the streets," *The Guardian*, March 21, 2011, http://www.guardian.co.uk/world/2011/mar/21/yemen-military-commanders-opposition-tanks.

11. *Ibid.*, p. 407.

12. April Longley Alley, "The Rules of the Game: Unpacking Patronage Politics in Yemen," *The Middle East Journal*, Vol. 64, No. 3 (Summer 2010), p. 402.

13. Robert F. Worth and Laura Kasinof, "Evasions by leader add chaos in Yemen," *The New York Times*, May 25, 2011, http://www.nytimes.com/2011/05/26/world/middleeast/26yemen.html.

14. For more on this, see: April Longley Alley, "The Rules of the Game: Unpacking Patronage Politics in Yemen," *The Middle East Journal*, Vol. 64, No. 3 (Summer 2010), pp. 385–409.

15. "Top Yemeni General, Ali Mohsen, Backs Opposition", *BBC News*, 21 March 2011, http://www.bbc.co.uk/news/world-middle-east-12804552.

16. Laura Kasinof and David E. Sanger, "US shifts to seek removal of Yemen's leader, an ally," *The New York Times*, April 3, 2011, http://www.nytimes.com/2011/04/04/world/middleeast/04yemen.html?pagewanted=1&_r=2&hp.

17. For more details, see: *Al-Sharq al-Awsat*, April 25, 2011.

18. Laura Kasinof, "Gulf nations repeat offer to mediate crisis in Yemen," *The New York Times*, April 10, 2011. http://www.nytimes.com/2011/04/11/world/middleeast/ 11yemen.html?scp=58&sq=Yemen&st=cse.

19. For more details, see: *Al-Sharq al-Awsat*, April 12, 2011.

20. Tom Finn, "Yemen resolution unlikely as president dismisses Gulf plan to end rule," *The Guardian*, April 8, 2011, http://www.guardian.co.uk/world/2011/apr/08/ yemen-president-gulf-saleh.

21. Laura Kasinof, "Yemen's loyalists clash with defiant troops," *The New York Times*, April 13, 2011, http://www.nytimes.com/2011/04/14/world/middleeast/14yemen. html?scp=6&sq=Yemen+al-Ahmar&st=nyt.

22. Tom Finn, "Yemeni forces kill 18 and wound hundreds as unrest escalates," *The Guardian*, May 12, 2011, http://www.guardian.co.uk/world/2011/may/12/yemen-protests-republican-guards-troops.

23. Gregory D. Johnsen, "Yemen's coming power struggle," *The National*, March 18, 2010, http://www.thenational.ae/news/world/yemens-coming-power-struggle?page Count=0#full.

24. Gregory D. Johnsen, "The al-Ahmar Family: Who's who," *Waq al-Waq*, June 3, 2011, http://bigthink.com/ideas/38715?page=all.

25. Laura Kasinof and Neil MacFarquhar, "Key tribal chief wants Yemen leader to quit," *The New York Times*, February 26, 2011, http://www.nytimes.com/2011/02/27/ world/middleeast/27yemen.html?scp=4&sq=Yemen+al-Ahmar&st=nyt#.

26. "Yemen transition deal collapses," *Al-Jazeera*, May 22, 2011, http://www.aljazeera. com/news/middleeast/2011/05/201152216373928689.html.

27. Tom Finn, "Yemen locked in power struggle as escalation of fighting leaves 38 dead," *The Guardian*, May 24, 2011, http://www.guardian.co.uk/world/2011/may/24/ yemen-saleh-ahmar-capital-fighting.

28. "Yemen airport shut as tribes battle Saleh," *BBC*, May 26, 2011, accessed March 7, 2012, http://www.bbc.co.uk/news/world-middle-east-13544243.

29. Uri Friedman, "Yemeni tribesmen advance on the capital," *The Atlantic Wire*, June 2, 2011, http://www.theatlanticwire.com/global/2011/06/yemeni-tribesmen-advance-capital/38405.

30. *Al-Jazeera*, July 17, 2011, http://blogs.aljazeera.net/liveblog/yemen-jul-17-2011-1211.

31. "Houthis control Sa'ada, help appoint governor," *National Yemen*, March 29, 2011, http://nationalyemen.com/2011/03/29/houthis-control-sa%E2%80%99ada-help-appoint-governor/.

32. Peter Beaumont, "Yemeni president arrives in Saudi Arabia as truce breaks in capital," *The Guardian*, June 5, 2011, http://www.guardian.co.uk/world/2011/ jun/05/yemeni-president-saudi-arabia.

33. Robert F. Worth and Laura Kasinof, "Yemeni president wounded in palace attack," *The New York Times*, June 3, 2011, http://www.nytimes.com/2011/06/04/world/ middleeast/04yemen.html?pagewanted=1&_r=1&sq=Yemen%20al-Ahmar&st= nyt&scp=7.

34. Laura Kasinof, "Yemen Swears In New President to the Sound of Applause, and Violence," *The New York Times*, February 25, 2012, http://www.nytimes.

com/2012/02/26/world/middleeast/abed-rabu-mansour-hadi-sworn-in-as-yemens-new-president.html?_r=2&ref=global-home&.

35. Karen DeYoung, "US Increases Yemen Drone Strikes," *The Washington Post*, September 17, 2011, http://www.washingtonpost.com/world/national-security/us-increases-yemen-drone-strikes/2011/09/16/gIQAB2SXYK_story.html.

36. "Islamist cleric Anwar al-Awlaki killed in Yemen," *BBC*, September 30, 2011, http://www.bbc.co.uk/news/world-middle-east-15121879.

37. Sudarsan Raghavan, "In Yemen, US airstrikes breed anger, and sympathy for al-Qaeda," May 30, 2012. http://www.washingtonpost.com/world/middle_east/in-yemen-us-airstrikes-breed-anger-and-sympathy-for-al-qaeda/2012/05/29/JQAUmKI0U_story.html.

38. "Salafis are taking heavy casualties as sectarian tensions continue in Sa'ada," *Yemen Post*, December 12, 2013, http://www.yemenpost.net/Detail123456789.aspx?ID=100&SubID=7428&MainCat=5.

# PART III
# Egypt and Sudan

# The Copts of Egypt: Fully Fledged Citizens or a New Dhimmi?

## Mira Tzoreff

Within the space of two and one-half years, Egypt experienced two regime changes: the revolution of January 25, 2011 that toppled its long-ruling autocratic president Hosni Mubarak, and the revolutionary *coup d'état* on June 30, 2013 that removed the elected president, Mohammed Morsi, from office. Neither was to the benefit of Egypt's Coptic minority, which constitutes approximately 10 percent of Egypt's 80 million people. In fact, they each occasioned a significant deterioration in their status, adversely affecting their daily lives both as individuals and as a group.

Egypt has long been considered among the most socially cohesive of all Arab states. But the increased difficulty faced by its Coptic minority raises serious questions about this idyllic image. This study will examine the status of Egypt's Copts in the post-Mubarak era, while providing the necessary background context.

## The Status of the Copts in Egypt — Historical Perspective

The Coptic Church was founded in Egypt during the first century of Christianity, six centuries prior to the arrival of Islam in the land of the Nile. However, during the formative period of the modern Egyptian state, the Copts did not flaunt their extended heritage in the country, even though their status as the "original Egyptians" (which would subsequently be emphasized in the Coptic discourse) might have helped them in their efforts to insure their status as full and equal citizens. Furthermore, the Coptic language, which evolved from ancient Egyptian and began to be written in Greek letters in the first century A.D., was a dynamic, vital, and vibrant spoken language until the seventeenth century, when Arabic replaced it, even in Church rituals.[1]

The history of the Coptic minority in Egypt in the nineteenth and twentieth centuries was characterized by an on-going effort of the community's leadership to achieve political, social, and cultural integration with the Muslim majority, which at times came at the price of blurring the Copts' cultural and linguistic particularism. The abolition of their obligation to pay *jizya* (a head tax paid by non-Muslims throughout the Ottoman Empire) in 1855 is considered to have formalized their full integration into Egyptian society. Moreover, throughout the nineteenth century the Copts were active in the country's modernization project: the Coptic Patriarch Kyrill IV (1854-1861) founded schools for boys as well as the first native school for girls. He also established a printing press that contributed to the renaissance of the Coptic theological and literary heritage; for these initiatives, Kyrill IV was called the "father of the reform movement" *(abu al-islah)*.[2]

The Copts were also involved in Egypt's broader political processes. For example, Copts were full-fledged members of the Council of Representatives *(Majlis Shura al-Nuwwab)* established by Khedive Isma'il (r. 1863-1879) with the aim of consolidating an Egyptian political community without reference to its members' religious or ethnic affiliation.[3] Figures from the Coptic community served in senior positions in the Egyptian bureaucracy and print media. *Al-Watan*, which first appeared in 1877,[4] had a Coptic editor, Micha'il 'Abd al-Sayyid, and its target audience was the Coptic community. *Al-Watan* was also supported by Isma'il, who aspired to imbue the Copts with a sense of belonging to the Egyptian political community. The Copts took also an active part in the Egyptian national struggle for independence and sovereignty while supporting the 'Urabi Revolt in 1882.

However, the Copts were opposed by some of the leaders and activists of the Egyptian national movement, who portrayed those employed by the British colonial bureaucracy, particularly those engaged in agriculture during the period of Lord Cromer (1883-1907), as collaborators who benefited from jobs that should have been occupied by the authentic Muslim *effendiyya* — the urban, highly educated, Westernized young Egyptians. For their part, Copts complained that Cromer's colonial regime preferred to fill governmental positions with Muslims, Syrian-Lebanese immigrants, and members of the Armenian community, rather than with Copts.[5] In order to refute these accusations Lord Cromer stated: "the only difference between the Copt and the Moslem is that the former is an Egyptian who worships in a Christian church whilst the latter is an Egyptian who worships in a Mohammedan mosque."[6] With this in mind, activists of the Egyptian national movement hardened their criteria for determining who was an Egyptian and left the Copts as merely a religious minority that was only a guest in the homeland *(watan)* of the Egyptian Muslims.

Mustafa Kamel (1874-1908), the popular leader of the Egyptian national movement, gave expression to the nationalists' ambivalent attitude toward the non-Muslims in Egypt. On the one hand, he introduced the idea of an Islamic-Pharaonic Egyptian identity that enabled the two religions, Islam and

Christianity, to co-exist, and defined the "Copts and Muslims as one united nation in their national identity, customs, character, and way of life. They cannot be separated one from the other since they are brethren in one homeland." On the other hand, he advocated the unity of Muslims, reaching across national boundaries and contributing to the strengthening of the leading Islamic power, the Ottoman Empire, against colonialism. This, according to Kamel should not be regarded as opposed to Egyptian *watani* patriotic priciples.[7]

Kamel's National Party program caused many previously-supportive Copts to rethink their position, as it positioned the Muslim Iranian, Afghan, and Tunisian on an equal footing with Egyptian Muslims, while the Copts were put at a lower level.[8] Thus, it was no coincidence that precisely at this juncture in history the Copts began to deviate from their assimilationist pattern of conduct. For example, in 1900 representatives of the young generation of Copts called for a cultural and linguistic revival and internal reforms in the Church. The group demanded the establishment of a seminary in Cairo to train divinity students and a Sunday school system for young Copts wherever needed. Members of the group called for the establishment of a Coptic political party whose main aim would be to defend the rights of Christians in general and the Copts in particular. The Coptic-Muslim feud peaked following the sudden death of Mustafa Kamel in 1908, as 'Abd al-'Aziz Jawish, then editor in chief of *al-Liwa*, the media organ of the Nationalist Party, wrote an ironic and offensive article in which he claimed that the Copts owed their survival to Islam.[9]

For the Copts, as "people of the book," *(ahl al-kitab)*, the rules of *dhimmi* (non-Muslim communities protected by Muslim rule) still applied (apart from the *jizya* payment). These rules provided for the protection of the dhimmi peoples' lives and property rights, but did not necessarily grant them full citizenship and civil equality. Yet in the eyes of many Muslim legal scholars, the status of dhimmi indicates religious tolerance, and even pluralism. To prove their point, they cite verses from the Qur'an, like Verse 256 of the *Surat al-Baqarah* (The Cow), "There is no compulsion in religion."[10] Another verse interpreted in the same spirit is Verse 6 of the *Surat Al-Kāfirūn* (The Disbelievers), "For you is your religion, and for me is my religion." [11]

At the end of World War I, many politically concious Copts joined the *Wafd* Party, whose platform was based on national unity and equality for all of Egypt's citizens. Its slogan was "religion belongs to God, the fatherland to all citizens."[12] Asked about the *Wafd*'s attitude towards the various religious faiths of its members, Sa'd Zaghlul, its undisputed leader, replied: "equal duties and equal rights for all."[13] To be sure, the first Egyptian constitution, which came into force in 1923, contained an explicit stipulation in Clause 2 that *shari'a* was the primary source for Egyptian legislation. Yet, during Egypt's first five years of (limited) independence, when Zaghlul was active in the political arena (1922-26), Copts held prominent ministerial positions, including minister of foreign affairs, communication, transportation and finance and budget. Sa'd Zaghlul's inclusive patriotism even resulted in a change in the Egyptian flag, which had been initially designed with the Islamic symbols of a crescent and three stars.

Tension between Muslims and Copts during this period peaked in the 1940s when Coptic activists established, at the initiative of a law student, Ibrahim Hilal, an organization called the "Coptic Nation Society" *(Jama'a al-Umma al-Qibtiyya)*, which became a political party in 1952.[14] The movement had its own flag and uniform, and it encouraged its members to learn the Coptic language. One of its demands was to receive a permit to open its own radio station.[15] The Free Officers *coup d'état* of July 23, 1952 and subsequent rise to power of Gamal 'Abd al-Nasser further deepened the cleavages between Muslims and Copts. Nasser's regime eventually carried out a sweeping nationalization program in the name of Arab socialism. Consequently, much property and many businesses belonging to Copts were nationalized, impoverishing many and thus damaging their social standing and influence.[16] Furthermore, during this period, the army increasingly served as a channel for social mobility. As Copts were not drafted into the army, they were denied access to many public offices reserved for army veterans. As a result, for the first time many Copts chose to emigrate to the United States, Canada, and Australia.

## Copts in the Sadat and Mubarak Eras (1970-2011)

Prior to the 2011 revolution, the public discussions surrounding the status of the Coptic community had always focused on the Copts' similarities to the Muslim majority. The heads of the Coptic community went so far as to refuse to view themselves as a minority group. Thus, in 1994, for example, the Coptic Patriarch Shenouda III claimed that, "We do not accept being distinguished from other Egyptians. We do not like to think of ourselves as a minority, and we are not interested in having others relate to us as a minority. We are Egyptians, part of Egypt, of the same nation." [17]

By Egyptianizing the Coptic collective identity the Coptic Church contested the constructions of "Otherness." One of the points of the Coptic narrative of sameness was the way Rubir Khalaf, the editor of the Coptic newspaper "The News of the Nation," described Shenouda III as an Egyptian through and through who loves "the sand of the nation and sanctifies his country's water from the Nile."[18] For an Egyptian the Nile is not simply an essential part of the national territory but it also molds the Egyptian identity regardless of religion, ethnicity or gender. Thus, Copts embody and are an integral part of the national organism. Milad Hanna, a Coptic intellectual and a former member of the People's Assembly emphasized the Coptic-Muslim mix that was put together under the auspices of the land of the Nile, and argued that Egyptian identity consisted of seven layers: the Pharaonic, Hellenistic (Greco-Roman), Coptic, Islamic, Arabic, Mediterranean, and African. According to Hanna, every Egyptian, no matter whether educated or illiterate, rich or poor, Copt or Muslim bears within himself all of these basic elements. Hanna claims also that Egyptian Islam has the peculiarity of having been influenced by all the layers of civilizations preceding it and hence its special flavor which one can notice in the Egyptian's high degree of tolerance.[19] Hanna added that the Egyptian personality consisted of a Sunni face, Shi'i blood, a Coptic heart, and Pharaonic bones.[20] The Coptic leadership translated the abstract idea of the double-faceted identity of the Copts into practical modes of action by organizing tours for both members of their own community (especially youth) and Christian tourists to monasteries, churches, and holy places aiming at illustrating the way the national, the religious, and the personal identities are intertwined. By touring the length and breadth of the national territory and at the same time traveling along the Egyptian-Christian topography, they were also able to demonstrate their authentic sense of belonging.[21]

The public discussions regarding the Copts' similarity to Muslims were connected to the debate over national unity. At the center of the latter debate was the claim that the Copts were an integral part of the Egyptian nation, they had all the characteristics making up the "Egyptian personality" (al-Shakhsiyya al-Misriyya), and for this reason they were integrated into Egyptian society in a harmonious way. Patriarch Shenouda III, in a documentary presented by the Al-Jazeera television news network, also expressed the deep linkage between the Copts and Egypt when he said that, "Egypt is not a land in which we live, but a nation that lives within us."[22]

These discussions overlapped with an additional one, the issue of the Copts' "firstness," or primordiality. Thus, for example, the Secretary-General of the Coptic Holy Synod, Anba Bishoi, said that the Copts are the native Christians of Egypt and the direct descendants of the ancient Egyptian Pharaohs. He claimed also that "The Copts were the first to put down roots in Egypt, but despite this, we welcome with love the guests (i.e., the Muslims) who came and settled in our land."[32] Nevertheless, according to the militant Copt narrative, following the Arab conquest that turned them into dhimmi, and especially after the "Pact of 'Umar" was formulated in the eighth century — according to which the Copts were prohibited from assembling, bearing arms, and building or renovating churches — Copts have felt like aliens in their homeland.

Indeed, despite the seniority of the Copts in Egypt and their efforts to integrate and assimilate into Egyptian society, throughout history, the Copts have remained second-class citizens. This was the case even though Clause 40 of the Egyptian Constitution of 1971 guarantees political, legal, and social equality to Muslims and non-Muslims. Moreover, Clause 46 asserts that the state shall ensure freedom of belief and worship, and Clause 8 promises equality of opportunity for all Egyptians, regardless of religion, ethnic identity, or race. However, besides the clauses promising equality, Clause 2 of the constitution states explicitly that Islam is the official religion of the state, the Arabic language is its official language, and the principles of *shari'a* are the main source of the state's legislation.

Copts engage in a very wide array of professions. Eighty percent of the pharmacists and 30 to 40 percent of the physicians in Egypt are Copts. Similarly, a high percentage of engineers and lawyers are Copts. A significant percentage of them are also active in the country's private sector. However, in addition to their large presence in the free and white collar professions, many Copts also work as sanitation workers *(zabaleen)*, as a result of which they are included in the category Donald L. Horowitz called unranked ethnicity.[24]

Although Copts constitute approximately ten percent of Egypt's population, their representation in government institutions is marginal, and their political representation in the bicameral Egyptian parliament is negligible. Thus, for example, in the elections held in the year 2000, only six Copts were elected to parliament, and in the 2005 elections, their number declined to just three. Moreover, in these elections only one Copt, Youssuf Boutrus Ghali, could be found among the ruling National Democratic Party's parliamentary faction. In 2007, the regime broke its promise to the heads of the Coptic Church to grant adequate representation to Copts in the list of candidates in the elections to the *Shura* Council. The Egyptian government before the January 25, 2011 revolution also included just two ministers from the Coptic community: Ghali, who served as minister of finance, and Maged George, who served as minister of state for environmental affairs.[25] In the elections that took place on November 28, 2010, only 6 Copts were elected to the Shura Council and 10 to the People's Assembly.[26] In 1942, by comparison, of the 264 members of parliament, 27 were Copts.[27] In addition, the community has had no representation in the army or the police, or even in the intelligence and diplomatic services, even though by law five percent of all jobs in these institutions are designated for them.

Their representation in the courts and the institutions of higher education is also negligible. For example, of the 17 public universities, with 274 deans, only one dean is a Copt. Of the 1,183 department heads, only 16 are Copts. Of the 71 senior administrative positions in academic institutions (president, vice president), not even one is held by a Copt.[28] It goes without saying that there is no Coptic university in Egypt, and that the Coptic language and Coptic history are not taught in any university. Copts are not allowed to enter Al-Azhar University, much less study there. In every school in Egypt there are mosques for the convenience of the students, but no places for worship are provided in educational institutions for Christians. All Arabic teachers in Egypt must be Muslim. Copts seeking to teach Arabic are rejected outright.

The four decades between Nasser's death in 1970 and the overthrow of Mubarak were marked by a further increase in religious tension in Egypt. Anti-Copt violence perpetrated by radical Islamists proliferated, including the torching of churches and the killing of Copts in church compounds. Such crimes were countered by protest demonstrations of inter-faith solidarity.

Nonetheless, this violence reached a peak on New Year's Eve, January 1, 2011, on the brink of the 2011 revolution, when a suicide bombing was carried out at the Elkedeseen (Two Saints) Church in Alexandria, just as worshippers were leaving the holiday service. The bombing left 21 dead and nearly 100 wounded. In the wake of the carnage, Hosni Mubarak urged both Christians and Muslims to unite in order to confront terrorism. Moreover, Hosni Mubarak called the victims of the church massacre "martyrs" (shuhada'), a term that is usually reserved in official discourse for Muslims only.[29] Youth of Mubarak's National Democratic Party announced that as a sign of solidarity with the Coptic community, they intended to take part in the upcoming Eastern Orthodox Christmas Mass. Among those who joined the initiative was 'Abd al-Mun'im Abu al-Futuh, previously a member of the Muslim Brotherhood's policy-setting Shura Council (he would subsequently leave the movement after the January 2011 revolution). In schools and universities, students stood in a moment of silence in memory of those killed.[30] Ahmed al-Taib, the Sheikh of Al-Azhar, paid a condolence visit to the Coptic Patriarch, Shenouda III, during which Coptic demonstrators attacked the Sheikh's automobile. Nevertheless, al-Taib insisted on demonstrating solidarity, and not from afar, in order to show that unity reigned between Muslims and Copts.[31] The Wafd Party recommended marking the Coptic New Year as "The Day of National Unity," and on the practical level, the government recommended monetary compensation to the families of the victims (20000EL – $3445) and wounded (5000EL – $861).[32] Participants in the solidarity demonstrations carried signs proclaiming slogans such as: "With my blood and my soul I will defend the cross. We are all Copts, we are all Egyptians, and we are all brothers and sisters."[33] Nor did the media remain indifferent. Thus, for example, Al-Ahram published an article by Abdel-Moneim Said, who defined three missions for the regime: 1) an uncompromising war on terror; 2) ensuring national unity; and 3) a reformulation of the social contract, the main point of which would be not only to combat those who advocated the creation of a fascist theocracy, but also to bring an end to the chaos and violence spreading through the country.[34]

# From the Tahrir Square Revolution (January–February 2011) to the Revolutionary Coup d'état (July 2013)

Religious tension reached a new high during the 2011 revolution. To be sure, Copts played an active role and helped give visibility to the anti-establishment character of the demonstrations, which crossed the boundaries of religion, ethnic identity, class, and gender. Among the slogans of the demonstrators were: "Muslims and Copts are brothers! Mosques and churches are one!"[35] However, the revolution eventually resulted in the sweeping victory of the Muslim Brotherhood's "Freedom and Justice Party" and the Salafi al-Nour Party in the elections to both houses of parliament that took place on December 3, 2011 and led to the victory of the Brotherhood's Mohammed Morsi in presidential elections on June 17, 2012. This aroused existential anxieties among the Copts.

When one adds to this the passing of Baba Shenouda III, the election of Tawadros II as the new Coptic patriarch, and the differences that have arisen between the Coptic Church and its independent-minded young members, then it is no wonder that the Copts are currently experiencing deep uncertainty regarding their status as equal citizens in their homeland.

# Yearning for an "Arab Spring", Experiencing an Islamic Frost

Copts were targeted several times during this two and one-half year period. At the beginning of March 2013, a church in the village of Sol in the Hilwan district of Cairo was destroyed. On March 23, 2013, a group of Salafis, in the village of Kina in Upper Egypt, cut off a Copt's ear because he was in a relationship with a young Muslim woman. When a Copt was appointed governor of the Kina district, resulting protests led to the suspension of the appointment. In April 2013, violent anti-Copt riots broke out adjacent to the Coptic cathedral in the 'Abbasiyya district in Cairo, in which two persons were killed and ninety injured. In this case, President Morsi quickly issued a condemnation, stating that he did not intend to allow anyone to fragment the nation.

The physical violence was accompanied by verbal attacks, which received backing from Muslim religious scholars who issued legal rulings justifying these positions. Some of these religious scholars were identified with the Muslim Brotherhood and others with Egypt's Salafi groups. For example, in connection with the Easter holiday that fell in May 2013, 'Abd al-Rahman al-Bar, a member of the bureau of the Muslim Brotherhood's Supreme Guide, Muhammad Badi' published a *fatwa* asserting that according to *shari'a* it was forbidden to greet the Copts on Easter, since this holiday by its very nature and essence stood in opposition to the Muslim belief that Jesus was never crucified, nor did he even die, but rather, he was taken up to heaven by Allah who gave him immunity from the Jews.[36]

This legal position contradicted the behavior of the Muslim Brotherhood's previous Supreme Guide, Mohammad Mahdi 'Akef, and his deputy, Hayrat al-Shater who customarily sent written greetings to the Coptic Patriarch and the leaders of the Coptic community on the Easter holiday. In April 2011, Muslim Brotherhood representatives also organized delegations that visited churches all over Egypt in order to greet the Copts on their holiday. What's more, in the past al-Bar himself had allowed Muslims to greet Copts on the latter's holidays. In fact, he personally paid a courtesy call to the St. Mark's Coptic Orthodox Cathedral in Cairo, the seat of the Patriarch, in order to greet him, and during this visit explicitly declared that "participation in the ceremony of appointment of the patriarch or greeting the Copts on the occasion of their holidays or ceremonies are not prohibited...." [37]

The extremism that became manifest in 2013 also sparked a lively debate among religious scholars who were not considered adherents of the Muslim Brotherhood. Egypt's incoming Mufti, Dr. Shawki Ibrahim 'Alam stated at a conference held by the Faculty of *Shari'a* Studies at Damanhur that "there is no obstacle to our greeting our brethren on their holiday or our consoling them in time of disaster...We are one nation, no matter what our political or religious affiliation."[38] A member of the Al-Azhar Islamic Research Academy went beyond the conciliatory and offered a legal justification for greeting the Copts on the Easter holiday. He argued that al-Bar's *fatwa* contradicted the precepts of monotheistic religions, which permit greeting the Copts on their holiday. He said al-Bar's ruling certainly contradicted Islam, which believes in Jesus and the Disciples. In a demonstrative act, the Sheikh of Al-Azhar, Dr. Ahmed al-Taib, led a delegation of al-Azhar scholars, to the Coptic Patriarch Tawadrus II to greet him on the occasion of Easter.

The issue of Muslim-Coptic relations in Egypt was not confined to religious law. There were journalists and intellectuals who expressed sympathy and solidarity with the Coptic minority in print, as well as in the digital media. Writing in the mass circulation *al-Masry al-Youm*, the prominent writer 'Ala'a al-Aswany laid out in detail the discrimination and persecution the Copts had been experiencing in Egypt.[39] Al-Aswany emphasized the discrimination suffered by the Copts, resulting in the fact that a Copt could "never attain a high position… no matter what one's qualifications." He also described the constant danger that Copts faced of "being driven from your neighborhood at any moment." Furthermore, being a Coptic male in Egypt, claims Aswany, means that one is unable to fall in love and marry the girl one really and truly wants, since "…in their [i.e., the Muslims] eyes you are an infidel who must not contaminate a girl of their religious community".[40] However, despite the discrimination described above, Aswany pleads with the Copts: "Don't hate your country and don't leave it…place your hands in ours and let us liberate our country from the gang of extremist savages that are trying to take it over."[41]

Another phenomenon that has gained momentum in recent years and offends Copts is the Islamization of public spaces, namely, the substitution of Coptic names of streets, squares or villages with Islamic ones. An example of this is the village of Dir Abu Hennis in the al-Minya district, in which approximately 30,000 Copts reside. The village contains remains of a church that was built in the year 413 A.D. and of monasteries from the tenth century, in addition to other sites through which, according to Coptic belief, the Virgin Mary passed. On April 12, 2009, a decision of the Office of Organization and Administration changed the name of the village of Dir Abu Hennis (Abu Hennis Monastery) to Wadi al-N'ana' ("Valley of Peppermint.") This phenomenon manifested itself in additional villages with Coptic names in Upper Egypt. Thus, the name of the village of *Umm al-Khamas* ("Mother of the Hegemon") was changed to *Umm al-Mu'minin* ("Mother of the Believers," the term used to designate the Prophet Muhammad's wife, 'Aisha). Victoria Square, located in the largely Coptic Shubra District of Cairo, was renamed *Nasr al-Islam* ("Victory of Islam"). The residents of these villages correctly viewed these changes as an attempt to erase Coptic identity and history, a kind of a cultural genocide. Therefore community leaders urged their followers to protest against this policy. Youths from the villages whose names were changed refused to change the name on their government-issued identity cards and declared that they would not agree to suppress their identity even if it cost them their lives. They carried banners with slogans such as "let us all die" and "may Abu Hennis live forever."[42]

This planned policy of Islamization of public spaces and expunging of Coptic and Christian history was the product of an ongoing debate between two schools of thought among Egyptian Muslim thinkers and activists regarding the status of Christians in Egypt. Both schools base their arguments on the corpus of sacred Islamic writings. One school holds that the Christians should be treated as *ahl al-dhimma*. The other school of thought views the Christians as equal citizens who should enjoy complete legal and civic equality.

The 2011 revolution in Egypt also sharpened the inter-generational struggle within the Coptic community. A clear expression of this was the appearance of the Maspero Youth Union, a Coptic youth movement that arose following a bloody attack on Coptic protesters on October 9, 2011, during which 25 Copts were killed and more than 300 injured in violent clashes with the army. This movement aimed at fighting for the rights of Christians in Egypt. They became known for their firm opposition to the post-Mubarak military government. Maspero's desire was to turn Egypt into a state for all of its citizens, by both reducing the power and influence of the Church and limiting the *"shari'a clauses"* in the new Egyptian constitution being drafted. To achieve these ends, on January 25, 2013, representatives of the movement met with members of the Constitution Drafting Committee that was working on the issue. Maspero objected to the constitution's Clause 2, which states that Islam is the religion of the state, Arabic is its official language, and *shari'a* is the state's main source of legislation. The Maspero Youth Union recommended framing Egypt as a civil state, with all that this implies. They also called for a change in Clause 11, which deals with ensuring gender equality in politics, society, culture, and economics. They wanted the words, "without impairing the principles of Islamic *shari'a*," deleted. This demand was based on Maspero's assumption that a patriarchal interpretation of *shari'a* laws not only does not strive for equality between men and women, but tends to perpetuate the existing gender hierarchy and continuous discrimination against women that are allegedly anchored in the legalistic texts. The Maspero representatives also called for adding a clause to the constitution stating that discrimination on religious grounds constitutes a criminal act for all intents and purpose.[43]

The heads of the Coptic Church, in contrast, repeatedly declared that they had no objections to retaining Clause 2. The discussion within the Coptic community about the constitution broadened and Coptic intellectuals joined the debate. One could discern the on-going dispute within the community, between the Church seeking to preserve its status among its flock and the youths and intellectuals working to restrict the Church's authority. The intellectual Kamal Zakher, for example, argued that the opposition was not to Clause 2 itself, but to the interpretation given to it by members of the Islamist factions. Zakher demanded that the Church not choose from among its own when it came to figures that would represent the Coptic community on the Constitution Drafting Committee. Instead, Zakher argued, the Coptic community should be represented by a qualified Coptic judge, one with the appropriate professional and religious qualities, who should be chosen from among the judges of the country's Court of Appeals.[44]

# The Crisis of Coptic Youth — Immigration is the Solution

In an April 2013 interview, the Coptic Patriarch-elect Tawadros II described a feeling of imminent disaster among the Copts, because Egypt was turning away from being a modern civil state into a different entity that no one yet knew how to characterize. Similar feelings of uncertainty about Egypt's future in general and the future of the Copts as citizens in particular were expressed by a 60-year old Coptic businessman, Osama Shehata. "My son the physician," said Shehata, "was attacked by toughs on the main street of the city in broad daylight and wounded badly in the head." According to Shehata, if a feeling of public security could be restored, then no one would think of emigrating from Egypt.[45] Patriarch Tawadros II went on to say that the Copt is first and foremost an Egyptian and therefore deserved equal opportunities.

For some young Copt men and women, the feeling of approaching disaster found practical expression in emigration. Many Copts have already left Egypt, and the number of those seeking to emigrate is increasing all the time. Thus, for example, Mina, a young Coptic man of 28, waiting at the entrance of the Dutch Embassy to receive an immigration visa, explained:

> I would be happy to continue living in my homeland, but circumstances work against me....The situation in Egypt is not stable, nor is it secure for us Christians. We are worried about the sexual harassment and indignities women suffer on the streets. I can't find work, so I am trying to emigrate.[46]

According to data published by the Washington Institute for Near East Policy, approximately 100,000 Copts emigrated from Egypt following the Muslim Brotherhood's sweeping victories in the parliamentary and presidential elections. According to Coptic organizations and the Egyptian Society for Human Rights, 100,000 Christians still in Egypt have applied for immigration visas to the US and Canada; 10,000 of them submitted their applications immediately after Morsi's election. However, senior sources in the Coptic Church described the figures above as exaggerated and claimed that according to the data in their hands, only 30,000 Christians had left Egypt since the beginning of 2013.[47]

Intriguingly, the country of Georgia has also become a potential destination for Coptic immigration. The Egyptian news agency MENA recently reported that 90,000 Copts had moved there. The Egyptian Foreign Ministry rushed to deny this data. Abir Habib, spokeswoman for the Georgian mission in Cairo, also claimed that the Egyptian news agency data do not meet the test of reality. According to her, "Only 643 Egyptians had been granted temporary resident visas and 12 Egyptians had received permanent visas.[48] According to Habib, although the choice of Georgia might seem strange, it can be explained by the fact that most of Georgia's citizens are Christian, and during this period, in which interfaith tension in Egypt was reaching unprecedented highs, the Copts seek to live in a state that will make it possible for them to conduct their lives as Christians freely.

Moreover, the Church establishment in Egypt not only recommends Georgia as a preferred destination for Coptic immigration, but also recommends that Copts volunteer to help their fellows seeking to immigrate to there as much as possible. One of those who would like to immigrate to Georgia and is supported by his Bishop is 35-year old Mark Maher, a government employee, who explained that Georgia, as an Orthodox Christian country, encourages Coptic tourism as well as financial investments as a means of stabilizing and strengthening the country's impoverished economy. Some young Egyptian Copts imagine Georgia to be in a place that would give them the possibility of establishing themselves economically, of getting married and raising a family, and of living a normal life as befits someone their age. None of this was possible in their homeland, because of the declining Egyptian economy. Alfred Gamil, a man in his late 20s, a graphic designer by profession, told a journalist that he had saved some money and planned to immigrate to Georgia and open a small business there. "I've been engaged for a year and a half," he stated, "and I can't get married, since I can't afford to buy an apartment. I want to dream, but I can't dream in Egypt."[49]

There are even more prosaic factors influencing immigration to Georgia. One is the fact that it is cheaper to immigrate to there than to the US or Canada. Another factor is that Georgia is viewed as a potential bridge to the Western European area. There are Copts, like 40-year old Ahmad Muhammad, who had convinced himself that by July 1, 2013, Georgia would join the European Union [which did not happen].

Although there are testimonies that one can hear Egyptian Arabic spoken on the streets of Georgian cities, official representatives of Georgia in Egypt emphasize the limitations their country has in absorbing immigrants. These officials note that it was the tourist companies that promised heaven on earth to those who expressed an interest, but as a matter of fact, Georgia was unable to issue a permanent residence visa to anyone, except for businessmen seeking to invest in the country. All that Georgia was able to do was issue tourist visas to those who applied. Those insisting on seeing Georgia as a destination for immigration were liable to find themselves without health and educational services, and their dream of a better life might quickly turn into a fantasy.

The verbal hostility towards the Copts reached a new high after the revolution of June 30, 2013, in the wake of Morsi's removal. In slanderous articles published on their Internet sites the Muslim Brothers blamed the Copts for the Morsi's overthrow. As proof, they pointed to the appearance of Coptic Patriarch Tawadros II beside the Minister of Defense 'Abd al-Fatah al-Sisi during the speech in which he announced Morsi's removal. The Copts were also accused of having supported the revolutionary movement *Tamarrud* ("Rebellion") that initiated the June 2013 protest. Naguib Sawiris, the Coptic Egyptian tycoon, joined millions signing a petition launched by *Tamarrud*. Furthermore, the "Free Egyptians Party" he founded, as well as his newspaper and television channel, helped their campaign by offering the use of branch offices. He also reportedly transferred over 28 million US dollars to fund the movement, although he firmly denied it, claiming that "there was no need to finance *Tamarrud* since the credit for bringing millions to the streets goes directly to Morsi."[50] According to Muslim Brotherhood-affiliated writers, Patriarch Tawadros II also encouraged the members of his community to take an active part in the *Tamarrud* demonstrations, and Coptic clergymen and monks were photographed as they were signing its anti-Morsi petition. Copts amounted to about 50 percent of the demonstrators, according to these articles, hence it was proper and legitimate for Brotherhood websites to label the June 30, 2013 revolution as the "crusader revolution." [51]

# Conclusion

While Mohammed Morsi was president, he missed an historic opportunity to encourage an interfaith religious dialogue that would promote full and equal citizenship for the Copts on the basis of *shari'a* legislation. In this context, he could have initiated legislation making it a criminal offence to injure, by word or deed, physically or emotionally, believers of other religions or their religious symbols, behavior frequently manifested by Salafi figures. If Morsi had brought about a shift from the dhimmi-tolerance *(tasamuh)* concept regarding religious minorities to a pluralistic *(ta'adudiyya)* and tolerant concept under the auspices of modernist Islam based on *ijtihad* (legal reasoning and hermeneutics on the basis of the Qur'an and the Sunna), then he might have brought about a significant reduction in interfaith tension and even the deepening of solidarity between Muslims and Copts.

The revolutionary *coup d'état* that took place on June 30 aroused hope and optimism among the Copts. However, the government's feeble response to the shooting at the Church of the Virgin Mary, on October 20, 2013, that resulted in the death of four and the injury of dozens, after a man fired 15 bullets at a wedding ceremony, demonstrated that the Copt's dilemma was not a top priority for the popular Defense Minister 'Abd al-Fatah al-Sisi. While on the declarative level all of the senior functionaries condemned the brutal attack — including Prime Minister Hazem al-Bablawi, al-Azhar Grand Imam Ahmed al-Taib, the spokesman of the Salafi *al-Nour* party, the leader of the Egyptian social-democratic party, and even members of the formerly violent, radical Sunni *al-Gama'a al-Islamiyya* — on the practical level, nothing was been done to reassure the Copts that the security of their lives and property would be guaranteed during the new transition period. Ultimately, it is the responsibility of those in power to defuse the tension between Egyptian Muslims and Copts that reached unprecedented highs during the past three years. It remains to be seen whether they possess the political will and capital to promote solidarity on the basis of the principle of civil equality without distinction of religious or ethnic affiliation.

# Notes

1. Makram Samaan and Soheir Sukkary, "The Copts and Muslims of Egypt," in Saud Joseph and Barbara L. K. Pilsbury (eds.), *Muslim-Christian Conflicts: Economic, Political and Social Origins* (Colorado: Westview Press, 1978), p. 141.
2. Subhi Labib, "The Copts in Egyptian Society and Politics 1882–1919," in Gabriel Warburg and Uri M. Kupferschmidt (eds.), *Islam, Nationalism and Radicalism in Egypt and Sudan* (New York: Praeger, 1983), pp. 302–303.
3. Thomas Philipp, "Copts and Other Minorities in the Development of the Egyptian Nation-State," in Shimon Shamir (ed.), *Egypt from Monarchy to Republic: A Reassessment of Revolution and Change* (Oxford: Westview Press, 1995), p. 133.
4. P. J. Vatikiotis, *The History of Egypt from Muhammad Ali to Sadat* (Jerusalem: The Magnes Press, 1983), p.181.
5. Philipp, "Copts and their Minorities in the Development of the Egyptian Nation-State," p. 133.
6. Lise Paulsen Galal, "Coptic Christian practices: formations of sameness and difference," *Islam and Christian-Muslim Relations*, Vol. 23, No. 1 (January 2012), p. 46.
7. Labib, "The Copts in Egyptian Society and Politics 1882–1919," p. 307.
8. J. D. Pennington, "The Copts in Modern Egypt," *Middle Eastern Studies*, Vol. 18, Issue 2 (1982), p. 160.
9. *Ibid.*, p. 308.
10. See http://quran.com/2.
11. See http://quran.com/109.
12. Labib, "The Copts in Egyptian Society and Politics, 1882–1919," p. 314.
13. *Ibid.*

14. Ami Ayalon, "Egypt's Coptic Pandora's Box," in Ofra Bengio and Gabriel Ben-Dor (eds.), *Minorities and the State in the Arab World* (London: Lynne Rienner, 1999), p. 55.
15. Pennington, "The Copts in Modern Egypt," p. 163.
16. Philipp, "Copts and Other Minorities in the Development of the Egyptian National State," p. 145.
17. Paulsen Galal, "Coptic Christian practices: formations of sameness and difference," p. 47.
18. *Ibid.*, pp. 50–51.
19. Milad Hanna, *Acceptance of the Other* (Cairo: Al-Ahram Center for Political and Strategic Studies, 2001), p. 131.
20. Paul Sedra, "Class, Cleavages and Ethnic Conflict: Coptic Christian Communities in Modern Egyptian Politics," *Islam and Christian-Muslim Relations*, Vol. 10, Issue 2, 1999, pp. 221–222.
21. Paulsen Galal, "Coptic Christian practices: formations of sameness and difference," pp. 53–54.
22. Michael Adel, "Copts Refuse Sectarian Conflict," *Al-Ahram Weekly*, http://www.weekly.ahram.org.eg/News/3879/17/Copts-ref.
23. L. Azuri. "Rising Tensions between Muslims, Christians in Egypt," Middle East Media Research Institute (MEMRI): Inquiry and Analysis Series Report, no. 646, http://www.memri.org/report/en/print4765.htm.
24. Donald L. Horowitz, *The Dimensions of Ethnic Groups* (Berkeley: University of California Press, 2000), p. 36.
25. Alessia Melcangi, "Before and After the Revolution: A Spring also for the Copts of Egypt?" *British Journal of Middle East Studies* (BRISMES), Graduate Section Annual Conference 2012, London School of Economics and Political Science (LSE), London, United Kingdom, 11 June 2012, p. 19.
26. "Elections in Egypt: Analysis of the 2011 Parliamentary Electoral System," *IFES*, November 2011, p. 11.
27. Rachel M. Scott, *The Challenge of Political Islam: Non-Muslims and the Egyptian State* (Stanford: Stanford University Press, 2010), p. 83.
28. *Ibid.*, pp. 9–10.
29. Dina Ezzat, "A Moment of Recognition," *Al-Ahram Weekly*, January 9, 2011, http://weekly.ahram.org.eg/2011/1030/eg1.htm.
30. Ekram Ibrahim, "Egypt's Citizens Launch Initiatives against Attack on Copts," *Ahram Online*, January 3, 2011, http://english.ahram.org.eg/NewsContent/1/64/3111/Egypt/Politics-/Egypt-Citizens-launch-initiatives-against-attack-o.aspx.
31. *Ibid.*
32. Yasmine Fathi and Salama El-Wardani, "Priest of Saint Church: Egypt Attack the Result of Blind Extremism," *Ahram Online*, January 2, 2011, http://english.ahram.org.eg/NewsContentPrint/1/0/3017/Egypt/0/Priest-of-Saints-Church-Egypt-attack-the-result-of.aspx.
33. *Ibid.*

34. Abdel-Moneim Said, "Our national Unity," *Al-Ahram Weekly*, January 2, 2011, http://english.ahram.org.eg/NewsContentPrint/4/0/3047/Opinion/0/Our-national-unity.aspx.

35. Jayson Casper, "Mapping the Coptic Movements: Coptic Activism in a Revolutionary Setting," *Arab West Report*, May 15, 2013, http://www.arabwestreport.info/sites/default/files/pdfs/AWRpapers/paper44.pdf.

36. "In Advance of Orthodox Easter in Egypt, Muslim Brotherhood And Salafis Issue Fatwas Forbidding Greeting Copts on Their Holidays," *MEMRI*, May 3, 2013.

37. *Ibid.*

38. *Ibid.*

39. 'Ala'a Al-Aswany, "The Situation of Copts in Egypt," *MEMRI*, April 2, 2013.

40. *Ibid.*

41. *Ibid.*

42. "The Cultural Genocide of Egypt's Christian Copts", *Assyrian International News Agency* (AINA), June 14, 2009, http://www.aina.org/news/20090613211135.htm.

43. Mounir Adib, "Coptic Church: Constitution's Sharia Provisions not at Odds with Civil State," August 13, 2013, *Egypt Independent*, http://www.egyptindependent.com/news/coptic-church-constitution-s-sharia-provisions-not-odds-civil-state.

44. *Ibid.*

45. Yasmine Saleh and Paul Taylor, "Egypt's Pope says Islamist Rulers Neglect Copts," *Reuters*, April 26, 2013, http://www.reuters.com/article/2013/04/26/us-egypt-pope-idUSBRE93P0B620130426.

46. Michael Adel, "The Copts Flee Egypt," *Al-Ahram Weekly*, April 30, 2013, http://weekly.ahram.org.eg/News/2402/24/The-Copts-flee-Egypt.aspx.

47. Suleiman Shafiq, "Al-Aqbat Yuhagirun ila Hadhan al-Watan" [The Copts will immigrate to the bosom of their homeland], *al-Mussawar*, June 27, 2012, pp. 32–37.

48. Yasmin Wali, "Egyptian Emigration to Georgia: Promised Land or Fool's Paradise?", *Ahram online*, June 10, 2013, http://english.ahram.org.eg/NewsContent/1/151/73088/Egypt/Features/Egyptian-emigration-to-Georgia-Promised-land-or-fo.aspx.

49. *Ibid.*

50. Edmund Blair, "Egypt Billionaire Sawiris Family to invest 'like never before'", *Reuters*, July 15, 2013. www.reuters.com/article/2013/07/15/us-egypt-sawiris-idUSBRE96E0FX20130715.

51. "Muslim Brotherhood beyond the *coup d'état* against Morsi," *MEMRI*, July 18, 2013.

# Nasser Nostalgia in post-Mubarak Egypt

## Joyce van de Bildt

"If Nasser were alive, he would make you wear a *tarha* (veil) and bracelets."[1] This was one of the slogans chanted against President Mohammed Morsi by Egyptian protestors in Tahrir Square on July 1, 2013. Waving pictures of Gamal 'Abd al-Nasser, the demonstrators were calling on Morsi to step down. The chant was just one of the many references to Nasser that have been made in post-Mubarak Egypt during the last three years.

A renewed interest in the nation's past usually coincides with periods of political upheaval. Indeed, after the January 25, 2011 revolution, a subsequent period of military rule and the short-lived government of the democratically elected Muslim Brotherhood, history has been invoked more than ever before in Egypt, as the country is searching for stability and strong leadership. Nostalgia for Nasser reflects a widespread Egyptian yearning for a unifying force that can confront the country's longstanding challenges of attaining greater social justice, economic development, and coping with the deep divisions and rivalries between Islamists and their opponents. Increased nostalgia for Nasser is also a reaction to what is perceived as continued Western domination in the region and the unquestioned decline of Egypt's standing and influence in the Arab world. Hence, the memory of Nasser has been invoked to demand all kinds of values, while largely ignoring Nasser's failures and the authoritarian nature of his regime. Instead, Nasser has been made into a symbol, one that is (temporarily) able to unite different forces. Desperately looking for a remedy to the continuing disarray in which Egypt finds itself, many Egyptians hope for a silver bullet; the emergence of a new Nasser-like leader.

This article devotes a special section to discussing "Nasser" fan pages on Facebook and the discourse they promote. Interestingly, over the past few years, Egypt has witnessed the emergence of Facebook pages with historical themes on which video, photo material, and historical documents are posted. Facebook pages have come to function as a platform from which people express their different views of a shared past, evoking rivalries but also dialogue. The pages' historical themes stand for a larger, more complex trend of nostalgia for the past, which is closely related to current social and political agendas.

# Nostalgia and the Nasserist Legacy in Egypt

The historian Carl Becker has argued that no matter what is written in history books, the memory of the past will always remain the dominant factor of how people perceive it, and that "this picture, however little it corresponds to the real past, helps to determine their ideas about politics and society."[2] As David Lowenthal argued, the accurate version of historical events is of minor importance in people's minds. Most important is what people *believe* happened, or what they *want* to have happened. The majority "does not seek historical veracity nor mind its absence."[3] They may believe in anything that unites them or strengthens their identity, which is something that is based on "faith, not rational proof." Scholarship on collective memory has further shown how groups construct versions of an imagined shared past, and how they employ them for self-understanding and legitimization in an ever-changing present.

Collective memory is not static but rather is constantly changing, usually under the influence of current events or in response to other narratives. Especially during periods of political upheaval, history can be invoked to reflect on contemporary contexts. While certain memories may be faint at one time, they may later on prove useful and be revived. This revival of the past is most common in times of a search for identity. Pierre Nora noted that "temporal and topographical memory sites emerge at those times and in those places where there is a perceived and constituted break with the past."[4] Shocking social changes, such as urbanization, demographic changes, or revolution, can encourage a renewed interest in the past and an awareness of personal and communal identity. Present grievances and mistrust regarding the future have led people to turn to history for answers, while glorifying past periods, and sinking into nostalgia.

The term *nostalgia* comes from the Greek words *algos* (pain) and *nostos* (to return home).[5] Nostalgia refers to actively missing the past. It is a sentimentality for the past, typically refusing its negative aspects. In the construction of collective memory, highlighting certain aspects of history and disregarding others is highly common. If collective memory is based on the selection of certain eposides of history, nostalgia is perhaps the most obvious manifestation of this selectivity, since it is partially detached from historical facts, being based more on sentimentality and imagination.

Nostalgia is a yearning for the past that can be the consequence of dissatisfaction with the present. Nick Hodgin argues that nostalgia has the important mnemonic function of connecting people to the past, "as a way of barricading themselves against the present," by clinging to talismans of continuity.[6] However scholars have questioned whether nostalgia constitutes a genuine desire to actually return to the past. Importantly, nostalgia can be a longing for something that may have never existed. Susan Stewart describes nostalgia as a form of sadness without an object, which wears a distinctly utopian face.[7] She argues that, like any form of narrative, nostalgia is ideological: the past it seeks has never existed, except as a narrative. In Egypt, a segment of the public has tended to glorify the Nasser period through such nostalgia. They express a longing not so much for what they have lost, but rather for an ideal situation that was not actually attained prior to 1970, yet is retroactively associated with a period of "real" freedom, prosperity, equality, and dignity under Nasser.

Gamal 'Abd al-Nasser is credited with attaining real sovereignty for Egypt, and for developing and "Egyptianizing" the national economy, mainly by introducing socialist measures. The successes of large Nasserist projects, such as the building of the Aswan Dam, the nationalization of the Suez Canal, and the expulsion of the British, are hardly debated. With his charismatic style of leadership, he succeeded in courting both Egyptians and a large part of the Arab world with his vision of Arab nationalism. Nevertheless, the darker, authoritarian side of his system of rule became clear already in the 1950s. Moreover, in the 1960s, Nasser's policies failed to fulfill the dream of Arab unity and social justice. Increased state control on the economy, land reforms, and nationalizations did not rid Egypt of rural poverty, unemployment, and social injustice. Though a champion of non-alignment during the Cold War, Nasser became militarily and economically dependent on the Soviet Union. Egypt's humiliating defeat in the 1967 war with Israel dealt the final blow to Nasser's image and the pan-Arabist ideology. Politically, Nasser died a broken man in 1970; yet, he had won the hearts of the Egyptian people. Nasser's successors, Anwar al-Sadat and Hosni Mubarak, gradually diverged from Nasser's domestic and foreign policies and at times went as far as reversing Nasser. But they too failed to solve Egypt's problems of poverty, unemployment, and inequality and succeeded in creating new reasons for public resentment as they opened up the economy and drew closer to the West.

The memory of Nasser and his legacy remained contested in Egypt. But during the Mubarak years, Nasser's reputation seems to have undergone a substantial popular revival. In a 1997 article, Joel Gordon argued that Nasserist nostalgia provides Egyptians with a sense of unity, stability, and civic culture that they had lost. He noticed the rise of Nasser nostalgia at a time when neither Islamism nor the state offered viable political alternatives. Nostalgia for Nasser, he said, should be interpreted as a search for "hope, purpose, Arab unity, and, not least, national unity and stability. [...] Nasserism produced a sense of nation and citizenship that transformed the way Egyptians looked at themselves and their world."[8]

In a critical assessment of the Nasserist legacy on the 30th anniversary of his death, Hosny Guindy and Hani Shukrallah acknowledged that "Gamal 'Abd al-Nasser continues to inhabit Egypt because [...] he is the representative of an age of certain national glory, despite any mistakes or setbacks. [...] Above all, he symbolizes for Egyptians the expression of their independent national will. It is this that remains. It is in this that we must seek our project for the future."[9] Gabriel Ben-Dor has argued that Nasser's legacy is not based on a system he left behind, but rather on his achievements in the realms of political psychology, such as "the restoration of pride in being Egyptians; the immense increase in the status of Arabism and Arabs throughout the region and the world [and] the confrontation with imperialism and the West."[10]

In times of dissatisfaction, Nasser is readily used as an icon that symbolizes better days. Mubarak's style of leadership contrasted sharply with that of Nasser, as did his relations with the West, his economic policies and his connection with the public.[11] During the Mubarak years, the image of Nasser was invoked, among other things, in opposition to the rise in food prices and education costs, unemployment, the privatization of companies, and cooperation with the United States and Israel. The icon of Nasser has the potential of symbolizing different ideals that are associated with him, yet were not necessarily achieved during his rule.

## Nostalgia for Nasser in post-Mubarak Egypt

Since the fall of Mubarak, the memory of Nasser has been revived in different ways, by different people, and in different contexts. One could say that the overthrow of Mubarak had the potential of turning the entire revolutionary legacy upside down, since Mubarak was often perceived as the continuation of a line of presidents that ruled Egypt since Nasser established the Republic. Still, efforts to erase Mubarak from the collective memory coincided with a renewed interest in Nasser. The slogans and goals of the 2011 revolution were often linked to that of the 1952 revolution because of their common call for change, freedom, social justice and dignity.[12]

The various actors in the effectively leaderless revolution of January 25, 2011 had one common objective, the departure of Mubarak. His resignation was followed by a nearly immediate campaign to rectify the past and to rewrite school textbooks. Already in April 2011, the Ministry of Education appointed a committee to this end, illustrating the urgently felt need by various groups in society to convey certain knowledge to future generations by taking the past — and hence the future — into one's own hands. Falsifications of history, it announced, would be scrapped from textbooks, while new chapters would be added: chapters on the January 25 revolution, but also on episodes of Egyptian history that had been suppressed until then. Among the proposed amendments was the addition of a chapter on the presidency of Mohammed Naguib. Another aim was to diminish the centrality of Mubarak's role in the opening days of the October 1973 war (Mubarak was Commander in Chief of the Air Force at the time) and give greater credit to Sa'd Eddine al-Shazli, then-Chief of Staff of the Egyptian armed forces.[13] The work of the committee coincided with several decisions to rename hospitals, schools, streets, and other public places that had been named after Hosni Mubarak or his wife, Suzanne.

Naturally, what initially seemed a concerted and united effort to rewrite history soon turned into the subject of disagreement, as various groups in society had specific interests in promoting certain parts of the past in order to promote their present goals. In Egypt, this became apparent just as the Muslim Brotherhood moved to the forefront of the political scene. Suppressed since 1954, the Muslim Brotherhood's narrative of the history of the Egyptian Republic is highly critical of the regime and reflects acute resentment towards past leaders of the Republic. In the aftermath of the victory of the Muslim Brotherhood's candidate Mohammed Morsi in the 2012 presidential elections, Nasser's legacy emerged as a particularly contentious issue. On June 29, 2012, the newly elected president addressed the crowds in Tahrir Square, blessing the 2011 revolution and commending the Egyptian people for their role in the struggle for liberation. He recalled the injustice committed by former regimes, and in reference to the campaign of harassment suffered by the leaders of the Muslim Brotherhood under Nasser, Morsi cried out "What do you know about the sixties!" It was considered an insult to late President 'Abd al-Nasser, and Egyptian intellectuals expressed their disappointment that Morsi had used the opportunity "to settle accounts."[14]

In April 2013, Morsi tried to rectify his words in a speech to workers on the eve of Labor Day, speaking at a steel factory in the Helwan district in Cairo. He promised to create thousands of jobs over the coming years, and not to privatize any state-owned companies, meaningfully adding the phrase, "That period is over."[15] Notably, Morsi explicitly praised Nasser for the role he had played in promoting national industries.[16] However, by that time, Morsi had was already under serious fire, and his gesture failed to impress.

Also on Revolution Day 2012, marking the sixtieth anniversary of the revolution, the history of the Muslim Brotherhood's persecution by Nasser put Morsi in a complicated position. In his televised address, Morsi acknowledged that the 1952 revolution was a defining moment in Egyptian history, stating that it "fought a great battle to achieve the full evacuation of occupying forces and independence; and was a model in support of liberation movements and the establishment of the concept of social justice and planned development."[17] But, he said, although the revolution succeeded in achieving certain goals, it had faltered in other areas, such as the promotion of democracy and public freedoms, owing to the fraud and tyranny practiced by the successive regimes that had ruled Egypt since the revolution. Morsi emphasized that the 25 January revolution was a crucial correction to what had gone wrong since 1952. Although trying to strike a conciliatory tone, in the eyes of many, Morsi's speech was an offense to Nasser's hallowed image. A ceremony at Nasser's tomb that day even turned into an anti-Muslim Brotherhood protest, with people reportedly chanting "Down with the rule of the [Brotherhood's] Supreme Guide" and "'Abd al-Nasser said it a long time ago, the Brotherhood is not to be trusted."[18]

This use of Nasser's image to claim that the Muslim Brotherhood was best marginalized in Egyptian politics became more common as dissatisfaction with Morsi's rule increased. The conclusion that "Nasser was right" was voiced more and more often. Video footage of Nasser from the 1960s, in which he made strong statements against the Muslim Brotherhood or mocked them in public, went viral on YouTube during October 2012.[19] In one of the videos, which dates from 1966, Nasser laughs off the Muslim Brotherhood and their idea to make the *tarha* (veil) mandatory for Egyptian women. Right before the large-scale protests of June 30, 2013 calling on Morsi to step down, anti-Muslim Brotherhood protestors carried pictures of Nasser through the streets of Egypt.[20]

Morsi was deposed by the military on July 3, 2013. Since then, the image of Nasser has proved to be very useful for the Egyptian military desirous of legitimizing their actions. At a time of severe instability, political and sectarian violence, and a faltering economy, the armed forces have presented themselves as embracing the ideals of stability, independence, and nationalism. These goals are allegedly personified through former Commander-in-Chief and Defense Minister General 'Abd al-Fatah al-Sisi, as they once were by Nasser. Hamdeen Sabahi, a Nasserist politician, made the following statement:

> Nostalgia for Gamal 'Abd al-Nasser is the result of the Egyptian people's awareness that the army has embraced the people's wishes and made sure that the revolution could take place. [...] Here the Sisi phenomenon is introduced. [...] He represents the Egyptian national identity that the Brotherhood wanted to steal away.[21]

Indeed, Sisi, who led the military in the ousting, has been compared to Nasser numerous times. Around Revolution Day 2013, an iconic photo started to be spread on social media and Egyptian news outlets. The black and white photo portrays a young boy holding a bouquet of flowers in his hand and saluting

'Abd al-Nasser, who is reaching out to shake the child's hand. Allegedly, the young boy was General al-Sisi.[22] Although his identity was not confirmed, the photo spread rapidly and was posted on Facebook pages and news websites.

Three weeks after Morsi's deposal, on the 61st anniversary of the revolution, hundreds of protesters in Tahrir Square carried posters of 'Abd al-Nasser.[23] On the same day, supporters of the "30 June revolution" gathered at Nasser's tomb carrying pictures of al-Sisi alongside pictures of Nasser, chanting anti-Muslim Brotherhood slogans.[24] At the same time, a Muslim preacher, speaking in front of a crowd of supporters of Morsi in Alexandria, described Sisi as the new Pharaoh — invoking an old idiom that had been used by the Islamists to delegitimize Sadat and Mubarak as well.[25]

Following weeks of violent street clashes between the military and protestors in Egyptian cities, as well as unrest in the Sinai, the army was eager to seize every opportunity to legitimize its rule. 'Adly Mansour, the chief judge who took over as interim president after the ouster of Morsi, used the 61st anniversary of the 1952 revolution to promote the military-backed interim government. "We will pursue the same goals [of the revolution] namely freedom and justice and are confident in our great people and its ability to overcome the difficulties of the present phase."[26] While excluding Mubarak, Mansour specifically praised Nasser, Sadat, and Naguib, Egypt's post-1952 "presidents from the armed forces."[27] Renewed emphasis on the military tradition (while ignoring Mubarak's continuation of this tradition) served the Egyptian army's goal of legitimizing their rule and actions in post-Morsi Egypt.

Nasserists in Egypt, that is those political players who continued to adhere to the leftist, Arab nationalist ideology as espoused by Nasser, adeptly capitalized upon the nostalgia for the late President. The fact that the most prominent Nasserist politician, Hamdeen Sabahi, placed third in the 2012 presidential elections, surprised observers, who argued that Sabahi "succeeded in reflecting Nasser's dreams" at a crucial moment in Egyptian politics.[28] In addition, one of Nasser's sons, 'Abd al-Hakim Nasser, increased his public appearances and was called on to run for president.[29] But the Nasserists are no longer the only ones evoking Nasser in the context of the during current unrest.

## The Emergence of Nasser Fan Pages on Facebook

A search for the words "Gamal 'Abd al-Nasser" in Arabic on Facebook results in a list of more than one hundred pages dedicated to him. A closer look at the content of the largest pages (the pages with the largest amount of "Likes") reveals recurring themes that characterize the memory of Nasser on Facebook.

Some posts are ideological and espouse ideas of Arab nationalism, defiance of Israel and resistance to cooperation with the United States, and a celebration of general revolutionary activities. Other pages are more directly related to current political goals and seek the promotion of current Nasserist politicians such as Hamdeen Sabahi, for example. Still other posts applaud the actions of the Egyptian army and General Sisi, or express resentment towards the Muslim Brotherhood.

The most popular pages were all established between 2008 and the present, and their amount of "Likes" range from a few dozen to one hundred thousand followers. The largest page is called *"Shabaka Nasser Ahbariya* — Nasser News Network 3.N,"* and has 134,000 "Likes." It was founded on 28 September, 2011, the 41st anniversary of Nasser's death. The second largest page, founded on July 24, 2008, is *"Gamal 'Abd al-Nasir"*, which managed to gather more than 62,000 "Likes". Another page with the exact same name was established on January 4, 2013, and has about 31,000 "Likes." There are other popular pages: e.g. "Jamal Abdel Nasser II By Mahmoud ElSheikh" (1,296 "Likes,"), "Gamal Abdel Nasser" (8,284 "Likes,"), "Nasser 56" (8,456 "Likes,") and *"Gamal 'Abd al-Nasir za'im al-umma al-'arabiya"* (1,054 "Likes,"), among others.[30] The pages are almost entirely in Arabic and rarely include posts in other languages.

Only limited conclusions can be drawn about societal trends based on Facebook statistics and trending topics. It is beyond the scope of this article to discuss whether Facebook can be considered an appropriate tool for examining collective memory, and to address the opportunities and limitations of such a methodology. There are many caveats to be taken into account in such an approach, especially regarding mediated memory, measuring reception, representativeness, and usership among different segments of the population. The viral nature of topics and fan pages may depend on marketing strategies and does not necessarily represent their actual popularity. Therefore, Facebook should not be taken as a tool for pinpointing trends in society because the pages represent only a limited slice of it. But Facebook does illustrate the content of certain trends within public discourse, particularly if these can be verified through other sources as well.

In this case, Facebook can illustrate the ways nostalgia for Nasser is expressed. The fact that there *are* Nasser Facebook pages, and that there is a recorded activity among the public on such pages, does indicate that the memory of him is alive for some people and that his image serves the purpose of promoting present political goals. Examining photos and videos considered memorable enough to upload gives an indication as to what Nasser embodies for the pages' founders and users. In addition, the Facebook pages show the links that users make between the past and the present, as they identify current events and current political leaders with Nasser.

The Nasser Facebook pages generally feature iconic pictures of Nasser: greeting the public, giving a speech, meeting world leaders, posing together with his family, etc. Moreover, they include pictures and written accounts of memorable Nasserist projects such as the Aswan Dam and the nationalization of the Suez Canal. The pages are also used as a platform to post all kinds of historical material such as photos, texts of speeches and songs, video archive material, postal stamps, old magazine covers, and cartoons. Posts also include political statements and slogans. In fact, they often include direct or indirect references to topics that are on today's agenda in Egypt, e.g. relations between religion and state, the role of the army, the status of the Copts, or ideas regarding the US-Egyptian relationship.

For example, the Facebook page *"Gamal 'Abd al-Nasir"* includes a picture of Nasser and 'Abd al-Fatah al-Sisi, both in uniform, with the text: "'Abd al-Nasir and 'Abd al-Fatah: Thank you. Signed by the Egyptian and Arab people."[31] This picture was posted on July 18, 2013, two weeks after the Egyptian army ousted President Morsi and the situation in the country remained very unstable. Examples of political criticism can be found on the Facebook page *"Shabaka Nasser Ahbariya* — Nasser News Network 3.N," which includes many photo shopped pictures that mock Morsi's relationship with US leaders. Also, the page *"Gamal 'Abd al-Nasir za'im al-umma al-'arabiya"* includes such references, e.g. a picture of Nasser meeting Che Guevara, placed next to a picture of Morsi meeting John Kerry.[32] Touching on another sensitive topic, the page "Jamal Abdel Nasser II By Mahmoud ElSheikh" includes a long post about "what Nasser offered Islam,"[33] and also *"Gamal 'Abd al-Nasir"* posted a picture of Nasser praying, with the text entitled: "Leader Gamal 'Abd al-Nasser and the correct understanding of Islam."[34]

In general, these Facebook pages romanticize the type of leader Nasser is thought to have been: a man of the people, and a family man. A post on *"Gamal 'Abd al-Nasir za'im al-umma al-'arabiya"* features a picture of Nasser in the middle of a crowd, with the caption: "He feels safe only among the people and the masses."[35] This emphasis on Nasser as a leader of the people demonstrates a desire for a strong, proud leader that acts in their interest and is close to the people.

The traditional Arabist outlook of many of the Nasser pages is also notable, echoing the psychological appeal of Nasser's promise to restore Arab dignity. *Shabaka Nasser al-Ahbariya*, for example, presents itself as "the voice of Arabism," declaring that "there is no place for neutrality here, we are biased in favor of the Arab homeland and the poor, who both have a leader: Gamal

'Abd al-Nasser."[36] Also "Jamal Abdel Nasser II By Mahmoud ElSheikh" relates to the Arab identity, while emphasizing Egypt's leadership position in the region, stating: "If Egypt is weak, the entire Arab struggle is weak. When Egypt is paralyzed, the Arab struggle is paralyzed. This is not a new fact but the effect of history and nature."[37] Furthermore it states that:

> Arab nationalism is not embodied in one man or group nor is it represented just by 'Abd al-Nasser and those who worked with him, but millions of Arabs carry the flame of nationalism in their hearts and it is irresistible and cannot be destroyed by any force in the world as long as one continues to believe in it with confidence.[38]

The majority of the followers of these Facebook pages are between 25 and 34 years old. Although this generation grew up long after Nasser had passed away, their activity expresses a certain longing for the values and principles Nasser espoused and promoted. As noted earlier in this article, nostalgia is often based on a narrative of history, instead of the actual experience of a certain event. Perhaps the arrival of a new generation of Egyptians was necessary in order to pave the way for such deep nostalgia for Nasser. His figure has become most appealing during this period of instability and insecurity in which Egypt currently finds itself.

# Conclusion

Reflections on Egypt's past have always been related to the current state of political and socio-economic affairs. Meir Hatina made the apt observation that Nasserism is one of the myths that "makes its presence felt in relation to abiding concerns that the political structure has been unable to resolve."[39] Despite his shortcomings, Nasser continues to serve as an icon for Arabism, independence, defiance of Israel, and economic reforms, and as such remains ideologically significant to Egyptians. In instances of political grievance, Nasser's principles and policies have been cited as a way to challenge the Egyptian authorities. In light of the public's complaints about the state of affairs under Mubarak, and the chaos that ensued after he was toppled, the serious flaws of the Nasser regime seem to have receded into the background as Egypt searches for a vision. After the overthrow of Mubarak and the subsequent dissatisfaction with the leadership of Morsi, the Nasserist nostalgia assumed a new dimension, that of "Nasser was right" when it came to the Muslim Brotherhood and his policy of suppressing it. As General al-Sisi came to power, Nasser's image was also used to legitimize the role of the military in Egyptian society.

The memory of Nasser is not a recollection of past events, but rather constitutes a set of "pre-established forms," images of the past that function as "screens" on which "present or timeless needs and desires" are projected.[40] The memory of Nasser reminds the disenfranchised of a dream they once had to empower the lower classes and establish social justice. A respondent to an interview with *Aswat Masriya* illustrated this very well when saying:

> "[Hamdeen Sabahi] wanted to liberate the people and give them their freedom back; and he knew how to reach out and speak to us, just like Nasser did […]. We've been broken for years and Sabbahi was going to bring us back our rights […]. Mubarak sold everything. Many of the factories that Nasser built for the Egyptians are now gone. […] I had a dream that Sabbahi would follow in the path of Nasser, but in a modernised way, with democracy."[41]

This may be a utopia that was not achieved during Nasser's days, but nevertheless provides people with a favorable understanding of the past that helps them look towards the future. This confirms David Lowenthal's assertion that "nostalgia is often for past thoughts, rather than past things."[42] In this case, nostalgia is less a longing for what actually was and more a cherishing of what was once thought possible by remembering these unrealized aspirations.

Digital tools such as Facebook have made commemoration of past events even more interactive and dynamic, and have encouraged the competitive preservation of history by civil society. The passage of memory, from the generation that experienced the event to the next generation, should not be taken for granted. Forgetting and fade-out are usually the rule.[43] This makes the existence of Nasser fan pages on Facebook significant. It illustrates that the memory of Nasser is alive, although we cannot say for certain among whom. We can safely assume, though, that promoting the memory of Nasser is meaningful for a younger generation of both Egyptians and Arabs from other countries.

In expressions of nostalgia, Nasser is very much elevated to the position of icon: on Facebook pages, he is often referred to as "the immortal leader." Obvious achievements of the Nasser regime, as well as the recollection of the heyday of culture and education that he encouraged, support this nostalgia for the past. Videos, music, slogans, and photos are easily invoked as a "weapon" in demanding reforms that are extremely difficult to achieve, such as democracy, social justice, and a healthy economy.

# Notes

1. Rana Ramadan, "Tahrir protesters return, burning pictures of Morsi and waving pictures of 'Abd al-Nasir," *Al-Misriyun*, July 1, 2013, http://almesryoon.com.
2. Carl L. Becker, "What are historical facts?" in Phil L. Snyder, ed., *Detachment and the Writing of History: Essays and Letters of Carl. L. Becker* (Ithaca: Cornell University Press, 1958), p. 61.
3. David Lowenthal, "Fabricating Heritage," *History and Memory*, Vol. 10, No. 1 (Spring 1998), p. 13.
4. Pierre Nora, "Between Memory and History: Les Lieux de Mémoire," *Representations*, Spring 1989 (*Special Issue: Memory and Counter-Memory*, 26), p. 7.
5. Svetlana Boym, *The Future of Nostalgia* (New York: Basic Books, 2001), p. xiii.
6. Nick Hodgin, *Screening the East: Heimat, Memory and Nostalgia in German Film Since 1989* (New York: Berghahn Books, 2011), p. 154.
7. Stewart, Susan, *On Longing: Narratives of the Miniature, the Gigantic, the Souvenir, the Collection* (Baltimore: Johns Hopkins University Press, 1984), p. 23.
8. Joel Gordon, "Secular and Religious Memory in Egypt: Recalling Nasserist Civics," *The Muslim World*, 87(2), April 1997, p. 105.
9. Hosny Guindy and Hani Shukrallah, "Liberating Nasser's Legacy", *Al-Ahram Weekly*, September 28 – October 4, 2000, Issue No. 501.
10. Gabriel Ben-Dor, Foreword to *Rethinking Nasserism: Revolution and Historical Memory in Modern Egypt*, edited by Elie Podeh and Onn Winckler (University Press of Florida: 2004), p. x.
11. Meir Hatina's "History, Politics and Collective Memory: The Nasserist Legacy in Mubarak's Egypt" analyzes the contested legacy of Nasserism and its use in contemporary politics under Mubarak. In: *Rethinking Nasserism: Revolution and Historical Memory in Modern Egypt*, pp. 100–124.
12. Ahmed el-Tonsi, "Nasser and Egypt's two revolutions", *Al-Ahram Weekly Online*, 29 September 29 – October 5, 2011, http://weekly.ahram.org.eg/2011/1066/focus.htm.
13. Sonia Farid, "Chapters praising Mubarak regime removed from Egyptian textbooks," *Al-Arabiya News*, April 21, 2011, http://english.alarabiya.net/articles/2011/04/21/146224.html.
14. Wala'a Morsi, "Intellectuals responding to Morsi's words 'What do you know about the sixties': We had wished for a speech to Egyptians, not a settling of accounts," *Al-Ahram*, July 1, 2012, http://gate.ahram.org.eg/News/226699.aspx.
15. "Egypt's Morsi vows more jobs, end to privatisations," *Ahram Online*, April 30, 2013, http://english.ahram.org.eg/News/70443.aspx.
16. "Morsi commends 'Abd al-Nasir's role in the industries in the sixties, what do you know about the sixties," *YouTube*, retrieved August 27, 2013, http://www.youtube.com/watch?v=KbhVHRqWXOI.
17. "President on July 23 Revolution Anniversary: We Will Go Forth for Better Future for Egypt," *Ikhwanweb*, July 23, 2012, http://www.ikhwanweb.com/article.php?id=30202.

18. "Ceremony at Nasser's mausoleum turns into anti-Brotherhood protest," *Ahram Online*, July 23, 2012, http://english.ahram.org.eg/News/48495.aspx

19. See, for example, these two videos: https://www.youtube.com/watch?v=TX4RK8bj2W0 and https://www.youtube.com/watch?v=EFvLz4FQ6vE.

20. See, for example: "Women of Suez demand Morsi out... while men wave pictures of 'Abd al-Nasir," *Al-Youm al Sab'a*, June 28, 2013, http://www.youm7.com/News.asp?NewsID=1137249 and "Ismaili demonstrators wave pictures of 'Abd al-Nasir in marches demanding the departure of Morsi," *Al-Watan*, June 30, 2012, http://www.elwatannews.com/news/details/213083.

21. Martin Chulov, "Egypt wonders if army chief is another Nasser", *The Guardian*, August 7, 2013, http://www.theguardian.com/world/2013/aug/07/egypt-morsi-nationalist-general-sisi.

22. Child "'Abd al-Fatah al-Sisi" gives military salute to 'Abd al-Nasir…" *Al-Fagr*, July 24, 2013, http://new.elfagr.org/Detail.aspx?secid=1&nwsId=389452&vid=2.

23. Fadi Francis, "Hundreds celebrate the 61ˢᵗ anniversary of the revolution in Tahrir square and raise pictures of 'Abd al-Nasir," *Al-Masry Al-Youm*, July 23, 2013, http://www.almasryalyoum.com/node/1974896.

24. "In pictures: 23 July commemorations in front of Nasir's tomb", *Al-Masry Al-Youm*, July 23, 2013, http://www.almasryalyoum.com/node/1973571.

25. "Nasserists raise pictures of al-Sisi in Qena while preacher in al-Sa'a Square describes him as the new pharaoh," *Al-Ahram*, July 26, 2013, http://gate.ahram.org.eg/News/376551.aspx.

26. "President Adly Mansour: Following the 23 July Revolution, mistakes have been made which we condemn... But that does not justify the revenge of the past," *Al-Ahram*, July 22, 2013, http://gate.ahram.org.eg/News/375214.aspx.

27. "Egypt's president hails ex-military presidents on 1952 revolution anniversary", *Ahram Online*, July 22, 2013, http://english.ahram.org.eg/NewsContent/1/64/77133/Egypt/Politics-/Egypts-president-hails-exmilitary-presidents-on-r.aspx.

28. Randi Ali, "From Nasser to Sabbahi, the dream of social justice lives on," *Aswat Masriya*, July 23, 2012, http://en.aswatmasriya.com/analysis/view.aspx?id=e4246118-0d9d-42b4-997b-34c9f3e24831.

29. Sheera Frankel, "Calls for Nasser's son to run for President", *The Times*, July 5, 2013, http://www.thetimes.co.uk/tto/news/world/middleeast/article3808334.ece.

30. The amounts of 'Likes' were retrieved on October 30, 2013.

31. "*Gamal 'Abd al-Nasir*" (2) on Facebook, July 18, 2013.

32. "*Gamal 'Abd al-Nasir za'im al-umma al-'arabiya*," March 7, 2013.

33. "Jamal Abdel Nasser II By Mahmoud ElSheikh" on Facebook, June 6, 2010.

34. "*Gamal 'Abd al-Nasir*" (1) on Facebook, July 25, 2013.

35. "*Gamal 'Abd al-Nasir za'im al-umma al-'arabiya*," March 30, 2013.

36. "*Shabaka Nasir Ahbariya* — Nasser News Network 3.N" on Facebook. See the "About" section.

37. "Jamal Abdel Nasser II By Mahmoud ElSheikh" on Facebook. See the "About" section.

38. *Ibid.*

39. Hatina, "History, Politics and Collective Memory: The Nasserist Legacy in Mubarak's Egypt," p. 101.

40. Marianne Hirsch, "The Generation of Postmemory," *Poetics Today*, Vol. 29, No. 1 (Spring 2008), p. 120.

41. Ali, "From Nasser to Sabbahi, the dream of social justice lives on."

42. David Lowenthal, *The Past Is a Foreign Country* (Cambridge University Press, 1985), p. 8.

43. Jay Winter and Emmanuel Sivan, *War and remembrance in the twentieth century* (Cambridge University Press, 1999), p. 31.

# Cohesion and Dissolution:
# The Case of Sudan

## Irit Back

On July 9, 2011, Africa's newest nation was born: South Sudan. After almost four decades of civil war (1955-1972; 1983-2005), an estimated death toll of more than two million and displacement of nearly four million persons, South Sudan's establishment attested to the ability of a long-suffering population to successfully challenge an oppressive and violent regime. Yet, at the same time, the dissolution of Sudan marked the first direct rejection of Africa's principle of maintaining the sovereignty and territorial integrity of all the continent's states.[1] Sudan's dissolution into two sovereign states was a dramatic event that has challenged many of the conventional, even sacrosanct notions of state cohesion, sovereignty, and territorial integrity. This chapter will analyze these challenges, in terms of both Sudanese politics and those of the African continent as a whole.

Since the establishment of the Organization of African Unity (OAU) in 1963, the promotion and maintenance of the cohesion of its member states, many of them newly independent, and respecting their sovereignty and territorial integrity, have been an integral part of the African discourse on unity. From the 1960s until the end of the 1980s, it became evident that the sovereign African states' commitment to these principles served to legitimize their disregard for neighboring intrastate conflicts, in spite of clear evidence of grave human rights violations which were often taking place. The OAU's unwillingness to formulate a clear joint position on such violations first emerged with regard to the secessionist efforts of Congo's Katanga region from 1960 to 1963, and again during the Nigerian-Biafran War between 1967 and 1970, and was reflected repeatedly in the organization's passivity towards numerous cases of intrastate conflicts in the 1970s and 1980s.[2]

This fierce commitment to sovereignty, however, was lessened in the post-Cold War era. In an article titled "Sovereignty Reconsidered," Letitia Lawson and Donald Rothschild examine developments in African positions on state sovereignty and cohesion in this period. They claim that the changing post-Cold War global environment triggered a shift that deflected Africans from their Cold War-era insistence on the inviolability of African state sovereignty:

Since the Cold War's end, the development of regional governance and globalization has diminished state authority. Transnational institutions increasingly handle critical problems such as currency control, mineral smuggling, taxation, corporate mergers, communications, defense, border security, broadcasting, and environmental controls. Meanwhile, the electronic and information revolutions have achieved a global reach that is not effectively regulated by states in Africa or elsewhere. And the international movement of migrants, goods, capital, and services continues to undermine borders.[3]

The change, the authors claim, was forced by a combination of external and internal pressures that affected "the African state, both as an autonomous institutional actor and as a set of patrimonial organizing principles," and created "insecure states." External pressures include "an emerging international individual rights regime" that restricts how sovereign states treat their citizens, and "external demands for structural economic adjustment, measures to combat corruption, and democratization as preconditions for continued resource flows." Internal pressures include factors such as "ethno-regional pressures for increased representation, autonomy, or self-determination" and "the proliferation of local international alliances in which local groups seek to affect [sic] change within their countries through international mechanisms while international actors seek change within nations by going around states."[4]

Changes in perceptions regarding state sovereignty were noticed at the continental level with the transformation of the OAU to the African Union (AU) in 2002. This transformation signified the member states' desire to establish a more effective model for African unity. Compared to the former organization's ambiguous commitment to the principle of "peaceful dispute settlement," the new organization seemed to have added checks and balances and other monitoring mechanisms that potentially made it a more effective, democratic, and autonomous organization.[5] The Constitutive Act of the AU was the core instrument for achieving goals such as peace, security, and stability in Africa. The Peace and Security Council (PSC), comprising 15 rotating members, was established to coordinate all responses to events involving grave human rights violations. Despite the AU's innovative legislation and regulation, which were designed to deal with these situations, the organization's commitment to the principles of state sovereignty, territorial integrity, and state independence was not (and, in some respects, is still not) clearly defined.[6]

Sudan, the biggest African state at the time, posed a special challenge to the re-invented continental organization. In 2003, while the AU struggled to define its policy positions toward intrastate conflicts, initial mediation efforts were held between the Sudanese state authorities and the rebel leaders from the south of

Sudan in search of a diplomatic breakthrough in their ongoing conflict. Those efforts were accompanied by rumors of a growing violence in Darfur, Sudan's western province. The African Union's efforts to find a comprehensive solution to Sudan's challenges of maintaining cohesion and preventing dissolution will be discussed later. Before delving into those issues, however, a short description of the roots of the inter-Sudanese processes that led to the disintegration of the Sudanese state is needed.

The civil war between the underdeveloped South and the politically dominant North erupted even before the British ceded colonial control in 1955, and continued uninterrupted until 1972 when the first phase of the war ended. In this period, persistent impoverishment and underdevelopment were exacerbated by chronic political instability. Under a cease-fire accord was signed between the rivals under the autocratic military rule of Ja'fr al-Numayri (1969–1985), the South was, to some extent, guaranteed autonomy. Yet it soon became apparent that the government of Khartoum had no practical intention of fulfilling its promises toward the South, and the civil war was renewed in 1983, continuing until 2005. This civil war, the longest in post-colonial Africa, accounted for approximately two million deaths and four million refugees and IDPs (internally displaced persons).[7]

The roots of the South's sense of deprivation stemmed from longstanding socio-economic characteristics of Sudan's state-building processes. The *Jellaba*, the class of wealthy merchants and officials whose origins can be traced to the Nile Valley, were thriving at the time of the Turko-Egyptian conquest in the nineteenth century, and they continued to prosper under British colonial rule. Through the British colonial system, the *Jellaba* created networks of political and economic alliances with British officials and traditional rulers, resulting in the spread of this elite group into the southern, eastern and western districts of the colony. As a result, the *Jellaba* were better prepared to inherit political and state power in 1956. Their dominant ideology, characterized by Nilo-centrism and Arabism, including the group's use of Arabic as the language of instruction in schools and Islamism as the state ideology, changed little after independence. The exclusion of Africa was illustrated by the emerging hegemonic discourse on the origins of Islam in Sudan, emphasizing its eastward origins (from the Arabian Peninsula and the Nile Valley) while ignoring the earlier West African carrying of Islam to some parts of Sudan (such as the old Sudanese kingdom of Funj and Western kingdom of Darfur) and minimizing the contribution of non-northern parts of the country to the Islamic renaissance in other periods (such as the nineteenth century *Mahdiyya* movement).[8]

There are some claims that the arguments regarding the Arabs' supremacist perceptions are derived basically from colonial literature that cultivated this myth, while a more nuanced historical perspective holds that "Arabs" are not an ethnic or racial group, but a cultural identity. Mahmood Mamdani, for instance, claims that in Sudan, Arab is "a political identity, one that is tribal, not racial. So to be an Arab is to belong to an Arab tribe."[9] R. S. O'Fahey claims that African and Arab influences combined to create a hybrid form of local Islam, which cannot be simplistically reduced to a model of "popular" or Sufi Islam, in contrast to urban Azhari "orthodoxy," and that Islam in Sudan (including the Islam of the ruling elite) was both an African "divine kingship" and an "Islamic Polity."[10]

Notwithstanding the different views regarding the origin and historical development of the riverine Northern Sudanese, there is common agreement that they cultivated the idea that they are not Africanized Arabs but trace their origins to outside of Africa. By doing so, they were ignoring inter-Sudanese historical processes such as migration, intermarriage, etc., thus enabling themselves to fortify their political and economic hegemony. For the rest of Sudan, the personalization of power by the Muslim Arabs in Khartoum and their efforts to create a homogeneous Sudanese culture without the requisite state infrastructure exacerbated the needs and desire for ethnic ties and consciousness among the groups excluded from the dominant ethnic identity. These expectations for ethnic unity were manifested in the formation of different groups who hoped to achieve what the dominant group within the central government had historically denied them, effective and significant decision-making capacity.[11] These common feelings of deprivation and neglect were not exclusive to the South of Sudan. There appear to be many similarities (as well as differences) between the ethnic-racial reactions developed in the South and in the west of Sudan and its impact on the attitudes of the northern-based elites toward Sudan's "non-Arab" citizens.

While the inhabitants of Sudan's predominately Christian and traditionalist South expressed their rejection of the hegemonic Nilo-Islamist discourse through ideological argumentation and guerrilla warfare, local "African" ethnic groups in Darfur (in western Sudan), such as the Fur, Masalit, and Zaghawa, were permanently deprived of political representation. In contrast to the South, then, it seemed that the Darfurian interests and hopes of better integration within Sudan focused more on socio-economic issues, rather than ethno-racial identity (religion was not a factor, as the Darfurians were Muslims, like the northerners). This assumption was valid until the end of the 1970s, when climatic changes, such as desertification and drought, affected the Sahara belt in particular, including Sudan's western and southern areas. These climatic effects intensified throughout the 1980s.[12]

The affinity between the country's South and Sudan's other regions had been predicted in the 1980s by John Garang, the visionary leader of the southern Sudan People's Liberation Movement/Army (SPLM/A). He cautioned,

> It is often forgotten that the Sudan is not just north and south. The Sudan is also west, east and center, no matter what definitions you wish to attach to these labels... All patriots must appreciate the reality that we are a new breed of Sudanese; we will not accept being fossilized into sub-citizens in the 'Regions.'[13]

Garang's predictions appeared to have been realized following the Islamic revolution of 1989, which led to the ruling party, the National Islamic Front (NIF), spreading a new Arab supremacist ideology. This was particularly evident after Omar al-Bashir established his dominance over the NIF, shoving aside Hassan al-Turabi, the ideological leader of the revolution.[14] Under Bashir's leadership, the NIF adhered to its traditional agenda of promoting Northern-Islamic hegemony, a tradition that became the target of attack by *The Black Book: Imbalance of Power and Wealth in Sudan*, which was published in May 2000. Demanding "justice and equality," the authors of the book tracked Northern dominance in all government agencies and powers including the police and military hierarchy, the judiciary, provincial administration, banks, and development administrations. "Every president had come from this region [and] most senior ministers and generals too," the authors claimed. The authors argued that most of the Sudanese wealth and political power had been controlled by three northern tribes since independence, and criticized the NIF for its "inability to depart from established patterns of injustice."[15]

The events of September 11, 2001 marked another milestone in the relations between the Sudanese center and its peripheries, as they had a direct effect on the struggle for power in the NIF. In the eyes of the West, and especially in the view of the Americans, Bashir was considered pro-Western and moderate in comparison to Turabi, who was known for his *al-Qa'ida* sympathies. In his efforts to reinforce his image in the West, and to secure the revenues from the country's fledgling oil industry, Bashir initiated intensive negotiations toward a peace accord from 2003 to 2005 between Sudan's two warring factions: the northern Sudan government and the southern SPLM/A in Naivasha, Kenya. These talks culminated in the Comprehensive Peace Agreement (CPA) signed in 2005.[16]

Continental efforts to mediate between the Sudan's North and the South had begun already in 1992–3, when the OAU initiated the Abuja peace talks. Yet, these talks failed and further efforts by the OAU were limited in scope.[17] Surprisingly, much of the success of the North-South dialogue could be attributed to a massive diplomatic effort by the regional Intergovernmental Authority on Development (IGAD). After the collapse of the talks, the NIF had approached the regional body of the Inter-Government Authority on Drought and Development (IGADD) in its summit meeting of 1993,[18] asking its leaders to mediate in the Sudanese conflict. In response, an IGAD sub-committee on conflict resolution in the IGAD sub-region was formed whose members were the presidents of Kenya, Uganda, Eritrea, and Ethiopia. It was the first political mediation effort of IGAD, which until then had mainly concentrated on natural disaster relief efforts.

The Sudanese government had agreed to IGAD's diplomatic initiative, especially because its Islamist policy had come under strong international diplomatic and financial pressure following the Islamic revolution of 1989. Despite its concerns about IGAD's disposition toward the Sudanese government, the SPLM/A had several reasons for joining the process, including its growing difficulty in achieving victory in combat. Eventually, the North-South mediation process continued for more than a decade, followed by ups and downs triggered by intra-Sudanese factors as well as external factors, such as the split within IGAD following the Ethiopia-Eritrea War between 1998 and 2000. The case of IGAD's intervention in the conflict between North and South illustrated how proactive intervention and mediation efforts by a regional organization can contribute to relatively successful conflict resolution.[19]

The 2010 elections in Sudan were another important step toward the implementation of the Comprehensive Peace Agreement (CPA). The first democratic local, national, and presidential elections in 24 years were originally scheduled to be held in 2009 as part of the implementation of the 2005 CPA agreement, but were ultimately held on April 16, 2010. According to official results, Bashir received 68.24 percent of the estimated 10.1 million votes. In the immediate period following the election, he took aggressive action against his opponents. Freedom House's critical report stated, "Bolstered by his victory, al-Bashir launched a crackdown on civil liberties in the North."[20] Still, the overwhelming victory (92.99%) of Salva Kiir Mayardit for the post of president of the country's southern region was one of the most significant results of the April elections. The SPLM won 87 percent of the South's regional Legislative Assembly seats (all but four seats) as well as nine out of ten governorships.

The election results had direct consequences for the subsequent referendum in South Sudan held on January 9, 2011, in which the population voted on whether or not to secede from the North and establish an independent state.[21] The result left no doubt as to their preference: 98.93 percent South Sudanese voted for independence marking a watershed of continental proportions. The dissolution of Sudan into two sovereign states could be considered the first direct deviation from the principle of sanctifying the sovereignty and territorial integrity of all member states. Notwithstanding the threat to state sovereignty, the African Union policies and actions almost unanimously supported the Southern Sudanese claim for self-determination and separation. From a historical perspective, this support constituted an almost inconceivable transformation in African perceptions since African states became independent of colonial rule.

African support for South Sudan's self-determination was expressed in advance of the referendum at an international meeting at the United Nations in New York on September 24, 2010, which was convened by UN Secretary-General Ban Ki-Moon to review the situation. African attendance at the meeting was impressive, and included the president of Malawi (chairperson of the AU), the prime minister of Ethiopia (the chairman of IGAD), other African heads of state, and representatives of other regional organizations. AU Commission Chairperson Dr. Jean Ping urged the leaders and people of Sudan to rise to the historic challenge of organizing a legitimate, credible referendum on the self-determination of South Sudan.[22] The unanimous support of African states for the South Sudan insistence on the right of self-determination (and eventually independence) is especially noteworthy in that the AU rejected such claims in other cases, such as Somaliland's longstanding efforts to secede from Somalia.[23]

Nonetheless, events following the referendum and subsequent establishment of an independent South Sudan demonstrated the incomplete nature of the agreements between the North and the South.[24] Thus, although the CPA dealt at length with political and wealth-sharing issues between the North and the South, it left some critical matters unresolved, particularly the delineation of precise borders between the two states and ownership of the oil-rich area of Abyei. During the five years of negotiations between the North and the South, it became evident that many of the oil fields were located in the future southern state. To cope with this reality, the CPA created an innovative deal in which the two sides agreed to split the country's oil wealth. However, the implementation of this decision was extremely problematic. In fact, oil plays a central role in the economies of both countries, and thus promises to be a matter of ongoing contention (and even confrontation) between them. [25]

Three other main issues are highly relevant in the post-CPA era: the demarcation of state borders, the risk of further fragmentation of the Sudanese state and the question regarding the cohesion of South Sudan.[26]

The controversy over Abyei has proven that issues of state cohesion and dissolution are often interwoven with additional factors, such as the need to define borders, which add further complexity to matters that are already highly contentious. Landlocked South Sudan is bordered by Ethiopia to the east, Kenya to the southeast, Uganda to the south, the Democratic Republic of the Congo to the southwest, and the Central African Republic to the west. As such, South Sudan is more likely to become embroiled in border disputes with its neighbors. A recent report of an incident between South Sudan and Uganda, its southern neighbor, illustrates the complexity of these borders issues:

> Ugandan police arrested three South Sudanese citizens last month for allegedly cultivating 300 hectares of land near the village of Abaya, about 12 km inside the Ugandan border. Edward Kala, a tractor driver, Simon Jangara, his employee, and Moses Mano, a herdsman, were detained in the village of Wano and later released after the intervention of the district chief. This sparked outrage from local residents, who threatened to stage demonstrations if the issue is not resolved. At the heart of the dispute is the difference between customary boundaries, which are not legally recognized, and international borders, which date back to British colonial rule. Police investigations revealed that South Sudanese rebels had used the disputed land as a training base in the 1950s during a revolt against the Khartoum government, and had regarded it as part of southern Sudan ever since. In conversations with people on both sides of the Ugandan border, the dispute is testing the limits of patriotism, friendship and neighborly relations.[27]

The border dispute issue is closely related to internal issues regarding the cohesion of both Sudanese states. Khartoum had to face the risk that the South's secession would have a ripple effect on other restive provinces, such as Darfur, Southern Kordofan, and Blue Nile. As was mentioned earlier, since the beginning of the negotiations over the CPA, the Sudanese government reacted with severe violence to the evolving conflict in its western province. In the case of the North-South conflict, which was portrayed as a predominantly religion-based matter, the inhabitants of Darfur are largely Muslims, and as such it was harder to justify the use of violence against them. In this context, Gerard Prunier claimed:

> The North-South conflict has been in many of its aspects a colonial conflict, while the Darfur uprising was from the beginning much closer to a genuine civil war. And civil wars are often the most relentless forms of conflict because they involve relatives. In Khartoum, the government panicked because it suddenly felt that the Muslim family was splintering, potentially with enormous consequences."[28]

From the political center, it seems that the Sudanese government is determined to retain control of the "remaining" country, even at the cost of further delegitimizing its international status.[29] From the perspective of the periphery, the success of the South Sudanese in determining their own fate serves, in some cases, as a stimulus and source of encouragement for secessionists' demands, like those raised by some, although not all groups in Darfur.[30]

As for the new state of South Sudan, its internal challenges are enormous. Its most pressing concerns are economic issues: the country is defined as the world's poorest, it is almost entirely lacking in infrastructure, more than half of its population is fed by aid agencies, and the country is utterly unable to absorb its numerous refugee communities.[31] Yet, from the perspective of the discussion on state cohesion versus dissolution, it is particularly intriguing to ask whether or not the new state will be able to create a national ethos and identity that can serve to unify its ethnically, linguistically, and religiously heterogeneous population. Currently, it seems that ethno-regional splits are clouding the prospects for state cohesion, as exemplified by the case of Jonglei State.

Prior to independence, in March 2011, after losing the election to another SPLM candidate, former SPLM General George Athor Deng led a militia that clashed with SPLM forces. Since independence, clashes between Athor's and SPLM forces resumed in the eastern Jonglei State, claiming the lives of many civilians. Athor justified his actions as a response to the undemocratic and corrupt behavior of the SPLM, and accused the ruling party of committing "crimes against humanity," mainly against the party's opponents. Indeed, recent reports from Jonglei State indicate a resumption of ethnic conflict, mainly between the Lou Nuer and the Murle tribes. Reportedly, these clashes claimed the lives of 30 people, and caused tens of thousands to flee from their homes to the safety of the bush. These events have caused an increase in the already significant number of internally displaced persons (IDPs) in this state.[32]

Beyond Jonglei, others have accused the SPLM of exercising a preference for the Dinka over other ethno-tribal and religious groups when appointing people to influential positions. Whether or not these accusations are well founded, South Sudan's ruling party has to find ways to democratize and incorporate its various ethnic, linguistic, religious, and regional interest groups. Failing to heed these early warning signs may lead to calamitous civil strife.

To conclude, the dissolution of Sudan into two sovereign states could be considered a turning point in Africa's commitment to maintaining the sovereignty and territorial integrity of all the continent's states. After witnessing the horrors of Africa's longest civil war, and one of its most brutal, it was encouraging to notice that a solution could be reached through negotiations. The signing of the CPA was not just a product of the willingness of both sides to end the conflict, but also could be attributed to broader African efforts. The active mediation of the regional organization IGAD, combined with the unanimous support of the continental organization (AU), was translated into the opportunity to implement the CPA in 2011, and is still felt in the continued efforts of both organizations to find solutions to ongoing disagreements between the two states.[33]

Yet, approximately two years after independence, the incomplete nature of the CPA is causing it to unravel. It turned out that many crucial issues were left unresolved, leaving the door open to renewed conflict. Moreover, the proliferation of ethnic violence in Sudan and South Sudan alike since the separation implies that many issues regarding the cohesion of both states remain unresolved. Sudan faces a growing wave of demands to redefine its relations with its peripheries (including ones with separatist movements), while South Sudan, struggles with growing demands for equal participation in its nation-building projecgt. The recognition of different ethnic, religious, linguistic, and regional "voices" and recruiting them into the process of building a more inclusive state still lies ahead for both states. Its successes and failures will serve as important lessons for other African and Middle Eastern states experiencing similar processes today.

# Notes

1.  Although it can be argued that Eritrea's secession from Ethiopia was a precedent for the Southern Sudan referendum, it was not quite the same case as Ethiopia was not colonized during the colonial partition of Africa in the late nineteenth century, and annexed Eritrea only in 1952.

2.  Adekeye Adebajo, "The Curse of Berlin: Africa's Security Dilemmas," *Internationale Politik und Gesellschaft* 4 (2005), pp. 83–98; W. Scott Thompson and Richard Bissell, "Legitimacy and Authority in the OAU," *African Studies Review*, Vol. 15, Issue 1 (April 1972), pp. 17–42.

3.  Letitia Lawson and Donald Rothchild, "Sovereignty Reconsidered," *Current History* 104 (May 2005), p. 229.

4.  *Ibid.*

5.  Omar A. Touray, "The Common African Defence and Security Policy," *African Affairs*, Vol. 104, No. 417 (2005), pp. 635–656; Thomas D. Zweifel, *International Organizations and Democracy: Accountability, Politics, and Power* (Boulder: Lynne Rienner, 2006).

6.  John Akokpari, Angela Ndinga-Muvumba, and Tim Murith, eds., *The African Union and its Institutions* (Auckland Park, South Africa: Fanele, 2008).

7.  For a detailed description of underlying causes of the ongoing civil war and the complex structure of racial/ethnic identities in the North and the South, see: Robert O. Collins, *Civil Wars and Revolution in the Sudan: Essays on the Sudan, Southern Sudan, and Darfur, 1962–2004* (Hollywood: Tsehai, 2005).

8.  Awad al-Sid Al-Karasani, "Beyond Sufism: The Case of Millennial Islam in the Sudan," in *Muslim Identity and Social Change in Sub-Saharan Africa*, ed. Louis Brenner (Bloomington: Indiana University Press, 1993), pp. 135–153.

9.  Mahmood Mamdani, *Saviors and Survivors: Darfur, Politics and the War on Terror* (New York: Pantheon Books, 2009).

10. R. S. O'Fahey "Islam and Ethnicity in the Sudan," *Journal of Religion in Africa,* Vol. 26, No. 3 (1996), p. 259.

11. Kelechi A. Kalu, "Resolving African Crises: Leadership Role for African States and the African Union in Darfur," *African Journal of Conflict Resolution*, Vol. 9, No. 1 (2009), pp. 9–40.

12. Ray Bush, "Hunger in Sudan: The Case of Darfur," *African Affairs* 87 (January 1988), pp. 5–23.

13. John Garang, *John Garang Speaks* (London: KPI, 1987), p. 93.

14. 'Abdel Wahhab Al-Effendi, *Turabi's Revolution: Islam and Power in Sudan* (London: Grey Seal, 1991).

15. For a translated version of the text, see: http://www.sudanjem.com/sudan-alt/english/books/blackbook_part1/blackbook_part1_20040422_bbone.pdf.

16. Marc Lacey, "Sudan and the Southern Rebels Sign Deal Ending Civil War," *New York Times,* January 10, 2005.

17. Steven Wondu and Ann Lesch, *Battle for Peace in Sudan: An Analysis of the Abuja Conferences 1992–93* (Lanham, MD: University Press of America, 2000).

18. That year, IGADD changed its name by dropping "Drought" and became known as IGAD.

19. For a detailed description of IGAD's mediation efforts in Sudan, see: Ruth Iyob and Gilbert M. Khadiagala, *Sudan: The Elusive Quest for Peace* (Boulder: Lynne Rienner Publishers, 2006), pp. 101–132.

20. "The Comprehensive Peace Agreement Between The Government of The Republic of The Sudan and The Sudan People's Liberation Movement/Sudan People's Liberation Army," available at: https://peaceaccords.nd.edu/site_media/media/accords/SudanCPA.pdf

21. Africa News, "Sudan; AU Commission Chairman Urges Country to Rise to Referendum Challenge in 2011," September 27, 2010.

22. Africa News, "Sudan: AU Commission Chairman Urges Country to Rise to Referendum Challenge in 2011," September 27, 2010.

23. Redie Bereketeab, *Self-Determination and Secessionism in Somaliland and South Sudan: Challenges to Postcolonial State-Building* (Uppsala: Nordiska Afrikainstitutet, 2002).

24. United Nations News Center. "Sudan: UN Civilian Protection Officials Voice Alarm over Violence in Abyei," March 16, 2011, available at: http://www.un.org/apps/news/story.asp?NewsID=37790&Cr=abyei&Cr1.

25. See, for example: Shannon Ding, Kelly Wyett and Eric Werker, "South Sudan: The Birth of an Economy," *Innovations: Technology, Governance, Globalization,* Volume 7, No. 1, 2012, pp. 73–90.

26. Christopher Zambakari, "South Sudan: Institutional Legacy of Colonialism and the Making of a New State," *The Journal of North African Studies*, Volume 17, No. 3, 2012, pp. 515–532.

27. Lodiyong Moritz, "South Sudan, Uganda in Border Dilemma," *The Niles Editors*, August 7, 2011.

28. Gerard Prunier, *Darfur: The Ambiguous Genocide* (Ithaca, NY: Cornell University Press, 2005), p. XI.

29. It is important to note that on March 4, 2009, the International Criminal Court issued an arrest warrant for Sudanese President Omar al-Bashir, accusing him of crimes against humanity in Darfur (an accusation that later was changed to genocide). This precedent setting court ruling, which included the first arrest warrant ever issued against an incumbent head of state, produced a highly contentious debate within Africa and beyond. See: Victor Peskin, "Caution and Confrontation in the International Criminal Court's Pursuit of Accountability in Uganda and Sudan," *Human Rights Quarterly*, Vol 31 (August 2009), pp. 655–691.

30. Khalid Mustafa Medani, "Strife and Secession in Sudan," *Journal of Democracy*, Volume 22, Number 3, July 2011, pp. 135–149.

31. See, for example, one of recent articles on this topic: "Food and fuel prices skyrocket in Nyala amid fears of famine," *Sudan Tribune*, July 31, 2013.

32. Charelton Doki, "S. Sudan detains Commander after human rights abuses in Jonglei", *The Niles Editors*, August 26, 2013.

33. "Relations Between Sudan and South Sudan: Launch, by the African Union and IGAD, of the AD HOC Investigative Mechanism," *African Union Press Release*, July 22, 2013.

# PART IV
# North Africa

# The Revolution's Aftermath: Tunisia's Road to a Renewed Polity

## Daniel Zisenwine

On January 13, 2011, Tunisia's president, Zayn al-'Abidin Ben 'Ali relinquished his official duties and fled the country. His departure followed several weeks of steadily intensifying anti-government protests that swept across Tunisia following the self-immolation of Mohamed Bouazizi, a 26-year old resident of the dusty provincial town of Sidi Bouzid, some 200 kilometers southeast of the capital, Tunis. His was an act of despair, protesting against economic woes and his confrontations with the authorities for selling fruits and vegetables from a street cart without a license. Many young Tunisians, jobless or underemployed, identified with Bouazizi's plight.[1] Frustrated by their dim economic prospects, increasingly irked at Ben 'Ali's authoritarian, repressive regime, and enraged by growing reports of endemic corruption amongst Ben 'Ali's family members and associates, Tunisians took to the streets in unprecedented anti-government rallies. As these protests gained momentum and made their way from the hinterland to the capital, the government initially clamped down on the protestors, but increasingly appeared hesitant and confused as to what an appropriate reaction would be. On January 12, 2011 Ben 'Ali delivered a televised address in which he acknowledged some of the protestors' complaints and promised to alter his policies. Visibly rattled by the protests' impact, the president announced that he would not run in the next elections, scheduled for 2014: "I understand you," he said. The address did not leave much of an imprint on the public. The next day's demonstrations in Tunis were the largest ever, as crowds called for Ben 'Ali's resignation. Less than 24 hours later, Ben 'Ali, who had ruled Tunisia since 1987, fled the country, finding asylum in Saudi Arabia.[2]

While the actual motives for Ben 'Ali's abrupt departure remain a matter of debate, one thing became clear on the morning after his flight: Tunisia had experienced what was for the Arab world an unprecedented event — a sitting authoritarian ruler had been forced out of office through largely peaceful protests. The news of Ben 'Ali's flight stunned the Tunisian public, which did not expect such an outcome and was uncertain how to proceed. Across the region, Ben 'Ali's ouster quickly became a source of inspiration. Crowds in Egypt and Yemen enthusiastically waved the Tunisian flag and cried out "Tunisia is the solution," as they protested against their own authoritarian rulers and demanded that they follow Ben 'Ali's example and step down. As international attention shifted away from Tunisia to the unfolding dramatic events in Egypt, Tunisians were left on their own to determine a new political future for their country. While this process has been more successful than in other countries confronting similar circumstances, it has hardly been a smooth one and its outcome remains uncertain. This chapter focuses on Tunisia's post-revolutionary reality and the efforts to transform its political system. These efforts have not seriously undermined the country's relatively high degree of social cohesion or its much-vaunted stability, but have exposed new political forces, social fissures, and economic fault lines that loom over Tunisian life.

At face value, Tunisia possesses qualities that set it apart from other Arab countries. The country is much smaller in population than many of them (10.5 million in Tunisia compared to over 82 million in Egypt, for example), has a relatively high degree of social homogeneity, owing to the absence of substantial ethnic or religious minorities, possesses fairly high literacy rates (79.1 percent[3]), and is characterized by a relatively high degree of gender equality. Many of these characteristics may be important factors underpinning the country's post-revolutionary trajectory. Before considering them, it is important to highlight several important chapters in Tunisia's political history, which serve as a backdrop to the country's recent upheavals.

Unlike other Arab states established after the Ottoman Empire's demise, Tunisia is not an artificially created polity designed to meet post-World War I European imperial needs. Its sense of "stateness" and its bureaucratic tradition reach back at least to the eighteenth century, when a local dynasty asserted itself, rendering Tunisia's ties with the Ottoman rulers in Istanbul nominal and symbolic only. In an unsuccessful quest to resist encroaching European colonialism in the nineteenth century, Tunisia's elite embraced a process of modernization and reform which laid the foundation for a constitutional tradition and introduced the notion of public involvement to political life. Tunisia's relatively short colonial experience (1881-1956) under French rule further reinforced the existing elements of modernization and embrace of Western culture and ideals. New political and social frameworks came to the fore, including trade unions and political parties that played a growing role in public life. Many Western ideals, including the promotion of a national identity, were later incorporated into Tunisia's nationalist movement, which led the largely non-violent anti-colonial struggle for independence, which was attained in 1956.

Under the leadership of Habib Bourguiba, the country's first president until his removal in 1987, Tunisia was known for its moderate positions on regional and international issues and pro-Western orientation. While the country did not foster genuine democracy and political pluralism, Tunisia stood out as an orderly society with a strong bureaucratic tradition, considerable degree of social tolerance, and emphasis on the rule of law. Under Bourguiba, religion was effectively pushed aside in favor of modernization and institution-building projects. A special emphasis was given to gender equality, which was demonstrated by the government's abolishment of polygamy, early adoption of a family planning program, and encouragement of women's education. Tunisia was one of the few Arab countries to witness the emergence of a middle class, which may have been more modest in its assets compared to a Western middle class but nevertheless possessed similar traits, such as stable employment, home ownership and financial solvency. This group would play a pivotal role in modern Tunisian society, as it supported Bourguiba's policies and later endorsed Ben 'Ali, who rose to power in a bloodless coup in 1987. Bourguiba's removal from office, or "the change" as it became known in Tunisian political parlance, was enthusiastically endorsed by the Tunisian middle class concerned with the president's declining health and worried about the lack of a political transitional mechanism. These Tunisians were optimistic regarding the new government's intent to promote a more open society.[4]

Notwithstanding Bourguiba's emphasis on a more secular state-building effort, a strong Islamist opposition movement emerged in Tunisia. This movement, which became a potent political and social force by the late 1980s, sought to restore Islam from its diminished position and impose a more religious character on Tunisia's national identity. Bourguiba viewed the Islamist current as a menace to his rule and to Tunisian society as a whole, and thus repressed it harshly. Initially, the Ben 'Ali regime made hesitant overtures towards the Islamists as part of its tentative steps towards greater political pluralism and a renewed social contract. However, by 1991 the regime viewed the Islamists as a serious threat to its existence, and cracked down on them with an iron fist. Their movement, *Ennahda*, ("renaissance") was effectively removed from public life. Its leaders were imprisoned or exiled, and any hint of *Ennahda* activity was immediately nipped in the bud. Notwithstanding this, it was clear to many observers that *Ennahda*'s messages continued to percolate clandestinely, although the extent of its public appeal remained unclear.[5]

As time went on, the Tunisian public's endorsement of the Ben 'Ali regime soured. The world financial economic downturn of the late 1990s affected the Tunisian economy. International investment in the country decreased, the number of tourists fell, and remittances from Tunisians working abroad (an important source of foreign currency) also dropped. These factors had a direct impact on the country's middle class, which was increasingly strained financially. At the same time, the Ben 'Ali regime veered towards crony capitalism, offering generous benefits to the president's associates and family members. Reports of corruption and extravagant expenditures within these circles increased the public's ire against a regime that had gradually lost touch with it and become increasingly repressive toward any form of dissent. This simmering discontent proved to be the backdrop of the uprising against Ben 'Ali which erupted in late 2010. As the protests against the regime erupted in the aftermath of Mohammed Bouazizi's self-immolation, one important force remerged from the shadow position it occupied in the later Ben 'Ali years-Tunisia's powerful trade union, *Union générale tunisienne du travail* (UGTT). The union staged anti-government rallies and was involved in bringing these protests from the peripheral countryside to the streets of the capital Tunis. The UGTT's role in the demonstrations against Ben 'Ali suggested that Tunisia's civil society, which many assumed had expired under the weight of the repressive regime, remained a formidable force in the country's political and social landscape. The UGTT would continue to be an active player in the post-Ben 'Ali era as well.

Within a short period after Ben Ali's overthrow, Tunisia set out to rebuild its political system, indicating that the revolutionary phase had ended and the transitional process had begun. Two major trends could be discerned: the first was a strong desire to restructure the country's politics and move towards a more pluralist, democratic framework that would incorporate a broad group of political and social forces. Somewhat contradicting that first trend was a second force: the inclination of Tunisia's middle class to maintain stability and oppose ongoing tumult.[6]

The last remaining relics of the Ben 'Ali regime were swiftly removed in the days and weeks following his departure, and were replaced by a transitional government led by Beji Caid Essebsi, a veteran Tunisian political figure from the Bourguiba era. Essebsi and his government negotiated with diverse political players regarding preparations for elections for a National Constituent Assembly entrusted with framing a new constitution for Tunisia and determining its future political system.[7]

As these talks continued throughout the early months of 2011, two significant developments ocurred. First, the Tunisian military retreated completely from political affairs, after playing an important role during the uprising against Ben 'Ali by refusing to open fire at the protestors. In doing so, it maintained its traditional distance from politics and society. Proportionally smaller in size than the armies of other Arab countries, the Tunisian army is generally "republican" in orientation, i.e. it has a non-political character, and does not hold a large stake in the national economy. Unlike in Egypt, where the military has overshadowed the post-revolutionary transitional process, the Tunisian army would be almost non-existent in the country's political life following Ben 'Ali's removal. Its absence from the scene helped the civilian transitional process move forward.

The second, and no less important development, was the Islamist movement's reemergence as a central actor. Within days of Ben 'Ali's departure, *Ennahda*'s London-based exiled leader, Rachid al-Ghannouchi, announced his intention to return to Tunisia and participate in the effort to reconfigure the country's political system. Although Ghannouchi contended that he did not see himself as a political leader in a new Tunisian political system, it was clear that he expected to play an influential role in politics.[8] Moving beyond Ghannouchi's own persona, it was not clear how many Tunisians would actually embrace *Ennahda*, which had been effectively removed from politics and society for nearly two decades. Moreover, it was apparent that if *Ennahda* would indeed seek to play an active role in a renewed political system, it would need to adjust its messages and ambitions to a new generation with which the movement was out of touch. The concerns of *Ennahda* officials regarding their status among Tunisians were quickly dispelled. Upon arrival, Ghannouchi was greeted at the Tunis airport by a crowd of enthusiastic supporters who, along with veteran *Ennahda* activists, provided the foundation of a revived movement. In retrospect, Ghannouchi demonstrated astute political instincts by returning to Tunisia at that particular moment. Still reeling from the shock of Ben 'Ali's unexpected downfall, few political figures or forces inside the country were ready to enter the political fray with a clear idea of what they sought to accomplish. Had Ghannouchi waited longer before returning to Tunisia, he may have ended up a spent force, detached from contemporary events and developments inside the country and unable to reconnect with a shifting political landscape. His arrival, shortly after Ben 'Ali's flight, indicated that he did not intend to squander the unexpected opportunity to play a leading role in post-revolutionary Tunisian politics.

Living in exile since 1991, Ghannouchi remained largely removed from the new generation of young Tunisians who were not involved with his movement in the late 1980s and early 1990s. Indeed, most in the enthusiastic crowd that greeted Ghannouchi at the airport in Tunis were virtually unknown to him. They were products of a new generation that had embraced *Ennahda* as a political force likely to implement an alternative vision for Tunisia. For his part, Ghannuchi announced that that it was time for a new generation to assume a leadership position.

Much has been written about *Ennahda*'s resurgence in post-Ben 'Ali Tunisia. By most accounts, the movement drew its support from a portion of the middle class that had gained traction during the early years of the Ben 'Ali era. While materially benefitting from the Ben Ali-directed economy, some of its members clung to tradition and religion as key components of their identity, seeking to inject greater meaning into their lives beyond the crass commercialism of the Ben 'Ali regime. Over time, their attachment to Islam became a means of protesting against a regime they grew to resent. This group's turn to *Ennahda* in the aftermath of the Tunisian revolution may have been a natural development. But given *Ennahda*'s lack of institutional frameworks, local leaders, and clearly articulated goals, its subsequent success in post-revolutionary Tunisian politics was nonetheless impressive.

To its credit, *Ennahda* demonstrated considerable political and organizational acumen as it took its place in post-revolutionary politics. Within weeks, the party had established local offices and branches across the country. Its rapid expansion stemmed from a combination of the movement's pent-up energy, suddenly released after years of repression, and the widespread public sympathy with its message of morality, social justice and faith. As it reestablished its presence, *Ennahda*'s success was also due to its embrace of a core characteristic of Tunisian politics — moderation and flexibility. The movement and its leaders tirelessly and repeatedly pledged that they were not an "Islamist" party that challenged the existing order, but rather a tradition-oriented social movement. *Ennahda* repeatedly emphasized its adherence to democracy and well-established societal values and norms, such as the active role and participation of women. The party also advocated the establishment of an inclusive political system and expressed interest in reaching out to a diverse group of political actors. Yet, critics of *Ennahda* asserted that this approach was a calculated decision to project a tolerant, inclusive public profile by a party still unsure of its electoral prospects and depth of public support.[9] Whether or not its motives in adopting these positions were genuine, the fact remains that *Ennahda* presented a far different image than the Muslim Brotherhood in Egypt, which expressed scant interest in reaching out to other parties.

When meeting European officials, *Ennahda* figures likened their movement to the veteran European Christian democrats: a traditional, conservative, yet democratic party seeking to allay any international concerns about the Tunisian transition. Given the harsh realities of post-revolutionary Egypt and Libya, the international community was quite keen to safeguard Tunisia's relative success in its transition. For the most part, *Ennahda*'s statements and entreaties were accepted by foreign parties.

A more cynical assessment of *Ennahda*, one articulated by its political opponents and critics, held that the movement's moderate, pro-democratic positions on key issues were nothing more than theatrical maneuvers intended to camouflage *Ennahda*'s true colors. Its critics assailed the movement's statements, vehemently denouncing them and dismissing the movement's pledge for a politics of inclusion and acceptance of opposing views. They argued that whatever positions *Ennahda* adopted on issues such as democracy or women's rights were not to be trusted, as they did not represent the movement's broader aspirations of establishing a religious state that would actually undermine these values. They contended that the movement sought to destabilize the country and undermine its core values, replacing them with a radical, religious ideology.

Secular opposition figures seized upon private or less-publicized statements of *Ennahda* leaders, which were not aimed at the general public or a foreign audience and presented a different vision than the one advanced by the movement. They contended that what *Ennahda* leaders told visiting European officials in French or English sharply differed from the more radical messages delivered in Arabic to a local crowd of supporters. Quotes of Rachid al-Ghannouchi's speech in Cairo, in which he spoke about establishing a "caliphate" as a long-term goal were presented as proof of *Ennahda*'s genuine intentions.[10] Overall, secular opposition forces treated *Ennahda* with a mixture of deep animosity, suspicion and mistrust. As these groups scrambled to gain their footing in a changing post-revolutionary political setting, they watched *Ennahda*'s reemergence with growing alarm. In contrast to *Ennahda*'s untested political record, these groups largely consisted of veteran participants in Tunisian politics, yet remained as weak and unsuccessful as they were throughout the Ben 'Ali years.

Indeed, Tunisia's secular opposition parties have historically commanded a weak political position. While the Islamists were always banned and restricted from assuming active involvement in politics, some secular opposition groups were granted legal status after 1981. These parties, such as the *Mouvement des democrats socialistes* (MDS) were allowed to function within the political system but were largely overshadowed by the ruling parties of the Bourguiba and Ben 'Ali regimes. In addition to the fact that they could not truly compete with the large ruling party, they suffered from a host of internal shortcomings. These included internal squabbles between leaders and factions, which further affected their ability to present themselves as a genuine alternative. Furthermore, they often found it difficult to clearly articulate their goals to the Tunisian public, which largely kept its distance from these parties. Compounding these parties' lack of clear vision and purpose prior to the Tunisian revolution was their alleged affiliation with the Ben 'Ali regime, which tarnished their reputation after his fall. Many Tunisians had little interest in endorsing minuscule parties associated with a past they sought to put behind them, and kept their distance even when it became possible to actively promote these parties. *Ennahda*, on the other hand, was considered by many Tunisians to be an uncompromised, yet untested movement whose leaders and activists paid a heavy price for their convictions during the Ben 'Ali years, and at the very least deserved a chance to prove themselves in a new setting.

Despite the weakened political standing and limited appeal of secular political parties, post-revolutionary Tunisia continued to boast a significant voting bloc of secular voters who opposed the notion of an Islamist party or a religiously oriented movement. These opponents represented a largely urban, Francophone population along with a large number of women activists seeking to protect and expand women's rights. While these voters ultimately did not deliver a victory to any of the veteran secular opposition parties in the 2011 elections for a National Constituent Assembly, they did not retreat from the political scene. The abovementioned general themes of *Ennahda*'s inclusive approach and the wariness of its opponents towards these positions, which underpinned Tunisia's post-revolutionary politics, played themselves out in the pre-election period. It was clear that, among the competing parties, *Ennahda* was the most eager to hold the elections as soon as possible and benefit from its near-instant popularity. Any delays in the vote could potentially thwart *Ennahda*'s position by allowing more time for competing parties to broaden their appeal among the voting public and subject *Ennahda* to political debates about its positions, goals, and ambitions, which at that point the party sought to avoid. Seeking to cultivate its image as a positive force in Tunisian politics, *Ennahda* (often reluctantly) accepted various developments in the period leading up to the elections. It agreed to postpone the vote from the original July date to October after the official agency entrusted with preparing for the vote announced that it would not be ready on time. *Ennahda* activists initially dismissed this argument, claiming that it was intended to undermine their party's potential success. Nevertheless, the party agreed to the postponement.

Throughout the campaign, *Ennahda* leaders reiterated their commitment to democracy and the rule of law. They placed a special emphasis on fundamental principles of Tunisian society, and expressed support for maintaining the existing status of women. The party even recruited women and fielded women candidates in a number of key voting districts, including women who refrained from wearing traditional Islamic garb. These moderate positions further enhanced the party's position among voters. But for *Ennahda*'s detractors, they were yet another example of the party's alleged deceit. *Ennahda* leaders repeatedly denied these claims. Indeed, the debate over *Ennahda*'s true colors became the focal point of the campaign, sidelining other urgent political and economic questions concerning Tunisia's future.

Beyond the larger meta-dispute between *Ennahda* and its rivals, the differences between the various competing parties in Tunisia's elections were insubstantial. Most parties offered similar remedies to the country's economic travails, including attracting foreign investment and creating new employment opportunities for Tunisians. Beyond these generalities, there was little most parties could offer on their own to ameliorate the country's deteriorating economic situation. The months that followed the revolution had not only failed to bring any improvement in the problematic areas of Tunisia's economy, such as a 17 percent unemployment rate,[11] but instead brought a further deterioration. These economic challenges included renewed efforts to reassure existing foreign investors of the country's stability and prospects, as well as attracting new investors. The Tunisian government also faced the need to reduce its deficit and the unemployment level, and address the economic disparities between the peripheral hinterland and the more vibrant economic centers along the Tunisian coast. These disparities could potentially drive a wedge between the more prosperous part of the country and the more depressed countryside. The magnitude of these economic challenges was far beyond the abilities of Tunisia's political parties to confront and required cooperation with the European Union (Tunisia's main trade partner), the International Monetary Fund, and the World Bank. Given the absence of a compelling blueprint for economic improvement, political parties had limited possibilities to offer voters, and so the main differences between parties throughout the campaign were the personalities of leading party officials and their backgrounds.

For the most part, veteran Tunisian opposition leaders and their small movements did not make serious inroads into the electorate during the campaign period. Parties such as the PDP (Progressive Democratic Party) the most established and stable of the opposition parties that survived the Ben 'Ali era, were expected to attract widespread support from voters who opposed *Ennahda*. Tunisian voters, however, ultimately preferred to pin their hopes on new political forces, and turned their back on the old opposition parties. Those who opposed *Ennahda* opted instead to vote for parties such as the *Congres pour la république* (CPR), led by veteran human rights activist, Moncef Marzouki, or the more centrist *Ettakatol* (Democratic Forum for Labor and Liberties) party. Marzouki, in a similar fashion to Ghannouchi, was recognized as an uncompromised political figure who had suffered under the Ben 'Ali regime, proven his sincerity, and thus worthy of endorsement. *Ettakatol*, led by Mustapha Ben Jaafar, was also absent from the Ben 'Ali-era parliament, and deemed a fresh political force.

The vote for the interim 2011 National Constituent Assembly was based on a proportional representation system in which the country was divided into voting districts. In a unique recognition of Tunisia's large expatriate community, Tunisians abroad were not only allowed to vote in the election but could also elect their own representatives for the interim assembly and play a role in fashioning the country's political future. Tunisian politicians, especially those who had lived abroad and maintained ties with the expatriate community, were well aware of this sector's power. They campaigned abroad amongst a population less affected by post-revolutionary economic ills and more concerned with the country's future political system. Overall, the election campaign was conducted in a civil fashion, unmarred by violence or threats, confirming anew Tunisia's historic moderation. Voter participation was not as high as had been hoped (54.1 percent, officially), but nevertheless was enough to legitimize the vote. International observers monitoring the elections reported few irregularities.

The results did not produce a decisive victory for any party. As expected, *Ennahda* received the highest number of seats in the new assembly (89, commanding slightly over 37 percent of the vote) but not enough for a governing majority, thus compelling it to form a coalition with other political forces.

Among the secular parties who did well in the elections were the CPR, which won 29 seats in the assembly (8.71 percent of the vote), and *Ettakatol*, which claimed 20 seats, ahead of the PDP (16 seats) and the MDS (2 seats). In what would have been previously considered an unlikely coalition, *Ennahda* joined with the CPR and *Ettakatol* to form an interim government: the CPR's Marzouki would become Tunisia's president while *Ettakatol*'s Ben Jaafar would serve as the newly elected assembly's speaker. The groundwork for the coalition was laid years earlier, when Marzouki and *Ennahda* activists maintained contacts while in exile.[12] Following the elections, the new government set out to draft a constitution and prepare for the country's new future.[13]

The newly elected assembly was entrusted with overseeing Tunisia's transition process, framing a new constitution for the country, and deciding on a new political system. Throughout this period, many of the hallmarks of Tunisia's transition period remained intact. Aware of the stakes they faced, no political force wanted to be accused of inflicting irrevocable damage to this process or of imposing its own positions on others. In that sense, Tunisia's political tradition of consensus and compromise continued to underpin political developments. A particularly contentious issue was the question of whether *shari'a* would be referred to as a basis for the country's legal system: *Ennahda* ultimately agreed not to include a direct reference to Islamic law, accepting Tunisia's 1959 constitution which declares Islam as the country's religion and accordingly rendering any such reference as unnecessary.[14] To be sure, the final draft brought to the National Assembly for approval in June 2013 was hardly flawless and many questions remain unresolved. For example, there has been a heated debate over article 141 in the proposed draft, which makes references to Islam in the constitution permanent and unchangeable. Secular parties have opposed this article, asserting that it seeks to strengthen the role of Islam at the expense of other ideals in Tunisian society.[15] More concretely, the powers of the president and the judiciary have yet to be finalized.[16] This process indicates the high value placed on avoiding divisive confrontations and seeking compromise that has been sorely lacking in Egypt and elsewhere. It also reflects the existing balance of power in society, with no one faction or current able to impose its will on the rest of the country.

To be sure, the situation in Tunisia is far from perfect. The transitional process has been marked by increasing polarization between Islamists and secular parties, street battles, and occasional political violence. The assassination of two left-wing political figures, Chokri Belaid in February 2013 and Mohamed Brahimi in July of the same year, shocked the Tunisian public, which is unaccustomed to political assassinations. The National Assembly's debate over the draft constitution was suspended in August 2013, as secular opposition members boycotted the proceedings and demanded the government's resignation. While the coalition government remained intact, the situation inside the country became increasingly perilous. As the summer of 2013 passed, the Tunisian government faced mounting pressure from opposition circles. Emboldened by the ousting of Egypt's Islamist government by the military, Tunisia's opposition sought to emulate the Egyptian example by staging large protests in the capital demanding the government's resignation. Frustrated by a lack of economic improvement, protesters expressed their disappointment with *Ennahda*'s overall performance in governing the country. *Ennahda* countered these protests by staging its own rallies. But *Ennahda* leaders also expressed their willingness to compromise.

By late September 2013, negotiations brokered by the UGTT had yielded an agreement between the quarreling sides. *Ennahda* agreed to transfer power to an independent interim government within three weeks as a first step towards new elections. The National Constituent Assembly was expected to ratify the proposed constitution and confirm appointments to the election commission. Although this agreement may augur a new phase in Tunisia's post-revolutionary development, the country's political parties are locked in a hard-nosed power struggle that shows no sign of ending.[17] Amidst this difficult reality, it is still conceivable that Tunisia's political tradition of moderation and compromise will be able to overcome the current violence and deadlock that has threatened to derail the entire post-revolutionary process. Whether this indeed turns out to be the case remains to be seen.

# Notes

1. Rania Abouzeid, "Bouazizi: The Man who Set Himself and Tunisia on Fire," *Time Magazine*, January 21, 2011, www.time.com; Yasmine Ryan, "The Tragic Life of a

Street Vendor," January 20, 2011, www.aljazeera.com; Hernando de Soto, "The Real Mohamed Bouazizi," December 16, 2011, www.foreignpolicy.com.

2.  David. D. Kirkpatrick, "Behind Tunisia's Unrest, Rage over Wealth of Ruling Family," *The New York Times*, January 13, 2011; "Tunisia: Ex-President Ben Ali Flees to Saudi Arabia," www.bbc.co.uk, January 15, 2011.

3.  See: www.cia.gov/library/publications/the-world-factbook.

4.  For more on Tunisia's modern history, see Kenneth J. Perkins, *A History of Modern Tunisia* (Cambridge: Cambridge University Press, 2004); L. Carl Brown, "Bourguiba and Bourguibism Revisited: Reflections and Interpretation," *Middle East Journal*, Vol. 55 No. 1 (Winter, 2001), pp. 43–57.

5.  Emad Eldin Shahin, *Political Ascent: Contemporary Islamic Movements in North Africa* (Boulder: Westeview Press, 1997), pp. 63–111.

6.  Marina Ottaway, "The Revolution is Over, Can Reform Continue," *Carnegie Endowment for International Peace*, July 13, 2011.

7.  David D. Kirkpatrick, "Interim Leader with Ties to Old Ruler Defends a Gradual Path", *The New York Times*, October 3, 2011.

8.  "Tunisian Islamist Leader Rachid Ghannouchi Returns Home," www.bbc.co.uk, January 30, 2011.

9.  Marc Lynch, "Tunisia's New al-Nahda", www.foreignpolicy.com, January 29, 2011; Elizabeth Dickinson, "Secularists Voice Dismay at Election Gains for Tunisia's Islamist Party," www.csmonitor.com, October 25, 2011.

10. "Le Califat est notre objectif ultime," *Le Temps* (Tunis), August 3, 2011.

11. See: www.cia.gov/library/publications/the-world-factbook.

12. Bruce Maddy-Weitzman, "Historic Departure or Temporary Marriage? The Left-Islamist Alliance in Tunisia," *Dynamics of Asymmetric Conflict*, Vol. 5, No. 3 (2012), pp. 196–207.

13. "Final Tunisian Election Results Announced," www.aljazeera.com, November 14, 2011.

14. "Tunisia's Ennahda to Oppose Sharia in Constitution," www.reuters.com; Duncan Pickard, "The Current Status of Constitution Making in Tunisia," *Carnegie Endowment for International Peace*, April 19, 2012; Human Rights Watch, "Tunisia: Fix Serious Flaws in Draft Constitution," Sept. 13, 2012, www.hrw.org.

15. Robert Joyce, "Tunisia's Neglected Constitution", *The Cairo Review of Global Affairs*, October 14, 2013.

16. Shukri Hamad, "Depsite Flaws, Tunisia's New Draft Constitution Promising," www.al-monitor.com, July 1, 2013.

17. Carlotta Gall, "Islamist Party in Tunisia to Step Down," *The New York Times*, September 28, 2013.

# The Libyan "Arab Spring" and Its Aftermath: Challenges to State Order and National Cohesion

## Yehudit Ronen

The opening shot of the "Arab Spring" uprisings was fired in Tunisia, and its flames quickly spread to Egypt and beyond. Libyan leader Mu'ammar al-Qaddafi watched the intensifying upheaval on Libya's western and eastern borders with alarm. His fears were realized on February 13, 2011, two days before the appointed "day of rage" proclaimed on Facebook by Libyan anti-regime activists. Riots first erupted in the eastern city of Benghazi, Libya's second political-economic urban center after the capital Tripoli, and a traditionally powerful bastion of militant Islamist activity.

The rebellion quickly spread across the country, and particularly in its Mediterranean coastal areas where most of the Libyan population and the pulse of the country's economic and political activity is concentrated. As the rebels gathered strength and scored increasing diplomatic and military achievements, questions were raised both in Libya and among analysts and policy makers abroad regarding the identity and vision of the rebel camp. Deciphering the underlying characteristics and aims of what appeared at the time to be a generally monolithic anti-Qaddafi camp was essential in order to better understand the Libyan armed conflict — in fact, a civil war — and to discern the likely potential threats and challenges to the state's political system and national cohesion if Qaddafi's regime was to be toppled. However, deciphering the Libyan opposition was a tall order, and not only because Libya was still enshrouded in the fog of war. Qaddafi's harsh and persistent repression for more than 40 years had crushed any independent group that dared to deviate from the regime's political and ideological line, while at the same time he had fashioned a facade of national cohesion and political and ideological uniformity. The Qaddafi regime's heavy-handed and duplicitous approach to Libyan society, and the tactics it employed to cope with the realities of diverse identities and conflicting political loyalties were not substantially different from those employed by many other Arab regimes facing similar challenges, however harsh and repressive, they may have been.[1]

Two years after the bloody end of the Qaddafi era, the difficulty of reliably mapping the identities, agendas and motives of the relevant actors in the "New Libya" remained acute. The ongoing difficulty stems from the country's continued instability, high level of violence and multiplicity of actors, including new and lesser-known ones.

This essay explores the nature of the challenges faced by the Libyan state and society in the post-Qaddafi era, particularly the efforts — so far unsuccessful — to establish a reasonable degree of political order and stability, and fashion a societal consensus regarding the meaning of Libyan national identity.

Conscious of the fragile and chaotic post-Qaddafi state of affairs as of summer 2013, the study aims to better understand the religious, political, tribal, ethnic, socio-economic, intellectual and demographic forces that compose the post-Qaddafi Libyan state and society. It also seeks to clarify the race to fill the newly created opportunity-inviting vacuum in the Libyan political space. Who are these "new" and "old" actors? To whom and what are they ideologically and politically committed? How strong is the Libyan Islamist current? To what extent, if at all, do Libyan Islamists collaborate with, or ideologically identify with the global jihadist community? Are there active links to groups like al-Qa'ida, in which Libyan jihadists have held senior leadership positions in the past?

A particular focus of this essay will be on the newly emergent phenomenon of the armed militias. Acting to carve out an influential political and economic position and promote their interests, these militias — especially the jihadist ones — have played an especially powerful role in informing post-Qaddafi Libya.

# The Dividing Lines in Libyan Society: Fertile Soil for the Aggrandizement of the Armed Militias

The immediate post-Qaddafi scene was bereft of any effectively organized and confidence-inspiring authority, even if formally headed by the politically weak National Transitional Council (NTC).[2] Hence, it became fertile ground for the proliferation of frustrated ex-rebel, power-hungry armed groups determined to promote their specific interests and, often, to dictate the course of affairs in the chaotic "New Libya." The plethora of armed militias included groups that ranged from several dozen members to tens of thousands and possibly even more.[3] Many had prior military experience and were armed to the teeth with high-quality weapons. The militias were organized according to various combinations of geographic, religious, tribal and military loyalties, as well as political and economic connections. There is no detailed and reliable profile available of the armed militias that would provide essential information about their size, identity, leaders, goals, financial conditions, arms, or connections to various other Libyan militias. There is also little reliable information regarding the connection between the militias and the jihadist organizations active outside Libya, mainly along its southern borders in the African Sahel region, where al-Qa'ida in the Islamic Maghreb (AQIM) has been active.[4]

Yet, the Islamist-jihadist armed militias, whose active presence in Libya and its surrounding environs gained considerable momentum beginning in the 1990s following the return home of *mujahidin* from Afghanistan, Pakistan and subsequently Iraq, have attained an unprecedented power base in Libya, particularly in the eastern region of Cyrenaica near the border with Egypt. Upon their return to Libya in the wake of the withdrawal of the Soviet army from Afghanistan at the end of the 1980s, the *mujahidin*, believing that jihad was the ultimate and sole way to overthrow the "infidel" Qaddafi, had inculcated their militant views into the already active anti-regime Islamist opposition camp.[5] They grew in strength by intertwining their jihadist rhetoric with recruiting and military training in the regions of Benghazi, Derna, and Bin Jawad in eastern Libya, the stronghold of sworn anti-Qaddafi circles: tribal groups, Islamists, and supporters of Idris al-Sanusi, who Qaddafi had deposed in 1969. These militias, well-organized and highly motivated, were commanded by senior ex-*mujahidin*, with one of the most prominent among them being Abd al-Hakim al-Hasadi, a high-level military commander in al-Qa'ida who had recruited and trained *mujahidin* in Afghanistan's Khost camp.[6] This empowered nucleus of militancy has become the center for Islamist and jihadist armed militias in the aftermath of Qaddafi's overthrow.

The diverse armed militias have also included opportunistic elements that are bereft of any political and/or ideological motivation. These militias took advantage of the anarchic post-Qaddafi circumstances to arm themselves and promote their own narrow economic-financial interests, which included organized crime. A huge trafficking network dealing in arms, human beings, and drugs has spread across the country and the Maghreb-Sahel expanses.[7] These regions have served as major smuggling routes from South America to Europe. According to figures for 2011, some 30 tons of cocaine and almost 400 kilograms of heroin were smuggled through these routes, generating profits of between $3 and $14 billion.[8] The smuggling industry via Libya and neighboring countries has already earned the term "global economy," and the flourishing gun-running trade passing along these routes has already changed the geo-strategic and security conditions in Libya and its Arab and African surroundings, spilling into and exacerbating active conflict areas such as Syria, Mali, Sudan, Chad, the Sinai Peninsula, and Gaza. This prosperous alternative economy, during a time of economic stagnation and in some sectors even paralysis, has attracted increasing numbers of Libyans, who secure their interests through the leverage of these armed militias.

Whatever their agendas, all of the armed militias have endeavored to keep their presence off the Libyan and international community's radar as much as possible, which only thickens the veil of smoke that clouds our understanding of the armed militias' identity and role in the "New Libya." In any case, neither they nor the relatively moderate groups who won the elections on July 7, 2012, and have governed the country since then, are unified or cohesive. As a rule, Libyan society has never been homogeneous or cohesive, in national terms, despite being predominantly Sunni Muslim. Rather, it is a diverse and often fractious society, fragmented along ethnic, political, tribal, and geographic lines.

The major geographic dividing line stretches between Cyrenaica in the east and its main urban centers, al-Beida and Benghazi, and Tripolitania in the west, with Tripoli made the exclusive center of power by Qaddafi. Within each region, there are numerous rivalries, usually tribal-based, e.g., those in Tripolitania between the cities of Misrata and Beni Walid, and Misrata and Zintan, respectively. An additional important fault line is the one between the cities on the Mediterranean shores and the concentrations of nomads mainly in the Fezzan Desert in the southwest, or around Kufra in the west of Libya.

Ethnically, there are African and other minorities living among the Arab majority population. The ethnic mosaic includes the Toubou, the Berber Amazigh and Tuareg (one should not confuse these Libyan Tuareg with the Sahelian Tuareg soldiers, who became part of Libya's army under Qaddafi).[9] Libyan society is also traditionally made up of tribal frameworks, which during the Qaddafi rule were roughly divided between a) the Warfalla, Qaddadfa, and Muqariha tribes, who supported and protected Qaddafi's regime and which were immensely rewarded, economically and politically, in return, and b) the large number of tribes that stayed aloof from the regime even if not necessarily acting against it. The latter were relatively marginalized and suffered economic hardship and political exclusion, and have used the post-Qaddafi era to change the tribal balance of power, and attain the socio-economic and political capital that accompany such power.

At bottom, Libya's primary common denominator is its anti-colonial heritage: Italy controlled the territory from 1911 until its expulsion in 1942, and the Libyan opposition created a national ethos and forged the country's modern history. It is therefore difficult to point to any authentic Libyan framework promoting national cohesion. The post-Qaddafi power-vacuum has created ample space for all of society's components to struggle to protect and advance their particular interests and alter the rules of the game in their favor. This competition, characterized by spiraling violence, remains a defining characteristic of Libyan realities. [10]

The ubiquitous presence of the armed militias has resulted in lawlessness and high levels of violence across the country. In eastern Libya, jihadist militias have viewed the void created in the wake of the collapse of the state order as a one-time opportunity, not only to correct chronic injustices, deprivation, and neglect but also to generously compensate themselves as a form of affirmative action for the long period of deliberate marginalization and discrimination under Qaddafi.

## Bad Governance and Armed Militias: Poor Prospects for Domestic Security and Political Order

The chronic weakness of the government and its failure to build any new effective security apparatus has limited its ability to inspire confidence across the country. Furthermore, the armed militias have gathered political-religious and military strength and their actions pushed the state towards anarchy. The fact that the police and the army collapsed together with the regime and no effective replacement has emerged has been a critical element of Libya's lawless and violent reality. The police and armed forces have been unable to recruit enough manpower, and as a result are "weak and hollow," and "ill-equipped, understaffed, bloated at senior ranks and tainted by their association with the old regime."[11] In late 2012, while the number of the armed militias was estimated at 100,000, the number of soldiers in the state's army was reported to be somewhere between 3,000 and 4,000. The same source reporting these figures portrayed life in Libya as being governed by "fear, death and aspiration to split,"[12] referring first and foremost to the chronically inherent rivalry between Tripolitania in the west of the country with Tripoli as its center, and Cyrenaica in the east with Benghazi as its heart. Some groups based in Cyrenaica even advocate separatism. This rivalry has been shaped by various pre- and post-independence processes.[13] Other foreign, mainly Arab sources, have emphasized the atmosphere of anarchy (*fawda*) and terror (*irhab*) imposed by the Islamist armed militias in Libya, who are exploiting the inability of the democratically elected government to function properly.[14] Qaddafi's success in crushing civil society during his reign has compounded the failure of the non-militia forces to fill the void and establish effective security forces. Certainly, the government's dwindling financial resources (oil exports were severely hampered by the elimination of the experienced, professional economic leadership and by the violence and chaos that engulfed oil installations) has also played a crucial role in the state's slipping into the abyss of violence.

Desperate, the anemic government began collaborating with Islamist militias in the terror-plagued area of Benghazi in late 2011. These specific militias, which became known as the "Libya Shield," became the de facto police and army in the region. The government's integration of these militias into the state's formal security system had two goals: first, dismantling their motivation to initiate anti-government violence; and second, turning them into a stabilizing element in a chaotic situation. The "Libya Shield" militias patrolled the borders, arrested drug traffickers, and imposed some measure of order, yet they soon became "a law unto themselves, pursuing agendas that are regional, tribal, Islamist and sometimes criminal," all the while refusing to internalize their formal subordination to the government. Indeed, they evinced contempt for it, with one of its powerful commanders even demanding the resignation of Prime Minister Ali Zeidan.[15]As time went on, the government tried to disentangle itself from this collaboration, but soon after, in June and July 2013, had to deal with intense violence in Benghazi. The bloody clashes, which erupted outside the "Libya Shield" Brigade premises in Benghazi, took place as protesters demanded the disbanding of the government-sponsored militias.[16] Seven soldiers were killed and nearly 40 people were wounded,[17] leading to the resignation of the Army Chief-of-Staff Yussef al-Manqush, who was criticized by army officers for his poor performance. Once again the government's helplessness resulted in a strengthening of the militias and the further deterioration of security.

The government's ineffective rule was visible not only in the Benghazi area but also in the central Mediterranean coastal region, particularly in the city of Misrata, the third largest in Libya, as well as the Nafusa Mountains area in western Libya, which was controlled by the Berber Zintan armed militias. It was this militia — and not the state's almost non-existent security forces — that ultimately captured Saif al-Islam, Qaddafi's son and formerly heir apparent, in November 2011 after he had gone into hiding for three months in the desolate southwestern Libyan desert.[18] The Zintan's refusal to transfer him to Tripoli for trial, and the initiation in September 2013 of legal proceedings against him under their own jurisdiction, demonstrated again the central authority's helplessness. Indeed it clearly illustrates the reversal of power in Libya since Qaddafi's downfall: no longer is there a dictatorial government with absolute control over all the centers of power throughout the country; instead, diffuse centers of power, and especially the armed militias, are now exercising power and control over the weak and malfunctioning democratic government. Moreover, the armed militias' power, which can be seen by their ability to issue their "soldiers" identity cards, wages, arms, Toyota pickup trucks, and basic welfare services, has led many analysts in Libya and outside the country to refer to the armed militias' administrative and social services as "running a state within a state."

# The State's Disorientation in the Security-Political-Economic Cycle

Although they played the crucial role in tipping the scales of war against Qaddafi, the Western states have not been rewarded with the valuable economic, political, and geo-strategic fruits they hoped to reap in the wake of Qaddafi's downfall. The economy has stagnated and in various areas is even paralyzed, with oil production and exports intermittently disrupted. One of the major problems has been security around the oil and gas facilities. In April 2013, two armed militias from the towns of Zintan and Zuara engaged in a deadly battle over who should guard the international Eni oil company's complex in Mellita, a battle that interrupted exports from the facility.[19] There have been numerous instances of battles between armed militias over the right to control the security (and receive the compensation for it) of oil and gas installations, resulting in damaging fluctuations in Libya's oil and gas exports.

As if the weak Libyan government and the basic infrastructure insecurity were not a serious enough problem to deter foreign investment and forestall new economic and infrastructure development projects, the deteriorating security conditions along Libya's borders have further eroded the interest of foreign economic entrepreneurs in the Libyan state. The writer Robert Kaplan noted that Libya's borders "have given way in the direction of frontiers, a term implying overlapping movements of gangs, militias, and tribes. Modern states have borders," he argued, while "weak and failed states [such as Libya] have frontiers."[20]

Paradoxically, it was in the years preceding Qaddafi's downfall that Western financial interests profited in Libya, thanks to oil industry and infrastructure development projects. Moreover, Qaddafi had served other vital interests of the West, which had in turn deepened its political commitment and economic involvement in Libya. Qaddafi had reined in Islamist terror in Libya and the Sahel, limiting emigration from Africa to Europe, reducing the volume of drug and arms trafficking in the Maghreb and Sahel regions, and voluntarily dismantling its weapons of mass destruction (WMD) program. Yet, the collapsed public systems, the disappearance of state order, and the deteriorating domestic and regional security conditions — paradoxically generated by the crucial military aid from the West to end the Qaddafi regime — together with the increasing terrorist attacks against symbols of the Western presence in Libya, have led Western governments and the international business community to largely disengage from Libya.

This violent disarray has been expressed almost daily: armed militias have encircled and sporadically locked out the employees of the national television and government buildings, including the foreign, justice, and interior ministries, attacked the Treasury, closed down seaports and the international airport in Tripoli, and halted traffic to and from the country. They have also repeatedly closed down the oil terminals at Tobruk and Zueitina and the gas-exporting Mellita complex, taken over and blocked major traffic arteries and junctions, launched recurrent attacks in Tripoli and Benghazi, and engaged in organized crime — including the trafficking of weapons, people, and narcotics.

These waves of violence, and the utter failure of the government to effectively respond, underscored the numerous similarities between Libya and an increasing number of failing states in the Middle East and Africa. A new spike in the violence was reached in July 2013. On July 27, more than 1,000 inmates from the Queyfiyya prison near Benghazi escaped after "a day of extraordinary violence, even by the standards of [post-Qaddafi] Libya," and in the wake of a "long string" of political assassinations in Benghazi and Tripoli of security officers and political figures who had harshly criticized the Islamist militias. One of those killed in Benghazi was a prominent lawyer, Abdul Salam al-Musmari, who, just two years prior, had fought with the Islamist rebels to overthrow Qaddafi. At approximately the same time that political assassinations were taking place in Tripoli and Benghazi, a bomb detonated at a police station in Benghazi and rocket-propelled grenades were fired at the United Arab Emirates Embassy in Tripoli and at a Tripoli hotel where government figures live.[21] It was with good reason, then, that there was a growing concern that Libya was becoming a Somalia on the Mediterranean. The earlier attack on the US Consulate compound in Benghazi in September 2012, during which the jihadist armed militia *Ansar al-Shari'a* killed United States Ambassador J. Christopher Stevens and three other American members of the diplomatic staff, had already shaped the image in the West of anarchic post-Qaddafi Libya. Since then, there have been additional attacks against Western targets including a car bombing at the French Embassy in Tripoli in the spring of 2013.[22]

The deterioration of Libya's domestic security has been accompanied by increasing challenges in the Sahel region. In January 2013, the Mali-based jihadist militia *Ansar al-Din,* an off-shoot of AQIM headed by Mukhtar Belmukhtar, who was also known as "Mr. Marlboro" due to his control over cigarette trafficking in the Sahel, launched a strike on the oil and gas facility at In Amenas in south Algeria's Sahel, adjacent to Libya, resulting in heavy loss of life, as Algerian forces eventually regained control.[23] *Ansar al-Din* played a central role in the military and political anarchy in northern Mali, where the militant Islamists' political and religious aggrandizement reached its peak, threatening Western economic and strategic-military interests to the point of generating a French military intervention to evict them from the country's northern region in early 2013. This episode further illustrated the risk and danger for Western governments and companies doing business in Libya.[24]

The upheaval in the Sahel was largely a result of the toppling of Qaddafi. Sahelian Tuareg, who had served in Qaddafi's army and security apparatus until his final hours in power, abandoned Libya and returned, heavily armed, to the Sahel region, especially Mali, following the collapse of the regime, loss of livelihood, and cruel treatment by the victorious rebels. In Mali, they tipped the balance against the central government there, while in Libya, they left a large security void.[25] From another angle, the Arab Spring opened up new possibilities and opportunities for the Amazigh idée in Libya, Mali, and other Maghreb countries.[26]

# Libya Falling Apart? Conflicting Visions of Identities and Interests

The destructive combination of the Libyan leadership's powerlessness and the newly empowered armed militias has unstitched the seams that had fastened together Libya's diverse and often conflicting elements of society during the four decades of the Qaddafi era. Aware of the absence of underlying national cohesion and the existence of rival identities and interests,[27] and facing strong political opposition particularly in the Benghazi area—the bastion of the deposed King Idris — Qaddafi had invested great efforts into fashioning and maintaining a common Libyan identity out of the patchwork of numerous different collective affiliations and loyalties.

Yet, since the summer of 2011, Qaddafi's "tailoring" is no longer relevant to the Libyan state and society. Indeed, the Libyan fabric was quickly rent asunder leading to unbridled competition between primordial and newer factions without regard for the possible consequences of their struggles for the national cohesion and the integrity of the Libyan state.

In July 2013, a year after Libya's democratic elections, the elected government was still struggling with constitutional challenges, including the idea of drafting the post-Qaddafi democratic constitution. Therefore, it was not coincidental that the voice of the Libyan writer Abdel Malek al-Safrani was raised in sympathy with the tribal presence, declaring that it is very important that tribal allegiances should play a role in informing the political system. "We should not forget that the tribe, in spite of its known shortcomings, has remained one of the factors of stability in our country since the [Arab Spring] revolution until now." The tribe, he further commented, "will continue to play an influential role under our current circumstance. Therefore, all who are fighting to keep the revolution on course…must work to help the positive features of the tribe prevail."[28]

# Conclusion

More than two years after Qaddafi's regime had been relegated to the pages of history, post-Arab Spring Libya is a divided and anarchical country without effective domestic and regional security, political stability, and national cohesion. The weakness of the state has been demonstrated by the absence of a consensual government and an effective army and police to fill the huge political vacuum and enforce state order. In fact, post-Qaddafi's Libya has become an arena of violence, where "old" and "new" combatants have fought to fortify their political position and secure other essential interests. In the process, they have fed and fostered the monster of lawlessness and chaos. While the 2012 democratically elected government has adhered to the rule of law and a defensive policy, the "old" and "new" power-hungry forces, with the tribal, Islamist and jihadist armed militias in the lead, have resorted to unrestrained violence, perpetuating insecurity and instability throughout the country.

Although this phenomenon might eventually turn out to be a merely interim or marginal one along an agonizing road to reviving the Libya state, the period between 2011 and 2013 definitely saw, among others, the rising and active presence of the tribes in political affairs that served as a reminder of the theory of Abd al-Rahman Ibn Khaldun, the Arab philosopher, historian, and sociologist, who 600 years ago wrote about the phenomenon of the disintegration of internal solidarity (*'asabiyya*) as being an integral part of social and political life. Within this context, Ibn Khaldun also coined the term "decline" (*inhitat*) in order to portray the nadir of the state or dynasty (*dawla*, in his parlance) while referring to the process of political transformation.[29] One can see how Ibn Khaldun's theory might apply to the Libyan case.

Notwithstanding Libya's political tumult and violence, the state and its society have the potential to extricate themselves from this low point. Libya has huge reserves of oil, gas, and iron, and great potential for tourism. Not by chance, its oil production and export infrastructure remained almost untouched by the NATO bombings. Libya also has a significant intellectual class, an active business community, and a large population of young people who advocate democracy and lean towards a modern Western lifestyle. It is also important to note that Libya is not threatened militarily — as of summer 2013 — by any of its neighbors. Theoretically, this situation could allow the Libyan government to focus its efforts on putting its house in order.

Practically, however, the Libyan strife-torn society is deeply immersed in an identity crisis, seemingly sliding down the slippery slope of losing control. Moreover, the longer and deeper the Libyan domestic crisis lingers, the greater the likelihood that other regional and international actors will be tempted to militarily intervene in the oil- and gas-rich Libyan state.

On June 1, 2013, groups in the Libyan Cyrenaica region declared their aspiration for autonomy, announcing this area would be a self-governing federal territory within the framework of the Libyan state.[30] Separatist voices have been loudly heard also in the Fezzan region in southern Libya. Is this a sign of future challenges to the territorial integrity of Libya?

This is one of many broader questions regarding the future of the Libyan state and society in the aftermath of the Arab Spring upheaval: Should the Libyan rebellion be referred to as just another coup d'état (*inqilab*) or should it be termed a revolution (*thawra*), with all that the term signifies? And is Libya's transition leading to a new beginning for the country, or will its loss of control accelerate, and result in its becoming a failed state and even its disintegration?

The embers of the 2011 upheaval in Libya are still glowing and the post-Qaddafi challenges to the state's cohesion and territorial integrity continue to plague state and society. We are "still witnessing competing tracks drawn by opposing forces," correctly noted one Beirut-based analyst, "hence it is difficult to tell what the final outcomes will be" in post-Qaddafi Libya. [31]

# Notes

1. For a comparative discussion of this subject, see Asher Susser (ed.), *Challenges to the Cohesion of the Arab State* (Tel Aviv: The Moshe Dayan Center for Middle Eastern and African Studies, Tel Aviv University, 2008).
2. The NTC was headed by 'Abd al-Mustafa al-Jalil, the minister of justice from 2007 until his defection from the Qaddafi regime in early 2011. It formally ended its role in the aftermath of the democratic elections in summer 2012.
3. *Al-Usbu' al-'Arabi*, October 15, 2012.
4. For more details on AQIM, see J. Peter Pham, "The Dangerous 'Pragmatism' of al-Qaeda in the Islamic Maghrib," *The Journal of the Middle East and Africa*, Vol. 2, No. 1, 2011, pp. 15–29; and Yehudit Ronen, "The Empowerment of Political Islam in Algeria and its Sahelian Environ: The 'al-Qaeda in the Islamic Maghreb' as a Representative Phenomenon," *Hamizrah Hehadash (The New East)*, Vol. 52, 2013, pp. 55–79.
5. For more details on the Islamist-regime confrontation, see Yehudit Ronen, "Qadhafi and Militant Islamism: Unprecedented Conflict," *Middle Eastern Studies*, Vol. 38,

No. 4, 2002, pp. 1–16; and *idem*, "Radical Islam Versus the Nation-State: Violent Conflict in Northeast Africa and the Nile Valley," in Jonathan Fox (ed.), *Religion, Politics, Society and the State* (Oxford: Oxford University Press, 2012), pp. 131–146.

6. "A Golden Opportunity," a report from Cairo and Derna, *The Economist*, 2 April 2011; and an interview with al-Hasadi in Canada's *Glob and Mail*, March 11, 2011, http://www.theglobeandmail.com/news/world/africa-mideast/libyan-rebels-at-pains-to-distance-themselves-from-extremists/article1939636/.

7. See Matthew Levitt, et al., "Countering Transnational Threats: Terrorism, Narco-Trafficking, and WMD Proliferation," The Washington Institute for Near East Policy, *Policy Focus*, No. 92, February 2009.

8. Vanda Felbab-Brown et al., "Political Violence and the Illicit Economies of West Africa," *Terrorism and Political Violence*, Vol. 24, No. 5, 2012, p. 789.

9. For more details, see Yehudit Ronen, "Libya, the Tuareg and Mali on the Eve of the 'Arab Spring' and in its Aftermath: An Anatomy of Changed Relations," *The Journal of North African Studies*, Vol. 18, No. 4, September 2013, pp. 544–559.

10. For more general discussion of this issue, see William Zartman (ed.), *Collapsed States: the Disintegration and Restoration of Legitimate Authority* (Boulder, CO: Lynne Rienner, 1995).

11. Frederic Wehrey, a former United States military attaché in Libya, "Libya Doesn't Need More Militias," *The New York Times*, June 10, 2013.

12. *Al-Usbu' al-'Arabi*, October 15, 2012.

13. This rivalry has increased tremendously since the removal from power of the Cyrenaica-based Sanusi Kingdom by Qaddafi and his relocating the state's capital to Tripolitania. For more on the Sanusi kingdom (1951–1969), see Dirk Vandewalle, *Libya Since Independence* (London: I.B. Tauris, 1998), pp. 41–81.

14. *Al-Usbu' al-'Arabi*, November 12, 2012.

15. Wehrey.

16. *Al-Ahram*, a report from Benghazi, June 16, 2013.

17. *Tunis Afrique Presse*, June 15, 2013.

18. For more details regarding Saif al-Islam's key political position during Qaddafi's Libya, see Yehudit Ronen, "Libya's Rising Star: Saif al-Islam and Succession," *Middle East Policy*, Vol. XII, No. 3, Fall 2005, pp. 136–144.

19. Heba Saleh, "Libyan violence disrupts international oil company operations," *The Financial Times*, April 29, 2013.

20. Robert Kaplan, "A Libyan Report Card," *Real Clear World*, April 4, 2013, http://www.realclearworld.com/articles/2013/04/04/a_libyan_report_card_105055.html.

21. Suliman Ali Zway, "Amid Protests, Inmates Escape From Libyan Prison," A Report from Benghazi, *The New York Times*, July 27, 2013.

22. These events were chosen as a sampling, and not intended to provide the reader with a systematic survey of the terrorist acts that were called out across Libya in the post-Qaddafi era.

23. Cigarette smuggling in the Maghreb-Sahel region, which attests to the economically successful and consequently militarily powerful position of the armed militias in the region, with Libya as an inseparable part of the phenomenon, was estimated to net

approximately $775 million per year. See United Nations Office on Drugs and Crime (UNODC), "Transnational Trafficking and the Rule of Law in West Africa: A Threat Assessment" (Vienna: UNDOC, July 2009), p. 75; *Al-Sharq al-Awsat*, "Who is 'Mr. Marlboro' the leader of the kidnappers?", January 19, 2013.

24. The terrorism in Libya was an integral part of the rising time of Islamist violence in its geo-strategic setting. See John M. Nomikos et al., "Another Frontier to Fight: International Terrorism and Islamic Fundamentalism in North Africa," *International Journal of Intelligence and Counterintelligence*, Vol. 22, 2009, pp. 50–88.

25. For a detailed discussion, see Ronen, "Libya, the Tuareg and Mali," also published online 18 June 2013, http://dx.doi.org/10.1080/13629387.2013.809660.

26. For details, see Bruce Maddy-Weitzman, "Arabization and its Discontents: The Rise of the Amazigh Movement in North Africa," *Journal of the Middle East and Africa* Vol. 3(2), (June-December 2012), pp. 109–135.

27. For a broader discussion of the problem of national identity, see: Anthony D. Smith, *The Ethnic Origins of Nations* (New York: Blackwell, 1986) and *National Identity* (London: Penguin, 1991); and Ted R. Gurr, *Peoples Versus States: Minorities at Risk in the New Century* (Washington DC: United States Institute of Peace Press, 2000).

28. Kamel Abdallah, "Libyan Constitutional Challenges," *Al-Ahram Weekly*, July 18–24, 2013.

29. 'Abd al-Rahman Ibn Khaldun, *Al-Muqaddima fi Ilm al-Tarikh* (An Introduction to History), translated from Arabic to English by Franz Rosenthal (London: Routledge & Kegan Paul, 1958).

30. Kamal Abdallah, "Cyrenaica declares autonomy," *al-Ahram*, June 9, 2013.

31. Mohsen Saleh, "Future scenarios for the Arab uprisings," *al-Ahram Weekly*, July 12–18, 2013.

# Algeria in 2013: Confronting Change

## Gideon Gera

Algeria's post-civil war status quo, now fifteen years long, was maintained throughout the last three years of turbulence in the Arab region. Compared to the upheaval in the Arab East (*Mashriq*), Algeria has maintained a fair degree of overall stability, notwithstanding numerous, albeit localized protests and riots. Algerian politicians explained this "exceptionalism" by noting that their country had already undergone its "Spring" period in 1988–1991, from a youth uprising to constitutional liberalization and the rise and rebellion of radical Islamists, resulting in dark days indeed, almost a decade of civil war. Yet difficulties have been numerous, exacerbated by the diffuse but palpable impact of the continuing surrounding turmoil. The 80 day-long absence of President 'Abd al-'Aziz Bouteflika, due to a stroke (between April and mid-July 2013) — added to a general sentiment of uncertainty and impending change.

Algeria is now the largest country in Africa (in the aftermath of the splitting of Sudan). Its population is relatively homogenous, by Middle Eastern standards — the vast majority of its Arabic-speaking majority and Berber speaking minority are Sunni Muslims. Algeria also possesses large oil and gas resources, which provide its main source of government revenues (the official GDP/per capita is $7,500). Where, then, lie Algeria's vulnerabilities?

Since the early 1980s, Algeria has been confronted with severe and persistent socio-economic problems. Furthermore it had to overcome a violent Islamist challenge and faces Berber claims for cultural autonomy and perhaps more. The Islamists' attempt to usurp power was crushed in a long and painful civil war, but small armed groups survived and regrouped, mainly in the country's southern desert region. Today, half a century after independence, Algeria is undergoing a profound process of generational change during a period of political succession, whose urgency is symbolized by the deteriorating health of the President during the final year of his third term. This combination poses a significant challenge to the ruling elite (*le pouvoir*), resulting in internal power struggles.

# The Socio-Economic Crisis

Algeria is a rich country. The decade-long rise in revenue from its hydrocarbon resources not only enabled it to pay back most of its external debts (incurred mainly in the early 1990s) but endowed it with large foreign currency reserves, approaching $200 billion. However, the economy remains stagnant, imports are continually increasing, inflation rose to 8.9 percent in 2012, and much promoted plans for diversification to non-hydrocarbon sectors have not been implemented. Aside from a permanent concern about developments in the international oil markets that could cause a decline in exports, the main macro-economic worry is the looming depletion of oil and gas reserves.[1] This would endanger the rent system on which the regime's ability to nurture loyalty — and thus political stability — is based. On the micro-economic level, the average well-being of the continuously growing population (from 10 million in 1962 to an estimated 37 million today) has not improved. The "youth bulge" has been particularly affected: two-thirds of the population are under the age of 30, which make up most of the unemployed. Some of them describe themselves as *Alger-rien* ("Algerian nothing").[2] Elaborate five-year development plans have not provided employment for these youth, nor helped them overcome insufficient housing and poor infrastructure.

In January 2011, a wave of widespread unrest occurred in Algeria, at the same time the uprisings were taking place in Tunisia and Egypt. This unrest consisted of mainly local protests against economic grievances and a limited attempt by opposition politicians to promote reforms. These protests did not coalesce into a nation-wide movement for regime change, but were undoubtedly unsettling to the regime. They were quickly subdued by a combination of the repressive "stick" and the conciliatory "carrot." The latter consisted of annulling price increases on essential household goods and foodstuffs and targeted government spending, along with some cosmetic political reforms, such as lifting the 20 year old state of emergency and granting permits to a number of political parties. Furthermore, the constitutionally prescribed parliamentary and local elections were held on schedule. Since then, there have been no broad coordinated protests. Nevertheless, unemployment, lack of infrastructure, official neglect and corruption, and student and professional grievances persist, and, therefore, so do almost daily protests in various forms. The "riot" (*émeute*) is popularly considered the most efficient form of protest to get the authorities' attention: in addition to police repression, the government frequently responds to riots with injections of cash and budget adjustments.[3]

The question remains: why has there not been a country-wide uprising like those that have occurred elsewhere in the region? The conventional wisdom, and the explanation most widely provided by Algerians, is that the population is war-weary. After almost a decade of civil strife during the 1990s, which claimed the lives of an estimated 150,000 to 200,000 people (following the hundreds of thousands of dead in the war of independence a generation earlier), the people are tired of conflict. To this explanation, one should add the popular support for the regime's repression of violent jihadi groups and the decline of the "participating" Islamist parties, which was demonstrated by their poor showing in the 2012 legislative elections.

# Strategic Reassessment: The Radical-Islamist Threat and New Border Challenges

Algeria is a Muslim country. The jihadi-radical current, which aimed at overthrowing the "impious" regime, emerged during the 1980s, when it carried out its first violent acts. With the outbreak of the civil war, it expanded its operations exponentially. While the rebellion was crushed at the end of the 1990's, not least because of popular rejection of Islamist excesses, residual groups survived. In 2006 the most radical among them affiliated itself with al-Qa'ida and took the name of "al-Qa'ida in the Islamic Maghreb" (AQIM). Following the regime's continuous pursuit of its cadres in the north of Algeria, many surviving elements of AQIM fled to the arid south (a residual presence remains in Kabylia), where they regrouped. Their presence was accompanied by the spread of radical jihadi movements in the neighboring states of northwest Africa (Mauritania, Mali and Niger). These organizations engaged in the lucrative practices of smuggling narcotics as well as kidnapping and ransom of Westerners (reportedly earning "significant" sums since 2003),[4] enabling them to increase their arsenals of weapons and spread their influence.

From 2010 onwards, the deteriorating security situation was of steadily increasing concern to the Algerian high command. In response, it reinforced its forces in the south and established operational cooperation with the neighboring countries, with quiet US support. More unrest in the Sahara-Sahel region followed the overthrow of Qaddafi's regime in Libya in the autumn of 2011: not only did this create an additional 1000 kilometers of unsecured border for Algeria, which already has its hands full securing its 1,376 kilometers of border with Mali, but thousands of Tuareg fighters from Mali and Niger — mercenaries recruited by Qaddafi — returned home loaded with arms, reinforcing the destabilizing impact and audacity of jihadis and rebellious Tuaregs. Profiting from the collapse of the central Mali government, these forces took control of northern Mali in early 2012 and also sporadically attacked Algerian military installations across the border. The ensuing French military intervention — tacitly supported by Algeria, a first for a country whose self-definition posits it as a determined opponent of Western neo-colonialism and intervention in smaller nations' affairs — pushed the jihadi insurgents back into the desert but did not annihilate them.

The increasing vulnerability in the south was starkly demonstrated by the well-planned and traumatic raid on a major natural gas plant at In-Amenas, not far from the Libyan border, carried out in January 2013 by a platoon-size group affiliated with AQIM. Thirty-eight foreigners working at the plant died during the raid and the ruthless Algerian military crackdown on the hostage-takers. The shock caused by the raid made the regime realize that it had a multi-dimensional challenge on its hands:

1) Strategically, Algeria found itself surrounded by hostile forces (Mauritania excepted), as the Tunisian-Algerian border had become porous to jihadi groups. This in combination with the notion that Morocco has always been considered as adversary created a feeling in Algeria of siege, and damaged its self-image as a regional power. A strategic reassessment, carried out during the spring and summer of 2013, led to an increased investment of resources in border security and some organizational streamlining (including in the security service) and new appointments at senior levels.[5] Most conspicuous was the upgrading of General Salah Ahmad al-Qaid, the Chief of Staff of the Armed Forces, appointed as Vice-Minister of Defense (the minister is Bouteflika himself) in the Cabinet re-shuffle on September 11, thus eliminating the intervening level of the Minister-Delegate to the Minister of Defense since 2005 (on the political aspect, see below).

Securing the southern border became a central task of the Algerian military, which was on continued alert to prevent further AQIM raids on sensitive installations. A further immediate risk was the possible influx of refugees from Mali, including adherents of jihadi groups, who could stir Algeria's own Tuareg population (approximately 100,000) in the adjoining deep south and reinforce the weakened but not defeated AQIM groups in the northeast (mainly, but not only in the Kabylia region).

2) Economically, the prevailing hardship of the population of the south could worsen, with possible political repercussions. The ferment among the neglected population of the southern districts following the In-Amenas raid led the government to immediately appease them — especially the youth — by providing them with attention, employment, and budget allocations. On a wider scale, the In-Amenas episode held the prospect of reduced gas production and thus a loss of revenue, as well as the negative effect on current and future plans and investments of foreign gas and oil companies. Whether there would be a long-term economic effect in the aftermath of the attack remained to be seen.

3) Politically, Algeria's long cultivated image as a guarantor of regional stability, including its own emphasis on its counterterrorism capabilities, was substantially damaged by the raid, both domestically and internationally. Therefore Algeria decided to augment its active presence in the Sahel countries, especially Mali, stepping up its military and financial assistance and diplomatic involvement.[6]

An additional set of challenges was posed by Algeria's Berbers. During the half-century of Algeria's independence, a cultural-linguistic identity movement emerged among the Berber-speaking portion (20-30 percent) of Algeria's population, mainly among the traditionally militant and alienated Kabylians. Contrary to radical Islamists, it has not challenged the primacy of the state *per se*, but demanded official recognition of the Amazigh (Berber) language and culture. After repeated confrontations, most notably in 2001, the regime eventually acknowledged the legitimacy of the Berber identity as part of the Algerian common heritage, and recognized Tamazight as a national, albeit not an official language. However, the Kabylia region remained alienated, to a considerable degree, from state authorities.[7]

Three distinct groups may be observed among Berbers: a) a minority well integrated in the ruling elite (the current and previous former prime ministers are Kabylians); b) the defiant Amazigh current, whose formal political expression was articulated mainly by the *Front des Forces Socialistes* (FFS) — and the smaller, avowedly secular *Rassemblement pour la Culture et la Démocratie* (RCD), in addition to the amorphous and illegal "Berber Cultural Movement" (MCB); and, 3) the silent sympathizers of the jihadi groups, which still find refuge in the Kabylia and Aures mountains.

The permanent state of tension between the regime and the Kabyle Berbers resulted in a vicious circle: For years, development plans neglected the Kabylia region, thus increasing economic hardship and public alienation, until recent government attempts to repair the situation. However, as opposed to the deep-rooted socio-economic difficulties and the jihadi Islamist challenge, Kabyle Berber mlitants have not achieved a critical mass of support for actions that would imperil the cohesion and stability of the state.

# Politics — the Regime

Algeria is governed by a centralist, opaque, and, some even say, a *maquisard* (i.e., an underground guerrilla mentality) military regime.[8] Another apt characterization of the regime might be "pluralist autocracy." Real power is exercised by a group of senior (and elderly) generals and the presidential clan, which is hidden behind a screen of parliamentary institutions and parties. The regime has tried to control the country's numerous pre-modern cleavages, described as "tribalism without tribes,"[9] by selectively incorporating Islamists (while harshly pursuing unrepentant ones), secular, Berber, and various regional and bureaucratic groups, all nourished by a *rentier*, crony capitalist system of patrons and clients. The main weakness of this system is its inbuilt structural corruption, meaning the routine allocation of resources to clients — be it import licenses, public works contracts, or housing projects. Unavoidably, corruption trickles down to the local level, further exacerbating popular discontent. In 2010, proceedings in foreign courts exposed personal corruption at the highest level of the national hydrocarbon company, "Sonatrach," forcing the resignation of the well-connected Minister of Oil Resources Chekib Khalil and imprisonment of its CEO, Mohamed Meziane. The scandal may have caused tension between President Bouteflika's "clan" and the powerful head of the Security Service (D.R.S.), General Mohammad "Tawfik" Medienne, who was involved in the investigation.

Nevertheless, the parliamentary and local elections in 2012 maintained the political status-quo: the majority of the seats were retained by the veteran regime parties, the *Front de Libèration Nationale* (FLN) and the *Rassemblement National Démocratique* (RND); the participating Islamist parties, however, suffered a setback, notwithstanding the fact that three of their leaders joined in a common anti-government list, the *Alliance de l'Algérie Verte*. A score of smaller parties and independents won the remaining sieges.

## Politics — the Upcoming Presidential Election

The main political event on the Algerian horizon is the April 2014 presidential election. The ruling elite's overriding objective is to maintain a firm grip on power while allowing for some well-managed personnel changes, and to maintain the "clientelist" system based on the distribution of the petrol rent in order to retain its positions and privileges. Any major change — as already advocated by some politicians — particularly tackling the corruption issue, would entail the redistribution of positions and income. Thus, present corruption scandals may be seen as stemming from, and part of the increasing political maneuvering of various interested actors and political parties, such as the Berber opposition RCD.[10] The candidates will probably be announced officially only at the turn of the year but the maneuvering and jockeying has already begun. In addition to aspiring former prime ministers, such as Ali Benflis, who was defeated in the 2004 presidential election, three-time prime minister Ahmed Ouyahia, and

Mouloud Hamrouche, prime minister during the "reform period" of 1989-1991, and perhaps the current leaders of the main parties, the legal Islamist alliance has also considered fielding a candidate, notwithstanding its 2012 electoral setback.

In April 2013, the ailing 76 year-old President Bouteflika suffered a stroke (the public was never informed). He was hospitalized in Paris for 80 days, which left the running of current affairs to Prime Minister Abdel Malik Sellal. Bouteflika's ill health called into question the rumors (assiduously promoted by his clan and the FLN leadership) that Bouteflika may run for a fourth term. To publicly reaffirm authority, Bouteflika reshuffled his cabinet in early September, appointing more loyalist and some younger ministers and promoting the Chief of Staff, General Salah Ahmad Qaid to cabinet rank. The reassignment of some important provincial governors was also apparently part of his pre-election maneuvering designed to pave the way to his reelection.

Whether Bouteflika runs or not, it is not at all clear that he will promote reformers or let the system continue as is, with its mediocre and corrupt politicians. Attempts by his family to promote his younger brother and counselor Sa'id seem to have been obstructed so far. Another unanswered question is the position (or positions) adopted by the very influential and privileged senior generals (the estimated number of both active and retired Algerian generals is in the hundreds).

Be that as it may, one ongoing factor is irreversible — time: a generational change at all political levels is well underway. The "founding fathers" generation — *mujahidin* — of independent Algeria is passing on. This also means that among the younger generations, the entrenched elite's revolutionary legitimacy — based on the 1954–1962 war of independence — has been steadily declining, thus requiring the regime to perform substantially better than it has thus far. Furthermore, it is hard to know what the political attitudes are of the younger, better educated and more professional military officers.

## Outlook

More than three years after the outbreak of the "Arab spring" upheavals and the subsequent short-lived unrest in the country, the Algerian regime was undoubtedly relieved that the turbulence still shaking the Arab region to its east had passed it by without compelling fundamental changes. Undoubtedly, however, the turbulence has palpably affected Algeria. One of these effects has been the regime's increased sensitivity and responsiveness to local "riots," especially in the south.

The mounting insecurity along its borders, which created a sense of siege, led to a strategic reassessment aimed at containing a possible spillover of instability from Libya, Tunis, and the Sahel, which could fuel a nation-wide opposition movement as well as damage the image of Algeria as a regional power.

Yet, the major problem the country suffers from is the enduring socio-economic crisis, stemming from increasing social inequality, enduring unemployment, and lack of sufficient housing and infrastructure. All of these problems are exacerbated by a young and rapidly growing population, resulting in endemic, albeit localized unrest. The government has attempted to alleviate these tensions through a mixture of police repression and targeted distribution of oil rent.

However, the main issue facing Algeria in the coming year is the presidential election, the outcome of which may point the country either towards stagnation or reform and change. A sudden collapse of oil and gas revenues, similar to what took place in the mid-1980s, might lead to serious social disturbances that overtake electoral developments. And although in an recent index of failed states, Algeria was classified as being "in danger of instability,"[11] in no way can it be counted among the failing Arab states, such as its neighbor Libya, or Yemen and Syria.

# Notes

1. Recent oil revenues have reportedly decreased by 12%. Liberté, November 13, 2013.
2. Jose Garcon, "Un regime immobile au milieu des revolutions", *Esprit* 380 (December 2011), p. 104
3. For a recent example: following the raid on the In-Amenas gas field (see below) budgets likened to a "Marshall Plan" were directed to the southern provinces. *Liberté*, March 12, 2013; *El-Watan*, March 17, 2013.
4. US Department of State, "Country report on terrorism 2012, Ch. 2, www.state.gov/j/ ct/rls/crt/2012. A US Department of Treasury estimate put the earnings from ransoms between 2004-2012 at $120 million. Stratfor, "The unspectacular, unsophisticated Algerian hostage crisis", www.stratfor.com/weekly, January 24, 2013.
5. Among other measures, the criminal investigation branch (*police judiciaire*) of the military security service was disbanded. This may also have been a result of the ongoing power struggle within the regime — see below. *Journal Officiel*, Vol. 45, No. 18 (September 2013), p. 4.
6. *Liberté*, October 28, 2013.
7. Bruce Maddy-Weitzman, *The Berber Identity Movement and the Challenge to North African States* (Austin, TX: University of Texas Press, 2011), pp. 183–201.
8. Interview with Hugh Roberts, *El-Watan*, July 8, 2012.

9. Mohammed Hachemaoui "Y a-t-il des tribus dans l'urne? Sociologie d'une énigme électorale (Algérie)" *Cahiers d'études africaines*, 2012/1 (205), p. 151.

10. See also the open letter on the subject to the head of the Security Service, General Medienne, by a former general manager of Sonatrach. *El-Watan*, February 18, 2013.

11. "The Failed States Index 2013", *Foreign Policy*, June 24, 2013, http://www. foreignpolicy.com/articles/2013/06/24/2013_failed_states_interactive_map.

# How did the Moroccan Monarchy Survive the "Arab Spring"?

## C. Richard Pennell

### What does it Mean to Survive?

During the initial months of the "Arab Spring" protests, it was a cliché to argue that one Arab country was not another Arab country.[1] This made for easy journalism and provided a comforting daydream for dictators. Syria's president, Bashar al-Asad, assured the *Wall Street Journal* on 31 January 2011 that "at the end we are not Tunisians and we are not Egyptians:"[2] Similarly, Saif al-Islam al-Qaddafi was determined that the pattern would not be repeated in Libya, despite the growing rebellion. "Libya is not Tunis or Egypt. Libya is different, if there was disturbance it will split to several states. There are no political parties, it is made of tribes. Everyone knows each other."[3]

How did the Moroccan monarchy survive the Arab Spring? This is question-begging in three ways. Firstly, we cannot know that the Moroccan regime has indeed survived the Arab Spring. It could still collapse, because the protests have been a rolling process, although it does look unlikely. Secondly, it avoids a very important point: that the royal regime that took power in 1956 was still in place in 2011, despite the fact that between 1960 and 1990, the government of every other country in North Africa was overthrown in a coup (Algeria in 1965, and again in 1992; Tunisia, albeit not in the narrow military sense, in 1987; Libya in 1969) and the successor regimes in Tunisia and Libya were washed away in 2011 and 2012. Perhaps the clue to King Mohammed VI's survival is to be found in the successes of his father and grandfather. Finally, it avoids asking whether regimes fall or whether they are overthrown: should we look at the enemies of the regime rather than its defenders?

All this raises differences of perspective. One feature of the Arab Spring movements is that they did not have centralized leaderships, a point particularly made about the Tunisian uprisings,[4] and this "leaderlessness" has become attached to the idea that social media were critical to their success.[5] There is a suggestion that such ad hoc movements, facilitated by uncontrolled and instant means of communication, do not *need* leaders, although it lacks much historical depth: inchoate mass uprisings have a history in the Middle East and North Africa.[6]

But mass expressions of anger have still to be explained in terms of "why then?" Why did they not happen earlier? What moves individuals to come together collectively rather than, as individuals, suffer patiently or run away? Why did the reaction to state oppression shift from stasis or flight, to fight? What made fear, that had held populations in check, convert into anger, which then boiled over?

## Flight or Fight (or Acquiesce)?

There are three reactions to force. One is a fear so powerful that it paralyses action. In the early period of the Nazi occupation of France, Simone Weil used the *Iliad* to illustrate this consequence of force:

> Here we see force in its grossest and most summary form — the force that kills. How much more varied in its processes, how much more surprising in its effects is the other force, the force that does not kill, i.e., that does not kill just yet. It will surely kill, it will possibly kill, or perhaps it merely hangs, poised and ready, over the head of the creature it can kill, at any moment, which is to say at every moment. In whatever aspect, its effect is the same: it turns a man into a stone. From its first property (the ability to turn a human being into a thing by the simple method of killing him) flows another, quite prodigious too in its own way, the ability to turn a human being into a thing while he is still alive. He is alive; he has a soul; and yet — he is a thing.[7]

This was what nineteenth century colonialists did: they aimed to cow native populations into submission.[8] Some of them coped by using what James Scott calls the weapons of the weak: "foot dragging, dissimulation, false compliance, pilfering, feigned ignorance, slander, arson, sabotage, and so forth."[9] These do not challenge the regime and rarely produce any major change,[10] and may even have the opposite effect.[11]

Is this one explanation of the stability of the regime in Morocco: that personal forms of resistance may substitute for wider mass protests and leave the regime unscathed?

Another response to the fear of force is the famous flight-or-fight dichotomy. Either choice is a way to resist oppression. Those who fight threaten their oppressor directly, but those who flee threaten him by seeking to escape his control. In either case, the response is action, not paralysis, and carries with it the hope of change.[12]

Sometimes the fear leading to paralysis, or hidden forms of resistance, may change into fear leading to action. The structures of fear may be changed by particular circumstances. One way to understand this is through the concept of structural fear as compared to conjunctural fear, a distinction borrowed from analyses of poverty (and particularly the work of John Iliffe). Structural fear can be seen as the long term anxiety of people who suffer because of their personal or social circumstances — the categories of race, religion, social group and so on defined by the United Nations Convention relating to the Status of Refugees of 1951 (as revised in 1967). Conjunctural fear is the result of an immediate crisis that overwhelms people who would otherwise be able to cope; it is often the product of war, revolution, or sudden political change.[13]

The problem is to pin down these different forms of fear because they are by nature personal, and if they do not produce mass action they remain individual and hidden, so they are difficult to identify. By definition, those who flee must have done something, said something, or been something that led them to abandon paralysis and publicly reject the regime. One way to identify and hear them is to listen to their own accounts, understand them, and relate them to the conjunctures.

# Refugees in (and from) the Middle East and North Africa

Since the end of the World War II, the Middle East and North Africa has been a parade ground of refugees.The war for Palestine and the creation of the state of Israel in 1948 established the pattern. By 2008, the number of Palestinian refugees registered with the UN Relief and Works Agency (UNRWA) had reached 4,618,141.[14] Then came Iraq: three wars added another two to three million. The still-evolving civil war in Syria has uprooted over six million more (more than 25 percent of Syria's total population), and 2.5 million have fled the country, mostly to camps in Jordan and Turkey.[15]

No one has the time to collect stories on this kind of mass scale, and huge population movements of this kind indicate a fairly obvious conjuncture. They tell us relatively little about the nature of the regimes they were fleeing from — and nothing at all about the states that did not produce mass movement on this scale. But individual accounts, often detailed and nuanced, are recorded when refugees seeking political asylum tell their stories on arrival in Western countries. These are carefully collected by legal authorities and often made publicly available.

Refugee accounts cannot tell the whole story, but they are helpful in understanding the political history of Morocco over the past generation. Although compared with some Arab countries there are fewer accounts, this is not to deny the extraordinary level of violence during Morocco's "Years of Lead" (commonly denoting the 1970s and 1980s). By the time refugee tribunals were reporting individual asylum cases in detail and in an accessible way, the numbers had dropped. People continued to leave Morocco for fear of political persecution, but their numbers (2,775 asylum seekers in the industrialized countries in 2011 and 3,933 in 2012 according to the UNHCR[16]) were dwarfed by the huge number fleeing from countries such as Syria and Iraq, and by the numbers of "regular" Moroccan migrants (more than 3.3 million of them in 2012, according to the Moroccan ministry of the diaspora).[17]

The stories of Moroccan political refugees make certain themes very clear: that while there was widespread rejection of the regime, no one single issue pushed people to rebel (or to flee). And because the opposition was fragmented, it could be manipulated and even incorporated by a regime that was supple enough to use opposition as a source of strength rather than weakness.

# The Opposition

Asylum seekers' accounts cover the period from the 1980s to the present, and they show that there was a great deal of opposition to the regime, that it was fragmented, and that important elements were co-opted. That was a pattern that began with independence in 1956.

The central figure was the king. It is one of the clichés of political scientists and historians that the Moroccan monarchy enjoys almost unquestioned legitimacy, due to its lineage going back to the Prophet. Yet North Africa is littered with the tombs of *sharifs*. The 'Alawi family's prestige is based largely on its preservation by the Protectorate and then by the role of Mohammed V as he broke free of French control and became the lynchpin of the nationalist movement. Both the colonial authorities and the nationalist parties made use of a dynasty with roots in the early seventeenth century and which defined a certain territorial identity. There were two implications:

One was a tension between claims for absolute authority based on the sultan or king being *amir al-mu'minin* ("Commander of the Faithful"), and a conditional leadership based on a recognition of his rule on a locality by locality basis in exchange for his guarantee of justice. Both these "Moroccan" concepts were paralleled by French ones –"colonial" autocracy versus the democratic tradition of French politics.

The second implication was for the territorial identity of Morocco. Independence in 1956 reunited the French and Spanish zones of the protectorate and the international zone of Tangier. A further historic claim to territories to the south, including the colony of Spanish Sahara and, even further afield, Mauritania, and to the Spanish enclaves on Morocco's north coast remained unfulfilled. In 1959 the dominant, urban nationalist, predominantly Arabic-speaking *Istiqlal* party split, but both the left wing, which became the *Union Nationale des Forces Populaires* (UNFP), led by Mehdi Ben Barka, and the mainstream maintained irredentist claims on those territories. The other nationalist party, the rural and Berber-based *Mouvement Populaire* (MP), originated in the Liberation Army, part of which had fought a military campaign in the Sahara and southern Morocco against Spanish and French forces just after independence.[18] The MP rejected Istiqlal and its offshoots, declaring personal loyalty to Mohammed V, but accepted the same idea of a Greater Morocco. So all three big parties emphasized their loyalty to the king, whatever constitutional pattern they favored, and accepted the idea of a national identity that was still incomplete. By co-opting all these rival political factions, the king could broaden his support.

Labor and professional unions were harder to co-opt. They were a powerful force in Morocco because they played an independent and vital role in the nationalist movement. By mid-1958, the *Union Marocaine du Travail* (UMT) had organized 200,000 workers in the most important sectors of the Moroccan economy and civil service.[19]

King Hassan II inherited the throne in 1962, but not his father's charisma; he inclined towards autocracy. He designed a series of constitutions from 1962 onwards that maintained the formal shape of a parliamentary democracy with a multi-party system and a constitutionally guaranteed trade union movement. Yet each conferred ever more preponderant power to the Palace. In fraudulent elections that followed the revised constitutions of 1970 and 1972, the original nationalist parties were joined by a clutch of parties that contested elections that no one believed in, for a parliament that had only a minority of directly elected members in order to form governments that were subservient to the king. Some of them were effectively right-wing palace parties (the *Rassemblement Nationale des Indépendants* (RNI) founded in 1978) and the *Union Constitutionelle* (1983), others were breakaway factions from the *Mouvement Populaire* (MP), including the *Mouvement Populaire Constitutionel Démocratique* (MPCD) that for a long time was an empty shell of an organisation, but would not remain so. This was accompanied by growing repression including the murder of exiled opponents, like Ben Barka in 1965.

The high-water mark of repression followed the failure of the two attempted *coups d'état* in 1971 and 1972. Savage revenge was exacted on both the army officers and cadets who were involved, and the wife and children of the presumed author of the second coup, the country's former strongman and confidant of the king, General Mohammed Oufkir. The political parties shrank into insignificance, although they did not disappear. The only substantial opposition came from the trade unions (particularly in the mines), from the Marxist-Leninist *Ila al-Amam* group, and from a slowly emerging Islamic movement grouped, in particular, around 'Abd al-Salam Yassine, a former official in the education ministry. In 1974, Yassine composed an open letter to the king, calling on him to abandon the ways of wickedness, corruption, foreign anti-Islamic values, and reliance on Western and Zionist capital. He was incarcerated for three years in a mental hospital for this open letter.

The attempt to incorporate the former Spanish Sahara into the kingdom in 1975-76 after Spain left the territory was a response to these pressures. It not only provided the hope of revenue from phosphates but brought virtually all the political parties, and the army, into line. Since all the nationalist parties accepted the idea of taking over the Sahara, it boosted the king's authority and legitimized the parties as well. The only opposition came from those groups that refused to be co-opted: Ila al-Amam on the left, Yassine's supporters and the radical left-wing *Union Nationale des Étudiants Marocains* (UNEM), which had called for the abolition of the regime in 1963 and supported Algeria during a brief border war designed by Morocco to return Moroccan territory to its "historic" size.[20]

Despite the popularity of the Saharan cause, the ensuing conflict damaged the regime. It was immensely expensive at a time when oil prices were shooting up and the price of phosphates was falling fast. Inflation accelerated. The poor suffered and protested, and the unions organised numerous strikes in public services and the manufacturing and mining industries.[21]

In 1981 there were riots in Casablanca, and again in Tangier and elsewhere in 1984 (sparked by among other things a rise in the price of bread and cuts to education services).[22]The regime was reaching a watershed and Hassan II realised that consolidating state institutions by co-option and repression was not enough. If the economy did not improve, the regime risked collapse. Backed by, or under pressure from, the European Economic Community, the World Bank, and the IMF the government launched a structural adjustment program of liberalizing the economy, privatizing state assets, and encouraging foreign investment. It took the whole of the 1980s for the Moroccan government to extract itself from the economic crisis. But by 1985, external debt and the trade deficit had begun to fall, the GDP per capita had begun to climb, money was at last being put into rain-fed agriculture, the fishing industry expanded, and tourism from Europe boomed. The European markets were so important that in 1987 King Hassan applied to join the EEC. The application was rejected, but new trade preferences were negotiated. The government was feted as one of the favoured countries of the IMF: in 1986, a report from the influential *Economist Intelligence Unit* in London was subtitled, "Growth against the Odds," and a 1995 IMF report on Morocco was titled, "Resilience and Growth through Sustained Adjustment."

But Morocco's macroeconomic success in the 1980s came at a desperately high price. By the end of the decade it was becoming all too clear what the effects were of cutting capital expenditure, freezing the wages of state employees, and failing to provide employment opportunities for high school and university graduates. The trade unions fought back and in the first four months of 1987 there were more than 20 separate strikes.[23] In December 1990, major riots broke out in Fes, protesting against poverty and inflation.[24] By 1991, 21 percent of degree holders were looking for jobs. The UNEM protested loudly.

Another center of opposition, Islamism, had already emerged and was growing stronger. In 1981, in the aftermath of the Iranian revolution, 'Abd al-Salam Yassine, having been released from his mental hospital, re-established a political group which went through a variety of name changes to become the *Jami'at (later Harakat) al-'Adl wal-Ihsan* (The Society (Movement) for Justice and Spirituality). It was intended to spread his call for a state founded on morality and justice. Once again Yassine was confined in prison for two years in the mid-1980s, and then under house arrest for ten years in 1989. Ordinary members of the Society suffered much more.[25]

The years of repression affected diplomatic relations with important allies, particularly France. Danielle Mitterand, the wife of French President François Mitterrand, intervened in the case of General Oufkir's imprisoned children. In Morocco a growing human rights movement took shape.[26]

It is against this background that the account of Tahar Bouazza (not his real name) should be read. The son of a wholesale fishmonger who made a comfortable living selling to shops and restaurants, he completed his high school diploma and enrolled in university in 1984 to study physics and chemistry. In his second year he began a political journey that took him, via student politics and the trade union movement, to a modernist form of Islamism. His aims were always a bit unclear. Tahar wanted a political system such as existed in Europe and thought the Moroccan monarchy had run the country for too long; but he had no real prescription for change. Elections were no use because, he said, the heads of each party were always the relatives of the king, so there was no real political opposition to his rule. So Tahar joined an ad hoc and informal student group that held meetings and distributed leaflets. Although it posed no real threat to the regime, Tahar was arrested and tortured, and was released only after his father paid a bribe to a judge. He took a long time to recover from the aftereffects of torture and rape. He could not continue his studies, and in 1987 he began work as a maintenance technician for a textile company. He joined the UMT to fight for better wages and conditions for workers, attended union meetings, and photocopied and distributed leaflets, and wrote signs calling for fair wages and sickness leave. He was arrested in November 1987 and beaten again. Tahar was inactive for several years during which he studied German, did a course in Germany, and began to build a career. But he was an inveterate political activist. In November 1992, a man approached him while he was at a mosque and began talking about *shari'a*, the Qur'an, and the king. In January 1993, this man invited him to join an underground fundamentalist group whose members referred to themselves as "the brotherhood." They rejected the notion of elections, hoping to win power through protests in the streets, but talked of the people choosing their ruler once the king had gone. It was socially moderate in its vision of the ideal state: women should be allowed to wear skirts (as opposed to a traditional *jellaba*), and permitted to work freely. There would be no Islamic punishments of amputation. Tahar's talents as an organiser and speechmaker were soon recognized and he quickly became an assistant leader in his home town. Not surprisingly, the police soon arrived to arrest him but he escaped and eventually fled to New Zealand, on the grounds that it was as far from Morocco as he could be.[27] Tahar's political journey ended with the Islamists just when the regime was publicly adopting a new look that would seek to co-opt them. Islamists did not figure in the original nationalist identification in the post-independence period. But they became part of it, absorbed into its structures quite seamlessly. In 1997, one of the smaller Islamic groups, *al-Tawhid wal-Islah*, gave up the fight to be recognised as a political party and merged itself into the shell of the MPDC, signaling that it would play by the king's rules and accept the primacy of the palace. The following year the party changed its name to the *Parti de la Justice et du Développement* (PJD). Both sides gained. Islamists could contest elections and the palace could control them: by allowing them to take part under the king's rules they could be required to contest only some constituencies and so be prevented from winning a decisive victory (as the Islamists had done in Algeria in 1990-91).[28] Notably, though, Yassine's movement refused to play by the king's rules, stayed outside the political process and was formally banned.

The riots of 1990 showed the Moroccan government that it must respond to social tensions either by allowing greater political participation or by yet more repression. The scale of the riots meant that repression would be extremely difficult and openly opposed by the regime's political and economic allies in

Europe. So King Hassan chose co-option and controlled, limited liberalization over repression.

The process began with a series of amnesties for political prisoners and the establishment of a Human Rights Advisory Council (*Conseil Consultatif des Droits de l'Homme — CCDH*) in 1990, although it was not until 1993 that the Moroccan authorities agreed to even talk with Amnesty International. In 1994, the latter reported that "the use of torture and ill-treatment has greatly diminished," and that "over the last three years improvements have taken place."[29] Amnesty was even allowed to open its own office in Casablanca and the press became less restricted.

Hassan had a sense of urgency: he was 60 years old in 1989, and his health meant that the regime had to be settled if the dynasty was to survive him. It had to be placed above the party political arena, but without losing control. A rolling process of constitutional amendments ensued that appeared to make Morocco progressively more liberal: the first was in 1992 and another in 1996. On paper, they increased the prerogatives of the parliament, giving it the right to approve or reject any government appointed by the king, but in practice the king still appointed and dismissed the government. Power was centralized in the king's hands and the referenda to approve the new constitutions were won with suspiciously high majorities — a "yes" vote of 99.985 percent and voter participation of 97.4 percent in 1992. These were results that came from the interior ministry rather than the ballot box. The 1996 referendum, which produced a directly elected house of representatives, was supported by all the major political parties: only the small left-wing parties, the PADS and the *Organisation de l'action démocratique populaire* (OADP) opposed it.[30] So did al-'Adl wal-Ihsan.

In the 1997 elections, a coalition including the *Union Socialiste des Forces Populaires* (USFP; heir to the UNFP) and the Istiqlal won the most seats, and the now-domesticated opposition was rewarded by a policy of *alternance*, with government designed to pass to-and-fro between supposedly competing blocs. In 1998, 'Abd al-Rahman el-Youssoufi, a once-exiled socialist, became Prime Minister. The elected government was allowed to run the economy, but security remained in the hands of the Palace and its loyalists.[31]

Yet the opposition was not silenced. Various left-wing groups, including the PADS, lined up with the Moroccan Association for Human Rights (*Association Marocaine des Droits Humains*; AMDH) which had been founded nearly two decades before (in 1979). They rejected the royal discourse of the *Conseil Consultatif des Droits de l'Homme* and other organisations.[32] The PADS wasn't formally illegal, though its members were regularly arrested. Other human rights activists, mainly on the far left, set up the *Forum Vérité et Justice* (FVJ) which demanded a full accounting of the violence of the "Years of Lead," with a truth and reconciliation commission. They had nothing to do with the regime's human rights bodies either, nor much with the AMDH.[33]

The limits to liberalization were clear: some prominent exiles came home, some prominent prisoners were released, and those former opponents of the regime who accepted the consensus were reincorporated. But the people largely unknown to the general public, who still did not accept the dominant order, were persecuted, as they had been before. Idris Bennani, for instance,[34] did not benefit from the amnesties, because he fell outside the consensus in two ways:

Firstly, there was the inherited mark of treason on him. In 1988, when Idris was 19 years old and had just gone to university, his father, an army officer, deserted and went to Algeria where he joined the Polisario Front. His family never saw him again, although Idris's mother went to Algeria to look for him. State violence was unleashed on the family and all its members were summoned by the police from time to time, questioned, and sometimes beaten.

Idris' own politics marginalized him further. In 1991 (when he was 22) he joined the AMDH and in 1993, aged 24, the PADS, one of the AMDH's sponsors. He went to meetings and demonstrations, wrote pamphlets about human rights abuses and distributed them. Neither the AMDH nor the PADS was part of the consensus and the police started bringing him in once a week, and often questioned him about the Polisario. They hoped to turn him into a paid informer. When Idris failed some of his exams, he reduced his university studies in favour of his work for the AMDH and PADS. Now he was being detained even more frequently, and the brutality increased. In May 1996, there was a demonstration organized by trade unionists as part of the celebrations for May Day, just when the king was beginning a state visit to France.[35] Idris carried a banner among a crowd of students. Some demonstrators shouted slogans in support of Polisario and others burned Israeli and American flags. To avoid arrest, Idris hid on the university campus because the police did not like to enter it for fear of trouble. He stayed there until the end of the university year, then left. With the help of his sister, he raised $7,000 for his travel fare to New Zealand, which he arranged quite legally through Casablanca airport. Apparently the police thought he was still hiding in the university.

# Mohammed VI

The mixture of apparent liberalism and real repression continued after King Hassan died in July 1999. The new king Mohammed VI, like his father, had studied law in France but he had never held a formal military command nor indeed any substantial executive position. That meant that he was less touched by his father's policies but still able to claim that his policy was one of continuity. So the apparent openness could be maintained, and even apparently extended, nixed with the repression of those who would not be co-opted.

The liberalization was dramatic. Driss Basri, the architect of Hassan II's repression, was sacked as minister of the interior in November 1999 because Mohammed had always disliked him. Within months of taking power, he had released some 8,000 prisoners, some of them famous men like 'Abd al-Salam Yassine. Prominent political exiles like the widow and children of Mehdi Ben Barka, whom his father's security officials had murdered in 1965, and Abraham Serfaty, were allowed to return. Serfaty, an extreme left-winger exiled in France, was even given a stipend as adviser to the National Board of Oil Research and Exploitation.[36]

But neither Serfaty nor Yassine were completely reconciled with the regime, or the regime with them. Yassine had already written another of his famous open letters to the king, calling on him to reject his father's heritage of violence, oppression, and servitude to Zionism and to cleanse the Augean stables with a radical restructuring of the government.[37] In late 2000, Serfaty attacked 'Abd al-Rahman el-Youssoufi, the Prime Minister, when he turned the censorship laws on two news magazines, *As-Sahifa* and *Le Journal*, for suggesting that nearly thirty years earlier he had plotted to overthrow King Hassan. A third magazine, *Demain,* was closed before it could publish an investigation linking the regime with drug traffickers. By the end of the year, a military officer had been imprisoned for denouncing corruption in the military, some relatives of Yassine had been arrested, and forty-seven members of the AMDH had been detained after staging a sit-in demanding "the truth about the kidnappings, arbitrary arrests and acts of torture committed under the reign of Hassan II."[38]

Deep-seated social reforms were touted but took a long time to eventuate. In 2004, a truth and reconciliation commission, the *Instance Équité et Réconciliation* (IER), was set up to hear the stories of those who had been tortured under Hassan II. It was not allowed to investigate the new reign, and had no judicial powers, but it could inquire and listen. Seven of its public sessions that were broadcast on the television made the victims' stories very public, but the torturers were not named. It also produced a 1,500 page report that contained recommendations about reparations and safeguards against future repression, and victims were compensated.[39]

That same year another radical reform was put in place: a rewritten family law code, the *Moudawana*. At the very beginning of his reign, Mohammed VI had said he wanted to improve the status of women. He appointed women to high official posts, both at the palace and in religious roles, and ten percent of the seats in the Chamber of Deputies were reserved for them. Reform of the *Moudawana* marked a definite break with the past. Under Hassan II, Moroccan women's rights organizations had advocated reform of the code, but now there was a concrete proposal and it brought real opposition from religious conservatives. In 2000, they organised a huge demonstration in Casablanca (over 300,000 people took part) demanding that the *shari'a*, not secular ideas, should be the basis of the law.[40] The legislation was then shelved. But in 2003, when the regime was prepared to deal more roughly with religious opposition, the plans were revived. Citing his authority as Commander of the Faithful, the king imposed his solution. Parliament passed a new code that established eighteen years as the uniform minimum legal age for marriage, consensual divorce, gave women equal custody rights over children, and made polygamy conditional or the granting of permission of the first wife. It also gave an important role to judges and family courts in the resolution of family disputes.[41]

On this issue, the Islamists were brushed aside but otherwise they were courted. Both sides made accommodations: for the 2002 elections, the PJD agreed informally with the interior ministry to limit the number of seats it contested so that it was certain to remain a minority party afterwards.[42] It won 42 of the 325 parliamentary seats, four in the reserved women's section. The mainstream Islamist party had been co-opted and the hardline Islamist opposition — al-'Adl wal-Ihsan — was excluded by allowing itself to be excluded. It rejected the executive monarchy, and this core refusal to accept the rules of the game led it to call a boycott of the elections. Turnout was very low — probably less than half of eligible voters — and the USFP and the "centrist" Constitutional Union lost many seats. Istiqlal's votes, and number of seats, went up. These elections marked the end of *alternance;* the king appointed a non-party technocrat, Dris Jettou, as prime minister and other non-party palace loyalists as ministers of foreign affairs, religious affairs, justice, and interior. The USFP, Istiqlal, and three other parties got lesser government ministries and the PJD formed a "constructivist opposition."[43]

Al-'Adl wal-Ihsan did not contest the next election, in 2007, either. There was an even lower turnout (37 per cent), but the PJD increased its seats marginally, to become the second biggest party in parliament. The winner, though, was Istiqlal which then set up a coalition government with the USFP, which had lost yet more seats, the Parti du Progrès et du Socialisme (PPS) and the centrist RNI. Both the PJD and the Berber-oriented Mouvement Populaire formed the "loyal" opposition: co-opted but not in government.[44]

The real opposition came from those Islamists outside the system. After the 2002 elections, the weight of state repression had been turned on them. New anti-terrorist laws of May 2003 defined terror so broadly that it permitted arbitrary arrests, and long periods when defendants could be held silent while being interrogated. In June 2004, Human Rights Watch reported that around 2000 prisoners were being held in a prison camp at Tamara, where torture was routine. In June 2005, Nadia Yassine, the daughter of the founder of al-'Adl wal-Ihsan, was charged with "attacking the institution of the monarchy" after a weekly newspaper quoted her as saying the monarchy was ill-suited for Morocco and would soon collapse. Her father invoked a mystical basis for the same prediction: a vision that the next year, 2006, would see a *qawma,* a great uprising. That did not happen, but many of his supporters dreamed their own dreams of Yassine in the presence of the Prophet, surrounded by a heavenly light and angels.[45] More substantially, al-'Adl wal-Ihsan ran a mass-recruiting campaign in mid-2006 which the government fiercely supressed: in May and June between 300 and 400 of members were arrested, though not generally held for very long.[46]

If political liberalism was only partially realized, so was its economic equivalent. Morocco is repeatedly cited as a golden example of a modernizing economy. There was a huge investment in infrastructure: massive prestige projects like Tanger-Med, planned to be the biggest port in Africa, and the vast new business, residential, and leisure complex at Casa-Marina. The phosphate sector was particularly successful, accounting for about a quarter of the total exports and about 3.5 percent of GDP in 2009. The *Office Chérifien des Phosphates* (OCP) Group is the biggest exporter of rock phosphate and phosphoric acid in the world. Tourism grew from 2,602,000 arrivals in 1995 to 9,299,000 in 2010, making it the 24th biggest tourist market in the world. There was low inflation and unemployment fell from 13.4 percent in 2000 to 9.1 percent in 2009.

The undoubted economic success masked deep problems. Unemployment was proportionally much higher among youth, and this demographic was so skewed that the educational level of the unemployed was higher than the labor force as a whole. People with secondary and higher education found it harder to get a job.[47] While the number of extremely poor Moroccans fell, poverty remained much more prevalent in rural than urban areas (14.4 vs. 4.8 percent in 2007).[48]

One of the government's great failures was education. Morocco has the sixth highest expenditure on education as a percentage of total government spending in the world (25.7 percent in 2008) and that is a consistent figure (it was 26.1 percent in 1992). Adult literacy has improved from 30.3 percent in 1982 to 56.1 percent in 2009. Yet in that same year only 38 percent of young men and 32 percent of young women of secondary school age were actually enrolled in school.[49]

All this puts into perspective the experiences of Ahmad Idris, a hairdresser from Safi.[50] In 1994, aged 17, he joined a cell of the hardline Islamist opposition group, al-'Adl wal-Ihsan. Some of his friends were already members and he admired their plans to change Morocco without participating in the corrupt electoral system. In 1998, he finished his secondary education: it was a surprisingly late date which suggests he was determined to get his baccalaureate or some sort of diploma even after he had formally left school.[51] That was the year al-'Adl wal-Ihsan set up its new political section, the *"cercle politique"* to integrate regional and provincial branches with the youth, women, and trade union sectors.[52] Ahmad distributed leaflets and helped organize demonstrations, and he took part in intense private discussions. But he was a follower, not a leader, and he decided to protect himself personally by continuing his education and learning a trade. He went to a hairdressing college in early 1999 and qualified eighteen months later. Then he opened his own salon in Safi: just the sort of petit-bourgeois/ bazaar merchant among whom al-'Adl wal-Ihsan built its base. But Ahmad talked politics to his clients while cutting their hair, and someone eventually reported him. In October 2001, he was arrested, beaten and intimidated for six days. After he was released, the authorities withdrew his business licence and the salon closed down. He found work as the employee of another barber, and he became more circumspect: nothing very serious happened to him until 2005, when Nadia Yassine was put on trial for attacking the monarchy. Now Ahmad was arrested several times and often held for several days. In 2007, the king paid a royal visit to Safi, to lay the foundation stone for a nursing school, inaugurate a new regional library, and so on. Potential troublemakers were rounded up and Ahmad was one of them.[53] In 2008, another royal visit to Safi was announced, this time to inaugurate several infrastructure projects and a center for the handicapped.[54] Ahmad was told to report to the police station, but he decided to leave town rather than face the police again. He hid with his maternal aunt at a place about 100 kilometers away in the countryside. There he stayed for a few weeks until late November 2008, when he fled to Australia.

## Weathering the Global Financial Crisis and the Arab Spring

Ahmad's flight came just as economic crisis threatened to undermine the Moroccan success story and throw its political system into disarray. There were two waves. The first was a global increase in prices between November 2007 and May 2008, particularly in food and oil that bought riots to Morocco, as well as Egypt, Yemen, and other countries. Both food and oil prices fell in 2008 in time for the second wave: the Global Financial Crisis. The great danger of the GFC for Morocco was that so many Moroccan migrants were based in Europe, one of it epicenters. The IMF forecast that remittances would fall by between 7.7 percent and 13. 8 percent in 2009, enough to cut between 1 and 2 percent of GDP.[55]

In fact, Morocco weathered the GFC reasonably well. GDP held up at 4.8 per cent in 2009, fell slightly in 2010, and remained above 4.5 percent thereafter. Unemployment rose slightly in 2009 compared with 2008 but it was not an overwhelming problem because the government increased spending on subsidies, wages, and pensions to support living standards.[56] This deft economic management was accompanied by equally competent political control that gave the appearance of movement, without actually changing very much, but which laid the basis for future change. The Western Saharan question was an example of this phenomenon.

During the 1990s, negotiations with the Polisario Front had stalled because neither the Moroccan government nor Polisario could concede ground and preserve their legitimacy. For Polisario, autonomy would destroy its *raison d'être*. For his part, the king needed to maintain the political consensus on the incorporation of the Saharan territories. Yet the war impoverished the people on both sides and undermined both the Moroccan and Algerian economies; as the dispute dragged on it provided increasingly fewer returns.[57] So both sides kept a semblance of negotiations alive.

Mohammed VI began his reign by offering Polisario autonomy provided it acknowledged Moroccan sovereignty and territorial integrity, but he never made any detailed proposals. James Baker, the UN negotiator, provided a series of plans, but they could not satisfy both sides at the same time. In April 2007, the Moroccan government proposed a "Saharan Autonomous Region" run by an elected local administration, with executive, legislative, and judicial functions and control of education and justice, and adequate finance, some it to be raised locally. The US Congress liked the plan, so did French President Nicolas Sarkozy, and the UN Security Council. Yet it languished because neither side was eager to enter direct negotiations.[58]

Then, unilaterally in January 2010, Mohammed VI set up a Consultative Commission on Regionalization, ostensibly to examine how administration, regional development, and finance might function in a democratic system. When the Commission reported in March 2011,[59] it proposed a system of elected regional councils that would control the local budget. Although this was designed for the whole country, the ultimate aim was a solution of the Western Saharan question; the Saharan provinces would be brought together into two regions rather than shared between three provinces. A general political reform hid a mechanism for dealing with a particular problem.

All this political maneuvering made no difference to the hundreds of thousands of refugees in the camps around Tindouf in Algeria. Polisario claimed jurisdiction over their inhabitants, but they were in Algerian territory. In August 2011, the British refugee tribunal system ruled on a man who was born in Tindouf, had fallen afoul of Polisario, and had fled using false identity documents, via Mauritania, Spain, and Russia to Britain. He never had a valid passport of any sort, but gave his nationality as "Western Sahara." Initially, he was refused entry on the confusing grounds that that there was no such place as Western Sahara, that the area known as that was under Moroccan control and that he would not be at risk from the Algerian army if he returned there. Equally, if he returned to Algeria he would not be at risk as a failed asylum seeker and so "You will therefore be removed to either Western Sahara or Algeria." He appealed, saying that "The Home Office just does not understand the situation in Western Sahara. It is a huge place spread over the borders of Algeria and Morocco, but there is no government and it is just ruled by gangs." After a convoluted process, a higher tribunal found what was obvious: that he could not be returned to a non-existent state and that if he was returned to Algeria, in the area where he had been born, he would be attacked by the Polisario authorities. Whatever the process at the United Nations, and despite what the US Congress and the government of France might say, the reality was that the Sahara refugee population had no place of belonging and were subject to no government. The negotiations were essentially chimerical.[60]

By the time this refugee finding was delivered, the Arab Spring had reached Morocco. After the uprisings in Tunisia and Libya, the Moroccan government acted quickly to head off any repetition. It announced bigger subsidies of basic food stuffs and fuel, salary increases for civil servants, a job-creation scheme for unemployed graduates, unemployment benefits and an expansion of free health care. Yet there were demonstrations anyway, beginning on January 17, 2011, over unemployment and high utility prices. On February 19, there was one in Tangier. On February 20, Facebook-based activists called for demonstrations across the country with slogans attacking the king's closest advisors and supporters, but not the king himself. They demanded a constitutional monarchy, and the enshrinement of Amazigh culture as central to the Moroccan identity. A protest that began over economic circumstances had now become political, and a broad spectrum of political forces joined the protests: al-'Adl wal-Ihsan, AMDH, some smaller left-wing political parties (such as PADS) and segments of some larger ones (such as members of the youth wing of the USFP) and some Amazigh associations. But none of them predominated, and like elsewhere in the Arab

Spring, there was no central leadership. And although the demonstrations were large (240,000–300,000 participants according to the February 20 movement's organiser — or 37,000 according to the ministry of the interior) and took place in more than 50 cities, and five people were killed in Al-Hoceima on the northern Rif coast,[61] they were not as overwhelming as they had been in Tunisia or Egypt.

Yet there were some worrying echoes of Tunisia when Fadwa Laroui set fire to herself. When her home in a *bidonville* in the small town of Souk Sebt near Beni Mellal was redeveloped by builders, she could not replace it with government-allocated land because she was a single mother, and so could not be "the head" of a household. Her last words, recorded on a cell phone camera and uploaded to YouTube asked whether she would inspire people to "take a stand against injustice, corruption, and tyranny?"[62] The reformed Moudawana and the economic miracle made little difference to her.

## The Restructured Consensus

To show he was listening, Mohammed VI set up a constitutional reform committee, whose members he chose. He promised a new constitution to strengthen parliament, increase the independence of the judiciary, and allow greater regional and local power. It was prepared very quickly.

The new constitution strongly emphasised human and citizenship rights and made Tamazight (Berber) an official language, but it was not a radical political re-organization. It removed the "sacred" character of the king — but he remained "inviolable" and he continued to preside over the cabinet. Power remained firmly in his hands: he was not a ceremonial monarch. But one important section incorporated the regionalization plan that had been designed to contain the Saharan issue: a new regional structure for the whole country that was explained in terms of democracy. Swiftly prepared, the new constitution was quickly approved in a referendum in July by 98.5 percent of voters on a turnout of 73.5 percent of registered voters (who were estimated at only 60 percent of those eligible to vote).[63]

On July 30, the twelfth anniversary of his accession, Mohammed VI announced he was bringing forward parliamentary elections set for the autumn of 2012. He was answered with sizeable demonstrations across the country, demanding not elections as a political gesture but a real parliamentary monarchy with the king's powers reduced.

What the elections brought was the culmination of co-option. The PJD won 27 percent of the seats, nearly twice those of Istiqlal. This had two results: it gave the PJD leader, 'Abdelilah Benkirane, more popular legitimacy than any of his predecessors, and it made him the hostage of the monarchy. He formed a coalition with Istiqlal, the Mouvement Populaire, and the PPS but real power still lay with the king, who not only presided over the Cabinet, but controlled a huge part of the economy. In 2009 *Forbes Magazine* called him the "King of Rock" because his fortune of $2.5 billion was based on the export of phosphate rock,[64] though his holdings went far beyond that, through control of the Sociéte Nationale d'Investissement (SNI) group, whose revenues sometimes equalled 3 percent of GDP.

The king had insulated himself from criticism. With Benkirane as prime minister, the PJD could no longer criticize the policy of the regime: it now had to take the blame, which soon came. In late May 2012, the unions organized large demonstrations in Casablanca about unemployment and low pay. The government did not have enough money to spend its way out trouble. GDP growth slowed from almost 5 percent in 2011 to 2.7 percent in 2012 because of drought that brought bad harvests, a sharp decline in tourism revenues, a drop in remittance transfers from Moroccans abroad, and a fall in the price of phosphate (from $202.5 per metric tonne in December 2011 to $175 in May 2012). All that cut into government revenue and high world commodity prices made things worse. Consequently, in 2012 the fiscal deficit grew to 7.6 percent of GDP, compared with 6.8 percent in 2011.[65] The trade unions and the un-coopted Islamists of al-'Adl wal Ihsane now provided the main opposition — though there was a breathing space when 'Abd al-Salam Yassine died in December 2012 and a short leadership vacuum followed.

Things got slightly better in 2013, because the harvest was very good, but the phosphate price continued to fall, (to $127.5 per metric tonne in September) and non-agricultural growth slowed in the first half of the year. In May, the political consensus became less firm when Istiqlal announced it would leave the coalition, and did so in July.[66] By the autumn there was opposition across the country: the USFP, al-'Adl wal-Ihsane, and the far left were calling demonstrations to protest about virtually everything: education, health, the cost of living, and price increases for milk and petrol. And it was not just the big cities where this happened — from August through September and on into October the Rifi town of Targuist was gripped day after day by demonstrations about the roads, the hospital, and the rest of the infrastructure.[67] Al-'Adl wal-Ihsane refound its voice. Its General Secretariat issued a communiqué criticising the PJD-led government, for the deteriorating socio-economic situation, the decline in spending power and for allowing "despots and speculators" a free hand. It talked of the need for social justice and fair distribution.

Even the street politics of demonstrations, let alone the parliamentary politics of co-opted or unco-opted parties, were little use to those who actually lived on the streets. Between January 2012 and May 2013, in the the aftermath of the Arab Spring, the British refugee tribunal considered the case of a young man, 'Abd al-Salam Talbi, who had lived on the Moroccan streets from the age of 7 until he was 14.[68] He was one among an estimated 10,000 homeless children (in 2001).[69] He became a drug addict and while he was under the influence caused burns to a friend. For this he was prosecuted and sentenced to fifteen years in prison. He started his sentence in an adult prison, where he was raped and physically abused until he was eventually transferred to a juvenile detention center. From there he escaped and somehow reached Britain. His lawyers argued that if the Home Office returned him to Morocco, now that he was over 18, he would probably be held in adult detention. This was "a slight and young looking individual" who would once again be at risk of rape, sexual, and physical assault by other prisoners. The lawyers explained that street children in Morocco belonged to a particularly vulnerable group: without family protection, uneducated, and impoverished, they were exposed to sexual and physical abuse, which often led to mental health problems and drug addiction. The tribunal rejected this claim because he did not belong to a group that was persecuted for a "Convention reason" (under the United Nations Refugee Convention of 1951), but he was not rejected because they did not believe him.

'Abd al-Salam Talbi chose flight, not fight, as his response to degrading treatment: whatever the political changes in Morocco — whether the king and his government survived or not, the Arab Spring made no difference to him, nor to the thousands of other street kids like him. Seen from their viewpoint, the question was not whether the regime would survive the Arab Spring, but whether they would.

# Legal Cases Cited

United Kingdom Upper Tribunal (Immigration and Asylum Chamber)
    2013 I R vs Secretary of State for the Home Department, Birmingham 21 May 2013, AA/11907/2011.
    2011 Glasgow 2 August 2011, AA/13541/2010
Refugee Review Tribunal of Australia
    2009 Untitled Case. [2009] RRTA 856 (24 September 2009).
Refugee Status Appeals Authority New Zealand
    1997 Untitled Case. [1997] RSAA 2355/95.
    [2000] Untitled Case. [2000] RSAA 72022/2000.

# Notes

1. Baroness Emma Nicholson, a member of the British House of Lords, told the *Yemen Times* that "Yemen is not Egypt, Libya or Tunisia," *Yemen Times*, February 24, 2011. At the end of January, Tony Blair told the BBC that "Hosni Mubarak is not Saddam Hussein," on BBC radio 5, "Breakfast," January 31, 2011, http://www.bbc.co.uk/programmes/p00drq8w. Several weeks later, Robert Fisk, no admirer of Blair, agreed: "Gaddafi is not Saddam and it's a mistake to assume he's finished," *Irish Independent*, March 3, 2011, http://www.independent.ie/opinion/analysis/robert-fisk-gaddafi-is-not-saddam-and-its-a-mistake-to-assume-hes-finished-2563657.html.

2. "Interview With Syrian President Bashar al-Asad," *The Wall Street Journal*, January 31, 2011, http://online.wsj.com/article/SB10001424052748703833204576114712441122894.html.

3. Saif al-Qaddafi, "Gaddafi's Son in Civil War Warning," *Al-Jazeera*, 21 February 2011, http://english.aljazeera.net/news/africa/2011/02/2011220232725966251.html. The speech was, of course, in Arabic but the only transcript I have found that can be easily cited is the English version produced by *Al Jazeera*. I have kept its occasionally inaccurate English.

4. See the remarks on this by Nadia Marzouki in Nadia Marzouki, "The Call for Dignity, or a Particular Universalism," *Middle East Law and Governance*, Vol. 3 (2011), pp. 148–158.

5. Halim Rane and Sumra Salem, "Social Media, Social Movements and the Diffusion of Ideas in the Arab Uprisings," *Journal of International Communication*, Vol. 18, Issue 1 (2012), pp. 99–100.

6. See for example, Lisa Anderson's description of Tunisia, in Lisa Anderson, "Demystifying the Arab Spring," *Foreign Affairs*, Volume 90, No. 2 (2011), p. 2.

7. Simone Weil, "The Iliad, or the Poem of Force," *Chicago Review* 18:2 (1965), p. 7; this is a translation of Simone Weil, "L'Iliade Ou le Poème de la Force," *Les Cahiers Du Sud*, no. décembre 1940- janvier 1941 (1965).

8. See the fundamental work on colonial warfare by C.E. Callwell, *Small Wars: Their Principles and Practice* (London, 1899): e.g. page 82 "...This is the way to deal with Asiatics — to go for them and cow them by sheer force of will."

9. James C. Scott, *Weapons of the Weak: Everyday Forms of Peasant Resistance* (New Haven: Yale University Press, 1985), p. 25.

10. Susan Eckstein, "Power and Popular Protest in Latin America," in Susan Eckstein (ed.), *Power and Popular Protest: Latin American Social Movements* (Berkeley: University of California Press, 2001), p. 8.

11. Eckstein's description of Mexico in the 1980s provides an apt illustration: "The law is continually violated behind the scenes, not publicly in the streets. The regime, in particular, thrives on corruption. For decades such everyday defiance of the law enhanced the regime's stability.' *Idem*, "Formal Versus Substantive Democracy: Poor People's Politics in Mexico City," *Mexican Studies/Estudios Mexicanos* 6 (1990), p. 42, quoted in Matthew C. Gutmann, "Rituals of Resistance A Critique of the Theory of

Everyday Forms of Resistance," *Latin American Perspectives* Vol. 20, Issue 2 (1993), p. 85.

12. David Barlow, "Disorders of Emotion," *Psychological Inquiry*, Vol. 2, Issue 1 (1991), pp. 60–61.

13. For the original concepts of structural and conjunctural poverty, see: John Iliffe, *The African Poor: A History*, African Studies Series (Cambridge, Cambridgeshire: Cambridge University Press, 1987), p. 4.

14. UNRWA, "Number of registered refugees," http://www.unrwa.org/userfiles/reg-ref(2).pdf.

15. "Scattered by War, Syrian Family Struggles to Start Over," *New York Times*, October 16, 2013, http://www.nytimes.com/2013/10/17/world/middleeast/scattered-by-war-syrian-family-struggles-to-start-over.html.

16. Table 3: "Origin of asylum applications lodged in 44 industrialized countries: 2011-2012" in Asylum Trends 2012: Levels and Trends in Industrialized Countries (Geneva: UNHCR, 2013), http://www.unhcr.org/5149b81e9.html.

17. "Les MRE en chiffrres", http://www.marocainsdumonde.gov.ma/media/43064/mre%20en%20chiffres.pdf.

18. C.R. Pennell, *Morocco Since 1830: A History* (New York: New York University Press, 2001), p. 301.

19. Douglas E. Ashford, "Labor Politics in a New Nation," *Western Political Quarterly*, Vol. 13, Issue 2 (1960), pp. 312–331.

20. Clement H. Moore and Arlie R. Hochschild, "Student Unions in North African Politics," *Daedalus*, Vol. 97, #1 (1968), pp. 21–50.

21. Susan Walz, "The Politics of Human Rights in Morocco," in John P. Entelis (ed.), *Islam Democracy and the State in North Africa* (Bloomington: Indiana University Press, 1997), p. 82.

22. Amnesty International, *Morocco Briefing* (London: Amnesty International, 1991), p. 2.

23. Walz, "The Politics of Human Rights in Morocco," p. 82.

24. George Joffé, *North Africa: Non-Islamic Opposition Movements*, WRITENET Paper No. 11/2002 (Writenet, 2002), p. 24.

25. Francesco Cavatorta, "Neither Participation Nor Revolution: The Strategy of the Moroccan Jamiat al-'Adl Wal-Ihsan," *Mediterranean Politics* 12:2 (2007), pp. 381–397; Michael Laskier, "A Difficult Inheritance: Moroccan Society Under King Muhammad VI," *Middle East Review of International Affairs*, Vol. 7, No. 3 (2003), http://www.gloria-center.org/2003/09/laskier-2003–09–01/.

26. Pennell, *Morocco Since 1830*, pp. 365–366; Jean-François Daguzan, "France, Democratization and North Africa," *Democratization*, Vol. 9, Issue 1 (2002).

27. Refugee Status Appeals Authority New Zealand, *Untitled Case*, [1997] RSAA 2355/95 (1997).

28. Lise Storm, *Democratization in Morocco: The Political Elite and Struggles for Power in the Post-Independence State* (London: Routledge, 2007), pp. 86–87.

29. Amnesty International, *Morocco: The Pattern of Political Imprisonment Must End* (London: Amnesty International, 1994).

30. Dris Maghraoui, "Constitutional Reforms in Morocco: Between Consensus and Subaltern Politics," *Journal of North African Studies*, Vol. 16, Issue 4 (2011), pp. 685–686.

31. Pennell, *Morocco Since 1830*, p. 376; Joffé, *Non-Islamic Opposition Movements*, p. 25.

32. E.g. the Organisation Marocaine des Droits Humains founded in 1989.

33. Frédéric Vairel, "Morocco: From Mobilizations to Reconciliation?" *Mediterranean Politics*, Vol. 13, Issue 2, p. 233.

34. Except where noted, Idris Bennani's story is derived from Refugee Status Appeals Authority New Zealand, *Untitled Case*, [2000] RSAA 72022/2000 (2000). His name is left blank in this documentation and the one given here is entirely fictitious.

35. Paul Taylor, "France gives Moroccan king red-carpet welcome," *Reuters*, May 6, 1996.

36. Jon Henley, "Morocco's reforming king rouses fundamentalist wrath," *The Guardian*, February 2, 2000; "Morocco names radical leftist as oil adviser," *Reuters*, September 2, 2000; "Moroccan Muslim leader free to go where he wishes: government source," *Agence France-Presse*, May 16, 2000.

37. Jack Kalpakian, "A Tug-Of-War Over Islam: Religious Faith, Politics, and the Moroccan Response to Islamist Violence," *Journal of Church and State*, Volume 50, No. 1 (2008), pp. 126–127.

38. Lara Marlowe, "Torture survivor says he would do it all again," *Irish Times*, February 21, 2001.

39. Frédéric Vairel, "Morocco: From Mobilizations to Reconciliation?" *Mediterranean Politics*, Vol. 13, Issue 2, pp. 236–237; Haim Malka and Jon B. Alterman, *Arab Reform and Foreign Aid: Lessons from Morocco* (Washington, D.C.: CSIS Press, Center for Strategic and International Studies, 2006), p. 49.

40. Bohdana Dimitrovova, "Re-shaping Civil Society in Morocco: Boundary Setting, Integration and Consolidation," *Journal of European Integration*, Vol. 32, Issue 5 (2010), pp. 523–539.

41. Valentine M. Moghadam, "Feminism, legal reform and women's empowerment in the Middle East and North Africa," *International Social Science Journal*, Vol. 59, No. 191 (2008), pp. 9–16; Malka and Alterman, pp. 47–49.

42. Storm, *Democratization in Morocco*, p. 86.

43. James N. Sater, "Morocco after the Parliamentary Elections of 2002," *Mediterranean Politics*, Volume 8, Issue 1 (2003), pp. 135–142; Haim Malka and Jon B. Alterman, *Arab Reform and Foreign Aid: Lessons from Morocco* (Washington, D.C.: CSIS Press, Center for Strategic and International Studies, 2006), pp. 51–53; Storm, *Democratization in Morocco*, p. 110.

44. Lise Storm, "The parliamentary election in Morocco," September 2007; *Electoral Studies*, Vol. 27 (2008), pp. 359–364.

45. "Sheikh Yassine Passes Away, Visions Unfulfilled, Succession Uncertain," *North Africa Post*, December 30, 2012, http://northafricapost.com/1776-sheikh-yassine-passes-away-visions-unfulfilled-succession-uncertain.html.

46. Human Rights Watch, *World Report 2006: events of 2005* (New York: HRW, 2006); Moheb Zaki, *Civil Society and Democratization in the Arab World: Annual Report 2007*

(Cairo: Ibn Khaldun Center for Development Studies, 2007); Marina Ottaway and Meredith Riley, *Morocco: from Top-down Reform to Democratic Transition?* Carnegie Papers: Middle East Series Democracy and Rule of Law, No. 71 (Washington: Carnegie Endowment for International Peace, September 2006).

47. International Monetary Fund, *Staff Report for the 2011 Article IV Consultation* (Washington DC, September 2011).

48. Maroc. Haut Commissariat au Plan, *Carte De La Pauvrété 2007* (Rabat: Haut Commissariat au Plan, 2010).

49. World Bank, World Development Index.

50. Refugee Review Tribunal of Australia, *Untitled Case*, [2009] RRTA 856 (24 September 2009).

51. It is possible to get the baccalaureate after leaving school, which is quite expensive and not necessarily easy for a lower middle-class boy, or he may have obtained some sort of trade certificate that allowed him to continue his studies to qualify as a hairdresser. Personal information Francesco Vacchiano (Instituto Universitário de Lisboa), Doris Gray (al-Akhawayn University in Ifrane, Morocco).

52. "Qui sommes nous? Parcours : Période d'équilibre, épreuve du «Mémorandum» (1998–2001) Renforcement du front politique dans le cadre de l'affermissement spirituel", al-'Adl wal-Ihsane website, http://www.aljamaa.net/fr/document/1117.shtml.

53. Maroc Agence de Presse "SM le Roi procède à la pose de la 1ère pierre pour la construction à Safi de l'Institut de formation aux carrières de santé." November 11, 2007, http://www.indh.gov.ma/fr/activ_royale36.asp; Bibliothèque régionale de Safi, http://biblioregionalesafi.webs.com/inaugurationparsmleroi.htm.

54. "Le milliardaire citoyen" *Maroc-Hebdo*, N°813 (7–13 November) 2008, p. 54.

55. Adolfo Barajas, Ralph Chami, Connel Fullenkamp, and Anjali Garg "The Global Financial Crisis and Workers' Remittances to Africa: What's the Damage?" IMF Working Paper, January 2010, http://cid.bcrp.gob.pe/biblio/Papers/IMF/2010/enero/wp1024.pdf.

56. International Monetary Fund, Morocco: 2011 Article IV Consultation, IMF Country Report No. 11/341 (Washington DC: International Monetary Fund, 2011), p. 31, http://www.imf.org.

57. Michael Bhatia, "The Western Sahara Under Polisario Control," *Review of African Political Economy*, Vol. 28, Issue 88 (2001), p. 292.

58. J. Peter Pham, "Not Another Failed State: Toward a Realistic Solution in the Western Sahara, *The Journal of the Middle East and Africa*, Vol. 1, Issue 1 (2010), pp. 1–24; Anna Theofilopoulou, *Western Sahara — How to Create a Stalemate* (United States Institute of Peace Briefing, May 2007). http://www.usip.org/publications/western-sahara-how-create-stalemate.

59. Maroc. Commission Consultative de la Régionalisation Rencontre de la CCR avec la presse 28 mars 2011, http://www.regionalisationavancee.ma/PDF/cons1.pdf accessed 18 April 2013.

60. Upper Tribunal (Immigration and Asylum Chamber) Appeal Number: AA/13541/2010 Heard at Glasgow, August 2, 2011.

61. Irene Fernández Molina (2011), "The Monarchy vs. the 20 February Movement: Who Holds the Reins of Political Change in Morocco?" *Mediterranean Politics*, Vol. 16, Issue 3, pp. 435–441.

62. Bruce Maddy-Weitzman "Is Morocco Immune to Upheaval?" *Middle East Quarterly*, Vol. 19, No. 1 (2012), pp. 87–93, http://www.meforum.org/3114/morocco-upheaval.

63. Fernández Molina, The Monarchy vs. the 20 February Movement.

64. "King of Rock," *Forbes Magazine*, 17 June 2009.

65. World Bank. GEM Commodities. http://data.worldbank.org/data-catalog/commodity-price-data; Mass anti-government protest in Morocco: protesters in Casablanca accuse the government of failing to deliver on the pledges of social justice. *Al-Jazeera*, May 28, 2012, www.aljazeera.com/news/middleeast/2012/05/20125282530957495.html.

66. Abdelilah Benkirane: J'y suis, j'y reste *Maroc Hebdo*, 6–12 September 2013, pp. 10–13. http://www.maroc-hebdo.press.ma/Site-Maroc-hebdo/archive/Archives_1038/pdf_1037/mhi_1037.pdf.

67. Issue 1038 of *Maroc Hebdo*, 13–19 September 2013 covers this on different pages. http://www.maroc-hebdo.press.ma/Site-Maroc-hebdo/archive/Archives_1038/pdf_1038/mhi_1038.pdf.

68. Upper Tribunal (Immigration and Asylum Chamber) I R vs Secretary of State for the Home Department, Birmingham 21 May 2013, AA/11907/2011. "Abdesalam Talbi" is a fictitious name.

69. Abdeslam Maghraoui, "Political Authority in Crisis: Mohammed VI's Morocco," *Middle East Report 218* (2001), pp. 12–17.

# PART V
# The Palestinians

.

# Sunset at Dawn: The Disintegration of the Palestinian State Project

## Menachem Klein

The Palestinian situation is different from any of the Arab states that experienced popular uprisings in recent years. Although their discontent is ongoing, there has been no large-scale uprising among West Bank (or Gazan) Palestinians, unlike during the first Intifada (1987–91), or as occurred in Egypt in 2011 and again in 2013. The Palestinians do not seek to shift their ruling system from despotism to democracy. Rather, they hope to establish their own fully independent government. Whereas Arab states are in a post-colonial stage, the 3.76 million Palestinians living in the territories occupied by Israel in 1967 are stateless.[1]

Although a Palestinian state does not exist, the Palestinian Authority (PA) exercises a limited autonomy over designated areas. As in Arab states that experienced popular uprisings, the PA's ruling West Bank elite is losing legitimacy and having to rely more on sheer force and coercive measures. Keeping in mind that there are important differences between the Palestinians and the Arab states where uprisings erupted, still one cannot disconnect the Palestinians from developments in the Arab region as a whole. In its own way, the Palestinian Authority is also disintegrating and losing public trust.

The "Arab Spring" has raised fundamental questions about the structure of the Arab states: are they stable and based on a substantial degree of social integration, or are they artificial structures imposed on conservative societies by Western colonial and imperial powers with the help of local elites motivated by narrow self-interest? Are they the expression of modern societies with pockets of religious conservatives, or societies suffering from a distorted modernity and ruled, until recently, by a narrow stratum of educated post-colonial despots, mostly former army officers? In short, is the national Arab state project a failure? As fundamentally important as these questions may be, they are not relevant to the Palestinian case, not only because the Palestinian state has not yet been established but also because of its special status as being partially occupied and otherwise dominated by Israel. Palestinians have not formed a modern army, or established a fully-functioning administration. Israel did not rule over the West Bank and Gaza Strip through Palestinian administration but rather by Israeli military administration. Israel limited its Palestinian employees in the administration of the occupied territories to low ranks. Thus, the Palestinians lacked an administrative mentor as well as a chance to operate a national administration. At most, they managed municipalities, worker and student unions, and religious institutions. In other words, the current dynamics of Palestinian society and politics are distinct from those experienced in Arab societies during the last three years, but they are nonetheless influenced by them.

In this chapter I sum up almost one hundred years of the failed Palestinian state building project. I will argue that it was not only external forces that caused this failure. Many factors originated in the Palestinian Liberation Organization (PLO)'s and the PA's modes of operation. Still, the Palestinian state building project is not doomed to eternal failure. The crisis of the Arab states can teach them a lesson about how to attain greater cohesiveness and establish their state on durable foundations.

# The PLO State Project

The Palestinian national movement under the British Mandate (1922-48) did not inherit a state. Originating in the declining Ottoman Empire, it was confronted, upon its formal establishment in 1919, with the powerful British occupation and subsequent Mandate. At the same time, the fledgling movement struggled against the Zionist movement that was backed by British. The Palestinian movement chose not to integrate into Mandatory institutions due to the British commitment, expressed first in Lord Balfour's letter in 1917, to support the Zionists' goal of establishing a Jewish homeland in Palestine, where the native Arab Palestinians were the majority. The Palestinian national movement hoped to cause the British to withdraw their support of the Zionists and enable the Palestinian majority to establish an independent state, as had occurred in neighboring countries. Unlike the Zionists, the Palestinian national movement did not use Mandatory institutions as an instrument to build its own modern social and political institutions or to promote a greater degree of social cohesion. These strategies were among the reasons for the Palestinian defeat in the 1948 war.

The PLO inherited a shattered and fragmented society. When the PLO was established in 1964, there was no Palestinian self-rule anywhere. Moreover, half of the Palestinian population consisted of displaced refugees. Traditional social structures had been destroyed and the urban leadership of wealthy Palestinian notables had collapsed. A new generation filled the post-1948 vacuum. The PLO and Fatah founders were young, ambitious, lower middle class refugees without strong kinship ties, wealth, or elite connections. Based on the model of the Algerian revolt against French colonialism, this new generation hoped to liberate Palestine through armed struggle. Only later did they gradually change their tactics to diplomacy.

In order to overcome the consequences of the 1948 war, the PLO was founded as a state-like organization. The Palestinian National Council was formed as the equivalent of a parliament-in-exile, and the Executive Committee was modeled after a government-in-exile, complete with portfolios. But statehood remained out of reach, as the PLO's Executive Committee lacked real state power. The PLO was organized around a romantic vision (articulated by the Palestinian National Covenant, in both its 1964 and 1968 versions), not a focus on territorial sovereignty, and did not possess a monopoly on the legitimate use of force. It was guided by a national liberation ethos of revolution rather than by a gradualist, constructive state-building policy. The PLO state project suffered from other structural problems as well.

First, it operated outside the territory which it claimed on behalf of the Palestinian people, and was thus fully dependent on Arab host countries for operational, political and financial support. The PLO tried to maneuver through the thicket of inter-Arab rivalries but with only limited success.

Second, with no state mechanism to enforce its power, Palestinians accepted PLO authority only voluntarily or symbolically, and could not be substantially taxed by it.

Third, the PLO, which, since 1968 was dominated by the Fatah movement, remained an umbrella organization with limited authority. Each PLO member organization remained independently armed and more often than not operated independently.

Fourth, the PLO did not acquire substantial experience in running state-like departments such as education, economic and financial affairs, and its armed forces consisted of volunteers. The PLO also lacked management skills. Its leaders, from Yasir 'Arafat down, preferred to employ patron-client governing methods instead of modern institutions. The PLO suffered from financial corruption, lack of transparency, dysfunctional modes of operation, disobedience, and outright refusal to respect decisions made by the organization's leadership. Based in Jordan [1968-70] and in Lebanon [1971-82], the PLO violated its host countries' authority and intervened in their domestic politics. The term "Fakahani Republic" (named after the Beirut neighborhood where the PLO was headquartered from 1971-1982) expressed the PLO self-image but not the reality.

The Palestinian elite prior to 1948 war, and West Bank leadership from 1948 to 1967, were urban leaders supported by their clans and had limited experience running larger regional institutions. The PLO bureaucracy, for its part, was largely made up of people from small towns or villages, and was quite inexperienced. Thus, after the Six-Day War in June 1967, the PLO faced problems convincing West Bank residents, traditionally tied to existing political and social elites, to accept its leadership. Beginning in the mid-1970's, the PLO worked to incorporate and subordinate West Bank and Gaza Strip civil society and professional institutions (legal and engineering associations, labor unions, journalists bureaus of commerce, youth and student organizations, university student associations, the Palestinian Red Crescent Society, mayors and municipalities) to its leadership based outside of Palestine. The PLO was not interested in running these institutions, but rather in keeping them politically neutral and preventing the emergence of an alternative leadership based within the West Bank and Gaza Strip. In other words, the PLO's main concern was to maintain its leadership status while remaining safely outside of Israeli-controlled areas, rather than building and operating de facto state institutions. Concurrently, the Jordanian alternative to PLO leadership that the PLO so feared was gradually removed. Israel's "Jordanian option" approach to solving the Palestinian problem proved a failure, thanks partly to PLO resistance, and partly to Israel's unwillingness to meet Jordan's demand for a complete withdrawal of Israeli forces to the June 4, 1967 lines.

Until 1993, Israel and the West rejected the PLO's claim to self-determination and refused to recognize the right to Palestinian statehood. Paradoxically, this rejection helped the PLO to mobilize domestic and international support for its activities, regardless of its poor performance in the realm of state-building. Moreover, international support for the Palestinian cause increased despite the PLO's numerous failures.

Following the 1982 Lebanon war that Israel initiated against the PLO, and the 1987 Intifada, the PLO increased its symbolic capital and achieved a more prominent international standing and profile. This was temporarily damaged by 'Arafat's siding with Saddam Hussein in the 1990-91 Gulf crisis, but Israel was ultimately forced to recognize the PLO as the sole representative of the Palestinian people and negotiated the Oslo agreements with it, as well as the failed final status negotiations (1999–2001, 2007–2008). A further Palestinian achievement, thanks in no small measure to continued Israeli settlement expansion, was the UN General Assembly's acceptance, in 2012, of Palestine as a non-member state.

In short, the PLO achieved its status more through rhetoric, symbolic action, violence and coercion than through state-building practices. The PLO held endless theoretical discussions on the topic, but its actual institution-building activity remained at a low level. Moreover, there was a growing dissonance between the PLO claim to speak on behalf of all Palestinians and the reality on the ground. The 1987 emergence of Hamas, at the beginning of the first Intifada, led to a zero-sum game between the two organizations and further exposed the gaps in PLO rhetoric. "Hamas is the sole legitimate representative of the Palestinian people" was written often on Gaza city walls in 1991-92. The PLO responded by declaring that "each rival with the PLO is a rivalry with (our) homeland. The PLO is the state, not just a party within it."[2]

# The Palestinian Authority

The establishment of the Palestinian Authority in 1994 was the PLO's first constructive step toward state building. For the first time, its leadership entered into the territory of the people it purported to represent. It also began operating as a centralized governing power, and, while limited under the Oslo Accords' interim agreements, it ruled over most of the more than 3.5 million Palestinians residing in the post-1967 areas, excluding Jerusalem. The PA shifted the instrument of Palestinian legitimacy from armed struggle and international diplomacy to democratically elected institutions. Elections were held in 1996, 2005 and 2006.[3] A decade after self-nominating leaders established the PLO, it achieved international recognition when 'Arafat was invited to speak at the UN General Assembly in 1974, following the Arab League Summit conference's recognition of the PLO as the "sole legitimate representative of the Palestinian people." The PA's legitimacy, on the other hand, was from the outset derived from competitive elections held in the West Bank and Gaza. However, in practice, the PA suffered from many of the PLO's structural and operational problems. First, the Oslo agreements limited the PA's power. It was not allowed to have its own currency, run a fully independent import-export system or exit-entrance checkpoints between the areas under its control and neighboring authorities. It was not allowed to operate international air or sea ports, and was not entitled to manage its own electromagnetic spectrum (enabling control over radio and television emissions, radar, and mobile phone networks) or population registration, including the right to issue residency certificates. In short, the PA had no state authority, but rather limited autonomy in part of the post-1967 lands.[4] Civil society organizations are fully dependent on international, PA or Hamas funding. The society is deeply divided between the PLO and Hamas, while each of the two rival organizations claims exclusive legitimacy and allocates resources only to its loyal followers. Political debates between Hamas and Fatah (the PLO's, and PA's dominant faction), or inside Fatah often produce new struggles rather than solutions. The PA governing apparatus is fully dependent on foreign professionals for training and budgets.

American and European professionals train and supervise the Palestinian police and security forces; the PA civil administration is supervised by the donor countries and international agencies like the IMF (International Monetary Fund). The PLO negotiation affairs department (in charge of writing legal and diplomatic papers to assist the Palestinian negotiators with Israel) is funded by a British institute and most of its employees are young Palestinians from abroad. And most of the time, Israeli restrictions prevent PA citizens from enjoying free movement between their autonomous areas. Yet despite all of these limitations, the PA administers well-run education, health and police systems, in addition to supporting private sector enterprises.

Under 'Arafat, PA institution-building was slow.[5] Progress was registered only when 'Arafat's hand was forced either by pressure from donor countries or his own Legislative Council. When the second Intifada broke out in 2000, and particularly following the Israeli re-occupation of the West Bank in 2002, the PA institutions largely disintegrated, apart from the health and education systems. Under President Mahmud 'Abbas (since 2004) and Prime Minister Salam Fayyad (2007-13), state-building from the ground up was initiated, and in certain areas succeeded. The financial system is now transparent and government expenses are monitored; the PA citizenry enjoy much better personal security and the government is less corrupt than it was under 'Arafat. Within limits, the legal system has improved its performance. Whereas 'Abbas worked top-down to achieve independence directly through negotiating with Israel or indirectly by mobilizing international pressure to force it to make concessions, Fayyad preferred to build the fledgling state from the bottom up. But soon Fayyad reached the limits that the Oslo accords imposed on the Palestinians. The Oslo agreements created Palestinians cantons divided by West Bank Area C [about 60 percent of the West Bank]. Israel controls Area C and expands its settlements there. No Palestinian state will be viable without geographical continuity and control over most, if not all, of Area C. But Israel seriously limits the PA government's operations there. In addition, Israel constructed a separation wall that cuts into the West Bank in places, adding more division to the territory. Israel has also used financial sanctions against the PA by periodically delaying the transfer of customs and VAT revenues that it collects for it, contributing to the PA's chronic financial crisis and its dependence on foreign donors.[6]

When Hamas won the 2006 parliamentary elections, PA officials cooperated with Israel and the US in an effort to bring Fatah back to power. This policy generated a sharp debate inside Fatah between its senior leaders and second tier officials. The senior leaders won out, and Hamas bases of support in the West Bank were gradually dismantled, but their policy derailed the nascent state-building project in the West Bank as well as Gaza. It pushed Hamas to react aggressively in Gaza in 2007 against Fatah cadres and institutionalized the political-geographical division of an area that the PLO had always insisted was a single indivisible unit. Senior PA and Fatah elites chose to preserve their privileged standing and interests over national unity and geo-political integration. The zero-sum game with Hamas has had a negative effect on civil society and the PA's democracy. West Bank security forces enjoy growing power at the expense of civil society institutions. Security forces routinely flout the law and trample on civil rights; the Legislative Council, in which Hamas won a majority in the 2006 elections, does not convene; and the president's term in office expired in 2009, but no new general elections appear to be on the horizon.[7]

Indeed, the World Bank and the IMF stated in April 2011 that the PA is functioning like other poorly governed authoritarian Middle East states. Yet their statement related only to the financial and economic fields that they examined. A more inclusive approach led Yazid Sayigh concluded that the PA is simply a failed state.[8] Neither 'Abbas's top-down strategy nor Fayyad's bottom-up one brought the PA closer to statehood than it had come under 'Arafat; its improved performance in some areas did not, at the end of the day, result in its acquisition of greater authority or territory.

## The Impact of the Arab Uprisings

Once the Arab Spring upheavals began, the EU states, Russia and the US focused primarily on the internal affairs of each of the Arab states, and were less attentive to the Israeli-Palestinian issue.[9] Meanwhile, the international community subsidizes the Palestinian Authority and thus unintentionally helps to maintain the status quo. And while the UN General Assembly voted in November 2012 to grant non-member state status to Palestine, this did not change anything on the ground. In addition, the EU adopted regulations in 2013 to cut off any cooperation with Israeli companies or institutions operating beyond the June 4, 1967 lines, with the primary aim of stopping Israel from expanding its settlements, rather than forcing Israel to remove all or most of the existing settlements. In any case, the EU's action has only had a limited effect.

Moreover, similar to other Arab societies, the Palestinian public's concern has turned inward, as described by three Norwegian analysts:

> Palestinian youth have largely exited from politics, prioritizing personal affairs (family and job) when considering the current situation and their future. They are unhappy with a difficult job situation, although West Bank youth express more optimism about the future than young people

in the Gaza Strip. Corruption and political favoritism are experienced as a major problem on the personal level in both areas. The Palestinian Authority and Hamas governments are also criticized in regard to the state of democracy, freedom of expression and human rights, more so in the Gaza Strip than in the West Bank. However, neither government is completely condemned, on account of their success in raising the level of security (the Gaza Strip) and economic prosperity (the West Bank). Widespread discontent with their situation among the youth does not translate into increased political interest or engagement. Instead, the majority has abandoned organized politics and what they consider a political class associated mostly with Fatah and Hamas and to which few seem to see any alternative.[10]

The Arab uprisings greatly impressed young Palestinian activists. In the summer of 2012, large anti-PA demonstrations broke out in the West Bank. The young demonstrators combined economic and political complaints. They protested against the rising cost of living and unpaid PA salaries, called upon the PLO to withdraw from the Paris Protocol (signed with Israel, the economic chapter of the Oslo Accords) and demanded that Prime Minister Fayyad and President 'Abbas resign. According to a European Council on Foreign Relations report, they "voiced a lack of confidence in Palestinian politics, per se. The same is also true of those Palestinians who openly advocate for political change, whose demands include reform of the PLO, new elections for the Palestine National Council (PNC), the PLO's primary legislative body, and even the dismantlement of the PA".[11]

Although the demonstrators lacked leadership and a viable strategy, their claims found an attentive public. A June 2013 poll conducted by the Palestinian Center for Policy and Survey Research found that 40% believed that the PA had become a burden on the Palestinian people while 30 percent believed that it was an accomplishment for the Palestinian people. Generally, 52 percent said the PA, both in the West Bank and in the Gaza Strip, or at least in one of the two areas, was a burden on the Palestinian people.[12]

In July 2013, young Palestinians established the Facebook group *Tamarrud* ("Rebellion"), named after the Egyptian mass movement that in June–July 2013 pushed the army to abolish the elected President Morsi's regime.

> We are a youth initiative that aims at making the voice of the youth heard and enabling its political participation....Oh Palestinians, revolt against oppression and division, revolt against those impeding the elections. No one is legitimate; the mandate of everyone has ended. The only

legitimacy is that of the people. Our movement in the West Bank and Gaza is peaceful with a clear aim — returning legitimacy to the people.[13]

At the same time, senior Fatah member Dr. Sufian Abu Zayda, a member of the Fatah Revolutionary Council and a former PA minister, published an article, posted on several web sites, that condemned the 'Abbas regime as a one-man dictatorship:

> Honestly, no one dreamed we would ever arrive at the present situation, in which all authorities and all senior positions are in the hands of a single person ... We never imagined there would be anyone ... who would hold the authority that even 'Arafat, with all his greatness and symbolic importance, did not have.[14]

The PA's angry official response came from the security establishment, as if to confirm Abu Zayda's argument.

But the majority of the public was indifferent to the *Tamarrud* call, despaired of the possibility of change. Nasser Barghouti, a young Palestinian, published a poem on the Arab Spring that never was:

> I thought in numbers we could say what is
> or what was right
> placards drawn with blood and no fright
> young and old stay the course
> street by street
> and night after night
> where the stars have turned a page
> and time its stray discourse
> and the whole world a stage
> on my spring that never was
> Tell me if I am right
> if you happen to see my black from my white
> tell me if might had always made right
> in this Arab spring of mine
> that never was
> tell me if you can
> tell me if history
> or geography
> or a crude stereography
> have me and my story
> and our Arab glory
> in their jaws

or will it
in my night
and in my endless flight
ever shine?
Tell me if you can
Red is the new color of my sight
not white
red is the new word
on the streets of my Arab spring
that never was
red is the new color of my sight
or have I erred
tell me if you can
what have I stirred?
in this history
this geography
this Arab glory?
that turns right into wrong
weak into strong
and what is whole
into the absurd?
is it darker
is it bright?
Tell me if you can
Three years and counting
from Benghazi to Baghdad
have we forgotten how to count?
or have we laid to rest all
that which together
we have breathed
and dreamt
and defended stout
tell me if you can
was it sane or was it mad
to heed that call
for my Arab spring that never was
to drop all for what was unsheathed
and for that which was just and a cause
tell me if you can

I was there in every corner
and every turn
in every broken bone
and every moan
I was there
I touched and kissed every tear
year after year
one fading smile after the other
one hopeless yearn after another
I was there
street, capital, and
conference
I no longer dare
to speak
to face or stare
at
my Arab spring that never was
here or there.[15]

Other young activists targeted their criticism inward rather than against the Arab Spring as a whole. "We had our own revolution on March 15, 2011," declared Mahmoud Yahya:

Our defining chant was, "The people want to end the division!" They beat us, slandered us, broke our limbs, smeared our reputation and blackmailed us. "We believe in our strength, but we were romantic. When I saw all of the March 15 activists emigrating and traveling away from Gaza, I knew that we had failed to bring about our Palestinian Spring, so I decided to travel as well.[16]

A fellow activist, Ahmed Balousha, was openly self-critical:

We settled for raising banners demanding that the political system be reformed, not toppled … I feel that we only lied to ourselves, saying that we were representing the Arab spring, when really we failed to take any meaningful action.[17]

The bloodshed and chaos that resulted from the Arab uprisings in surrounding countries contributed to a profound pessimism among Palestinian youth. According to a 2013 opinion poll, 57 percent of Palestinian youth believe that future regional events would negatively affect the Palestinian situation, and only 18 percent believe they would have a positive effect on it. Moreover, West Bank youth did not endorse the Arab Spring model. Just 26 percent of them believed that an uprising similar to those that occurred in Egypt and Tunisia could occur against the Palestinian Authority in the West Bank, and only 15 percent would support it.

Activists that do not want to copy the Egyptian model but to establish an original Palestinian one suggest replacing 'Abbas's state discourse and calling upon the international community to put pressure on Israel by challenging it directly with an individual and collective human rights discourse. Occasionally they organize small protests against 'Abbas and the peace process; against Israeli settlers and the IDF; or in favor for national reconciliation between Fatah and Hamas. Palestinian activists conduct intensive discussions on the Internet, but without building their own institutions or transferring the virtual discussion groups into sustained and coordinated action in the real world. Beyond the limited success of its anti-normalization campaign (i.e., ending joint activity with Israeli grass-roots organizations because it creates the impression of normal relations in a highly abnormal situation), the young generation of activists has not achieved much in the real world. To be sure, it can potentially serve as an agent of change, and is fully aware of the deadlock the PA has reached. However, it lacks political and organizational skills.

The PA administration is confused and lacks a coherent strategy to secure the state-building project, other than simply keeping the PA alive and waiting for change to come from the outside and rescue it. Sporadically, PA leaders have helped the younger generation organize anti-Israeli non-violent protests, but in many other cases they prevented them from challenging Israel because they were afraid that non-violent protests would quickly turn violent or anti-'Abbas in nature. 2013 finds the Palestinian society in crisis, without a united polity, a clear vision or any real optimism. One can find clear expression of this in a Palestinian Center for Policy and Survey Research public opinion poll from September 2013: 49 percent of the post-1967 Occupied Territories Palestinians opposed President 'Abbas' decision to return to direct talks with Israel in 2013. Only a slim majority, 51 percent, supported the two-state solution, which is 'Abbas and the PA's sole political goal, and 48 percent opposed it. Moreover, 59 percent of them believed that this goal is no longer practical. Sixty percent supported popular non-violent resistance, which 'Abbas opposes and tries to prevent. No less telling is the fact that 59 percent of the Palestinian population in the West Bank and Gaza Strip believed that the Oslo accords damaged vital Palestinian national interests, and 60 percent opposed their continued implementation. In this context it is worth mentioning, that a)'Abbas was in charge of the Palestinian team that negotiated the initial Oslo agreement and personally signed it, on 13 September 1993, on the White House lawn; and, b) the primary Palestinian share in implementing the Oslo agreements is the PA's security cooperation with Israel, which the 'Abbas administration sees as its guarantee to receive financial and political support from the US and the EU. The Palestinian majority not only opposes 'Abbas' policy, but also his argument that Israel is a genuine partner for a two-state solution. According to the same poll cited above, 59 percent believe that Israel's long term goal is to expand its borders over all of the land occupied in 1967 and expel its Palestinian population, and 21 percent believe that Israel "only" aims to annex the West Bank and deny Palestinian rights.

# Conclusion

The PA not only faces a strategic crisis, but also lacks democratic legitimacy.[18] The PA does not rule through democratically elected political institutions: the Legislative Council is frozen due to the Hamas–Fatah struggle, while the official tenure of the president ended 4 years ago and, consequently, the president rules only by decree. There is a growing political vacuum that the younger generation, those who grew up during the second Intifada, has tried to fill, albeit unsuccessfully thus far. The PLO "old guard" and the leaders of the first Intifada that hoped to gain from Oslo are deeply frustrated, disappointed and tired. Fearing not only US anger but also the possibility of an Arab Spring-like uprising against them, the PA leadership agreed in July 2013 to accept US Secretary of State John Kerry's proposal to resume peace talks with the Netanyahu government under certain terms and conditions, which included a $4 billion pledge of economic investment. 'Abbas' administration hopes that the US promise to base the talks on the June 4, 1967 lines with land swaps, together with the injection of new funds, will improve its status domestically and internationally and hold at bay the waves of popular unrest unleashed throughout the region during the last three years.

# Notes

1. The figure is that of the Palestinian Bureau of Statistics, http://www.pcbs.gov.ps/Portals/_pcbs/PressRelease/census2007_e.pdf.

2. Quoted from Menachem Klein, "Competing Brothers: The Web of Hamas-PLO Relations", *Terrorism and Political Violence*, Volume 8 (Summer 1996), Number 2, pp. 111–132, the quote is from page 115. The two rival movements failed to stick to their many modis operandi and cease fire agreements. Their last violent confrontation broke out in June 2007 in Gaza City. The PLO call it "armed revolution against legitimate government," whereas Hamas argue that it was a self defense act against PLO-Fatah attacks on its people. Since 2007, the division between them has been institutionalized, politically and geographically.

3. Presidential and legislative elections were held in 1996, presidential elections in 2005 and legislative elections in 2006.

4. Nathan Brown, *Palestinian Politics After the Oslo Accords Resuming Arab Palestine* (Berkeley: University of California Press, 2003), pp. 94–137; Rashid Khalidi, *The Iron Cage: the Story of the Palestinian Struggle for Statehood* (Boston: Beacon Press 2006), pp. 140–218.

5. Menachem Klein, "'Arafat as a Palestinian Icon", *Palestine-Israel Journal*, Vol. 11 (2004/5), pp. 30–38.

6. Menachem Klein, *The Shift: Israel–Palestine from Border Struggle to Ethnic Conflict* (New York: Columbia University Press, 2010), pp. 21–45, 89–117; Khalidi, *The Iron Cage*, pp. 140–218.

7. Nathan Brown, "Are the Palestinians Building a State?," *Carnegie Commentary*, June 2010, http://carnegieendowment.org/files/palestinian_state1.pdf; Brown, "Fayyad Is Not the Problem but Fayyadism is not the Solution to Palestine's Political Crisis," *Carnegie Commentary*, September 2010, http://carnegieendowment.org/files/fayyad_not_problem_2.pdf; Brown, "Palestinians: the Unsustainable May No Longer Be Sustainable," *Carnegie Commentary*, February 2011, http://carnegieendowment.org/2011/02/22/palestinians-unsustainable-may-no-longer-be-sustainable/2dt9; Brown, "Requiem for Fayyadism", *Foreign Policy*, April 17, 2013, http://www.foreignpolicy.com/articles/2013/04/17/requiem_for_fayyadism; *International Crisis Group*, "Ruling Palestine 1: Gaza Under Hamas," *Middle East Report*, No. 73, March 2008, http://www.crisisgroup.org/en/regions/middle-east-north-africa/israel-palestine/072-ruling-palestine-I-gaza-under-hamas.aspx; *International Crisis Group*, "Ruling Palestine 2: The West Bank Model," *Middle East Report*, No. 79, July 2008, http://www.crisisgroup.org/en/regions/middle-east-north-africa/israel-palestine/079-ruling-palestine-II-the-west-bank-model.aspx; Yezid Sayigh, "Hamas Rule in Gaza Three Years On, Crown Center for Middle East Studies," *Middle East Brief*, Vol. 41, March 2010, Brandeis University, http://www.brandeis.edu/crown/publications/meb/meb41.html.

8. Yezid Sayigh, "War as Leveler War as Midwife — Palestinian Political Institutions, Nationalism, and Society since 1948," in Steven Heydemann (ed.), *War, Institutions, and Social Change in the Middle East* (Berkeley: University of Californian Press, 2000), pp. 200–239.

9. Mark Katz, "The Arab Spring and the Israeli/Palestinian Conflict: International Implications," *Russia in Global Affairs*, April 15, 2013, http://eng.globalaffairs.ru/number/The-Arab-Spring-and-the-IsraeliPalestinian-Conflict-international-implications-15933.

10. Mona Christophersen, Jacob Høigilt and Åge A. Tiltnes, *Palestinian Youth and the Arab Spring*, February 2012, NOREF [Norwegian Peace Building Resource Center] Report, http://www.peacebuilding.no/var/ezflow_site/storage/original/application/562d62ccb49d92227b6865a8b2d11e1a.pdf.

11. Alexander Kouttab and Mattia Toaldo, "In Search of Legitimacy: The Palestinian National Movement 20 Years After Oslo" (London: European Council on Foreign

Rlations, October 2013), p.2, http://ecfr.eu/page/-/ECFR89_PALESTINE_BRIEF_AW.pdf.

12. "Poll No. 48: Full Analysis," Palestinian Center for Policy and Survey Research, http://www.pcpsr.org/survey/polls/2013/p48e.html. For another poll on youth attitudes with similar findings, see Kouttab and Toaldo, "In Search of Legitimacy".

13. Asmaa Al-Ghoul, "Tamarod Comes to Palestine," *Al-Monitor*, July 11, 2013, http://www.al-monitor.com/pulse/originals/2013/07/hamas-tamarod-palestine-gaza-egypt.html#ixzz2YqCsIDSk.

14. For additional information, see *Ha'aretz*, July 12, 2013, http://www.haaretz.com/weekend/week-s-end/in-rare-scathing-article-prominent-fatah-member-calls-abbas-tyrant-and-dictator.premium-1.535449.

15. *The Palestine Chronicle*, August 25, 2013, http://www.palestinechronicle.com/my-arab-spring-that-never-was-a-poem/#.UkVoBYZmidk.

16. Asmaa al-Ghoul "Palestinian Activists Bemoan Their Lost Arab Spring", *Al-Monitor*, January 18, 2013, http://www.al-monitor.com/pulse/originals/2013/01/palestine-failed-arab-spring.html#ixzz2g5UMEc2O.

17. *Ibid*.

18. Jonathan Schanzer, "The Slow Death of Palestinian Democracy," *Foreign Policy*, April 19, 2013, http://www.foreignpolicy.com/articles/2013/04/19/slow_death_palestinian_democracy_fayyad_abbas?page=full.

# The Palestinians:
# A Test of Governmental Stability and Social Cohesion

## Ephraim Lavie

Palestinian society in the West Bank and Gaza is embroiled in an ongoing struggle for national independence. Its traditional social and political structures have undergone considerable change in recent decades, resulting in challenges to existing norms. High fertility rates have led to an especially high proportion of youth. These youth are being educated in high schools and universities, and over one-half of all university students (in the West Bank) are female. Yet, at the same time, the Palestinian economy has retained many of the features of that of a Third World state. It is still critically dependent on external aid, food aid, medicine, and equipment from UN agencies, United Nations Relief and Works Agency (UNRWA), and other non-governmental organizations (NGOs). The labor market in the West Bank remains largely dependent on Israel and its settlements. In these conditions, the disparities between the quality of life in cities versus the villages and refugee camps continue to grow, obstructing the path to greater social and economic mobility.

On the eve of the popular protests and uprisings in the Arab world that were first sparked in late 2010, the Palestinian Authority (PA) already suffered from a lack of legitimacy. The internal political split between Fatah and Hamas, and the lack of geographic contiguity between the West Bank and the Gaza Strip, raised the question of who represented the Palestinian people. The Palestine Liberation Organization's internationally recognized status as the sole legitimate representative of the Palestinian people had been shaken, especially after the Hamas victory in the PA's parliamentary elections in January 2006 and the PA's subsequent loss of control over the Gaza Strip. The fact that the PA failed to hold presidential, parliamentary, or local government elections after their terms had officially ended in 2009/2010 also contributed to the decline in the government's legitimacy. The PA's government, comprised mainly of technocrats, does not include representatives of society's political power brokers, and operates without constitutional foundation or parliamentary oversight. Law-making stemmed from the president's authority to publish emergency resolutions, due to the fact that the legislature had ceased to convene. Therefore, bills on civil issues that government ministries sought to promote were formulated by the ministries' legal advisors and submitted to the president to be published as laws. Thus, in the absence of separation of powers, the government as the executive branch had kept extensive powers of legislation and execution, with no public oversight.

Beginning in 2008, after years of violent confrontations with Israel (the Second Intifada, 2000-2004) and the continued stagnation in diplomatic negotiations, the PA took steps to rehabilitate its institutions and establish effective rule. Since then, it has executed multi-annual development plans with the generous financial assistance of the international community and with Israel's support and encouragement, which eliminated roadblocks and relaxed restrictions on mobility in the West Bank. The PA's official goal was to abandon violence and build the Palestinian state from the bottom up: to reorganize governmental institutions, reinforce the PA's social and security foundations, and develop a sustainable economy, so that the Palestinian Authority could become a *de facto* state.

Despite this new orientation and technocratic emphasis, the PA was heavily criticized by Palestinians for failing to share the fruits of development with large sections of the population, who suffered from economic hardship. It was also taken to task for its security cooperation with Israel (one-third of the PA's budget was consumed by the security sector) and for human rights violations committed by PA security personnel. Critics also bemoaned the absence of genuine multi-party politics in the PA: the Fatah party was in the throes of a chronic internal crisis, Hamas activities were prohibited in the West Bank, and the smaller parties failed to promote a new agenda or gain significant public support. The result was widespread cynicism, and even despair, among large sectors of the public.

Palestinian society had displayed a considerable degree of cohesion during the First and Second Intifadas (1987-92; 2000-04). However, this weakened in subsequent years. The leadership's continued impotence in managing domestic affairs and revelations of corruption in its ranks gradually eroded society's sense of collective solidarity and diminished its willingness — Palestinian women included[1] — to bear the burdens imposed upon them by the national leadership. Particularly noteworthy was the frustration and disappointment of commanders and activists of the Second Intifada, who had sacrificed their best years to partake in the national struggle. They believed that they had not received the appropriate material or political rewards for their sacrifices: political appointments and/or political influence in decision-making.

These decade-long developments have contributed to a gradual weakening of a Palestinian national collective identity in favor of sub-state identities associated with groups such as the family and the locality, as well as a strengthened religious identity. In addition, Palestinian youth have prioritized individualist goals at the expense of allegiance to the collective aims advocated by the national leadership.

## Preemption: Diverting Potential Protests to "Appropriate Goals"

PA leaders were not totally unprepared for the negative public sentiments directed against it, fueled, in part, by the "Arab Spring" protests. Senior PA and Fatah leaders attempted to improve the unfavorable image created by the PA's security coordination with Israel, emphasizing (especially to young Palestinians) that Palestinian interests were served by such coordination.[2] They hoped that the public would accept their explanation that the national agenda demanded precedence over the political struggle against Israel and over internal disputes with the Palestinian government.

Against the backdrop of the uprisings in Tunisia and Egypt, the PLO executive committee announced on February 12, 2011, that presidential and parliamentary elections would be held before September 2011. The announcement was accompanied by statements explaining that the elections were the only way to end the split between the West Bank and Gaza and restore national unity.[3] The public was assured that the elections would be fair and free, and would take place under international supervision.[4] One month later, however, Mahmud 'Abbas, president of the PA and chairman of the PLO, stated that general elections could not be held due to the continuing divisions among the Palestinians and the disconnection between Gaza and the West Bank.[5] On February 13, the government took another step in response to the regional environment by announcing the government's dissolution and its reconstitution to include representatives from Fatah and other factions. Members of Fatah's revolutionary council told 'Abbas, that while they understood that reappointing the non-affiliated Salam Fayyad as prime minister was necessary to guarantee continued US support for the PA, they still believed they ought to receive senior governmental posts as members of the ruling party. As it happened, however, the plans for forming a new government were suspended following 'Abbas's proposal to Hamas Prime Minister Isma'il Haniyeh in Gaza to establish a provisional technocratic government until elections were held.

Preceding these moves was a PA decision to accede to a Palestinian Supreme Court injunction, which had ordered it to hold local elections. Left-wing Palestinian parties including the Popular Front, the People's Party, and the

National Palestine Initiative Party had actively campaigned for elections, after they had been originally scheduled for Summer 2010 and then cancelled. The parties filed a petition to the Supreme Court, which in December 2010 ordered the PA to set a date for the elections, explaining that any delay constituted a violation of the court's order. In response, the Palestinian Minister of Local Government announced that the elections would take place in the Summer 2011. Party activists praised the Palestinian Supreme Court's decision and rejected the claims that elections in the West Bank only deepen the existing fragmentation of the Palestinian people. They explained that their job was to save democracy from the internal split and external intervention in matters of the Palestinian people.[6]

Hamas leaders in Gaza, who had seized sole power in 2007, refused to recognize the legitimacy of Fayyad's government or its decisions. Hamas persistently objected to elections or any reconciliation with Fatah until the key issues related to the future of Hamas' forces and their role in security affairs in the West Bank were settled, and as long as PA institutions remained linked to the Americans and maintained their security cooperation with Israel. Nonetheless, under the influence of the Arab Spring and calls by various Palestinian factions to end internal divisions, Haniyeh invited 'Abbas and Fatah to begin a comprehensive national dialogue to satisfy the public's demand for reconciliation. In response, 'Abbas announced that he was ready to come to Gaza to put an end to the split and set up a government of independent officials, whose job would be to organize elections for the presidency, the PA's legislative council, and the PLO's national council.[7]

In the civil sphere, Palestinian journalists began to promote a public debate on the role of the Internet and Facebook as agents of influence. They urged young people to exploit social networks only for purposes that serve the national Palestinian cause, such as ending the internal division and the Israeli occupation.[8] PA leaders and Hamas leaders in Gaza quickly appropriated this debate for their own purposes, in order to demonstrate their appreciation of hardships faced by the public.[9] At the same time, they began to make practical use of online media and social networks to recruit youth for what the leaders believed were "appropriate goals" — ending the Occupation and mending the split — in order to eliminate the potential risk that the social media would be used against them.[10] However, the response to their efforts was minimal.

No more than several thousand young people attended demonstrations organized by the PA. The officially-sponsored "Young People's Demonstration" on March 15, 2011 consisted of mainly Fatah activists, students who were dismissed from their classes for the event, and PA employees who were bused to the site. The signs they held proved that the demonstrators had no common goal. In addition to the conventional slogans calling for the end of the internal division and the Occupation, left-wing activists also waved signs that called for reforming the PLO. Security forces indicated their sponsorship of the event by distributing food, beverages, and banners. Inspired by the sights of Egypt's Tahrir Square, the security forces even participated in the clean-up after the event as a symbolic gesture of their shared civic responsibility.

Although the calls from some quarters to end the split did not trigger mass demonstrations, Fatah and Hamas leaders recognized that action was needed if they were to survive. They were concerned by the flow of young people joining smaller, alternative organizations, a process that had been going on for several years. Leftist factions such as the Popular Front, the Democratic Front, the Communist People's Party, and the Initiative (*al-Mubadara*) Party, whose leaders were considered uncorrupt, proposed a civic-national agenda that was not inconsistent with the PA's state-building programs. These leftist groups began to attract young people to their ranks. One of the expressions of this shift was the lively participation of youth in the demonstrations organized by these factions as alternatives to the official March 15 event. A commemoration of the establishment of the People's Party turned into a joyful celebration of solidarity with the Egyptian nation.

In contrast to the West Bank, the Gaza Strip has become a breeding ground in recent years for salafi-jihadist groups that pose a challenge to Hamas' rule. Although limited in numbers and organizational skills, these groups' power lies in their ability to restrict Hamas' freedom of action. They criticized it for failing to fight against Israel or impose *shari'a* law in Gaza. Their militant attitude and aggressive approach in and outside Gaza attracted activists from the ranks of Hamas' own military arm, and posed a threat to political stability and security in Gaza.

Consequently, although the dynamics that led to the crumbling of Arab regimes elsewhere in the region originated from conditions that differed from those prevailing in the Palestinian territories, both Fatah and Hamas leaders were concerned that changes in the region would resonate with young Palestinians, and bring together rival forces from the left and right to oppose the existing leaderships. The leaders of both movements remained apprehensive of a grassroots awakening seeking to emulate the unaffiliated activist organizations that had ignited events in Tunisia, Egypt and other countries.

These developments, along with the threat to Bashar al-Asad's rule in Syria, and Egypt's attempt to retain its status as a major regional player, prompted Hamas and Fatah leaders to accelerate their reconciliation efforts. In the spring of 2011, they responded to a new Egyptian initiative that recognized their right to maintain effective control in their respective territories until general elections were held for the presidency, the parliament, and the Palestine National Council (PNC), and to defer a resolution of security-related and other disputed issues until after the elections. Hamas and Fatah leaders presented this reconciliation document (in early May 2011) as a response to the demands of the Palestinian youth and the general public. However, Hamas leaders began to recalibrate their position in the aftermath of the Muslim Brotherhood's rise to power in Egypt (One of their leaders, Mohammed Morsi, was elected president in June 2012.) They believed that the Brotherhood's success in Egypt would cause a significant change in Egyptian policy, shifting Egyptian support from the PA to Hamas, an offshoot of the Brotherhood. In contrast, the PA viewed reconciliation with Hamas as a move that might undermine its persistent state-building efforts and resolute efforts to achieve UN recognition.

# Public Opinion in Palestinian Society

Most of the public was in no mood for activism. Their overwhelming preference was the maintenance of domestic stability and calm, and avoiding a major violent confrontation with Israel. They had resigned themselves, at least temporarily, to the internal national split, and adopted an acquiescent, if cynical, attitude towards the chances of achieving a diplomatic solution to the Israeli Occupation in the foreseeable future and consequent social and economic prosperity.[11]

Public opinion polls and studies indicated low levels of political interest and participation in Palestinian society, and suggested that young people felt alienated from, and mistrustful of the political system.[12] They were disappointed with the various parties and factions that had failed to successfully transform themselves from revolutionary movements to political parties and appeared to be dedicated to promoting personal or narrow party interests at the expense of national ones.[13] A minority of the young people who remained politically active belonged to existing nationalist and Islamic-religious factions. The majority of young people, however, showed no inclination to set up new organizations to promote political or social change. In recent years, their passion for participating in student council elections and demonstrations was much more limited than the rebellious youth elsewhere in the Arab world. For the most part, Palestinian youth confined themselves to participating in annual commemorations of "Land Day" (an annual protest against the Israeli government's confiscation of Palestinian lands), the "Nakba" ("the catastrophe" of the 1948 defeat), or the "Naksa" (the "setback" of the 1967 Six-Day War).

This phenomenon predated the popular uprisings in the Arab world,[14] and has continued since. In 2013, independent groups of young people tried and failed to stimulate economic protests in the West Bank through social media networks.[15] Many Internet users expressed their frustration at the repeated failures to mobilize the public for protest, which they blamed on external factors such as the Israeli Occupation, and internal factors such as their powerlessness against Palestinian commercial enterprises and economic corporations. In mid-2013 *Tamarrud*, an independent protest movement of young people, was established in Gaza.[16] It attempted to use social media to mobilize a campaign for civil disobedience designed to topple Hamas' rule in Gaza. It hoped to generate massive support among young people, especially Fatah activists in Gaza, and eliminate the barriers of fear that prevented them from moving against Hamas. These efforts, however, failed to stir the public or stimulate any significant action in Gaza.[17]

The public was similarly unresponsive to Hamas' attempts to garner public support for the "Resistance" (*al-Muqawama*). The organization known as the Intifada Youth Coalition ("*Ahlaf Shabab al-Aqsa*"), which began operating in social networks in the second half of 2013, failed to recruit young people to date. Its call to unite for a new Intifada against Israel, its declared intention to organize a demonstration at sea to remove the naval blockade against Gaza and extend the area permitted for fishing, and its repeated cries to hold "days of rage" protests at various sites to protect the Al-Aqsa Mosque — have attracted limited response.

Evidently the social and political changes that have occurred in Palestinian society have led young Palestinians to withdraw into their personal "cocoons" and seek refuge in the extended family or in a return to religion. Most of the public no longer distinguishes between the political right and left and is irked by the leading political movements, Fatah and Hamas, because neither of them have succeeded in ending the conflict with Israel or resolving social and economic concerns in the West Bank and Gaza. The younger generation has gradually turned away from politics and adopted an individualistic attitude that prioritizes personal concerns for education, employment, and professional advancement over national collectivist issues. They reject the slogan commonly used by the leaders (placing the national campaign against Israel at the top of the agenda), which for many years had freed these leaders from addressing society's fundamental social and economic problems. This rejection is also a product of the steadily growing public perception that the diplomatic process with Israel would come to nothing.

This phenomenon has been reflected in the PA leadership's policy in recent years, which has focused on a state-building strategy. The PA leadership has promised that its campaign for independence would be conducted using non-violent tactics, in line with its declared position there would be no return to an armed struggle. PA President 'Abbas and Prime Minister Fayyad reiterated that lessons had been learned and the Palestinian people would not revert to a third armed Intifada, but instead would limit themselves to popular, non-violent resistance, similar to ongoing local protests against Israel's separation barrier. Following these protests, the PA took steps to contain the intensity of political demonstrations that might possibly turn violent by organizing local and international soccer matches, festivals, and performances of local and foreign entertainers.

## The Public Discourse around the Arab Spring

In the months that followed the eruption of the Arab Spring, the Palestinian discourse included criticism of the public's own lassitude and stupor, on the one hand, and optimism in view of the unfolding of the Arab Spring, on the other.

Khalil al-Asli, a Palestinian journalist, claimed that the Palestinian nation's acclimation to the Occupation was so complete that it coexisted with it. To illustrate his point, he described how the recent Nakba Day was commemorated:

> This nation observed the 63rd anniversary of the Nakba by holding a soccer match and a sports tournament costing several million dollars; and they even called it the 'Return Tournament'...On the 'Mountain of Fire' (*Jabal al-Nar*) [Nablus] in the West Bank, the bastion of the revolution, the neo-Palestinians commemorated the Nakba with rallies complete with impassioned speakers and artistic performances, including the Debka dance. Yet even before the celebration ended, everyone returned to their business and you could almost believe that no one there was a refugee or that the Nakba had nothing to with them; merely a hollow, meaningless ceremony!"

Al-Asli described a similar situation in Ramallah, and noted that the Palestinian police forces were stationed to maintain order at all the entrances to the city from the direction of Jerusalem, and prevented Palestinians from reaching the Qalandia border crossing.

> The faces of the Palestinian policemen were etched with determination to follow official orders to prevent any demonstration or parade outside the cities? Based on an official decision to prevent something called the 'Third Intifada'! Woe, people! How strange is your situation!

Al-Asli noted that not a single rally in commemoration of the Nakba was held in Jerusalem, and he ended bitterly:

> Have I not told you that the situation of the Palestinian people is going downhill in all respects, and the only thing that interests most people is their salary, and nothing else matters! Have I not told you that the nation's condition is bewildering and perplexing? And for anyone who wishes to contemplate this, all that remains is to wonder about the situation that has befallen the nation that was once called 'The Nation of Giants' ("*Sha'b al-Jabrin*")."[18]

Another writer, the poet Tawfik Amarna, wrote a poem denouncing the reconciliation agreement between Fatah and Hamas, known as the "Mutual Consent." Amarna argued that the "Mutual Consent" method implemented by the Palestinians in their dialogue with the Jews had become a ridiculous course of action, and the Palestinians repeated the same mistakes in the reconciliation between Fatah and Hamas, thereby mocking the people. He ended by writing, "And if one side imposes a veto, the other folds without a thought to its own interests, the homeland, or [public] sensitivities."[19] Following Israel's temporary freeze on transferring tax revenues to the PA in response to the unity agreement with Hamas, journalist Khalil al-Asli published a column titled "I don't want a state — I want a salary." He related the story of an employee in the education sector who entered the teachers' room after having gone to the bank and discovered that her salary hadn't been transferred to her account by the PA. She said, "Give me my salary, I don't want a state!" The woman added,

> What should I do? I have a lot of obligations that are much more important than any talk about Jerusalem and the homeland. Our heads ache from talking about these slogans, which some people used to get rich while the rest of the nation goes hungry!

According to al-Asli, that is the situation of civil servants, while all the while the government blames the delay on Israel's failure to transfer tax revenues.[20] According to the Palestinian News Network (PNN), a local correspondent in Nablus stated that new slogans and jokes on this issue were making the rounds in text messages and social media, convenient vehicles of expression for citizens who feared expressing an explicit political opinion [in public].[21] PNN also reported that a well-known newspaper vendor in the center of Nablus, commenting on the delay in salary payments, proclaimed sarcastically that "The people want to bring back the split" [between Fatah and Hamas]. Another young man added the following line to his wedding invitation: "We apologize for the nature of the event due to the delay in salary payments."

Alongside this pessimistic outlook were expressions of optimism, viewing the "Palestinian Spring" as an integral part of the popular uprisings in the Arab world. Journalist Hani al-Masri wrote that while March 15, 2011, a day of demonstrations and other activities across the West Bank and Gaza in support of national reconciliation, was not a turning point, it was a promising start. In his opinion, such popular activities would soon become a steady and irrepressible stream of action.[22]

The writer and deputy minister of public relations, Dr. Mutawakel Taha, published an article, "Tsunami on the Border," arguing that "just as the masses had succeeded in shaking the thrones of kings, so too are they capable of uprooting the barbed wire fences separating Palestine from the rest of the Arab World." He added:

> These masses are capable of sowing confusion among the security forces who have prevented them and continue to prevent them from getting to the border...it is possible that the initial attempts to move en masse to the border will become great national events, comparable to the Nakba or Naksa...but the miracle of Tahrir Square and the millions of demonstrators created a new energy similar to the strength of a Tsunami, the energy of millions of demonstrators before the barbed wire fences will make the disconnected island of occupation [Israel] ripe for defeat, and in this situation the state's feeble military organization, comprised of and developed on the totem of nuclear terror, will not help it because its hands will be tied and it will be helpless against the raging tide of flesh, and as it breeds the spilling of blood, it will not be able to stem the tide of the flood...everything that has happened on the border is but a preliminary exercise for those enormous forces that will appear soon...who come to restore the lost paradise, Palestine, and the steps of its masses come to shake the whole world...what characterized the "Revolutionary Spring" was the great exodus from the darkness of political parties, and the forces and ideas of mummies, to the dawn, with its own tools and improvisations — these tools and improvisations are only able to be used and understood by the generation of this period — a younger generation.[23]

Similarly, Dr. Mamduh al-'Aker, head of the Palestinian Independent Commission for Human Rights (ICHR), pointed to a new spirit among the Palestinian people, one that demands a revival of the Palestinian cause and a return to the place where it belongs — as the struggle of a national liberation movement. In his opinion, the PLO should be reestablished as the leadership of the Palestinian people, with new leaders, and the role of the PA should be modified to retain the powers of a large township. Al-'Aker declared that he felt the "winds of change" blowing, indicated by demonstrations in villages, and in the activities of non-governmental BDS (boycott, divestment, and sanctions) organizations that campaign for boycotts, such as the boycott of products from Jewish [West Bank] settlements, the imposition of cultural and other sanctions against Israel, and prevention of investments in Israel.[24]

In an article, "At last, breaking the barrier of fear,"[25] the Palestinian Jerusalemite author, Liana Bader, asked: "Is it possible for us to dream of a Palestinian Spring? ... Can we hopefully learn and know that there is a new world around us that is moving forward, and that it will leave us behind if we do not courageously leap forward on our way?" Bader finds the first signs of a "Palestinian Spring" in a connection she makes between the spring of women's freedom and the spring of young people's freedom. She referred to the brutal murder of a young Palestinian woman named "Aya," from the village of Tzorif, which was believed to be an "honor killing." Bader pointed out that the murder garnered widespread attention in the mainstream Palestinian discourse. It was evident among the residents of Tzorif, who publicly came out against the murderers and expressed solidarity with the family of the young murdered woman, and in the reaction of the president, who signed a presidential decree removing all lenience against crimes of this nature. "This is a Spring against fear, silence, and collaboration of the strong against the weak," Bader wrote.

The "Second Spring," noted Bader, "was the spring that occurred on the 1948 *Nakba* border, when groups of young people crossed the border with Palestine, and one of them even succeeded in reaching the city of Jaffa, and was pleased to visit despite being arrested by the Israeli army." "Migrating birds," Bader wrote, "know the way [to Jaffa] without guidance, and this young man has proven that we know how to get to Jaffa." "No one expects that everything will come true at once, but this is springtime," Bader continued. "What matters is the barrier of fear has been broken." Bader concluded by observing:

> There is also the freedom of the Arab Spring where young people redeem their country in more bloodshed in the street than has been spilled in all the Arab-Israeli wars. Two fronts have emerged: the front of oppressors of domestic enemies, and the enemy army front that prepares for racial cleansing and extermination.

## Summary and Assessment

Three years have elapsed since the outbreak of the popular protests against the regimes of the Arab world, yet no "Palestinian Spring" has occurred, despite a situation that appeared to satisfy the conditions for a popular uprising: declining PLO legitimacy as the exclusive representative of the Palestinian people, the enduring diplomatic stagnation and Occupation, economic distress and growing unemployment, governmental corruption and human rights violations, and a leadership that seems to have reached the end of its road. As in other Arab societies, there is a big gap between Palestinians' expectations from their government and their actual social and economic conditions. Like the long-ruling FLN in Algeria, the National Democratic Party in Egypt and the Ba'th Party in Syria, the Fatah movement has experienced an ideological decline over the years, failing to keep its promises, achieve its national goals or even formulate an agenda that would be relevant to society's fundamental concerns.

During both the first and second intifadas, grassroots demonstrations and protests against the Israeli Occupation heightened Palestinian society's awareness of its own power as an actor, vis-à-vis Israel and the Palestinian leadership as well. In the 2006 elections, Palestinian society marked a dramatic change by voting for Hamas in the PA's legislative elections. Thus, the Palestinians barrier of fear vis-à-vis repressive authoritarian rule (whether Israeli or Palestinian) was breached long before the outbreak of the popular uprisings in the Arab world in late 2010.

Palestinians have gained considerable experience organizing the public from the bottom-up, controlling public spaces, using the media to formulate and express national goals, and managing a national struggle against an occupier. They possess a variety of means of expression, both electronic and print, and the rate of Internet and social media use is high in comparison to neighboring Arab societies.[26] Young people also believe they can influence public life, particularly in the wake of the uprisings across the Arab world, which emphasized the growing power of civil society.[27]

Still, the fact is that the dramatic events in the Arab world have not yet led to a Palestinian uprising. This has been occasionally attributed to the relatively liberal rule of PA President 'Abbas and Prime Minister Fayyad (2007-2013), in contrast to other Arab regimes. Palestinian society in the West Bank did benefit from a degree of freedom of expression and respect for human rights, as well as exposure to satellite television stations, radio stations, private television channels and the rapidly expanding social media networks. Demonstrations and protests were permitted, under certain conditions. Some of the protests focused on the split between the PLO and Hamas, others on the PA's financial crisis (mainly in September 2012). Protests against Israel focused on a variety of immediate issues such as land expropriations, the popular committees' opposition to the separation barrier and campaigns to release Palestinian prisoners from Israeli prisons. These acts of protest did not trigger any violent clashes with the security forces, and no fatalities were recorded. The Palestinian public was evidently hesitant to return to the violence and internal anarchy of the Second Intifada that severely damaged the foundations of society. It was therefore important for the public to maintain stability and calm, despite the continuing diplomatic stalemate with Israel, and despite continued economic and social hardships.

At the same time, a deeper explanation for the lack of a Palestinian uprising in recent years seems to lie in the shrinking social cohesion of Palestinian society, which is related to the declining status of Palestinian national symbols since Oslo. The PLO was assimilated into the Palestinian Authority and largely lost its stature as the sole representative of all segments of the nation. Fatah, the leading force in the Palestinian nationalist movement for more than four decades, became substantially weaker, and declined in popular support. National unity disintegrated and the public seemed resigned to live with two separate governing entities: one in the West Bank, and the other in the Gaza Strip. In addition, the unifying concept of "armed struggle" was officially abandoned in favor of state building.

Confronted with this reality, young Palestinians were left with no definitive collective social or political goal. The public was witness to the PA's continued corrupt administration, including the multiple security arrangements that consumed a significant part of the budget at the expense of education and welfare. All of these issues gnawed at the sense of collective solidarity and ultimately contributed to a retreat from a national collective identity into a family-centered or religious identity.

The general public began to doubt the ability of Fatah or Hamas to liberate the people from the Israeli Occupation or to resolve society's fundamental social and economic problems, yet it also doubted its own ability to change reality through street demonstrations. Young people had much less belief in the efficacy of trying to establish a new political force that would successfully mobilize the public for dramatic change. They developed a more individualist approach to life, and now preferred to devote themselves to their studies, employment, and personal development, rather than to national concerns.

These changes have been fueled by similar processes that have taken place across the Arab world. First, national Palestinian identity did not fully displace older primordial identities. Clan-related factors have remained a dominant feature in Palestinian society. The PLO, when it established the Palestinian Authority, obtained its legitimacy and support mainly from society's traditional structure. As traditional societal groups were integrated into state structures, the state became the means for reinforcing these older, enduring identities. Second, Palestinian society developed no significant liberal-secular stream that could effectively promote the ideas of democracy and popular sovereignty. The PLO, like neighboring autocratic Arab regimes, had oppressed and weakened rival "nationalist" forces that tried to offer an alternative. Like these regimes, it gave a free reign for a time to the Islamists, which were not considered a threat as long as they focused on social welfare issues. These tactics allowed the PLO and other Arab regimes to maintain domestic calm, or at least a semblance of serenity, but in effect they purged political life of all significance. And while the majority of Palestinians are not overly religiously observant, society continues to retain a traditional character, and there appears to be a growing return to religion and conservative conduct, and a rejection of the trappings of a Western lifestyle.

# Notes

1. On the role of Palestinian women in the Intifada, and on the nationalization of Palestinian motherhood, see Mira Tzoreff, "The "female others" — women, gender, and nationalism in Palestinian society in the shadow of the Intifadas," in Ofra Bengio (ed.), *Women in the Middle East — Between Tradition and Change* (Tel Aviv University: Dayan Center Papers, No. 134, 2004), pp. 114–125 [Hebrew].

2. For example, PA spokesperson Adnan Damiri told students at Al-Najah that "security coordination is an interest of the Palestinian people and is designed to facilitate everyday life." WATAN, local Ramallah television channel, February 28, 2011.

3. See statements by Yassir 'Abed Rabbo and 'Azzam al-Ahmad, *Radio Ajyal*, February 12, 2011; statements of Dr. Muhammad Shtayyeh on *Sawt Filastin*, February 13, 2011, http://www.palvoice.com/index.php?id=29012.

4. Statements of Nabil Sha'at on Sawt Filastin, February 13, 2011, http://www.palvoice.com/index.php?id=29015.

5. *ASharq al-Awsat*, March 6, 2011.

6. Elections were ultimately not held due to the fact that reconciliation efforts were unsuccessful.

7. *Al-Hayat Al-Jadida*, March 16, 2011; www.palestine-info.info, March 15, 2011.

8. See for example op-eds by journalists Baker Abu Baker, Akram Muslim and Salah al-Wadi'a in *Al-Hayat Al-Jadida*, February 16, 2011; *Al-Ayyam*, February 20, 2011; *Ma'an*, February 17, 2011.

9. Prime Minister Fayyad initiated a direct discourse with the public on Facebook and responded to questions he received from the public using short films. He also delivered a weekly speech on *Sawt Filastin* radio and other local stations.

10. "Appropriate goals" is a type of Facebook campaign that calls for the return of Palestinian refugees. See The *Middle East Media Research Institute* (MEMRI), March 8, 2011, http://www.memri.org.il/cgiwebaxy/sal/sal.pl?lang=he&ID=107345_memri&act=show2&dbid=articles&dataid=2714.

11. See Palestinian Center for Policy and Survey Research, directed by Dr. Khalil Shikaki, Ramallah, September 2013, http://www.pcpsr.org/.

12. See Bernard Sabilla, "The Influence of the Family on the Political Participation of Youth," in Rafi Netz (ed.), *The Palestinian Family* (Tel Aviv University, Tami Steinmetz Center for Peace Research, 2005), pp. 74–91 [Hebrew].

13. Statements of youngsters on the program *"Shu Birasak?"* ("What's on your mind?"), *Radio Raya*, March 17, 2011.

14. For example, during Israel's "Operation Cast Lead" (December 27, 2008 — January 17, 2009), young people in the West Bank did not demonstrate against Israel or demonstrate in solidarity with the residents of the Gaza Strip.

15. For example, a continued campaign to boycott mobile telephone companies in view of the high cost of services they charged, and repeated attempts to organize protest demonstrations against government actions such as raising the VAT rate.

16. The official name of the movement is the "Movement of Rebellion against Wrongdoing in Gaza" *(Harakat Tamarrud 'Ala 'Al-Zulm fi Gaza)*. These activists began their campaign against the Hamas on July 1, 2013, one day after the *Tamarrud* movement's massive demonstration in Egypt (June 30, 2013) that led to the toppling of the government by a military *coup d'état*. The movement is supported by elements from Fatah and the PA.

17. A survey by the AWARD institute, which was conducted in July 2013, of a population of young adults, indicated, that since early 2012, there was a significant increase in the willingness of young adults in Gaza (between the ages of 18 and 30) to participate in demonstration against the government. In January 2012, 29% of this group was willing to participate, compared to 42% in July 2013.

18. Khalil al-Asli, "Using rocks, soccer, and debka" *(bial-hajar, wal-kura wal-debka)*, *PNN*, May 16, 2011.

19. Tawfik Amarna, "Mutual Consent" *("Tawafuk")*, *Al-Hayat Al-Jadida*, June 15, 2011.

20. Khalil al-Asli, "We don't want a state, we want a salary" *(lanurid watan… nurid rateb)*, *PNN*, May 8, 2011.

21. "The people want a return to a split? Late salary payments lead to puns and jokes" *(al-sha'b yurid i'adat al-inqisam)*, *PNN*, May 11, 2011.

22. Hani al-Masri, "Elections at Bir Zeit and popular action" *(intikhabat Bir Zeit wal-hirak al-sha'bi)*, *PNN*, April 6, 2011.

23. Mutawakel Taha, "Tsunami on the Border" *(Tsunami 'ala al-huddud)*, *PNN*, 13 June 2011.

24. See interview with Dr. Mamduh al-'Aker: *Haaretz*, February 3, 2001, and *PNN*, March 13, 2011.

25. Liana Bader, *Al-Ayyam*, May 19, 2011, http://www.al-ayyam.com/article.aspx?did=166266&date=5/19/2011.

26. Rafi Netz (ed.), *Palestinian Media* (Tel Aviv University, Tami Steinmetz Center for Peace Research, 2003).

27. See a poll conducted by the AWRAD Institute, under the supervision of Dr. Nader Said-Foqahaa, in July 2013, of 1,200 young people (18–30) in the West Bank and Gaza: http://www.miftah.org/Doc/Polls/AWRADPoll120813.pdf.

# PART VI
## Turkey and Iran

# Gezi Park: From "Father State" to Custodianship

## Hay Eytan Cohen Yanarocak

*"O you who have believed, obey Allah and obey the Messenger and those in authority among you."*

*Nisa Surah — Verse 59*

The police brutality in the Summer of 2013 against environmental activists who wanted to protect Istanbul's Gezi Park ("Park of Excursion") from demolition, in order to convert a former Ottoman artillery battalion fort into a shopping center, triggered one of the most important episodes of political dissent in modern Turkish history.

Unlike previous political demonstrations against government policies, the Gezi Park confrontations brought about an unusual alliance: Green movements; communists; socialists; nationalists; Kemalists; Kurdish and women's rights activists; workers' unions; anti-capitalist Muslims; and "Istanbul United," the alliance of fans of rival leading Istanbul soccer clubs (Fenerbahçe, Galatasaray, and Beşiktaş).

Many commentators across the globe argued that the protests constituted the initial steps of a Turkish version of the "Arab Spring" protests that swept across the region in the last three years. In light of the AKP's[1] democratic election and referendum victories, such an analogy is problematic. Unlike the pre-Arab spring dictatorships that were swept up in the tumult, Turkey had a competitive democratic electoral system. The AKP of Erdoğan achieved decisive victories in 2002 with 34.28 percent of the total vote, in 2007 with 46.4 percent, and finally in 2011 with 49.9 percent. As a result, the AKP and Erdoğan enjoy a certain amount of legitimacy that the deposed Arab dictators, for the most part, did not possess.

Erdoğan also rejected the claim that the Gezi riots triggered a "Turkish Spring." Immediately after founding the AKP in 2001, Erdoğan himself referred to his party's emergence as "the fall of the leading oligarchy."[2] In retrospect, Erdoğan interprets his party's establishment as a "Turkish Spring" in response to the secular elite and the TSK's[3] previous domination of the political and social order.[4]

Although demonstrators' attempts to topple Erdoğan and his government failed and left his, and his party's legitimacy intact, the Gezi Park protests nonetheless caused a political earthquake that shook the foundations of the Turkish authoritarian state tradition, which can be traced from Ottoman times.

According to Selçuk Akşin Somel, the first Ottoman history textbook of Ahmet Vefik Paşa's *Fezleke-i Tarihi Osmani*[5] (1869), published under the reign of Sultan Abdülaziz (1861-1876),[6] was designed in a state-centered authoritarian environment. Similarly, Avner Wishnitzer has indicated the same conditions existed for Ottoman textbooks published under Abdülhamit II (1876-1909) and the Committee of Union and Progress (CUP; 1909-1918).[7]

Turkish historian İsmail Kaplan argues that, similar to the Ottoman period, modern Turkey's education system is traditionally designed to create an obedient citizen from birth until death. Kaplan sees the trinity of *holy-state, holy-nation*, and *holy-head of the state* as the most important tool to create the obedient citizen.[8] "The Religion Knowledge" textbook written by Ethem Ruhi Fığlalı supports Kaplan's claim. Fığlalı's textbook devoted a subsection to the need to obey state leaders, justified by the Holy Quran's "Nisa Surah," verse 59.[9]

The patriarchal and paternal tradition of state authoritarianism can also be seen in the Turkish language and social structure. Turks attributed gendered definitions to the most important conceptions of nationalism, naming their homeland "motherland" (Anavatan) while the geographic name "Anatolia" was Turkified to "Anadolu," meaning "mother-filled" or "filled with mothers."[10] Contrary to the land, the state that must protect the motherland from extra-territorial "rape", required a masculine character and was therefore named "father" or the "Father State" *(devlet baba)*.

The "Father State" concept is known to all Turks and to those who experienced Ottoman rule throughout the Empire. This idea, therefore, is not an invention of Mustafa Kemal Atatürk, the founder of modern Turkey.[11] Ottoman sultans enjoyed absolute power due to the absence of an hereditary aristocracy, self-governing cities, a strong merchant class and artisan guilds. There was an absolute obedience to state authority. Moreover, the sultans' task of protecting his subjects' welfare and meting out justice reflected the paternal identity of the Ottoman state tradition.[12]

The Kemalist revolution that emerged as the founding ideology of the 1920 revolution, which, via its radical reforms, established the secular nation-state, also inherited the Ottoman tradition of the "Father State". The most prominent example can be found in the surname of the founder of modern Turkey: Mustafa Kemal *Atatürk*. Prior to 1934, the Turks did not use surnames; instead, they used their fathers' names or different secondary names. As a result, the Turkish parliament adopted the Surname Law of 1934, making usage of surnames compulsory for all Turkish citizens.[13] Moreover, the TBMM[14] enacted a special law granting Mustafa Kemal alone the surname Atatürk, "father of Turks," which could not be used by other citizens. Hence, many Turks still refer to Atatürk as "Ata," literally "father."[15]

In the post-Atatürk period, despite occasionally forming coalition governments, Turks tend to unite under one strong charismatic leader, or "father," such as İsmet İnönü, Adnan Menderes, Süleyman Demirel, Turgut Özal, and Recep Tayyip Erdoğan. The election system enshrined in the 1982 constitution also encouraged and reflected this tendency. Despite claiming "the stability of the government" and "justice in the representation" as the *sine qua non* values, with the former requiring the highest threshold in the world for political parties' election to parliament — 10 percent — the Turkish electoral system openly ignores the "justice in representation" principle. Therefore, the current election system paves the way for a hegemonic governing party system, while small parties and interest group politics are constantly threatened with extinction.[16]

Certainly, the general elections of 2002, 2007, and 2011 were conspicuous examples of power concentrated in the hands of one leader, Erdoğan. Following his victories during his second term in 2010, Erdoğan, called by his comrades the "reis," or "chief,"[17] began to eliminate the country's system of checks and balances, namely the TSK and the judiciary.

On September 12, 2010, the 30th anniversary of the 1980 military coup, Erdoğan overcame the checks and balances obstacle provided by the judiciary via a referendum package that paved the way for a constitutional amendment designed to weaken the judicial system in favor of executive powers.[18] Another crucial milestone in his accumulation of power was the resignation of former Chief of Staff General Işık Koşaner in 2011, in protest against the arrest of senior TSK officials.[19] General Koşaner's resignation opened the way for Gendarmerie Forces' General Necdet Özel to become chief of staff. This nomination changed the TSK custom wherein only the ground forces' commanding general could be nominated as chief of staff. Aware of this custom, General Özel accepted the TSK's defeat and its removal from the Turkish political arena as a key player. This was evident in the 2011 Supreme Military Council's seating arrangements. Prior to Özel's nomination, the chief of staff and the prime minister had presided over the council together from the head of the table. However, from 2011 on, Erdoğan has been the only one who sits at the head of the table presiding over the council.[20] The elimination of the two most important checks and balances on the executive — the TSK and the judiciary — led to Erdoğan's increasing authoritarianism, or the "Putinization" of Turkey.

As a direct consequence of his high concentration of power, Erdoğan was increasingly seen as the ultimate leader by his fellow AKP members. Some AKP members even took this to a more radical dimension. AKP Bursa Member of Parliament Hüseyin Şahin stated that "touching…Erdoğan is a way of worshiping by itself." Moreover, the head of the AKP in the city of Aydın İsmail Eser declared Erdoğan a "prophet," for which Erdoğan later berated him, emphasizing that the last prophet was the Prophet Muhammad.[21] Not only members of Parliament and junior party members were enamored with this personality cult. The Minister of European Union Affairs and Chief Negotiator Egemen Bağış declared that the cities Rize (Erdoğan's parents' hometown), Siirt (where Erdoğan began his political career), and Istanbul (Erdoğan's birthplace) are sacred since they contributed to the birth of "the most important leader of the entire Turkish history," hinting that Erdoğan is a greater leader than Atatürk.[22]

Senior Turkish columnists also alluded to Erdoğan's competition with Atatürk's legacy. Tülin Daloğlu of *Al-Monitor* argued that Erdoğan was attempting to overcome Atatürk's legacy, first, by being the first elected president after three consecutive premierships and, second, by being the ultimate peacemaker with the PKK[23] and the Kurds in Turkey.[24]

Unquestionably, consecutive election victories, his fellow party members' attitudes, and traditional obedience to the leader concept have encouraged Erdoğan to become increasingly authoritarian., Some have even labeled him the "Tek-Adam" monarch, a "despot," or literally, the "sole-man."[25]

With the repeated defeat of his opponents in the elections, and through referendums and reforms, Erdoğan has begun to act as the lone social engineer of the Turkish Republic. While explaining his grandiose ambitions for the Republic's 100th anniversary in 2023, he appeared to be single-handedly designing Turkey's foreign and domestic policies, including family structure, abortion, caesarean births, alcohol and cigarette consumption, education, health, and art.

The most striking accusations against Erdoğan came after the demolition of the "Humanity Monument" that symbolized Turkish-Armenian friendship in the border city of Kars. Erdoğan, who visited Kars in January 2011, termed the statue "ucube" ("monstrous") and asked for it to be demolished. After six months, the statue was destroyed by officials with cries of "Allahu Akbar" (God is the greatest).[26] A similar demolition decision was made by the Turkish court for the Onaltıdokuz Towers in Istanbul, since the towers obstructed the view of Istanbul's mosque silhouette, according to Erdoğan.[27]

Turkish popular culture was also among the targets of Erdoğan's criticism. The TV series, "The Magnificent Century" (*Muhteşem Yüzyıl*), which depicts the days of Suleiman the Magnificent, was repeatedly denounced by Erdoğan due to the program's open décolleté clothes and intimate *Harem* (women's chambers) scenes that he claimed were anachronistic and unrepresentative of the Turks' Ottoman ancestors *(ecdad)*.[28]

Erdoğan's ambitions to engineer Turkish social life were not limited to monuments and television series, but also permeated into family life. For example, he asked Turkish women to give birth to at least three babies. Moreover, he called for restrictions on abortions and sought to make it more difficult for women to have cesarean sections, on the grounds that the procedure impedes a woman's ability to give birth to more than two children.[29] Many argue that Erdoğan's "at least three babies" policy is designed to balance the high Kurdish birth rates.[30]

The penetration of Erdoğan's social policies into secular Turkish life was further exacerbated by the alcohol regulations recently approved by parliament and ratified by President Abdullah Gül. The regulations ban the sale of alcoholic beverages after 10:00 p.m. and put in place many other restrictions on beverage companies and their consumers.[31] In an interview with Habertürk's Fatih Altaylı, Erdoğan called regular wine drinkers "alcoholics."[32] Moreover, he accused those protesting the new alcohol regulations of being followers of the "two heavy drinkers," in reference to Mustafa Kemal Atatürk and his comrade Ismet Inönü, the first and second presidents of Turkey, respectively. Despite the public outcry, Erdoğan has not admitted that he was referring to Atatürk and Inönü.[33]

At the same time, Erdoğan has also begun to uproot very prominent symbols and pillars of Kemalist Turkey by enacting regulations that restrict celebrating Atatürk Remembrance Youth and Sports Holiday in stadiums[34] and prohibiting celebrations of the most important secular holiday, Republic Day, in the former Turkish Parliament plaza. The measure resulted in clashes between secular Turks and police forces in Ankara on Republic Day, October 29, 2012.[35]

In some segments of Turkish society, the public disapproval of Erdoğan grew with his promotion of the third bridge project over the Bosphorus. After the construction of the first and second bridges (1973 and 1988), Turkish environmentalists concluded that the accompanying highways led to urban sprawl, and therefore organized protests against the construction of a third bridge. Another element arousing public anger was the Neo-Ottoman dimension of this bridge. Erdoğan named the bridge, which is currently under construction, after Yavuz Sultan Selim (Selim I), the first Ottoman caliph. To the minority community of Turkish Alevis, Yavuz Sultan Selim is known as the butcher of 40,000 Alevis.[36] Indeed, this insensitivity to a minority for the sake of glorifying the Ottoman past has been an outrage to the Alevis of Turkey.[37] Moreover, Turkish Transportation Minister Binali Yıldırım's statements referring to the "Alevi Massacre as a legend" in July 2013 further angered the Alevis and deepened the rift between them and the AKP.[38]

As a result of Erdoğan's far-reaching changes, the "Tek-Adam" accusations reached their peak during the Gezi Park protests. Erdoğan's dismissal of the protestors, declaring that "no matter what you do, we have made a decision and we will implement it," further escalated the situation.[39] According to a survey conducted by Istanbul Bilgi University, 92.4 percent of respondents specified that they took part in Gezi Park protests due to Erdoğan's authoritarian attitude.[40] Despite the public outcry, Erdoğan refuted the accusations, stating he was a servant of the people, and not their master.[41] Instead of compromising with the demonstrators, Erdoğan chose to marginalize them by calling them *Çapulcu*, or "Looters," which was later taken as a compliment by the protestors. Soon the term was Anglicized into "Chapullers" and began to attract more international attention.

Despite the high volume of international media coverage of the Gezi events, the Turkish media's self-censorship aroused skepticism about the resilience of Turkish democracy and strengthened accusations of authoritarianism against the Erdoğan administration. The Turkish media's self-censorship reached an absurd level when, at the critical early moments of the protests, CNN Türk broadcast a documentary film about penguins. The decision to broadcast this documentary came to symbolize the Turkish media's self-censorship. Following vociferous protests, however, these channels began to broadcast the unfolding events.

Yet it is important to bear in mind that the AKP-opposition Doğan Media Group was punished by an unprecedented $2.5 billion tax audit in 2009, and the main news channels — CNN Türk of Doğan, NTV of Şahenk, and Habertürk of Ciner Group — ignored or downplayed the street protests to avoid provoking the government, fearing that the owners' business interests would be targeted for retaliation by the government or pro-government groups. The aftermath of the Gezi protests justified their fears. On July 24, 2013, the Turkish police raided Koç Group's nine provincial offices, after the Koç Group had opened the gates of Divan Hotel to protect the demonstrators from the police's tear gas during the protests. Many Turkish columnists call this act a government "witch hunt."[42]

It is also vital to note that not only rich corporate executives but also journalists were targeted in the "witch hunt." According to the Press Institute Association, dozens of journalists were fired from their jobs, intimidated, wounded, and even detained. Moreover, the Union of Turkish Journalists reported that during the Gezi protests, 36 journalists resigned, 20 were fired, and 14 were sent on compulsory leave.[43] According to the opposition CHP,[44] Turkey is "the biggest journalist prison" in the world. The CHP's "imprisoned journalists report" indicates that there are 64 journalists who are currently imprisoned while 123 more journalists are on trial without being jailed.[45]

As a direct result of the censorship and the intense pressure on the media, the demonstrators turned to social media. With the assistance of Twitter and Facebook, people could circumvent the state's control over information flow. Turkey is eighth in the world in Twitter usage,[46] and Turkish Facebook[47] use is first among the European states. These high numbers manifested themselves in the Gezi Park protests. Due in part to smartphones and Twitter, the protests quickly spread across Turkey.

Kadri Gürsel of *Al-Monitor* argues that this smartphone-based internet and social-media-driven public consciousness, against the background of the Gezi Park protests, has led to the "Newest Turkey." By using this term, Gürsel differentiated the post-Gezi period from the "New Turkey" period of the AKP. During its election campaigns, the AKP always distinguished itself from Kemalist "Old Turkey" and identified itself with the concept of "New Turkey." Gürsel took this term one step further.

Hence, it is not surprising that Erdoğan labeled Twitter and other social networks a "menace" to all societies in general and to Turkish society in particular. Ironically, and notwithstanding such criticism, Erdoğan himself has almost three million followers on Twitter. In fact, Erdoğan and his supporters have formed their own Facebook and Twitter accounts and have been confronting the protesters in the virtual arena. By creating new hashtags with creative names, parties on both sides of the debate have attempted to expand or to halt the ongoing demonstrations. Turkish police have acknowledged the importance of social networks and launched an operation against those who tweeted information in support of the riots. Many demonstrators were taken into custody.[48]

Due to the Gezi Park protests, Erdoğan's authority and his stance towards the demonstrators was questioned by some AKP party members, such as İdris Bal and Ertuğrul Günay. Bal's critical report on the AKP's attitude regarding Gezi Park indicated his unwillingness to further subordinate himself to an authoritarian party handed by a charismatic leader. Furthermore, in his report, Bal indicates that the AKP regarded the Gezi protests as an attempt to pave the way for a new *coup d'état*.[49] Like Bal, Günay claimed that Erdoğan's closest comrades misinformed and misled him during the crisis.[50]

Erdoğan's non-compromising policies were also indirectly criticized by his fellow party officials. President Gül's statement that "the ballot box is not everything,"[51] Deputy Prime Minister Arınç's apology to environmentalists, Education Minister Avcı's "we unified the opposition against us" statement,[53] and EU Affairs Minister Egemen Bağış's linkage of the free Turkish civil society concept to the Gezi riots marked a blatant contradiction of Erdoğan's harsh statements.[54] While Günay and Bal's statements were taken as an act of opposition against Erdoğan, the statements of Gül, Arınç, Avcı, and Bağış were acknowledged as pro-Erdoğan and were perceived as intended to defuse the tension of the riots. In reality, both types of statements constituted resistance to Erdoğan's absolute authority.

In their book *Gezi Direnişi* ("Gezi Resistance"), Emre Kongar and Aykut Küçükkaya designated the most important effect of the riots as the collapse of the "walls" of the "Horror Empire" that were created by the state authoritarianism and its biased post-2010 constitutional referendum judicial mechanism.[55] Actually, as far as the authoritarian Turkish "Father State" is concerned, the "horror of empire" did not belong to a certain class of society. Throughout modern Turkish history, the dominant forces, whether representing the "Old Turkey" or the "New Turkey," always tended to use the "Father State" concept for their own benefit. However, globalization, the free flow of information, social media, a multilingual pluralist and well-educated society, and the realization of the Turkish Constitution's Article 34 enablisng the organization of non-violent demonstrations shook the traditional authoritarian Turkish statehood model. The Gezi Park protests undermined the holy trinity of state, nation, and the head of state. Due to social media, individualism began to constitute a threat to the holy state that to some extent existed at the individual's expense. The unity between the supporters of the Atatürk-postered Kemalists and the Kurdish supporters holding posters of PKK founder Abdullah Öcalan during the Gezi Park protests indicates the erosion of the classical holy nation definition of the trinity. What is more, the Gezi protests regarded the head of the state, Erdoğan, as the least respected part of this trinity, so one might say that this trinity has been bankrupted.

In conclusion, the Gezi protests put an end to the indisputable holiness of the patriarchal and paternal Turkish "Father State". Instead, Turkish society has begun to see the state as a custodianship or a mechanism that should serve the common interests of its citizens. Hence, the citizen's perception of the state has posed an alternative to the traditional state-oriented "Father State" authoritarianism. Only time will tell which course Turkey is embarking on.

# Notes

1.  AKP: Adalet ve Kalkınma Partisi ("Justice and Development Party").
2.  Hüseyin Besli and Ömer Özbay, *R.Tayyip Erdoğan bir liderin doğuşu* (R. Tayyip Erdoğan a birth of a leader) (Istanbul: Meydan, 2010), p. 285.
3.  TSK: Türk Silahlı Kuvvetleri ("Turkish military").
4.  "Başbakan Erdoğan: Türkiye'nin Baharı biziz," (PM Erdoğan: We are Turkey's Spring), *Euronews*, June 16, 2013, http://tr.euronews.com/2013/06/16/basbakan-erdogan-turkiye-nin-bahari-biziz/.

5. "Summary of Ottoman History".

6. Selçuk Akşin Somel, *The Modernization of public education in the Ottoman Empire 1839–1908* (Leiden: Koninklijke, 2001), pp. 194–195.

7. Avner Wishnitzer, "Teaching Time: Schools, Schedules and the Ottoman Pursuit of Progress," *New Perspectives on Turkey*, No. 43, 2010, pp. 5–32.

8. İsmail Kaplan, *Türkiye'de Milli Eğitim İdeolojisi* (National Education Ideology in Turkey) (İstanbul: İletişim, 2011), p. 392.

9. Ethem Ruhi Fığlalı, *Din Kültürü ve Ahlak Bilgisi 8* (Religion Culture and Morality Knowledge 8) (Istanbul: Milli Eğitim Basımevi, 2000), pp. 50–51.

10. Carol Delaney, "Father State, Motherland and the Birth of Modern Turkey," in Sylvia Yanagisako and Carol Delaney (eds.), *Naturalizing Power* (New York, Routledge, 1995), p. 187.

11. *Ibid.*, p. 179.

12. Ergun Özbudun, "State Elites and Democratic Culture in Turkey," in Ali Çarkoğlu and William Hale (eds.), *The Politics of Modern Turkey* (Oxon: Routledge, 2008) vol. 1, pp. 296–297.

13. Temuçin Faik Ertan et al. (eds.), *Başlangıcından Günümüze Türkiye Cumhuriyeti Tarihi* (Ankara: Siyasal Kitabevi, 2011), p. 214.

14. TBMM: Türkiye Büyük Millet Meclisi ("Turkish Grand National Assembly").

15. Delaney, p. 187.

16. Bülent Tanör and Necmi Yüzbaşoğlu, *1982 Anayasasına göre Türk Anayasa Hukuku* (Turkish Constitutional Law according to 1982 Constitution) (Istanbul, Beta, 2004), pp. 204–213.

17. Hüseyin Besli and Ömer Özbay, *R.Tayyip Erdoğan Bir Liderin Doğuşu* (R. Tayyip Erdoğan A Birth of a Leader, (Istanbul: Meydan, 2010), p. 10.

18. Leyla Köksal Tarhan et al. *Referandumdan sonra HSYK* (HSYK after the referendum) (Istanbul: Tesev, 2012), p. 14, http://www.tesev.org.tr/Upload/Publication/dc5126d0-8dfa-4658-9720-fe03e97e1760/HSYK%20Rapor.pdf.

19. "Orgeneral Işık Koşaner İstifa Etti" (Chief of Staff Işık Koşaner resigned), *Milliyet*, July 29, 2011, http://siyaset.milliyet.com.tr/orgeneral-isik-kosaner-istifa-etti/siyaset/siyasetdetay/29.07.2011/1420393/default.htm.

20. "Artık Ortak Yok," (From now on there is no partner) *Sabah*, August 2, 2011, p. 1.

21. "Başbakana dokunmak bile bence ibadettir" (Touching to PM is a sort of worship), *CNN Türk*, July 21, 2011. [Last accessed: July 28, 2013] http://www.cnnturk.com/2011/turkiye/07/20/basbakana.dokunmak.bile.bence.ibadettir/623516.0/.

22. "Bağış: Rize Siirt ve İstanbul Mübarektir" (Rize Siirt and Istanbul are sacred), *Hürriyet*, February 10, 2013. [Last accessed: July 31, 2013] http://www.hurriyet.com.tr/gundem/22567341.asp.

23. PKK: Partiya Karkeren Kurdistan ("Kurdistan Workers' Party").

24. Tülin Daloğlu, "Turkey's Erdoğan Problem," *Turkey-Pulse*, *Al-Monitor*, July 17, 2013, http://www.al-monitor.com/pulse/originals/2013/07/turkey-erdogan-gul-problem-president.html.

25. Güngör Mengi, Vatan, ""Tek-adam'a" Tepki Birikmiş", June, 2, 2013, http://haber.gazetevatan.com/%93tek-adam%94a-tepki-birikmis /542924/4/yazarlar.

26. "İnsanlık Anıtı artık yok" (Humanity Monument now does not exist), *Milliyet*, June 14, 2011, http://gundem.milliyet.com.tr/-insanlik-aniti-artik-yok/gundem/gundemdetay/14.06.2011/1402439/default.htm.

27. "Siluet Yıkımı" (Silhoutte Demolish), *Radikal*, May 25, 2013, http://www.radikal.com.tr/turkiye/siluet_yikimi-1134867.

28. "Bizim böyle bir ecdadımız yok" (We don't have these kind of ancestors), *Milliyet*, November 26, 2012, http://siyaset.milliyet.com.tr/bizim-boyle-bir-ecdadimiz-yok/siyaset/siyasetdetay/26.11.2012/1632951/default.htm.

29. "Her Kürtaj bir Uludere'dir" (Each abortion is an Uludere), *Radikal*, May 27, 2012, http://www.radikal.com.tr/turkiye/basbakan_her_kurtaj_bir_uluderedir-1089235.

30. Emre Aköz, "Kürt nüfusu Türk nüfusundan çok daha hızlı artıyor," (Kurdish population growth's rate is higher than the Turkish), *Sabah*, October 22, 2011, http://www.sabah.com.tr/Yazarlar/akoz/2011/10/22/kurt-nufusu-turk-nufusundan-cok-daha-hizli-artiyor.

31. Alkol Düzenlemesi Yasası'na Cumhurbaşkanı Gül'den onay, (President Gül ratified alcohol regulation law), *Sabah*, June 11, 2013, http://www.sabah.com.tr/Gundem/2013/06/11/alkol-duzenlemesi-yasasina-cumhurbaskani-gulden-onay.

32. Teke tek, Inteview Fatih Altaylı–Recep Tayyip Erdoğan–*Habertürk TV*, June 2, 2013, http://tv.haberturk.com/programlar/video/teke-tek-recep-tayyip-erdogan-2-haziran-2013-23/90553.

33. "Başbakan: İki ayyaşın yaptığı muteber de..." (What two heavy drinkers do is acceptable but...), *CNN Türk*, May 28, 2013, http://www.cnnturk.com/2013/turkiye/05/28/basbakan.iki.ayyasin.yaptigi.muteber.de/709778.0/.

34. "19 Mayıs Gölgelendi" (May 19th overshadowed), *Cumhuriyet*, January 12, 2012, http://www.cumhuriyet.com.tr/?hn=307316.

35. "Ulusta ortalık savaş alanına döndü" (Ulus became a warfield), *Hürriyet*, October 29, 2012, http://hurarsiv.hurriyet.com.tr/goster/haber.aspx?id=21802912&tarih=2012-10-29.

36. Cafer Solgun, "40 bin Alevi nasıl öldürüldü," (How forty thousand Alevis were killed), *Taraf*, May 31, 2013, http://www.taraf.com.tr/haber/40-bin-alevi-nasil-olduruldu.htm.

37. "Alevilerden Yavuz Sultan Selim köprüsüne tepki," (Reaction of Alevis to Yavuz Sultan Selim Bridge), *Radikal*, May 30, 2013, http://www.radikal.com.tr/turkiye/alevilerden_yavuz_sultan_selim_koprusune_tepki-1135626.

38. "Alevi katliamı efsane gerçeklikle alakası yok" (Alevi massacre is a myth it has nothing to do with reality), *Habertürk*, July 15, 2013, http://www.haberturk.com/polemik/haber/860478-alevi-katliami-efsane-gerceklikle-alakasi-yok.

39. "Erdoğan Gezi Parkı için son sözünü söyledi" (Erdoğan had his last word on Gezi Park), *Yeni Şafak*, May 29, 2013, http://yenisafak.com.tr/politika-haber/erdogan-gezi-parki-icin-son-sozu-soyledi-29.05.2013-525860.

40. "Gezi Parkı direnişçileriyle yapılan anketten çıkan sonuçlar" (Results of the survey that was conducted among the Gezi Park protestors), *T24*, June 4, 2013, http://t24.com.tr/haber/gezi-parki-direniscileriyle-yapilan-anketten-cikan-ilginc-sonuclar/231335.

41. Semih İdiz, "Erdoğan denies he is a king," *Turkey Pulse*, *al-Monitor*, May 31, 2013, http://www.al-monitor.com/pulse/originals/2013/05/erdogan-authoritarian-turkey-king.html.

42. Kadri Gürsel, "Is audit of Koç Companies Erdoğan's revenge for Gezi Park?" *Turkey Pulse*, *Al-Monitor*, July 29, 2013http://www.al-monitor.com/pulse/contents/articles/opinion/2013/07/koc-audit-raid-turkey-interest-rate-lobby-gezi.html.

43. Kadri Gürsel, "Gezi Cleansing in Turkish Media," *Turkey Pulse*, *Al-Monitor*, July 26, 2013, http://www.al-monitor.com/pulse/originals/2013/07/turkey-journalists-censorship-press-freedom-erdogan.html.

44. CHP: Cumhuriyet Halk Partisi ("Republican People's Party").

45. "Dünyanın en büyük gazeteci cezaevi Türkiye" (Turkey is the largest journalist prison of the world), *Hürriyet*, July 25, 2013, http://www.hurriyet.com.tr/gundem/24355074.asp.

46. "16.6% Turkish Internet Users are on Twitter," *Webrazzi*, May 30, 2011, http://en.webrazzi.com/2011/05/30/turkish-twitter-user/.

47. "Facebook'ta Avrupa lideriyiz" (We are Europe's leader in Facebook), *Sabah*, January 21, 2012, http://www.sabah.com.tr/Teknoloji/Haber/2012/01/27/facebookta-avrupa-lideriyiz.

48. Twitter, "baskınlarında gözaltı sayısı 34'e yükseldi" (Number of custodies increased to 34), *Radikal*, June 5, 2013, http://www.radikal.com.tr/turkiye/twitter_baskinlarinda_gozalti_sayisi_34e_yukseldi-1136449.

49. "Gezi'de stratejik hata yapıldı" (A strategic mistake was done in Gezi), *Radikal*, August 12, 2013, http://www.radikal.com.tr/turkiye/gezide_stratejik_hata_yapildi-1145699.

50. "Günay: Başbakan yanlış bilgilendiriliyor" (Günay: PM is misinformed), *Haber7*, June 8, 2013, http://www.haber7.com/partiler/haber/1036312-gunay-basbakan-yanlis-bilgilendiriliyor.

51. "Gül'den Gezi Parkı açıklaması: Demokrasi sadece seçim değildir mesaj alınmıştır," (Gezi Park statement from Gül: Democracy is not only the ballot box, we got the message), *Akşam*, June 3, 2013, http://www.aksam.com.tr/siyaset/cumhurbaskani-gul-demokrasi-sadece-secim-degildir-mesaj-alinmistir/haber-212133.

52. "Bülent Arınç ilk gün için özür diledi" (Bülent Arınç apologized for the first day), *Hürriyet*, June 4, 2013, http://www.hurriyet.com.tr/gundem/23431837.asp.

53. "Muhalefetin yapamadığını 5 günde başardık" (In 5 days we succeded what the opposition failed to do), *İHA*, June 3, 2013, http://www.iha.com.tr/gundem/muhalefetin-yapamadigini-5-gunde-basardik/279340.

54. Egemen Bağış, "Turkey's Democratic Path," *New York Times*, July 29, 2013, http://www.nytimes.com/2013/07/30/opinion/global/turkeys-democratic-path.html?_r=0.

55. Emre Kongar and Aykut Küçükkaya, *Gezi Direnişi* (Gezi Resistance) (Istanbul: Cumhuriyet Kitapları, 2013), pp. 67–68.

# Turkey, Its Kurds, and the Gezi Park Protests

## Duygu Atlas

Turkey's Gezi Park protests, a series of historic mass anti-government demonstrations in Summer 2013 the likes of which Turkey had not experienced in decades, were highly relevant to Turkey's ongoing "Kurdish question." The degree of Kurdish participation in the protests and their overall reaction to them have been the subject of much speculation. The calm which prevailed in the formerly conflict-ridden areas of eastern and southeastern Turkey contrasted sharply with the unrest in Istanbul and other large cities in Turkey's west. Hence, the question posed repeatedly by analysts and activists alike was "Where are the Kurds?" After all, this unprecedented anti-government outburst came amidst a recently reinvigorated peace process between the Turkish state and the Kurds. The Kurdish political movement, the vanguard of the struggle for genuine democracy in Turkey for decades, found itself in a dilemma, between a natural impulse to participate in a democratic movement with which it shared common denominators, and the desire to ensure the completion of a fragile peace process that had made unprecedented progress.

The Kurds' position in the Gezi Park protests, therefore, cannot be analyzed outside the specific context of the democratic opening initiative *(demokratik açılım)*, which the Justice and Development Party *(Adalet ve Kalkınma Partisi,* AKP) government launched in 2009. The democratic opening initiative, which introduced limited improvements in Kurdish civil rights, most notably in the use of the Kurdish language, heralded the beginning of genuine efforts to solve Turkey's decades-old Kurdish problem. This process had reached a crucial juncture at the time of the Gezi Park protests, as the withdrawal of the Kurdistan Workers' Party *(Partiya Karkerên Kurdistan,* PKK)'s armed units from Turkish soil was under way, and expectations were running high that the Turkish government's new democratic package would guarantee more democratic rights for them.

# A Novel Approach to the Kurdish Question: The AKP and the Democratic Opening Initiative

Turkey's Kurdish question has embroiled the country in a state of conflict for almost thirty years. The traditional argument advanced by the Turkish authorities, that citizens of Kurdish origin enjoy rights equal to their ethnic Turkish counterparts and that the issue was solely a matter of defeating terrorism, trumped any attempt to address the core issues at stake. The underlying reasons for the conflict, namely the injustice and inequality stemming from the lack of recognition of Kurdish identity and resulting restriction on Kurds' civil liberties, were glossed over by the dominant security discourse. The Kurdish question was portrayed as an existential threat to the unitary Turkish state, which was built on the principle of an overarching Turkish citizenship melding together the heterogeneous society of its predecessor, the Ottoman Empire. In fact, the Kurdish question, along with the threat of Islamic *irtica* ("reaction"), was perceived as the archenemy of the secular Republic, especially during the 1990s.[1] The army and the Kemalist elite, fearing disruption to the very foundation of the state, used these threats to consolidate their absolute control over politics. This perception, sustained by the military and bureaucratic elites, impeded the implementation of democratic reforms and civil initiatives, a sine qua non for solving the Kurdish question and the consolidation of democracy in Turkey.

Following decades of internecine fighting between the Turkish state and the PKK, which left many tens of thousands dead and hundreds of villages destroyed, the Justice and Development Party's mid-2009 launch of the democratic opening initiative began a new chapter in Turkey's Kurdish saga. The new strategy for solving the issue and ending the violence and terror which had bedeviled the country for decades was the democratization of political life and the adoption of comprehensive policies to address the political, economic, and sociological dimensions of the heretofore intractable problem. This novel governmental approach marked a transformation of Turkey's official stance, from the historical denial of Kurdish existence and assimilation attempts to that of recognition of the Kurdish reality and Turkey's multi-cultural makeup.

Several factors explained this historic shift:
1. The expectations for greater cultural freedom and protection of rights grew among the Kurds in the wake of European Union (EU)-prodded reforms, which had been legislated as part of Turkey's EU accession bid and consequent efforts to meet the Copenhagen Criteria.[2]
2. The restructuring of civil-military relations, epitomized by the "Ergenekon" affair, presented new opportunities to address the

Kurdish question.[3] Beginning in 2008, the controversial "Ergenekon" affair unearthed the ties of the Turkish military and security forces to the "deep state,"[4] which allegedly conspired to overthrow the AKP government by assassinating a ring of minority members and intellectuals in order to destabilize the country. The image of the military was greatly tarnished as a result of these accusations, which ultimately resulted in the conviction and lengthy imprisonment of hundreds of leading military figures, including İlker Başbuğ, former chief of the Turkish armed forces, and retired Brigadier General Veli Küçük. Most importantly, the military's domination of political life, including its traditional blocking of civil initiatives regarding the Kurdish question, was brought to an end. The ruling AKP was thus able to embark on a new initiative to address the matter.

3. The developments in neighboring Iraq added a new sense of urgency to solving the Kurdish question in Turkey. Iraqi Kurds had registered significant political gains, especially following the US invasion of Iraq and ousting of Saddam Hussein in 2003. Not only did the Iraqi Kurds retain their autonomy, but they also garnered substantial political strength. The impact on Turkey's Kurds of the Iraqi Kurds' consolidation of their increasingly independent entity in northern Iraq marked a new chapter in the the historical overlapping between the Kurds of Turkey and Iraq — a worrisome matter for the Turkish government. Ofra Bengio explains the convergence in regional terms:

> From the regional angle, developments in neighboring Iraqi Kurdistan decisively influenced Turkey's Kurds. Actions by Iraqi Kurds, known in the pan-Kurdish discourse as "Southern Kurds," have intersected with those of their brethren in Turkey at a number of important junctures: in the mid-1970s when the PKK's establishment coincided with the war between the Iraqi Kurds and the Ba`th regime; the establishment of PKK headquarters in Iraqi Kurdistan following the Iraqi Army's retreat in 1992; and the 2004 renewal of the Kurdish struggle in Turkey after the entrenchment of the Kurdish entity in Iraq. Additionally, over the years the borders between Turkey and Iraq have blurred, becoming more and more porous and thus facilitating the exchange of ideas and trends between the two Kurdish communities. In general, the weakening of the classic nation-state paradigm and the rise of multiculturalism as a preferred normative value have emboldened the demands for recognition of Kurdish identity and culture in both Iraq and Turkey.[5]

Therefore, the AKP saw in the launch of a Kurdish initiative a preemptive act that would help the government avoid a domino effect spilling over from its southeastern neighbor.

4. It was not only the pro-reform discourse of Erdoğan that drew Kurdish votes to the AKP in the 2007 parliamentary elections, but also Erdoğan's drawing of a parallel line between his experience as a political figure, who had been brought to trial and penalized by the repressive establishment, and that of Kurds suffering from decades of state repression. It was Erdoğan's own struggle as an Islamist politician that enabled him to adopt a softer, more accommodating approach towards the Kurdish problem, based on an understanding and acknowledgment of Kurdish discontent. He pointed to his personal story in a 2005 speech in Diyarbakır, the southeastern city often referred to as the "Kurdish capital":

> During the days of my imprisonment for reciting a poem, I sent out this message to my people; "I am not angry [and] upset with my state. This state, this flag, this homeland belong to all of us. A day will come when these wrongdoings will be corrected." For this reason, it is a dream of mine and my colleagues that everyone will live as first class citizens and our children will look to the future with hope in every place where our flag flies high.[6]

By empathizing with the Kurds and underlining the mutual history of suppression of both Kurds and the Islamists by the secular state, not only did Erdoğan increase his credibility in the eyes of the Kurds but he also demonstrated that his party was the political "address" for solving the Kurdish issue. The Kurds easily identified with Erdoğan's gesture of political solidarity, for his struggle for more religious freedom appeared similar to their struggle for the recognition of their ethnic identity. The Kurds' own religiosity and traditionalism served as additional factors contributing to the government's appeal, resulting in major electoral gains for the AKP in the last three general elections at the expense of Kurdish parties.

The incongruity between the Kurdish demands and what the AKP was willing to provide, however, soon caused the democratic opening initiative to run cold. There were a number of reasons for the negative turn of events.

Firstly, the entrance of 34 PKK militants from the Habur border crossing between Iraq and Turkey on October 22, 2009 in their guerrilla attire, and the jubilant welcome they received from ecstatic Kurdish crowds, signaled the beginning of a downward spiral in the democratic opening process.[7] In the eyes of those who wholeheartedly opposed the initiative from the beginning, this incident reaffirmed their fears that the government was trying to appease the PKK, a dangerous move in their view. Indeed, although the government hoped that the initiative would eventually result in the dissolving of the PKK, it did not take into consideration the force of Kurdish nationalism and how such events would resonate among the Kurdish public. The Habur incident not only exacerbated Turkish nationalist fears but also turned the supporters of the initiative against it by leaving them with a negative impression of the initiative's achievements. The deterioration of relations between the government and the Kurds continued with the closure of the Kurdish Democratic Society Party (*Demokratik Toplum Partisi*, DTP) in December 2009 and the round-up of its representatives in the same month in a crackdown against the Kurdish Communities Union (*Kürdistan Topluluklar Birliği, Koma Civakên Kurdistan*, KCK), the urban wing of the PKK. The DTP's closure, which increased Kurdish suspicion towards the initiative, was preceded by a PKK ambush on December 7, 2009, which killed seven Turkish soldiers in the Reşadiye district of Tokat, a city located in the mid-Black Sea region of Anatolia. Four police officers in the Dörtyol district of the Southeastern city of Hatay were also killed, and the subsequent attack by Turkish nationalists on the local headquarters of the Peace and Democracy Party (*Barış ve Demokrasi Partisi*, BDP) only exacerbated the growing Turkish-Kurdish rift. The government continued its security-oriented policies regarding the Kurdish question, despite the fact that an important threshold had been crossed when tape recordings of the state's 2010 dialogue with the PKK in Oslo, led by the representatives of the Turkish National Intelligence Agency (*Milli Istihbarat Teşkilatı*, MIT), were leaked and did not generate a negative public reaction. It is important to note that holding talks with the PKK's imprisoned leader Abdullah Öcalan had long been considered a political taboo, as the Turkish public regarded him as Public Enemy Number One.

Secondly, the failure of the democratic opening initiative was also partly due to the AKP government's inability to explain its contents to the public. The officials thus failed to calm the wave of anxiety which arose from fears that the opening would ultimately threaten the country's territorial integrity. Therefore, from the very start, the initiative was handicapped by the public's concern for the existential problems of the Turkish territorial state.

Thirdly, the failure to integrate the opposition parties into the policy-making process regarding the initiative caused them to oppose it unreservedly.

Fourthly, the government's attempt to bypass the Kurdish political movement also proved to be damaging to the process. Although Erdoğan held a meeting with Ahmet Türk, the leader of the BDP's predecessor, the DTP, shortly after the launch of the initiative, the BDP insisted that the PKK's leader, Öcalan, be the government's counterpart in the process, thus torpedoing any possible dialogue. And although it was later discovered that the Turkish government had held secret talks with Öcalan, it is reasonable to assume that it preferred to do so covertly so as not to antagonize its ethnic Turkish constituency.

Notwithstanding its initial failure, the democratic opening initiative nonetheless transformed the political space in Turkey by opening channels of discussion on the Kurdish question. Not only did this new political space allow the Kurdish political movement to challenge the state discourse, it also presented a rare opportunity to rally the Kurdish populace around Kurdish nationalist ideals. Kurdish politics were thus transformed, and Kurdish groups jumped into the political scene with their own proposals, demands and initiatives. Hence, the post-2009 period was crucial for the Kurdish movement, marking a surge in Kurdish identity politics. The exponential increase in Kurdish activism was an outward sign of a solidified Kurdish national identity in Turkey.

The government's approach to the solution of the Kurdish question, as laid out in the democratic opening initiative, its subsequent policies and its overall political tone played a major role in shaping the evolution of Kurdish identity politics since 2009. Through its interaction with, and reaction to, the government, the Kurdish political movement has built an internal platform on which to challenge government policies. It has realized the importance of increasing its appeal to the various sectors of Kurdish society, and therefore has included a conglomerate of groupings from across the Kurdish political spectrum. It has also prompted and supported civil activism by the Kurdish public, hence further contributing to its politicization. The movement has thus re-conceptualized itself as one with multiple strands of activism rallying around the causes of ethno-national recognition and civil and collective rights. In this process, the gap between the vision of the democratic opening initiative and the tightening grip of the state around the Kurdish political movement provided the grounds for heightened Kurdish activism.

This new phase of the Kurdish political movement is exemplified by three developments that have dominated domestic politics in the post-initiative process. The first was the emergence of a new political actor in the Kurdish political scene, the Democratic Society Congress (*Demokratik Toplum Kongresi/ Kongreya Civaka Demokratîk*, DTK). In a political environment where multiple Kurdish actors occupy the political landscape, the DTK acts and functions like a congress. It encompasses not only the former DTP and current BDP members, but also a variety of civil society groups and intellectuals, both Kurdish and Turkish. Hence the DTK is not merely a local organization or an exclusively Kurdish civil society platform. It serves as a higher, supra-party organization that brings together Kurds of different political associations and leanings, and is the product of the attempt to carry the Kurdish struggle into the civil realm in accordance with Öcalan's plans. It acts as the foundation for a future "autonomous Kurdish structure," advocated as the ideal solution to the Kurdish question by Öcalan and the Kurdish political movement. The rise of the DTK in the political arena and the central role it has come to play is an unmistakable sign of the crystallization of Kurdish political identity in the wake of the democratic opening initiative.

The rise in acts of civil disobedience was the second development which attested to a growing wave of Kurdish nationalism. Kurdish disgruntlement with the turn that the government's initiative had taken was marked by increased acts of civil disobedience, coordinated by the DTK. For example, on March 24, 2011, 20,000 persons held a sit-in in the eastern city of Batman. The third indication of growing Kurdish nationalism was the DTK's unilateral declaration of democratic autonomy on July 14, 2011 during a congress in Diyarbakır. This was another example of the existence of a more solidified Kurdish political identity and the growing distance between the Turkish state and the Kurdish community in the post-initiative period in Turkey. It also testified to the increasingly prevalent Kurdish tendency to take matters into their own hands in order to produce their own solution against the background of the continued impasse with the Turkish state.

Taken as a whole, the initiative ended up aggravating existing grievances and suspicions on both sides: the Kurds continued to feel ostracized while the Turkish side remained suspicious of Kurdish intentions. However, the stalled peace process was jump-started again in January 2013, eighteen months after the AKP emerged victorious for a third consecutive time in the June 2011 general elections. It appears that the renewal of the peace process was a result of the contacts between MİT and Öcalan.[8] The news regarding the government's intention to resume the peace process was announced to the public by Prime Minister Erdoğan during a television interview in late December 2012. Attempts to "sabotage" the peace process were apparently undertaken by unknown parties, including the killing of three PKK members in Paris, the bombing of AKP headquarters in Ankara, and the leaking of details of the meeting between Öcalan and the parliamentary delegation from the BDP. Despite such hiccups, much-anticipated progress was made when Öcalan's letter calling for an end to armed struggle was read to the public during the Newroz celebrations in Diyarbakır in March 2013.

The road map for peace, which was agreed upon during the government-Öcalan meetings held through the course of 2012, was composed of three phases. The first leg of the peace process called for the withdrawal of the PKK's forces from Turkish territory into bases in northern Iraq. The actual withdrawal, which started in early May 2013, was expected to be completed over a five-month period. The second phase was to be the implementation of constitutional reform, which would guarantee civil rights for Kurds and thus allow greater recognition of their ethnic identity. The completion of the PKK's withdrawal was ultimately dependent on the reform package, which the government had agreed to produce by September 1, 2013 and to pass the relevant laws by October 15, 2013. Deemed by many as the real test that would determine the fate of the peace plan, the contents of the reform package were announced at the end of September. They included decriminalizing the use of the Kurdish letters "q, w, x" which are not found in the Turkish alphabet, allowing classes in Kurdish, albeit only in private, fee-paying schools, permission for villages to use their old names, allowing election campaigns to be conducted in languages other than Turkish, and the abolition of reciting the oath of allegiance, which begins with the line "I am a Turk." However the reforms fell short of meeting Kurdish expectations, which had been centered on the right of education in one's mother tongue and the elimination of the ten percent electoral threshold for attaining seats in parliament. In the meantime, the PKK slowed down its withdrawal of forces and the two sides blamed each other for delaying the process. Both the PKK and the BDP expressed dissatisfaction with the government's slow pace. PKK leader Cemil Bayık openly stated that should the second phase fail, the whole process would be reversed and PKK forces returned to Turkey.[9] Similarly, BDP Co-Chair Selahattin Demirtaş warned that his party would begin to conduct "a tough opposition" to the government.[10] Simultaneously, there were reports indicating that young people are joining the PKK's ranks at an increasing rate.[11] If and when the second phase is successfully completed, the third phase envisions a normalization process, which entails a general amnesty as well as the Kurds' reintegration into society.

## Kurds at Gezi Park

The Gezi Park protests erupted during the height of this fragile peace process. The Kurdish attitude toward the protests was, therefore, largely dictated by their concern about how their participation in the protests might affect the unfolding peace process. In fact, Kurdish politicians expressed concerns that ultranationalists, who oppose the rapprochement reached between the government and the Kurds, might exploit any Kurdish support for the protests to torpedo the ongoing peace talks. Reflecting the degree of concern on the issue, BDP Co-Chair Selahattin Demirtaş stated that they would not "allow the events in Gezi Park to turn against the peace process."[12] The ultranationalist tone, which indeed dominated the public squares at times, contributed to Kurdish reticence and increased Kurdish suspicion of the protests.[13]

Nevertheless, Kurds were not entirely absent from Gezi Park. The most outspoken protester was a deputy from the Kurdish BDP, Sırrı Süreyya Önder. Before the small-scale environmental sit-in snowballed into a mass protest movement, Önder was the first politician to go to the park and place himself in front of the municipality's bulldozers, and was even shot in the shoulder by a police tear gas canister. Önder's involvement in the protests, done on an individual basis and not a result of a party-sanctioned position, was a microcosm of the overall Kurdish participation in the protests. Kurdish political organizations opted to remain more on the sidelines and settled for making declarations of support at the beginning of the protests. The Democratic Society Congress saluted the Gezi protests while heavily criticizing the AKP government for its "arrogant" attitude towards the protestors in its group meeting held on June 9, several days after the start of the protests. Moreover, the DTK pointed to the 1982 Constitution, which is the product of the 1980 military coup, as the "main source of all problems" and argued that all democratic opposition groups should come together in their demand for a "pluralistic, egalitarian, liberal and democratic constitution."[14] Similarly, the KCK issued the following statement nine days after the start of the protests:

> As those who have experienced the worst kind of it, the people of Kurdistan knows very well what state violence is. The police violence which is being exercised by the AKP government stands in contrast with the spirit of the Democratic Peace Process. [...] The Kurdish people should take initiatives in this process [referring to the Gezi Park protests] and should do their part with the [other] democratic forces in order for this process to move in the right direction."[15]

Some BDP members also made similar statements showing support for the protestors and criticizing the heavy-handed police intervention.

As it quickly became apparent that the protests were the product of a widespread political reaction to the AKP's growingly authoritarian mode of governance, and that it brought together many different segments of the Turkish society, the Kurdish movement also changed its course and more actively supported the protests. However, the lukewarm Kurdish stance of the earlier period still drew criticism. Sırrı Süreyya Önder was the first to fiercely criticize the Kurdish party and organizations' failure to properly address the issue.[16] Önder's criticism was also shared by Öcalan, who had earlier sent out a message saying that he viewed the Gezi Park protests as "meaningful and important."[17]

In an interview given in July, the prominent Kurdish politician Ahmet Türk, who serves as the head of the DTK, stated that Öcalan had criticized the Kurdish political movement for "not reading" the Gezi events well.[18]

The most significant aspect of the protests, from the Kurdish angle, is the new linkage made by many Turks between the protests and the Kurdish question. The brutal police crackdown on protestors and the unyielding government determination to put an end to the protests led many to shed prejudices and question state policies against the Kurds. It was not only the suppression of democratic demands by state authorities but also the delegitimization of dissident voices by the government and the ease with which it labeled them as "marginals" and "terrorists" that generated a collective re-evaluation of the conflict within the Turkish society. A statement by Mehmet Kaya, the head of Tigris Communal Research Center (*Dicle Toplumsal Araştırmalar Merkezi*, DİTAM), aptly described this situation:

> [The Kurdish question] was represented [in the past] in a way as if the [PKK] members came down to the cities to create chaos. This is why the public always found justification in 'state terror.' When four thousand villages were evacuated and a million people were forced to migrate, the media created the perception that these people were all PKK members, [thus] finding justification to these undemocratic practices. During the Gezi protests, people's self-expression was also depicted as terror. [...] It seems that it is very easy for the state to call its people terrorists.[19]

In addition, the Gezi protests created a rare opportunity for different segments of Turkish society to get better acquainted with one another's grievances and political affiliations. Even the physical barriers seemed to have been lifted at Gezi Park, as PKK flags were waved side by side with flags of the Turkish Republic. It was possible to see Atatürk and Öcalan's faces in the same frame and to hear Turkish nationalist chants such as *"Mustafa Kemal'in askerleriyiz"* ("We are Mustafa Kemal's soldiers") in the same public space as *"Bijî Serok Apo"* ("Long live Apo", i.e. Öcalan). As such, the Gezi Park protests served as a much-needed first step at building mutual understanding between two peoples whose perceptions of one another had been largely shaped by the dynamics of a bloody conflict. Notwithstanding sporadic instances of clashes between Turkish nationalist groups and Kurdish protesters, the Gezi Park protests constituted a significant first attempt at deciphering and internalizing the codes of real coexistence.

Further contributing to the new feelings of solidarity between Turks and Kurds was the lack of coverage of the Gezi events by mainstream Turkish media. This raised important questions as to how well informed the Turkish public was with regard to the conflict in the regions populated by Kurds. In this respect, author Tuna Kiremitçi's tweet that read, "Wait a second... Did we follow [the events in] Diyarbakır from this media for 30 years?"[20] is an apt example. In social media venues such as Twitter and Facebook, statements that empathized with Kurdish suffering were abundant. These were even accompanied by apologies to the Kurdish people, for the protestors in the west of Turkey were stunned by the disregard shown in the media towards their own ill treatment, prompting them to question the Turkish state's treatment of its disadvantaged minorities.

## Conclusion

One of the most important lessons of the Gezi Park protests was the realization that democracy is a much sought-after commodity among all sectors of the Turkish society that have been alienated over the years by state policies reflective of one government ideology or the other. Even more importantly, the dynamics of the Gezi Park protests indicated to many that a democratic culture that both the Kurds and other Gezi protestors yearned for could only be built if demands for civil liberties voiced by different segments of society were considered inseparable. As Gültan Kışanak, co-chair of the BDP, aptly put it: "There is no such thing as democracy for Kurds and flogging for Turks."[21] The cornerstones of mutual understanding between Kurds and Turks, albeit in a limited manner, seems to have been laid with the Gezi Park events, as both sides were now more attentively attuned to the social, political, and historical factors that have shaped their respective political positions.

As Turkey braced itself for the possibility of renewed conflict with the PKK and a second round of mass protests, it remained to be seen whether the AKP government would act to ease the social tensions or continue with its heavy-handed authoritarian ways, which were likely to bring dissident voices even closer together in opposition.

## Notes

1. For a detailed analysis of this subject, see Omer Taspinar, *Kurdish Nationalism and Political Islam in Turkey: Kemalist Identity in Transition* (New York: Routledge, 2005).
2. The Copenhagen Criteria are a key set of rules that define a country's eligibility to become a member of the European Union. They require that the candidate country have "stable institutions that guarantee democracy, the rule of law, human rights and respect for and protection of minorities; a functioning market economy" and "the ability to assume the obligations of membership, in particular adherence to the

objectives of political, economic and monetary union." "Conditions for Enlargement," European Commission, http://ec.europa.eu/enlargement/the-policy/conditions-for-enlargement/index_en.htm.

3. Ümit Cizre, "The Emergence of the 'Government's Perspective on the Kurdish Issue," *Insight Turkey*, Vol. 11 No. 4 (2009), p. 4.

4. The term deep state (*derin devlet*) refers to a clandestine network composed of secular and military forces that acted as the self-appointed guardians of the secular order. It used techniques like intimidation, fear-mongering, and murder of dissidents who posed a perceived threat to the secular Republic.

5. Ofra Bengio, "'The Limping Giant': Turkey and the Kurdish Question," *Tel Aviv Notes*, Vol. 5 – Special Edition, No. 8, June 27, 2011, http://www.dayan.tau.ac.il/pdfim/TA_Notes_SE8_BENGIO_27_06_11.pdf.

6. "Erdoğan'ın Diyarbakır Mesajı: Devlet Geçmişte Hatalar Yaptı," ("Erdoğan's Diyarbakır Message: The State Made Mistakes in the Past"), *Radikal*, August 13, 2005, http://www.radikal.com.tr/index.php?tarih=13/08/2005.

7. Halil M. Karaveli, "Reconciling Statism with Freedom: Turkey's Kurdish Opening," *Silk Road Paper* (October 2010), p. 19, www.silkroadstudies.org/new/docs/silkroad papers/1010Karaveli.pdf.

8. İlter Turan, "Turkey's Second Kurdish Opening: Light at the End of the Tunnel or Another Failed Attempt?" *GMF*, April 12, 2013, http://www.gmfus.org/wp-content/blogs.dir/1/files_mf/1365796547Turan_TurkeysSecondOpening_Apr13.pdf.

9. "Bayık: 1 Eylül'de Adım Atılmazsa Geri Çekilme Durur," ("Bayık: If No Steps Taken By September 1, Withdrawal Will Stop"), *Fırat News*, August 27, 2013, http://www.firatnews.com/news/guncel/bayik-1-eylul-de-adim-atilmazsa-geri-cekilme-durur.htm.

10. "Muhalefeti Sertleştiririz," ("We Will Put A Tough Opposition"), *Radikal*, August 30, 2013, http://www.radikal.com.tr/politika/muhalefeti_sertlestiririz-1148410.

11. "PKK'ya Katılım Patladı," ("The Numbers of Those Joining the PKK Skyrocketed"), *Milliyet*, April 27, 2013, http://gundem.milliyet.com.tr/pkk-ya-katilim-patladi/gundem/gundemdetay/27.04.2013/1699351/default.htm.

12. "Turkey Protests Unite A Colourful Coalition of Anger against Erdogan," *The Guardian*, June 3, 2013, http://www.theguardian.com/world/2013/jun/03/turkey-protests-coalition-anger-erdogan.

13. Müjde Küçükkeleş, "Istanbul Protests: What Consequences for Turkey's Peace Process?" *Open Democracy*, June 10, 2013, http://www.opendemocracy.net/müjge-küçükkeleş/istanbul-protests-what-consequences-for-turkey's-peace-process.

14. "DTK'dan Gezi Parkı Yorumu: Artık Hiçbir Şey Eskisi Gibi Olmayacak," ("DTK's Gezi Park Comment: Nothing Will Be the Same"), *T24*, June 10, 2013, http://t24.com.tr/haber/dtkdan-gezi-parki-yorumu-artik-hicbir-sey-eskisi-gibi-olmayacak/231672.

15. "KCK'dan Gezi Parkı Açıklaması," ("KCK's Gezi Park Statement"), *Sol Portal*, June 6, 2013, http://haber.sol.org.tr/devlet-ve-siyaset/kckden-gezi-parki-aciklamasi-haberi-74225.

16. "Sırrı Süreyya Önder: Türkiye Yanıyor, DTK'dan Tek Cümle Yok," ("Sırrı Süreyya Önder: Turkey is Burning, Not A Single Word from DTK"), *Radikal*, June 20, 2013,

http://www.radikal.com.tr/politika/sirri_sureyya_onder_turkiye_yaniyor_dtkdan_
tek_cumle_yok-1138415.

17. "Öcalan Hails Gezi Protests, Warns against Ergenekon Supporters among Protesters," *Today's Zaman*, June 7, 2013, http://www.todayszaman.com/news-317630-ocalan-hails-gezi-protests-warns-against-ergenekon-supporters-among-protesters.html.

18. "'Öcalan'ın Gezi Konusunda Bize Eleştirisi Oldu,'" ("Öcalan Criticized Us about the Gezi Park"), *Radikal*, July 29, 2013, http://www.radikal.com.tr/yazarlar/ezgi_basaran/ocalanin_gezi_konusunda_bize_elestirisi_oldu-1143839.

19. "Diyarbakır: Biz Acı Çekerken Neredeydiniz?" ("Diyarbakır: Where Were You When We Were Suffering?", *BBC Türkçe Servisi*, June 19, 2013, http://www.bbc.co.uk/turkce/haberler/2013/06/130619_diyarbakir_gezi.shtml.

20. Tuna Kiremitçi (140darbe), "Bi saniye...Biz Diyarbakır'ı da 30 sene bu medyadan izledik di mi?", Twitter, June 2, 2013, 3:38 a.m, https://twitter.com/140darbe/status/341141747633635328.

21. Zümray Kutlu, "Türkler, Kürtler ve Gezi," ("Turks, Kurds and the Gezi Park"), *Radikal*, June 30, 2013, http://www.radikal.com.tr/radikal2/turkler_kurtler_ve_gezi-1139903.

# The 1979 Iranian Revolution in Historical Perspective

## Meir Litvak

The 1979 Islamic Revolution has justifiably been considered a profound turning point, not only in the history of Iran but also for the modern Middle East. This event put an end to the monarchy that had existed, albeit with interruptions, for 2,500 years, and introduced in its stead an "Islamic Republic," the first regime of its kind. This regime relies on religion to provide its ideological *raison d'être*, and aspires to have Islam provide the foundation of its policies in all areas of life.

## Between Modernity and Tradition

The revolution in Iran reflects several paradoxes related to the dialectics of modernity and change in the Middle East. On the one hand, the victors in the revolution rejected modernity as a worldview and as a system of values and institutions. They aspired to recreate a utopian past, specifically the Islamic government that is said to have existed during the times of the Prophet Mohammed and his son-in-law 'Ali (the fourth Caliph, 664-660 C.E.). The two primary forces that led the revolution — the merchants and the clerics — were indeed traditional groups that had been adversely affected by the Shah's modernization project. On the other hand, the revolution was a modern one in terms of its method of resource mobilization and the definition of several of its goals. Key aspects of modernity included, for example, the novel integration into political life of broad population groups — especially the broad lower classes, women, and educated young people — and the clerics skilled use of technology, including audio cassettes and satellite broadcasts. Israeli sociologist Shmuel Eisenstadt defined the aspirations of the Iranian Islamic revolutionaries, similarly to other fundamentalist activists, as being essentially Jacobin, with an affinity to the ambitions underlying the modern world's great revolutions, the French and the Bolshevik. In other words, theirs was a desire to totally reshape individual and collective identities through political action, and to completely assimilate the individual into the utopian community that the revolution was designed to create.[1]

A second modern feature is the persistence of the historical process of building strong nation states. Similar to Marxist thinkers who believed that a proletarian revolution would lead to the gradual disappearance of the state, Khomeini also believed that the implementation of Islamic ideology, largely through imposing of a universal system of religious justice, would obviate the mechanisms of governmental bureaucracy. According to Khomeini, when Islamic rule is established, there will no longer be any need for anything but "a judge with a pen and inkwell and a few enforcers" in every city to administer justice and maintain public order.[2] Khomeini's statements reflected a lack of understanding of social and economic realities, and were ultimately disproven by subsequent developments in Iran. The traditional Islamic state had confined itself to the maintenance of public order and personal security, imposed minimum governmental intervention in society, and set its sights on global expansion. In contrast, the state established by the revolution reinforced the Iranian government and did so within the state's boundaries. From the beginning, the government was intensely involved in the life of society, strove to achieve national and economic integration, and sought to impose an Islamic lifestyle on the population. It also assumed socio-economic obligations that were a function of its ambition to establish Islamic social justice. These trends were reflected in a policy designed to inject the Islamic regime's ideology into peripheral regions, especially villages, and to increase the Islamic state's involvement in economic management. State mechanisms were harnessed to disseminate the regime's ideological as well as its pragmatic, mundane messages. These developments expanded the state bureaucracy by several hundreds of thousands of employees, and confirm the opinion — voiced by Said Arjomand, relying on de Tocqueville's commentary on the French Revolution — that the revolution in Iran was similar to other revolutions that strengthened the very state that they intended to destroy. These developments also confirm Max Weber's comment that a bureaucracy is indestructible once it has been fully established.[3]

A strikingly modern aspect of the new regime, one that extended Pahlavi policy, was the cultivation of education and science. By 2012, literacy rates in Iran reached 93 percent of the entire population (and the rate was even higher among the younger generation).[4] Under the Islamic government, the number of universities increased to 54, and they are currently attended by over 3 million students. The government Islamicized the social sciences and humanities curricula, although it refrained from intervening in the exact sciences. Scientific output increased from 1,300 papers published annually in 2000 to 15,000 papers in 2009, and Iran's share in global scientific output increased impressively from less than 0.2 percent in 2000 to 1.3 percent in 2009. One of the fields in which

Iran has made prominent progress is nuclear technologies.[5] Another expression of this trend was the expansion of Iran's Internet network: the number of users rose from 250,000 in 2000 to 42 million in 2012, although the government's acts of oppression since 2009 have limited what was once an animated arena of activity.

Iran's attitude to the West is yet another aspect of the dialectics between modernity and tradition. In the last 200 years, Iran has alternated between a desire to follow its original social, cultural, and political tradition, and its need and desire to adopt Western patterns of culture and government in order to meet the numerous challenges that the West itself has posed. One of the Shah's gravest errors was his determination to rapidly adopt key features of Western culture — many of which were superficial in nature and only a few that were related to principles and values — at the expense of the local culture and Islamic-Persian identity, which were consequently marginalized. Khomeini's ideology was the complete opposite. It strived to erase all signs of Western culture's influence, and to place Iran within a utopian Islamic framework. Both leaders erred in their extreme approaches, ignoring the complexities of life and society and the impact of historical developments. The Shah's simplistic approach occasioned a sense of loss of cultural and national identity. Khomeini's approach was similarly unrealistic. After two hundred years of contact with the West, in an era of global economic systems and international media, it was no longer possible to obliterate the presence of the outside, non-Islamic world. Despite the desire to establish an Islamic system that was free of foreign influences, the Islamic government's own actions reflected Western cultural-political influences. For example, it retained Western patterns and institutions such as a constitution, a parliament, and parliamentary and presidential elections, and called itself a republic, even though these terms and institutions have no roots in traditional Islam.

The country's political-intellectual discourse also extensively corresponded to the discourse in Western countries, apparently based on the understanding that the Iranian audience has been thoroughly exposed to this discourse and its effects cannot be ignored. Attempts to erase Western cultural influences are manifest in small details such as the imposition of a style of dress and a prohibition on certain music, and have met with opposition, especially from the younger generation. Since the revolution, the government has become increasingly aware that many young people, who are the large majority of the population (more than 60 percent of Iranians were born after the revolution), will not willingly disassociate themselves from Western culture, whether external trappings such as music and dress code, or deeper features such as the concepts of liberty and progress. The Islamic Republic has tried to create a compromise by offering a synthesis of these extremes. Islamic reformist thinkers have been placed in charge of these attempts, and have stressed Islam's pluralism and the need to combine religious views and the people's rule.

The change in women's status also reflects the revolution's dilemma of choosing between tradition or change. Immediately after the clerics seized power, they enacted a series of personal status laws related to marriage, divorce, and the custody of children after divorce. In the spirit of the strictest interpretation of *shari'a* law, they restricted women's rights compared to the Shah's era. For example, the new laws defined the age of majority as nine for girls: at this age a girl could legally marry or be prosecuted for a crime. For boys, the age of majority was fixed at 13. Clerics took steps to exclude women from the labor market and ban them from major fields of study in universities. Outward expressions of these efforts included the imposition of Islamic attire and strict rules of modesty. In several cases women were stoned to death for adultery. At the same time, the clerics did not restrict women's right to vote and be elected to the parliament or engage in political activity. In any case, socio-economic necessities forced the Islamic government to relax several of its principles. In view of the labor shortage during the Iran-Iraq War, and evidently in response to pressure brought to bear by the women themselves, the authorities were forced to re-open fields of study at universities and permit women to return to the labor market. Although literacy among women remains lower than literacy among men in Iran, more women than men have at least a high school education (60 percent and 50 percent respectively), and there are more female university students than male university students. Nonetheless, several scientific fields remain closed to women, and the employment rate for women is lower by one-third compared to the employment rate for men.[6]

In the mid-1990s, a new stream of Islamic feminism emerged, one that attempted to promote women's rights by offering a liberal interpretation of Islamic law. As a result of these efforts, women played a primary role as a force pressing for change and democratization, manifested in the election of reformist president Mohammad Khatami on June 23, 1997, and in the rise of the reformist camp in the parliamentary elections of February-April 2000. In recent years, various clerics even demonstrated some flexibility in interpreting laws related to personal status matters. For example, they have raised the minimum age of marriage of girls to 13, and of boys to 15, evidently out of recognition that the country's needs and changing mores required a more modern approach.[7]

From the outset, Iranian Islamic revolutionaries defined their goal in primarily cultural rather than socio-economic terms. They sought to reshape people in the spirit of Islam and create a countrywide and global community of righteous believers. However, the presumptuous goal of creating a new man failed in Iran, as it did in all the major revolutions that sought the same goal. The Iranian Revolution repeatedly encountered materialism, greed, and widespread corruption, even within government and clerical circles. Human nature proved to be stronger than the ability of any preacher to change it. Paradoxically, and perhaps inevitably, the very attempt to impose a religious lifestyle, at least in the public sphere, diminished the people's connection to religion, and fueled the secularization that was embraced by significant segments of Iranian youth.

By the authorities' own admission, Iranian society at the beginning of the twenty-first century suffered from grave problems, including drug addiction and prostitution among youth. These problems were exacerbated by the country's social crisis and high unemployment, but were mainly fueled by a sense of despair. In the first decade after the revolution, revolutionary fervor substituted for everyday wants and needs to some extent, but as time passed, initial passions dulled and the desire to satisfy more earthly needs were expressed with increasing regularity. Widespread frustration ensued — especially among young people who had no experience of the government's misdeeds under Mohammad Reza Shah — when they learned that Islamic slogans failed to be translated into an alternative that was superior to Western civilization's offerings.[8]

## Between Islam and Nationalism

The Islamic government's attitude to the question of nationalism also reflected a blending of Western influence and internal state-building processes. At the purely ideological level, Khomeini rejected nationalism, which he viewed as a Western concept that was alien to Islam and designed to dissolve Islamic unity. However, since Iran's Shi'i identity distinguished it from other Middle Eastern countries, and had also been a key element in Iranian national identity in the past, the revolutionary government found it difficult to separate the components that bound together religious and national identities, especially since Iran's distinct existence over centuries reinforced its own self-awareness, as did the distinctiveness of the Shi'i creed.

Moreover, in many ways the revolution was a national one as well. One of the revolution's goals was to extricate Iran from its status as a subordinate client of the United States, and put an end to the intervention and influence of foreign powers in its domestic affairs. From this perspective, the revolution was successful, and the new government and its accompanying discourse adopted specifically national features, including the constitutional determination that the state president must be a Shi'a of Iranian origin (which caused one presidential candidate, Jalal al-Din Farsi, to be disqualified in 1980 because his father was an

Afghan).[9] The long war with Iraq (1980-1988) precipitated a return to national, and not merely Islamic, symbols as a means of rallying the public around the struggle against Iraqi, Sunni, and Arab "others." Like the monarchy, the Islamic Republic also suppressed separatist movements and pursued a policy of disseminating Persian language and culture among the country's minorities. Recent studies show that even the Islamic education system continued to convey what were clearly national messages that emphasized Iran's unique role in and contribution to Islam and Islamic culture. Moreover, the new textbooks include numerous favorable references to the pre-Islamic period, which is considered to be *jahili*, a period of ignorance and barbarity according to basic Islamic tenets. In 1971, the clerics attacked the Shah for his lavish festivities celebrating the ancient Persian Emperor Cyrus, but in 1991, 'Ali Akbar Hashemi Rafsanjani, then president of Iran, during a visit to Persepolis, the ceremonial capital of the Achaemenid Empire (ca. 550–330 C.E.), emphasized that it was very much a part of the Iranian heritage; in 2010, Iran held ceremonies celebrating the return to Iran of the original Cyrus Cylinder from the British Museum. According to Iranian scholar Farhad Khosrokhavar, Iranian society has become more homogeneous than ever, as the vast majority of young people, who come from all parts of the ethnic spectrum, now speak Persian and have been exposed to the intense government programs of Islamic socialization and social integration. Nonetheless, some researchers argue that this heightened homogeneity has, instead, reinforced the country's minorities' awareness of the patronizing attitude of Persian speakers and reduced their willingness to accept it.[10]

# Between Religion and State

The institutionalization of Khomeini's *velayat-e faqih* principle represented a major change in the religious leaders' traditional Shi'i worldview. Since the mid-nineteenth century, the Shi'i establishment was comprised of an informal hierarchy headed by the supreme sources of imitation (*marja-e taqlid*) that every believer must follow. The climb up the Shi'i echelon was never formalized: instead it depended largely on a religious scholar's popularity among the believers, recognition of his learnedness and scholarly accomplishments by colleagues, and one's reputation as a man of justice. The 1979 Constitution revoked the believers' right to elect a spiritual leader for themselves, as the clerical oligarchy appointed the Supreme Leader at the top of the ruling pyramid. For the first time in Shi'i history, the Constitution defined a formal ranking, by placing one specific *marja-e taqlid* above his colleagues, and even granting him power to veto his colleagues' religious rulings.

The revolution and the clerics grip on power created another, political rather than religious, hierarchy involving official religious appointments. At the top was the spiritual leader, *Rahbar*, also known as *Vali-ye faqih* (Guardian Jurist or the *faqih* who fills the place of the *imam*), with the Council of Guardians alongside him. In this manner, a division was created between clergymen who gave preference to studiousness and those who turned to the political sphere or who became part of the various state systems. In effect, they were politicians in clerics' clothing, and they wielded more power than their colleagues bearing higher-ranking religious titles.

At the political level, the revolution put an end to the monarchy, conferring the power to rule upon the clergy for the first time in Iran's history. The new rulers professed their intent to end earthly tyranny and replace it with divine law. Ayatollah Khomeini's status as *Rahbar* effectively granted him freedom of action that was very similar to the powers of the deposed Shah. The Islamic political system, however, proved to be much more complicated than the monarchy it replaced. Unlike the Shah's autocratic rule in the final years of his regime, the Islamic government in Iran was not constructed as a centralized monarchy. Rather, it was designed as an oligarchy, or even a system with multiple power centers, where the Supreme Leader balances or negotiates between them and functions as the ultimate arbiter. This system makes it possible for different social groups to influence decision making.

## Priests Defeating Prophets?

The Shah had tried but failed to base his legitimacy on the grandeur of Iran's pre-Islamic monarchs. Khomeini, in contrast, established his government on the concept that the clergy are the legal heirs of the Prophet and the twelve Shi'i imams, and on his own personal reputation as a pure, impeccable individual and longstanding opponent to the Shah's tyrannical government. To these, Khomeini added modern and legal-rational elements of legitimacy: elections and public referendums as the means of garnering popular support.

Like all revolutions in modern history, the revolution in Iran triggered the rise of new elite groups and the integration of new social elements in the political arena. The monarchy's aligned political elites were removed in a series of arrests, executions, and flights into exile. Their positions were seized by groups of clergymen, lower- middle class technocrats, and bazaar merchants. The changes in the elite groups and the establishment of new governing institutions ignited a wave of upward social mobility of hundreds of thousands of young people, who assumed vacated and newly created positions. These masses became the government's mainstay. The expansion of education at all levels also facilitated and promoted such mobility, although class differences remained.

Under Qajar rule (1794-1925), the relationship between state and religion was characterized by mutual dependency and cooperation, but also by tension. In the twentieth century, the clergy retained its important status in the political sphere despite the Pahlavi monarchs' attempts to weaken it. Khomeini's creed was largely shaped as a response to this policy. His doctrine called for religion's domination of politics, but also for the incorporation of political elements into religion. On the face of things, Khomeini's *velayat-e-faqih* doctrine reflected an authentic aspiration to subjugate politics to religious values. However, the three decades that elapsed since the revolution show that one practical outcome of this doctrine was also the bending of religious doctrine to suit political needs. David Menashri has demonstrated that in almost all the cases in which the government was forced to choose between revolutionary principles and state interests, Khomeini decided in favor of pragmatic, national, worldly interests. This fact has led researchers such as Sami Zubaida to doubt whether the Iranian government should be called an Islamic regime and whether its functioning is truly dictated by the fundamental principles and values of Islam.[11]

Subjugation of the holy law to political needs peaked in a series of statements made by Khomeini in late 1987 and early 1988, in response to a legislative crisis. Khomeini criticized what appeared to be the obvious assumption that the government in an Islamic regime is subject to *shari'a*, and determined that the sanctity of government is one of God's most important commandments. The Iranian Islamic government possesses the "absolute authority" that was delegated by God to the Prophet, and from him to the clergy. This sanctity surpasses all secondary commandments including prayer, fasts, and the *hajj* (pilgrimage to Mecca), and therefore the leaders of the Islamic government may even temporarily suspend fundamental commandments, and even destroy mosques, if such actions served the state's interest.[12]

The legislative process also reflected the state's supremacy over religion. The government's official intention was to effectively make Islamic law, the *shari'a*, the foundation for legislation, canceling all laws that were inconsistent with the *shari'a* and adapting all new laws to Islamic values. To this end, the Council of Guardians was established with a right to veto any law enacted by the parliament if it was incompatible with the *shari'a*. Reality, however, proved to be more complicated than such simplistic formulas. In several cases, contradictions were discovered between different interpretations of Islam, or between opposing Islamic values such as the sanctity of private property and the desire to impose social justice. In other cases, contradictions emerged between the religious law and the requirements of a modern economy, such as the use of interest by modern banks, or contradictions between Islamic law and government interests. In such cases, the government created legal arrangements that allowed it to enact laws even if they seemingly contradicted traditional Islamic principles.[13]

In the decades preceding the revolution, the clergy had been divided over the need to intervene in politics, on the desirable attitude towards the state, and on various social and economic issues. In place of the ideological diversity that characterized religious sages, Khomeini aspired to ideological unity under the legal Islamic expertise and authority of the supreme jurist. This idea did not stand the test of time: political power exacerbated internal differences, especially when these were added to conflicts between rival power centers and factions. In the 1980s, these disputes became official with the consolidation of two religious factions: *Jame'e-ye Ruhaniyat-e Mobarez* (the Association of Combatant Clerics), considered to hold right-wing views on the economy, Western culture, and political openness, in contrast to the *Majma'-e Ruhaniyun-e Mobarez* (the Militant Clerics Association), which was considered more leftist in orientation. These factions ostensibly argued about the correct interpretation of Islam, but in practice most disputes were power struggles cloaked in religious terminology. These disputes typically were decided through political means rather than legalistic or scholarly arguments. The growing factionalism illustrated the illusion of Khomeini's demand for ideological uniformity, as well as the illusion that Islam offers a comprehensive solution to all problems of complex modern societies. It also exposed the fallacy of Khomeini's simplistic view that ruling a modern country could be reduced to the imposition of justice through religious-legalistic rulings.

Thirty years on, an analysis of the revolution shows that it failed in the most important area of its initial vision — the vision of rule by a learned Islamic legal scholar. The appointment of Hojjat al-Islam Sayyid Ali Khamenei as *Rahbar*, the new leader, immediately after Khomeini's death in 1989, represented a victory for the "Politicians" faction in the religious establishment, over the "Theologians." The choice of a spiritual leader who lacked outstanding scholarly credentials, never published a decent legal essay, and did not hold the rank of Ayatollah, was equivalent to a declared withdrawal from the ideal on whose behalf Khomeini had led the revolution. Instead of Khomeini the cleric, circumstances led to the rise of Khamenei a politician in clerical guise, and proved that the ruling elite had failed to produce scholars or religious jurists who were able to make policy. From this perspective, the revolution seems to have lost its soul when Khamenei was appointed. At the same time, however, it is important to note that, lacking in scholarly accomplishments, Khamenei failed to achieve status at the pinnacle of the religious leadership, despite his political powers, which indicates that the Shi'i tradition of leadership was not compromised. After close to two decades of rule, Khamenei has failed to acquire for himself status or reputation as supreme spiritual leader or successor to Khomeini's power. As the leader of the revolution and head of the state, he enjoyed complete political freedom, but his rule appears to lack solid religious legitimacy. Khomeini's vision thus failed, and the Islamic government of Iran became one more government led by a human hand, and arguably, one of the most tyrannical.[14]

The Islamic regime is not democratic, and has not hesitated to use oppressive means against its rivals. Significantly more political prisoners were executed in the 1980s than during all of the Shah's years in power. On the other hand, the Islamic regime contains elements of popular participation in politics that were absent during the Shah's rule, and they facilitated some degree of political pluralism, reflecting divisions in the religious establishment itself. The Supreme Leader is not elected by the people, the power of the Majlis is limited by the Council of Guardians that is appointed by the Supreme Leader, and political opponents are punished and persecuted. But this is not the dictatorial rule that traditionally characterized many Arab countries, for example. The presidential and parliamentary elections in Iran also reflect the complexity of its system: These are not democratic elections, because the ruler disqualifies any candidate who is not to his liking, but the results are not determined in advance. The elections are thus a struggle between several streams within the government, and the elected president does not win 99 percent of the votes or anything close to that.

Occasionally, the regime absorbed surprising defeats, such as the election of Khatami as president in 1997 and the reformists' victory in the 2000 Majlis elections. These surprises also stemmed from the entry of new groups into politics, the existence of rival power centers within the government, and from external cultural influences that penetrated Iran's society, to the regime's chagrin.

# Continuing an Economy of Dependence

The final analysis of the revolution's economic achievements is equally unimpressive. The belief that Islam has a solution to the problems of Iran and other countries, that it offers an alternative to Western capitalism and socialism, has proven to be an illusion. Disagreements and disputes among senior Iranian leaders on the features and implementation of an Islamic economy show that, here, too, Islam offers no single course of action but rather multiple interpretations and contrasts grounded in the holy sources. No religious answer has yet been found to resolve the contradiction between the aspiration for social justice and protection of the sanctity of private property. These debates reflected the economic and political interests of opposing groups more than they reflected theoretical scholarly disputes. As for the economic steps themselves, even though they were couched in Islamic terminology, they differed little from the solutions applied to similar situations in the West. During Khomeini's rule, efforts focused on attempts to build statist socialism or economic populism in religious attire, but after his death, his successors shifted to a more capitalist economy, with the same Islamic dress. From time to time other economic ideas were proposed in an attempt to infuse economic development with some moral-legalist content, but these efforts were fleeting. Scholarly sermons and appeals to individuals to allow their economic conduct to be guided by their inner conscious and moral considerations were no effective substitute for policy.

Even after three decades of revolution, Islamic economics failed to extricate Iran's dependency on exports of a single raw material, oil, and on the importation of finished products from the West. Even the leaders themselves understood that escaping this situation required a much deeper internal transformation that was beyond their capabilities. Iran's economic crisis remains grounded in this fundamental factor. The crisis obviously worsened after the long war with Iraq, its enormous expenses, and the damage to its infrastructure, but also as a result of long years of economic sanctions imposed by the United States and other countries, as well as mismanagement, widespread corruption, and preference for populist action at the expense of long-term planning.

# Foreign Relations: Between Vision and Constraints: Iran Before Islam?

Foreign relations also posed a dilemma for the regime, which was forced to choose between its commitment to the ideals of the revolution, especially the vision of disseminating the revolution to the entire world and leading it against the West, on the one hand, and the state's tangible interests and constraints, on the other. This dilemma was added to another dilemma of choosing between the need to open up to the outside world in order to make an impact on it, and the apprehension that such opening might erode Iranians' commitment to the Islamic revolution. These dilemmas and other issues were not decided in theological seminaries but through power struggles involving the factions of the religious establishment. According to Menashri, the more time that passed since the outbreak of the revolution, the more strongly national state interests overshadowed the revolutionary vision, as the rulers were increasingly forced to consider Iran's circumstances and the limits of its power. Indeed, pragmatic considerations typically prevailed in Iran's relations with neighboring or geographic proximate countries, while revolutionary terminology came to the fore as distances grew — and risks diminished. Alongside their revolutionary worldview, Iran's leaders adopted a cost-benefit approach to policy making. For example, Iran refrained from extending assistance to the Shi'i rebellion against Saddam Hussein's rule in Iraq in 1991 because it feared a renewal of hostilities with Iraq. It steadfastly maintained this position even when Iraqi soldiers massacred Shi'is. Iran also refrained from providing aid to the Chechen rebellion against Russia, even though its leaders viewed the rebellion as a Muslim campaign against the government of a Christian country. Evidently friendship with Russia was more important to Iran's leaders than the edicts of their religion. Iranian leaders were also motivated by the fear that the success of ethnic movements on its borders would affect its own minorities. Regarding distant Israel, Iran chose to adhere to a rigid ideological line because it believed that pursuing such a policy promoted its leadership in the Pan-Islamic world, and pursuing this policy carried no direct risks.[15]

The revolution's success in seizing power in Iran inspired other Islamic revolutionaries in the region and worldwide, but it is doubtful whether Iran's Islamic government served as a role model. As the years passed, it became evident that the revolution's impact was limited mainly to Shi'i populations in the Muslim world. Iran's shared Islamic vision did not repair the historical divide and differences that separated Sunnis and Shi'is. No revolution modeled after Iran occurred in other countries, in part because local circumstances and opposition movements there differed in composition and strength, and also because the rulers learned the lessons of the Shah's failed regime.

## Iran and the World: From Defense to Offense

The revolutionary regime fundamentally transformed Iran's dialogue with the outside world in the modern era. During the Qajar era, weak Iran was subject to economic exploitation and political manipulation by Russia and Britain, the two imperialist powers on its borders, which incessantly intervened in its domestic affairs. Mohammad Reza Shah Pahlavi adopted a clear pro-American line, which went as far as subservience, as a means of strengthening his own rule and standing up to the Soviet Union. The Islamic government liberated itself from such international pressure, and transformed Iran into an independent, proactive actor. The backbone of Iran's foreign policy was to stand defiantly against the United States, and to take actions that strengthened the regime's domestic status and added to its weight in the global arena. Today, Iran seems to have set its sights on achieving hegemony in the Middle East region. In the view of its ruling elites, Iran is already on the world map. In this respect, as it continues to trigger strategic high-stakes dramas, Iran has embarked on a new historical course of action.

The degree of Iran's defiance towards its surrounding countries is largely — but not entirely — dependent on the internal balance between its more and less zealous elements. The election of President Khatami in 1997, and the Majlis elections in February 2000 in which the conservatives were handed a crushing defeat at the hands of the reformists, reflected the desire of Iran's younger generation for cultural, social, and political openness. Khatami did indeed allow such openness, but in 2001, the conservatives launched a counter-attack against him and managed to reverse his changes.

Conservative forces also regained control of all elected state institutions through a clever combination of controlled oppression, superior recruitment skills compared to their reformist rivals, a populist social platform, and exploitation of the internal split in the reformists' ranks and their diminishing ardor. In 2004, the conservatives defeated the reformists in the Majlis elections, and in June 2005, Mahmud Ahmadinejad, mayor of Tehran and a former officer in the Revolutionary Guards, won the presidential elections. By proving that they still controlled the real power in Iran, the conservatives' achievements exposed the limitations of liberalization within an Islamic government.

During Ahmadinejad's tenure (2005-2013), Iran pursued a confrontational foreign policy designed to promote itself as a regional power and as a leader of the Third World. It renewed its efforts to advance its nuclear capabilities by installing centrifuges to enrich uranium. While it denied any intention to produce nuclear weapons, many of its measures appeared illogical unless they were designed to attain a nuclear weapon capabilities.

On the regional level, Iran worked to consolidate the so-called "Axis of Resistance" composed of Iran, Syria, Hizballah in Lebanon, as well as Hamas and Islamic Jihad in the Palestinian Territories. It exerted concerted efforts to transform Iraq into its client state working on three levels: government to government, vis-à-vis specific Shi'i and Kurdish movements, and towards the Shi'i clerical establishment in Najaf. Iranian companies also competed for major commercial and infrastructure projects in Iraq. Yet, in view of the complexities of Iraq's internal dynamics, the results were mixed as it faced increasing competition from Turkey, as well as Turkish support for Sunni parties in Iraq. Iran persisted in its conflict by proxy against Israel by supplying the Lebanese Hizballah with thousands of missiles and in extending weapons supplies to Hamas and Islamic Jihad. It also actively disseminated anti-Zionist and anti-Semitic propaganda, culminating in Ahmadinejad's repeated statements denying the Holocaust, as well as the Iranian foreign ministry's sponsorship of an international conference on Holocaust denial.

Domestically, Ahmadinejad's tenure was characterized by increasing political repression coupled with economic populism that was designed to consolidate support for the regime among Iran's lower classes and residents of the provinces, but which came at the expense of long-term economic growth and stability. It was also marked by an increasing role for the Revolutionary Guards, as thousands of former guards officers were appointed to administrative offices ranging from provincial governors to ambassadors.

Populist policy and nationalistic rhetoric, however, could not disguise the regime's failure to solve Iran's structural socio-economic problems of insufficient economic growth, economic mismanagement, and widespread corruption which resulted, inter alia, in increasing youth unemployment, rising drug consumption, and a growing sense of cultural suffocation. Rising disaffection was manifested in the June 2009 presidential elections when Mir Hossein Musavi, the former radical prime minister in the early 1980s, and Mehdi Kerrubi, a former Majlis Speaker, ran against the incumbent Ahmadinejad as two relatively reformist candidates calling for some opening.

Ahmadinejad won in the first round by a majority of 62 percent, thanks to what appeared to be the government's engineering of the election. Feeling cheated, hundreds of thousands of mainly young people took to the streets in protest chanting the slogan, "Where is my vote?" The protests, the largest since the 1979 Revolution, were fueled by a feeling of deep frustration. The protestors felt that while they were willing to abide by the political rules, however restrictive, established by the regime, and which granted the system legitimacy, the regime itself had violated these very rules. The protests were eventually crushed with relatively few fatalities but with thousands of arrests. The regime also proved effective in neutralizing the use of the internet by the protesters, revealing a high level of technological sophistication.

The "Green Movement" protests failed due to a combination of factors. The opposition lacked organization and leadership. Historically, leaders in Iran usually required charisma which derived from either religious position, as was the case with Ayatollah Khomeini in 1978-1979 — or from the prestige of leading an extended national struggle, as was the case with Mohammad Mosaddeq in the early 1950s. By contrast, Mousavi and Karrubi lacked the necessary charisma or skills, but equally important refrained from breaking away from the regime.

In all past protest movements in Iran, the clergy had played an important role. By utilizing the corpus of Islamic symbols and slogans that were familiar to the entire population or the recruitment apparatuses of the mosques and the other religious institutions dispersed throughout the country, the clergy had always managed to build a coalition of various social groups. At times the clergy themselves led the protest movements, while on other occasions they essentially served as a front for other actors. Once the clergy was in power, they could use the same means to sustain the regime and of course deprive them from the opposition

The protesters limited their agenda to the election fraud and later to the question of dictatorship, but failed to expand it to the socio-economic realm. Consequently, the demonstrations were confined to mostly young middle class people and failed to attract the workers, the lower classes or the formerly powerful bazaar merchants. It appears that the lower classes were still attracted by Ahmadinejad's populism. Factory workers, despite their economic troubles, had previously gone on strikes. Yet, they had focused on questions of salary and working conditions, and did not translate their demands to the political sphere, whether because of a lack of awareness, organizational and recruiting difficulties, or their sense of alienation from the youth. The bazaar merchants, who had been the heart and soul of the past protest movements, had lost much of their political power. Conceivably, many of them refrained from joining the opposition, either because of their conservative social approach, their revulsion towards liberal ideas, or because their economic situation was not all that bad. Another reason for the passivity of various groups was probably weariness after thirty years of revolution, a war, and great hopes for reform that had not materialized. The public no longer possessed the strength for a prolonged struggle against the government. Or, as the *Economist* explained earlier, Iranians learned a bitter lesson after the fall of the Shah: as bad as it may be, an insurrection can make matters worse.[16]

While Arab countries have experienced major upheavals since 2011, Iran remained relatively calm. Iranian exceptionalism can be explained as a combination of several factors:

Increased political repression, particularly following the suppression of the 2009 protests. In 2011 and 2012, Iran lagged only behind China in the number of executions, 660 and 522 respectively.[17] Concurrently, the regime was wise enough to refrain from employing brutal means of oppression along the lines of Saddam Hussein. While in various Arab countries the barrier of fear had been broken, in Iran it survived. In addition, the regime's populist economic policies, particularly compensating the poorer classes for rising prices following the removal of food subsidies, bought it popular support among the groups which had been its mainstay since 1979.

Most Iranians have supported the regime's public position on the nuclear issue, mainly defending Iran's rights to peaceful nuclear development and capability. Large groups may support the unannounced goal of achieving a military capability, and may regard international sanctions against Iran as an inherently unjust attempt to keep Iran technologically backward. Differences emerged, however, regarding the degree to which the leadership should adopted a confrontational posture vis-à-vis the international community.

An additional likely factor explaining the calm was the growing bloodshed, destruction, and economic hardship in Arab countries: this probably deterred many Iranians from seeking a violent overthrow of the regime, fearing that Iran would follow the same tragic course.

Concurrently, while the Iranian regime was a dictatorship, it was never an autocracy. The ruling class was composed of the clergy, which comprised of several hundreds of thousands of men, but with their families and dependents their numbers reached millions. Millions more, including members of the revolutionary guards, employees and political clients of the six major trust-funds (*bonyads*) that controlled approximately 20 percent of the economy benefited from the regime's largesse and had a vested interest in its long-term survival. While the regime's social basis of support became narrower following the marginalization of reformists, it appeared to be wider than that of any Arab regime.

The overall effect of these factors has been to produce a culture of political apathy among large segments of the population. This was manifested, inter alia, in the increasing consumption of foreign literature, as well as books on psychology, and the trend of walking in the mountains outside the city, reading poetry in the bosom of nature, movies, study groups, and dreaming of immigration.[18] The regime enabled these groups to behave the way they wanted as long as they confined their activities to the private sphere.

At the same time, however, Ahmadinejad's erratic and turbulent policies, as well as mounting international economic pressure, obliged the conservative ruling elite to take public opinion into consideration. With the coming of the presidential elections, the regime vetted close to 600 presidential candidates before approving eight of them, all veteran regime stalwarts, who reflected different approaches to domestic and foreign policies within the ruling establishment. Significantly, Hasan Rouhani, who eventually won, emphasized several themes in his election campaign, among them the need to balance realism and the pursuit of Iran's strategic goals, declaring that while installing nuclear centrifuges was a major achievement, the Iranian people also needed to eat. He promised to improve Iran's relations with the international community, saying he would restore the honor of the Iranian passport and currency, whose value had plummeted during Ahmadinejad's tenure. In the domestic field, he promised moderation, saying he would do his best to ensure the release of political prisoners.

The rallying behind Rouhani of reformists such as former president Khatami and mainstream pragmatists led by former president Rafsanjani awakened the seemingly apathetic or demoralized public opinion and resulted in a fairly high voter turn-out. Rouhani's victory by a fairly high margin and the poor showing of the radical hardliners, Saeed Jalili and 'Ali Akbar Velayati, reflected a clear message from the Iranian public to its leaders that they rejected the idea of a siege economy as the price for Iran's nuclear ambitions and that they wanted an accommodation with the international community. It also implied that most people were once again willing to abide by the rules set by the regime for the time being, as long as they would have some way to express their wishes or have influence on the government's policies even if in a limited fashion only.

While the elections revealed a gap between much of the public and the regime's hard core, they also demonstrated the resilience of the Iranian system. The ruling establishment knew that it could not ignore public opinion, especially in view of the Arab upheavals. Yet, leadership was strong and flexible enough to contain a vote of protest within the system, and offer sufficient latitude for the popular voice, while preserving political control and maintaining policy in the hands of the ruling elite. Still, in the long run, socio-economic change, the expansion of education, and heightened expectations of the younger generation, on the one hand, and structural economic problems on the other hand, will continue to pose significant challenges for the Islamic government.

# Notes

1. Shmuel Noah Eisenstadt, *Fundamentalism, Sectarianism, and Revolution: The Jacobin Dimension of Modernity* (Cambridge, U.K.: Cambridge University Press, 1999).
2. Cited from Graeme Newman, "Khomeini and Criminal Justice: Notes on Crime and Culture," *The Journal of Criminal Law and Criminology*, Vol. 73, No. 2 (Summer, 1982), p. 561.
3. Said Amir Arjomand, *The Turban for the Crown*, Oxford 1988, p. 173.
4. http://www.tradingeconomics.com/iran/literacy-rate-youth-total-percent-of-people-ages-15-24-wb-data.html.
5. Yair Even Zohar, Daphna Getz, and Uri Kirsh, *A Comparative View at the Development of Scientific and Technological Research in Israel and Middle Eastern Countries According to Quantitative Indices* (Haifa; Technion, 2011).
6. Djavad Salehi-Isfahani and Daniel Egel, *Youth Exclusion in Iran: The State of Education, Employment and Family Formation* (Washington DC: Wolfensohn Center for Development at Brookings, 2007), pp. 18–19.
7. Literature on women is extensive. Following is a selection of references: Parvin Paidar, *Women and the Political Process in Twentieth Century Iran* (Cambridge, 1995), pp. 221–355; Ziba Mir-Hosseini, *Islam and Gender the Religious Debate in*

*Contemporary Iran* (Princeton, 1999); Mahnaz Kousha, *Voices from Iran: The Changing Lives of Iranian Women* (Syracuse, 2002); Mahnaz Afkhami and Erika Friedl (eds.), *In the Eye of the Storm: Women in Post-Revolutionary Iran* (London, 1994); Asghar Fathi, *Women and the Family in Iran* (Leiden, 1985); Guity Nashat, *Women and revolution in Iran* (Colorado, 1983).

8.  On the crisis of Iranian youth, see Meir Litvak, "Iran's Rebellious Youth," in Asher Susser (ed.), *The Middle East: The Impact of Generational Change* (Tel Aviv: The Moshe Dayan Center, 2005), pp. 119–132.

9.  See: David Menashri, *Post-Revolutionary Politics in Iran: Religion, Society and Power* (Portland, Oregon: Frank Cass, 2001), p. 255.

10. Farhad Khosrokhavar, "Toward an anthropology of democratization in Iran", *Critique: Critical Middle Eastern Studies*, Vol. 9, Issue 16 (Spring 2000), pp. 3–29.

11. Menashri, *passim*; Sami Zubaida, "An Islamic State? The Case of Iran", *Middle East Report*, Vol. 153 (July–August, 1988), pp. 3–7.

12. Meir Litvak, "The Rule of the Jurist (*Velayat-e Faqih*) in Iran: Ideal and Implementation," *Ha-Mizrah He-Hadash*, Vol. 42 (2001), pp. 170–172 [Hebrew].

13. For an extensive debate on this issue, see Asghar Schirazi, *The Constitution of Iran: Politics and the State in the Islamic Republic* (London, 1997).

14. Arjomand, *The Turban*, pp. 177–188; Mohsen Milani, "The Transformation of the Velayet-e Faqih Institution: From Khomeini to Khamenei", *The Muslim World*, Vol. 82 (1992), pp. 175–190.

15. Meir Litvak, "Israel through Iranian Eyes: From Holocaust Denial to Negation of Existence," in Uzi Rabi (ed.), *Zman Iran* ["Iran Time"] (Tel Aviv: Hakibbutz Hameuhad, 2008), pp. 49–67 [Hebrew].

16. *The Economist*, December 9, 2004; Stephen C. Fairb, "End Note: Iran's Distant Second Revolution,'" *RFE/RL Iran Report* 6: 6 (February 10, 2003).

17. http://www.iranhrdc.org/english/publications/3420-executions-in-iran.html#.UtPFaJ6Irmg.

18. Megan K. Stack, "In Clerics' Iran, Children of the Revolution Seek Escape," *The Los Angeles Times*, December 26, 2004.

# Contributors

**Duygu Atlas** is a doctoral candidate in the School of History, Tel Aviv University, and a Junior Researcher at the MDC.

**Irit Back** is a Lecturer in the Department of Middle Eastern and African History, Tel Aviv University, and a Research Fellow at the MDC.

**Ofra Bengio** is a Professor (Ret.) in the Department of Middle Eastern and African History, Tel Aviv University, Senior Research Fellow at the MDC and founder of its Kurdish Studies Program.

**Brandon Friedman** is a Research Fellow at the MDC and Lecturer in the International Programs, Tel Aviv University.

**Gideon Gera** is a Principal Research Fellow Emeritus at the MDC.

**Menachem Klein** is a Professor in the Department of Political Studies at Bar-Ilan University.

**Ephraim Lavie** is a Research Fellow at the MDC, and the Director of the Tami Steinmetz Center for Peace Research at Tel Aviv University.

**Meir Litvak** is a Professor in the Department of Middle Eastern and African History, Principal Research Fellow at the MDC, and the Director of the Alliance Center for Iranian Studies at Tel Aviv University.

**Elisheva Machlis** is a Research Fellow at the Alliance Center for Iranian Studies, and Lecturer in the International Programs, Tel Aviv University.

**Bruce Maddy-Weitzman** is a Principal Research Fellow at the MDC, Lecturer in the Department of Middle Eastern and African History and Lecturer in the International Programs, Tel Aviv University.

**Joel Parker** is a Researcher at the MDC and Lecturer in the International Programs, Tel Aviv University.

**C. Richard Pennell** is a Professor in the School of Historical and Philosophical Studies at the University of Melbourne, Australia.

**Uzi Rabi** is a Professor in the Department of Middle Eastern and African History, Tel Aviv University, and the Director of the MDC.

**Paul Rivlin** is a Senior Research Fellow at the MDC and Lecturer in the International Programs, Tel Aviv University.

**Yehudit Ronen** is a Professor in the Department of Political Studies at Bar-Ilan University.

**Asher Susser** is a Professor Emeritus in the Department of Middle Eastern and African History, Tel Aviv University, and the Stanley and Ilene Gold Research Fellow at the MDC.

**Mira Tzoreff** is a Lecturer in the Department of Middle Eastern and African History, Tel Aviv University, and a Research Fellow at the MDC.

**Joyce van de Bildt** is a doctoral candidate in the School of History, Tel Aviv University, and a Junior Researcher at the MDC.

**Esther Webman** is a Senior Research Fellow at the MDC, and the Head of the Zeev Vered Desk for the Study of Tolerance of Intolerance in the Middle East at the Stephen Roth Institute for the Study of Contemporary Antisemitism and Racism, Tel Aviv University.

**Hay Eytan Cohen Yanarocak** is a doctoral candidate in the School of History, Tel Aviv University, and a Junior Researcher at the MDC.

**Ronen Zeidel** is a Research Fellow at the MDC, and a Lecturer in the Department of Middle Eastern and African History, Tel Aviv University and in the international programs at the University of Haifa and the Hebrew University of Jerusalem.

**Daniel Zisenwine** is a Research Fellow at the MDC, and a Schusterman Scholar and Visiting Professor at Georgetown University.

**Eyal Zisser** is a Professor in the Department of Middle Eastern and African History, Senior Research Fellow at the MDC, and Dean of the Faculty of the Humanities, Tel Aviv University.

# Index